American Disaster Movies of the 1970s

American Disaster Movies of the 1970s

Crisis, Spectacle and Modernity

Scott Freer

BLOOMSBURY ACADEMIC
NEW YORK • LONDON • OXFORD • NEW DELHI • SYDNEY

BLOOMSBURY ACADEMIC
Bloomsbury Publishing Inc, 1385 Broadway, New York, NY 10018, USA
Bloomsbury Publishing Plc, 50 Bedford Square, London, WC1B 3DP, UK
Bloomsbury Publishing Ireland, 29 Earlsfort Terrace, Dublin 2, D02 AY28, Ireland

BLOOMSBURY, BLOOMSBURY ACADEMIC and the Diana logo are
trademarks of Bloomsbury Publishing Plc

First published in the United States of America 2024
Paperback edition published 2025

Copyright © Scott Freer, 2024, 2025

For legal purposes the Acknowledgements on p. xi constitute an
extension of this copyright page.

Cover design: Eleanor Rose
Cover image © Joe Webb

All rights reserved. No part of this publication may be: i) reproduced or transmitted in
any form, electronic or mechanical, including photocopying, recording or by means of
any information storage or retrieval system without prior permission in writing from
the publishers; or ii) used or reproduced in any way for the training, development or
operation of artificial intelligence (AI) technologies, including generative AI technologies.
The rights holders expressly reserve this publication from the text and data mining
exception as per Article 4(3) of the Digital Single Market Directive (EU) 2019/790.

Bloomsbury Publishing Inc does not have any control over, or responsibility for, any
third-party websites referred to or in this book. All internet addresses given in this
book were correct at the time of going to press. The author and publisher regret
any inconvenience caused if addresses have changed or sites have ceased
to exist, but can accept no responsibility for any such changes.

A catalog record for this book is available from the Library of Congress.

Library of Congress Cataloging-in-Publication Data

Names: Freer, Scott, 1967- author.
Title: American disaster movies of the 1970s : crisis, spectacle and
    modernity / Scott Freer.
Description: New York : Bloomsbury Academic, 2024. |
    Includes bibliographical references and index.
Identifiers: LCCN 2023015196 (print) | LCCN 2023015197 (ebook) |
    ISBN 9781501336836 (hardback) | ISBN 9781501375620 (paperback) |
    ISBN 9781501336843 (pdf) | ISBN 9781501336850 (epub) |
    ISBN 9781501336867 (ebook other)
Subjects: LCSH: Disaster films–United States–History and criticism. |
    Motion pictures–United States–History–20th century. | Nineteen seventies.
Classification: LCC PN1995.9.D55 F74 2024 (print) | LCC PN1995.9.D55 (ebook) |
    DDC 791.43/6556–dc23/eng/20230607
LC record available at https://lccn.loc.gov/2023015196
LC ebook record available at https://lccn.loc.gov/2023015197

ISBN: HB: 978-1-5013-3683-6
     PB: 978-1-5013-7562-0
     ePDF: 978-1-5013-3684-3
     eBook: 978-1-5013-3685-0

Typeset by Integra Software Services Pvt. Ltd.

For product safety related questions contact productsafety@bloomsbury.com.

To find out more about our authors and books visit www.bloomsbury.com
and sign up for our newsletters.

Disaster brings out the best and the worst in people.

This book is dedicated to the many 'vulnerable' workers who lost their jobs at the University of Leicester during the Covid-19 pandemic.

Contents

List of figures   viii
Preface: Escape from Lockdown City (2020)   x
Acknowledgements   xi

Introduction: Don't look up   1

1. Purging the American Dream in the 1930s   13
2. Melodrama in high modernity: *Airport* (1970)   31
3. The dark carnivalesque: *The Poseidon Adventure* (1972)   55
4. Skyscraper apocalypticism: *The Towering Inferno* (1974)   77
5. Los Angeles – a 'convicted' city: *Earthquake* (1974), *The Day of the Locust* (1975), *Smash-Up on Interstate 5* (1976)   99
6. Modern arenas of pleasure and violence: *Rollercoaster* (1977), *Two-Minute Warning* (1976), *Black Sunday* (1977)   123
7. Bee ecohorror: *The Swarm* (1978)   145
8. The destructive gaze: *The Medusa Touch* (1978)   169
9. Aftermath   177

Notes   201
Bibliography   234
Index   251

Figures

1.1 Blackie (Clark Gable) praying to, and thanking, God — 23
1.2 Mother O'Leary (Alice Brady): 'It was a city of wood, and now it's ashes. But out of the fire will be coming steel' — 26
1.3 Ma Joad (Jane Darwell): 'We'll go on forever, Pa. We're the people' — 29
2.1 The adulterous 707 captain, Vernon Demerest (Dean Martin) envisaging the stewardess, Tanya (Jacqueline Bisset) — 46
2.2 Inez (Maureen Stapleton), with 'tired and dull eyes', and Guerrero (Van Heflin), 'the defeated man in his fifties' — 47
2.3 The fractured relationship between work and the family — 51
3.1 Reverend Frank Scott (Gene Hackman): 'God wants winners, not quitters' — 68
3.2 Reverend Frank Scott (Gene Hackman): 'What is it you want – another sacrifice? More blood?' — 73
4.1 Death by fire — 93
4.2 Michael O'Halloran (Steve McQueen): 'You know, one of these days, they're gonna kill 10,000 in one of these firetraps' — 95
5.1 The ubiquitous Charlton Heston reclaims the *cock*pit from Karen Black in *Airport 1975* — 105
5.2 Richard Roundtree as 'a black, second-string Evel Knievel', alongside Rosa Amici (Victoria Principal) — 109
6.1 The synergy of the disaster spectacle and the amusement park is affirmed in *Rollercoaster* — 133
6.2 John Blane (James Brolin) is shot, and the reality of death disturbs the theme park fun — 137
6.3 The spectator (David Janssen as Steve) is the target of violence in the big spectacle — 138
7.1 The helicopter pilot (Steve Marlo) identifies 'a moving black mass' — 162
7.2 Maureen (Olivia de Havilland) looks on in horror at her school children who have been killed by a swarm of bees during a flower festival — 164

7.3	Eco-sadism	166
8.1	Richard Burton as Dr Morlar	170
9.1	Superman (Christopher Reeve) retrieves the dead body of Lois Lane (Margot Kidder), though her life is soon restored *à la* Lazarus	180

Preface: Escape from Lockdown City (2020)

Revisiting the golden age of American disaster movies during a coronavirus pandemic that has, so far, resulted in a 15 million death toll has been both disheartening and compelling.[1] When I eventually recovered from a semi-comatose state, brought on by severe Covid-19, Leicester was in Lockdown. I likened the experience to *The Day of the Triffids* (Steve Sekely, 1962), when Bill Masen wakes up to find the hospital deserted: 'What's been happening in this post-apocalyptic world?'[2] I lay in bed for weeks, too fatigued to visit the toilet unassisted, and my online friends recommended I watch, on my laptop, *Contagion* (Steven Soderbergh, 2011). At the time, Albert Camus's *The Plague* (1947) was a popular read. Other post-apocalyptic forms of pop culture, such as the 1975 television series, *Survivors* (Terry Nation), were revisited. I designed a T-Shirt with the words '2020: Escape from Lockdown City' that included a map of Leicester in the spirit of John Carpenter's *Escape from New York* (1981) – there was little hope of escape from what felt like a maximum-security prison-city. Existentially, the disease had invaded my body, like an alien force disrupting my embodied self, but at the same time the disease was a distant spectacle. I lost friends, and yet it was still hard to comprehend the epic scale of tragic suffering. Onlookers (and participants) invariably liken disturbing, horrific events to a film genre (apocalyptic, zombie, disaster). It is not to trivialize the horror – death, destruction and disease – but it is a reaching to a reassuring reference point as a means of articulating jarring, and unfamiliar, sensations and sights. Life imitates art, and art helps to confront and contain life. The dreaded disease will in the future be written about as a disaster that temporarily dethroned global capitalism and revealed the powerlessness of individual agency. But we have been here before. Many times.

Acknowledgements

My first debt is to my partner, Dr Rebecca Styler, for her intellectual companionship and for nursing me during long Covid. Molly – the Queen of Catopia – is the third member of our inter-species household and she makes me feel humane. This world is a better place thanks to people who are willing to support and to share the gift of knowledge. In this respect, I wish to express my gratitude towards the following people: Professor Phil Shaw, Dr Chris Horn, Dr Mark Duffett, Dr Guy Barefoot, Dr Christopher Harrington, David Watts and Dr Jenny Stewart. Finally, to all my former students, especially William Wolstenholme, who carry forth the light through the darkening days.

Introduction: Don't look up

The disaster film is a modern, demotic form of tragedy via which painful truths are processed and as a result ignored. As Irwin Allen once stated, 'people are observers of the macabre. It is a trait of all of us, to one degree or another.'[1] In this respect, the title of Adam McKay's 2021 film, *Don't Look Up*, suggests that, while screened apocalypticism allows for a vicarious indulgence in the macabre, humanity prefers not to confront the reality of an impending apocalyptic event. In this case, the instrument of disaster is a 'planet-killer comet', yet the film title is a metonym for various disaster deniers (e.g., those against climate-change). The film is a satire of the mediation of the macabre as a spectacle of mass destruction, and the concomitant disaster movie tropes: the tough-talking, hard-bodied white saviour, the spaceship for the select few, the silenced scientist of rational truth. The film continues the vogue for disaster comedy, exemplified in *The Big Bus* (James Frawley, 1976) and *Airplane!* (Jim Abrahams, David and Jerry Zuzker, 1980), as the repetitious and familiar formula of the disaster genre invites parody. But in turn, the cautionary warning is trivialized. What is lost is the serious message, the apocalyptic revelation of an unheeded vision of doom. Hence, the anti-mimetic, self-fulfilling prophesy, and the need to revisit the disaster cycle of the seventies.

The film's immediate context is the Covid-19 pandemic in which the disease disaster has been played out through social media, when numerous scientists have received death threats, and when libertarians have protested and rioted against State infringements of their individual rights. Peter Isherwell (Mark Rylance), a tech billionaire CEO, is a stand-in for super-rich tax-evaders, such as Jeff Bezos, Elon Musk and Richard Branson, who invest in lucrative space tourism whilst global warming ensues. *Don't Look Up* is a comment on the performance of emotional pain as opposed to the painful truth voiced by Kate Dibiasky (Jennifer Lawrence), an MSU doctoral candidate in astronomy: 'We're all gonna die!'. It is a familiar discourse: the hubristic faith in the triumph of technology and the nihilism at the heart of capitalism. And *Don't Look Up* also mocks the therapeutic, aesthetic, filtering of disaster: *Total Devastation*, a big budget, 'popcorn' spectacular, with a 'stellar cast' directed by Devin Peters (Chris Evans), is to be released in advance of the actual disaster. In other words, *Total Devastation* (a fictional film within the film's narrative) implies we have been here before – big-screen events foreshadowing the apocalyptic event. The fate of planet earth and humanity has been rehearsed on numerous occasions via a demotic art form. The disaster movie is a bearer of bad news. So, why aren't people terrified? Why do the cinematic prophets of doom go unheeded? The film begins with an intertitle, quoting the American humourist, Jack Handey: 'I want to die peacefully in my sleep like my grandfather, not screaming in terror like his passengers.' The implication is paradoxical: while mass hysteria is provoked by alarmists, to prevent such a fate one must heed their message. And so, visions of doom are contained via an appeasing form, like a one-liner joke or *Total Devastation*, which, in the words of Jack Bremmer (Tyler Perry), the co-host of *The Daily Rip*, is a 'ton of fun'.

Don't Look Up is both funny and depressing. The Last Supper scene when people gather at the family home of Dr Randall Mindy (Leonardo DiCaprio), an astronomy professor, and calmly accept their deaths and the fate of total destruction is a rare cinematic moment of resigned fatalism that undercuts default Hollywood triumphalism. The end of humanity has been prophesied many times. This is such a tale, though with a dystopian acceptance of oblivion, without overcoming solace or survivors. The closing *schadenfreude* scene is of Isherwell, and his elect passengers, landing on a habitable planet and being eaten alive by a seemingly cute, exotic creature, the Bronteroc. Janie Orlean (Meryl Streep), the President of the United States, cannot avoid the genetic forecast of her death. The Adam and Eve new dawning is denuded by a generic invocation of H. G. Wells's *The Time Machine* (1895) and *Planet of The Apes* (Franklin J. Schaffner, 1968): human evolution is doomed to prehistoric regression. For this is not an Anthropocene world. It is a revenge of nature finale that follows a montage of sublime nature – polar bears, hummingbirds etc. – prior to the dissolution of the Mindy house. Amidst the satire that brings levity to the horror, the fractured flashes of the natural order – echoing the pastoral euthanasia of Sol Roth (Edward G. Robinson) in *Soylent Green* (Richard Fleischer, 1973) as he listens to the main themes from Symphony No. 6 by Tchaikovsky, Symphony No. 6 by Beethoven and the 'Peer Gynt Suite' by Edvard Grieg – are a depressing reminder of the sublime beauty that has already been destroyed by a human existence tied to the death drive of capitalism and an infantilizing mass media. How do we cut through the oppressive symbolic space to avert disaster?

The film appears to have taken its cue from Arnold Schwarzenegger, who in 2015 was chosen by the French government to help make the moral case for the world to act urgently on climate change: 'I've starred in a lot of science fiction movies and, let me tell you something, climate change is not science fiction, this is a battle in the real world, it is impacting us right now. [...] This is bigger than any movie, this is the challenge of our time'.[2] George Monbiot, in response to *Don't Look Up*, sees the media's obsession with actors as spokespeople as vindicating Guy Debord's predictions in *The Society of Spectacle* (1967) and indicative of the 'absence of moral seriousness': 'Substance is replaced by semblance, as even the most serious issues must now be articulated by people whose work involves adopting someone else's persona and speaking someone else's words.'[3] The film's message, too, is that spectacle is at the 'heart of the unrealism of the real society'. Reality cannot compete with the movies.[4] The film endorses what Douglas Kellner (with reference also to Debord) sees as 'the triumph of the spectacle', concomitant with media sensationalism, that results in 'pacification and depoliticization', especially when 'consumption has attained the total occupation of social life'.[5] Spectacle dominates to such an extent that a disaster heading our way cannot be averted. For Kevan Manwaring, the 'postmodern neutering' of the future 'shuts down hope' offered in 'trans-apocalyptic' narratives that dramatize 'the transition from our current civilization to what comes after'.[6] In this sense, *Don't Look Up* is complicit: for it does not break through the mediating screen. A fixation on the death-drive event and its media multiplicity does not, according to Slavoj Žižek, 'destabilize the symbolic order we dwell in'.[7] Prophecies of doom are encoded in the entertaining capitalist discourse of trauma and reassurance. This said, another way of reframing the iteration of the disaster genre is to see it as modern tragedy. Humanity cannot confront the horror of mass self-annihilation, so the disaster film is a means, through tragic pleasure, of confronting and containing the Dionysian chaos that threatens to undo the superstructures of high modernity.

Crisis, spectacle and modernity

This is the first scholarly book dedicated to the cycle of disaster movies that dominated the American cinema screens and television in the 1970s. Rather than limiting the perspective to what Stephen Keane terms 'the classic phase lasting from 1970–74' (when disaster movies were most popular), this book spans from *Airport* (George Seaton, 1970) to *The Swarm* (Irwin Allen, 1978).[8] Film cycles are often, according to Zoë Wallin, 'tainted labels' because of their association with 'formulaic repetition and imitation'.[9] However, the objective is to demonstrate that the disaster cycle did not follow a unidirectional trajectory, and neither was it, in the words of Michael Ryan and Douglas Kellner, 'unidimensionally conservative'.[10] The golden age of the disaster movie was made up of successes, imitations, mutations, aberrations and major or minor disappointments, produced according to fluctuating, turbulent times as well as other cinematic trends (e.g., New Hollywood, blaxploitation and vigilante films). When it comes to the disaster cycle, mainstream Hollywood and art films are not so diametrically opposed. The seventies cycle was a zeitgeist counterblast to America's hubristic mastery of nature's destructive power (via technology or divine power), exposing the built-in vulnerability of high modernity.

For many scholars, the Hollywood output constitutes a popular time-bound cycle, distinctive from the durable 'conventionalized group' considered the film genre.[11] Invariably, disaster movies in this period are read as metaphorical responses to when the United States underwent a 'legitimacy crisis' or 'when major institutions lost the confidence of the American people'.[12] This has led to a general account of the films as a 'reactionary culture' in which to 'exorcise greater fears':[13]

> Overall, the disaster movie [...] is a way to displace contemporary problems into simple, physical confrontations – for example, man versus shark, or airline versus hole in the tail section. These confrontations are generally resolved via old-fashioned, virtues: hard work, individual initiative, group cooperation. The disaster movie is thus a conservative response which "solves" the 1970s malaise by drastically simplifying and reframing it.[14]

For Keane, despite 'their critique of corporate greed', they were 'edgy but ultimately reassuring'.[15] Ryan and Kellner, to a degree, concur: 'The disaster films [...] provide therapeutic narratives, which enact crisis, then assuage it.'[16] John Sutherland sees elemental disaster (flood, earthquake, meteor, fire, shark) narratives as rendering 'society docile to its masters and managers' by syphoning off 'rebellious and cynical' sentiments'.[17] And for Nick Roddick, the reactions to corporate disaster point to 'a shared ideological stance', because most films reassured by showing the audience that the system could cope.[18] However, the focus of these studies is on commercial successes, assuming a shared cathartic effect, and while ignoring the subgenre variations (e.g., ecohorror), the anti-genre (e.g., *The Day of the Locust*), made-for-TV movies (e.g., *Smash-Up on Interstate 5*) and post-*Jaws* films (e.g., *Black Sunday*).

The cycle was, to some extent, determined by the market, yet, to echo Stuart M. Kaminsky, this does not answer the question why a certain popular narrative form rises, persists and fades.[19] According to Steve Neale, 'films made within a specific and limited time-span' are founded 'for the most part, on the characteristics of individual commercial success'.[20] However, it is difficult to ascertain what constitutes the winning formula (as a means of reducing risk in production investment) in the disaster cycle. For instance, *Airport* was the second highest grossing film in 1970, thus prompting Universal Pictures, more than any other Hollywood studio, to invest in a financially stabilizing genre.[21] But, at the time of its release it was not typed as 'disaster' and was noted more for its *Grand Hotel* narrative approach.[22] The importance of *Airport* lay in Arthur Hailey's 1968 novel transposing portmanteau-melodrama into a setting of high modernity, and the film did not obviously conform to expectations in terms of exploiting 'the spectacular potential of the screen'.[23] It is not a film of mass death and destruction. A suicide bomber is blown up in a toilet and the Boeing 707 lands safely. George Seaton's screenplay – an exemplar of classical Hollywood storytelling – suppresses a key subplot of crisis and trauma in the novel, and consequently downplays the structural fault lines that Hailey had shown existed in a complex, big industry. So, to regard *Airport* as establishing a genre template or ideological model for subsequent imitators is misleading.[24]

Yet, the view that persists is that *Airport* spawned a series of imitators. It was only following the success of *The Poseidon Adventure* (Ronald Neame, 1972) that *Airport* was retrospectively typed. *The Andromeda Strain* (Robert Wise), released in 1971 – a Universal production – fared relatively poorly, even though it was more of a straightforward disaster movie. The use of multiple-screen and close-up images of gruesome death in *Andromeda* proved that for the disaster formula to commercially work the right balance between a horror spectacle and a fantasy filter had to be struck. Roddick rightly points out that *Poseidon*, though not the first movie of the cycle, 'confidently established its basic narrative model'.[25] *Poseidon*, in contrast to the 'old-fashioned nonsense' of *Airport*, was described by Vincent Canby as a 'fun' 'Ark movie' (when a group of assorted characters are placed in an unsafe situation).[26] By 1974, following the combined success of *Poseidon* and *Airport*, Hollywood studios were willing to invest more in the genre, and aimed bigger in terms of what Pauline Kael referred to as 'destruction orgies'.[27] The peak year featured *The Towering Inferno*

(John Guillermin), *Earthquake* (Mark Robson) and *Airport '75* (Jack Smight) in the top-ten highest grossing films. But even though *Inferno* was the apotheosis of the cycle, as Stirling Silliphant (the screenwriter) noted, the genre had been reduced to a logistics formula that privileged spectacle above the multiple unfolding stories that had made *Airport* so popular:

> Now you have a script of 130 pages. You have eight major story/character blocks – 8 goes into 130 around 16+ times. So you know, going in, that you can only put Holden on 16 pages of the movie in terms of foreground action or any kind of meaningful dialogue, unless you unbalance everything and give him 22 pages and cut Chamberlain to 10, etc., etc., etc.[28]

The overall result was of the reduction of characters to superficial stereotypes, with less expositional or melodramatic dialogue.

For Andrew Britton, 'the differences between *The Poseidon Adventure* and *The Towering Inferno* are primarily decorative', in staging 'the purification and resurrection of capitalism'.[29] However, set in the modernist superstructure of a skyscraper, *Inferno* is apocalyptic on a grander scale and resonates more as a crisis film in the year of Richard Nixon's presidential resignation. In comparison to *Airport*, which was released before the Watergate scandal and oil crisis, *Inferno* was a nihilistic rendering of the cycle. The scenes of death by fire were too close to reality for Kael: 'What emotion are we meant to feel for Robert Wagner [...] and his secretary (Susan Flannery), who have a little fling, get out of bed, and die hideously, the camera lingering on their agonies? [...] The realism here is very offensive'.[30] Disaster movies do not necessarily ennoble suffering and are inseparable from the big question of tragic catharsis. The idea of a reassuring effect ignores the potential for the reality of tragic suffering to break through the 'protective shield' of the spectacle.[31] Various prominent American reviewers – Roger Ebert, Pauline Kael and Vincent Canby – found certain movies to have been disturbing spectacles of disaster. So, *Inferno* was part of a commercially successful stage in the cycle, but it did not contain 'similar, easily exploitable features' that spanned the decade.[32]

Because of 'their sudden quantitative importance (number of films, audience numbers)', by the mid-1970s a group of French critics were prompted to analyse the ideological context of 'film catastrophes' in a set of short articles, published in *Positif* (March 1976).[33] The shared view is that the films represent a crisis in Western capitalism out of which a new male order emerges. For Joel Magny:

> The metaphor is clear: for a new man, for a new birth, we must refuse morality and the current way of life (symbolised in almost all these films by a social function

or party which unfolds, unawares, at the time of the disaster) to return to the primitive values of religion and wild capitalism. The apparent contradiction between technocracy and primitive thought is resolved in the fact that this return to fundamental values concerns the masses, while the heroes, the leaders, the chosen ones, the elite lead the world by manly strength (physical and moral) and knowledge. This is the answer that the West is currently trying to find to the collapse of its values and hierarchies. Such films are a perfect illustration of the struggle currently being played out between the liberal ideology of advanced, but dying, capitalism and the return of a primitive ideology (free enterprise, individualism, etc.) which is trying to make itself new.[34]

Many of the disaster movies dramatized survival scenarios in which supposedly a regressive masculine type takes hold of the situation. Stéphane Sorel concurs in a piece entitled, 'Catastrophic Masculinity', that the re-evaluation of values called for the 'glorification of masculinity' at the expense of female stars:

Immersed in a breathtaking fiction, the audience follows (literally) the hero carrying all the hopes, the leader, the man. Because the leader can only be a man. Gene Hackman in *The Poseidon Adventure*, Charlton Heston in *Airport 1975*, Charlton Heston again in *Earthquake* (with Arthur Kennedy), Newman and Steve MacQueen in *The Towering Inferno*, Richard Harris in *Juggernaut*.[35]

Women either serve an ornamental function or an ethical model, or as in the case of the stewardess played by Karen Black in *Airport 1975*, 'can only act if the men are *physically* out of the picture'.[36] Disaster movies convince us: 'of the inherent inferiority of women, of their inability to take responsibility for themselves, to take action and of the imperative need for them to put their fate in the hands (both literally and figuratively) of men'.[37]

There is certainly a degree of truth in this established gender reading of the cycle. Female stars were not represented as leaders emerging out of survival scenarios, and male-centred apocalypticism dominated mainstream cinema at the expense of feminist utopias that envisioned alternative societies in the medium of literature.[38] As a rule, the male spirit of destruction, as opposed to female optimism, lends itself to cinematic spectacle. For instance, the 1978 screen adaptation of Arthur Herzog's *The Swarm* (1974) is a throwback to the pre-Rachel Carson era of environmentalism, with the matriarchal bee colony obliterated and the anthropocentric status quo restored. This theme of 'eco-sadism' is replicated in *Empire of the Ants* (Bert I. Gordon, 1977), when Joan Collins playing the overbearing careerist perishes at the same time as the queen ant during a Darwinian face-off that empowers the primitive male.[39] But again, the trajectory is not ideologically uniform. As the chapter on the 1930s cycle argues, the purging of a fallen capitalist order and the re-evaluation of male types is a long-established convention in the disaster film. In *Deluge* (Felix E. Feist, 1933), for example, the deep anxiety was one of regression to a Wild West state of nature in which lawless men return to a primal, predator type, and which is averted by a reconstructed male in the form of Martin (Sidney Blackmer) – albeit at the expense of the non-monogamous female. The moral purge precludes the re-evaluation of sexual mores. In the 1970s, the noble religious patriarch, embodied in Martin, is tragically undone in *The Poseidon Adventure*, and in *Airport* the traditional patriarchal family is challenged, via the privileging of romantic relationships with working women above familial ties. Nonetheless, materialistic men who honour money and ambition above familial duties are generally part and parcel of an institutional purging of bad capitalists.[40] Ultimately, the disaster genre is male-centred, for as the chapter on *The Medusa Touch* (Jack Gold, 1978) argues, toxic masculinity was, and remains, integral to disaster spectacles, in channelling male grievance and reasserting dominance via violent means.

The 1970s cycle was also a secularized riposte to movies that implied a sense of 'God's abiding support' in the very midst of disaster.[41] The final scene in *The War of the Worlds* (Byron Haskin, 1953) invokes the *deus ex machina* of divine intervention, when global Martian victory seems imminent, and the survivors take refuge in a Los Angeles church. The invasion abruptly stops, and Dr Clayton Forrester (Gene Barry), seeing that an alien has expired, says: 'and we were all praying for a miracle'. He looks up to the sky as church bells chime. The narrator (Sir Cedric Hardwicke) observes that while the Martians were impervious to humanity's weapons, they had 'no resistance to the bacteria in our atmosphere to which we have long since become immune. After all that men could do had failed, they were destroyed and humanity was saved by the littlest things, which God, in His wisdom, had put upon this Earth.' Bacteria is God's way of guarding humanity in this best of all probable worlds against an alien invasion. In *The Devil at 4 O'Clock* (Mervyn LeRoy, 1961), just before a volcano erupts and destroys the whole Pacific Island in French Polynesia, Father Doonan (Spencer Tracy) comforts the dying Charlie (Bernie Hamilton) and says: 'Don't be afraid of God. Call on him, if you want to.' Re-joined by Harry (Frank Sinatra) on the other side of the chasm, Doonan gives the dead Charlie the last rites, and Harry also gives the sign of the cross. However, in *Poseidon* and *Earthquake*, the sacrificial deaths of Reverend Frank Scott (Gene Hackman) and Stewart Graff (Charlton Heston) subvert the assurance supposedly given by strong religious patriarchs. Scott's blasphemous monologue – 'What is it you want – another sacrifice? More blood?' – raises the question of God's benign purpose (or existence) in a world of innocent suffering. The ignominious drowning of Heston (an Episcopalian actor) is poetic justice for the drowning of the biblical Egyptians – or the ideological punishment of Atheist-Communists – in *The Ten Commandments* (Cecil B. DeMille, 1956). Where is the parting of the waves now, Heston? Perhaps the audience is meant to exult in the cinematic fall from grace for Heston, whose career trajectory mirrored the shifting, post-war codes of apocalypticism in American cinema: from biblical epics to secular disaster movies.

An enduring feature of the cycle is the spectacle of disaster which has been dispersed into various other cinematic genres. *Inferno* and *Earthquake* – marketed as 'event' films – paved the way for the big-budget blockbusters of *Jaws* (Steven Spielberg, 1975) and *Star Wars* (George Lucas, 1977). Consequently, comic book fantasies, starting with *Superman* (Richard Donner, 1978), became an affirmative substitute for the destruction orgies, which for Kael represented a 'death wish for film art' and the only way Hollywood knew 'to make money'.[42] To create big spectacles about the flawed and failed nature of modernity, the event film involved epic feats of cinematic engineering. *Inferno* was described by Canby as an 'end-of-the-world' movie for 'movie technology buffs': 'The special effects are smashing, better than those in "Earthquake" even without the brain-bending Sen-surround effect of "Earthquake." The technological work is old-fashioned Hollywood make-believe at its painstaking best.'[43] *Inferno* as a superstructure blockbuster starred the world's tallest skyscraper, 'The Glass Tower, soaring 138 stories into the air, but the film's bigness also involved two books, fifty-seven movie sets, a big stunt crew, two Hollywood studios, and the biggest all-star cast since *Grand Hotel*.' The overpowering drama of the disaster movie was also defined by its immersive horror spectacle. Canby referred to *Earthquake* as 'the Big Splat' movie, alluding to ingenious technical devices to augment the horror of mass death and destruction. The film is notable for its pioneering use of Sensurround – low-frequency sound vibrations, emitted from speakers near the screen and at the back of the cinematic theatre to induce the sensation of being 'physically unhinged'.[44] This complemented the visual effects created by, for example, the shaker mount camera and the splat camera effect. Such participation gimmicks aimed to imitate the thrill of the fairground ride, and *Rollercoaster* (James Goldstone, 1977), which also used Sensurround and is another Jennings Lang production for Universal Pictures, is illustrative of the synergy between event cinema and the theme park.

The focus on the 'most strident and successful disaster movies' of the cycle has meant that movies from the latter half of the decade have been overlooked.[45] According to Keane, the cycle 'became increasingly redundant as the 1970s progressed'.[46] Yet, if anything, the cycle was becoming more experimental by incrementally implicating the spectator within 'the realm of the possible'.[47] *The Hindenburg* (Robert Wise, 1974) is notable for revisiting an actual disaster when a German zeppelin crashed and burned on 6 May 1937. It was a relative disappointment for Universal, in the same year *Jaws* was released.[48] For Roger Ebert: 'This isn't fun. We go to disaster movies for fun.'[49] The use of newsreel coverage and Herbert Morrison's radio eyewitness report ruptures the fantasy filter. Subsequent films brought disaster closer to home. While *Rollercoaster* capitalized on Hollywood's return to its fairground origins, *Two-Minute Warning* (Larry Peerce, 1977) and *Black Sunday* (John Frankenheimer, 1977) challenged the 'Roman-circus mentality in the audience' by returning the cinematic gaze of horror towards 'observers of the macabre'.[50] For A. A. Klein: 'the film cycle eventually bores or annoys the audience […] And the moment that a film cycle begins to falter at the box office, film studios will either heavily revise the original formula or cease making the cycle altogether.'[51] It would be truer to say that the cycle had exhausted itself because spectacles of mass destruction had fallen out of favour in a Jimmy Carter era of post-Vietnam nostalgia films. *The Swarm* (Irwin Allen, 1978) marks the end of the cycle, but if it had been released earlier as planned, shortly after the publication of Herzog's novel that was responding to the African bee scare, perhaps it may have fared commercially, and critically, better. The film belongs to a series of what I term 'bee movies' and is illustrative of how the cycle was also constituted by subgenres (e.g., ecohorror), a mixture of separate genres that were shaped by cinematic tropes as well as contemporaneous conventions and concerns.

Therefore, rather than submitting to Maurice Yacowar's over-arching typology, this book treats the cycle as a time-bound phenomenon that is also defined by disaster subgenres according to their various sites or contexts of modernity in crisis:[52]

- Airports
- Luxury Ocean Liners
- Los Angeles

- Skyscrapers
- Modern Arenas
- The African 'bee scare'.

For instance, in 'The Towering Inferno (1974): Skyscraper Apocalypticism' attention turns to the American skyscraper as a site of the inherent precarity of vertical capitalism. Central to this chapter is the question of how genre cinema can represent the violent reality of mass destruction while mitigating audience responses to the socio-political resonances of historical disaster, both in terms of their troubling causes – the modernist architect as capitalist overreacher and the worker as sacrificial victim – and their unsettling consequences. To establish a context in which to approach this question, a critical account is provided of the long cinematic tradition of inferno films, ranging from *The Life of an American Fireman* (Edwin S. Porter, 1903), *The Workman's Lesson* and *The Crime of Carelessness* (Harold M. Shaw, 1912) and *The Fireman* (Charlie Chaplin, 1916) to made-for-TV-film, *The Triangle Factory Fire Scandal* (Mel Stuart, 1979). If *Inferno* helped to establish a superstructure blockbuster tradition, its central tropes – the heroization of firemen and the exoneration of wicked capitalists – belong both to the origins and tendency of disaster capitalism. The chapter also considers how *Inferno* negotiates its indulgence in the spectacle of sublime terror, while offering itself as a cautionary tale about high modernity and its uncertain future.

The chapter on *The Poseidon Adventure* considers the subgenre of the 'ark' movie, a group jeopardy drama set in the single, enclosed setting of a luxury ocean liner, in relation to hubristic faith vis-à-vis the extreme forces of nature. Films, such as *Titanic* (Jean Negulesco, 1953), that depicted the 1912 sinking of RMS *Titanic* – one of the most famous tragedies in modern history – generally focused on stoical heroism and a closing sense of salvation. While not an overt 'crisis film', *Poseidon* nonetheless addresses the problem of evil – how to reconcile tragic suffering with the notion of a benevolent God, and as such redresses both the retributive justice of biblical epics and the rise of American Protestant evangelism.[53] But what distinguishes *Poseidon* from *Inferno* is a dark carnivalesque that blends Dantean symbolism, derivative of *Dante's Inferno* (Harry Lachman, 1935), with the *parodia sacra* of New Hollywood films (e.g., Robert Altman, *M*A*S*H*, 1970). It also owes much to Irwin Allen's penchant for fantasy adventure, which started with *The Lost World* (Irwin Allen, 1960) and continued until *When Time Ran Out* (James Goldstone, 1980). So, rather than only examining the cycle according to the commercial demands of a movie industry, this book also shows how films dramatized modern disaster via cinematic precursors and concurrent trends.

Finally, to view the cycle as a 'box-office fad', or as providing 'a foretaste of what was about to become the main tradition' of Reaganite entertainment, overlooks the fact that it roughly spanned the same cinematic period of New Hollywood, which also conveyed a dark and unsettling vision of American society.[54] Therefore, Andrew Britton's synergy of the blockbuster and the disaster movie is disingenuous. 'A disaster movie could be a blockbuster, but not all blockbusters were disaster films.'[55] Disaster cycles mirror, in part, the cyclical rise and fall of American modernity. Therefore, the opening chapter examines a crop of films from the 1930s, a foreshadowing mini cycle that responded to the Wall Street Crash of 1929 and the subsequent Great Depression by imagining the social gospel purging of an ethically unrestrained capitalist society.

1

Purging the American Dream in the 1930s

In *The Dry Salvages* (published in 1941 during the London Blitz), T. S. Eliot recalls the Great Mississippi flood of 1927, the most destructive river flood in the history of the United States. Millions of acres across seven states were flooded, with evacuees totalling 500,000:

> I do not know much about gods; but I think that the river
> Is a strong brown god-sullen, untamed and intractable,
> Patient to some degree, at first recognised as a frontier;
> Useful, untrustworthy, as a conveyor of commerce;
> Then only a problem confronting the builder of bridges.
> The problem once solved, the brown god is almost forgotten
> By the dwellers in cities-ever, however, implacable.
> Keeping his seasons and rages, destroyer, reminder
> Of what men choose to forget. Unhonoured, unpropitiated
> By worshippers of the machine, but waiting, watching and waiting.[1]

Eliot (born in St. Louis), like American authors and dust-bowl balladeers in the 1930s, was well aware that soil erosion was the cause of numerous floods, and here he pays homage to the 'intractable' destructive force of nature that city dwellers and worshippers of the machine 'choose to forget'.[2]

America's manifest destiny – the conquering of the West – has come at a big cost. Calamitous events that cause a high level of human suffering and material loss are more likely to affect low-income earners and developing countries. Nonetheless, as an advanced industrialized country, America is and has been particularly prone to natural disasters – cyclones, floods, droughts, earthquakes – as well as human-instigated disasters: oil spills and fires. The great Dust Bowl drought is 'considered the worst climate tragedy of the twentieth century in the United States and the worst prolonged environmental disaster in its recorded history'.[3] But the disaster was also man-made, the ecological result of mushroom growth: rapid urban and industrial expansion and the concomitant exploitation of natural resources (hence the extensive ploughing of topsoil in the Great Plains and subsequent Dust Bowl storms). The devastating environmental catastrophe also resulted in 'economic ruin, and great human hardship', intensifying the deprivations of the Great Depression, brought on by the Wall Street stock market crash of 1929 that had signalled the end of prosperity politics and that had raised questions about business leadership and capitalism itself.[4] One could take a longer view and regard, though certainly not equal in terms of the suffering involved in the colonial destruction of indigenous communities, the greatest disasters of American history – the Great Chicago Fire of 1871, the Johnstown Flood of 1889 and the San Francisco Earthquake of 1906 – tragic consequences of America's manifest destiny.

Earlier movie scriptwriters had made it clear that 'natural disaster was God's retribution for the sins of the trapped people', and this is evident in the Old Testament spectacles of Cecil B. DeMille, Henry King and Michael Curtiz.[5] For Stephen Keane, the disaster films of the 1930s could be distinguished 'from Roman and biblical epics'.[6] Yet, while the seventies cycle could no longer assume moviegoers would accept Christian moral edicts, a group of films, beginning with Felix E. Feist's *Deluge* (1933) and ending with John Ford's *The Grapes of Wrath* (1940), continued to harness religious apocalypticism and themes of Christian redemption. Films, such as *Dante's Inferno* (Harry Lachman, 1935), typify how Hollywood, as a moral guardian, reworked an actual disaster (SS *Morro Castle*, 1934) into a story of spiritual renewal to address the corrupt prosperity politics of the American dream that had placed profit before social responsibility. It is 'a film notable for its blatant exploitation of Dante, [and] for its terror-inducing sets [...]' and is the frame for holding in place 'the unfolding moral narrative'.[7] The Dantean symbolism frames the opening scenes, when Carter is seen working as a stoker in the bowels of a ship, and it later becomes apparent that the coal-fuelled flames of the steam engines are part of the film's inferno conceit and a fire and brimstone corrective to the capitalist decadence of the 1930s. Typical for the thirties cycle and its underlying theme of Christian repentance, Carter eventually renounces the degradation of unbridled capitalism. It is indicative of how the revised disaster genre generally deployed, instead of Old Testament retributive visions, a 'social gospel' perspective reflective of F. D. Roosevelt's new social theory of community cooperation rather than economic individualism.[8] Out of disaster, the American dream was morally purged and restored.

The thirties crop also shows that the disaster genre is inseparable from a biblical myth of America: from the exodus of the pioneering pilgrims to purging 'deluge' narratives. The national trauma of the 1929 crash and the persistent depression had punctured the teleological drive of a nation: the conquering of the Wild West to build a modern nation. In other words, the frontier myth had reached its own end times. It is unsurprising that Noah's Ark, the biblical story of divine judgement and renewal, frames *Deluge*, whereas a reversed version of Exodus underpins John Steinbeck's 1939 novel – for the migratory exodus brought no happy end nor final arrival. However, the on-screen cycle fulfils the apocalyptic pattern of an end with a new beginning, reflecting the New Deal's emphasis on nation rebuilding through the millenarian traditions that underpin the social gospel expectations of bringing the kingdom of God into the earthly realm.

The 'social gospel' was a religious social-reform movement, whose chief proponents, such as Washington Gladden and Lyman Abbott, influenced to an extent by Walter Rauschenbusch's *Christianity and the Social Crisis* (1907), advocated that the 'Kingdom of God' require social as well as individual salvation. According to William H. Brackney, Rauschenbusch envisioned a Christian social order where bad men can be made to do good things.[9] And Roosevelt's New Deal policies of the 1930s demonstrated how 'earlier reform initiatives supported by the social gospel were becoming part of American national policy'.[10] This new moral spirit of anti-capitalist collectivism and national reconstruction was reflected too in disaster movies.[11] The Great Depression cycle both challenged and reasserted the optimistic logic of the frontier myth through a series of narratives that married the older biblical theme of decadence and divine retribution with an emphasis on social concern and reform.

Noah's Ark (1928) and *Deluge* (1933)

The first film to initiate the 1930s' cycle and its apocalyptic pattern of purging and renewal that underwrites the biblical deluge narrative was *Deluge* (Felix E. Feist, 1933), an adaptation of Sydney Fowler Wright's 1928 novel. According to *The Oxford Companion to World Mythology*, the flood myth usually carries aspects of the creation/genesis story, as in Hebrew mythology, and the floodwaters become a 'second version' of the primeval maternal values – a vehicle for 'rebirth as well as a cleansing element'.[12] In other words, the deluge narrative is one of violent eruption and re-creation, a chance to start again by removing the wrong. To quote Frank Kermode: 'The moments we call crises are ends and beginnings.'[13]

Conventionally, the American deluge narrative serves a kind of eschatological pattern: the old stagnant order is purged to make way for a 'second coming' (to start afresh, to create a more satisfactory balance between virtue and money). In Wright's novel, the 'deluge is neither a self-inflicted tragedy [...] nor the judgment of an angry deity', but the opening intertitle signals that the film version is modelled on the paradigmatic flood and creation of Genesis:[14]

> *Deluge* is a tale of fantasy – an adventure in speculation – a vivid epic pictorialization of an author's imaginative flight. We, the producers, present it now purely for your entertainment, remembering full well God's covenant with Noah: "And I will establish my covenant with you; neither shall all flesh be cut off any more by the waters of the flood; neither shall there any more be a flood to destroy the earth." (*Genesis* 9:11)

While reassuring American audiences that this world is a 'monument of mercy, according to the oath of God', and so they are secure from another deluge, nonetheless *Deluge* underscores the recurring cinematic link between the flood myth and the biblical story of Noah's Ark that was established in Michael Curtiz' film.

Noah's Ark, a 1928 hybrid silent-talkie film, which had been released with a 'Vitaphone music and effects tracks and talking sequences', is in keeping with Cecil B. DeMille's spectacular epic *The Ten Commandments* (1923) by drawing parallels between biblical and modern times to suggest a tapeworm of moral continuity.[15] The film also appropriates the parallel editing from D. W. Griffith's *Intolerance* (1916) that interweaves timeless and time-bound parallels to stage, in the words of Tom Gunning: 'an allegory of providential progress moving through historical catastrophe to religious redemption'.[16] The film opens, after the deluge, with an intertitle expressing God's covenant: 'neither will I again smite anymore everything living, as I have done'. The film then juxtaposes depictions of the building of the Tower of Babel and the worshipping of the golden calf (which, in the context of Exodus 32, can signify the idolization of a false god, such as Mammon – the personification of the greedy pursuit for wealthy gain) with shots of New York skyscraper construction and uncaring stockbrokers. The preceding intertitle reads: 'But men continued to remain wicked in their hearts. And they said: Let us build a city and a tower whose top may reach unto heaven and make us strong on against God's vengeance.' We witness palimpsestic images of suicide, a gambling roulette and dancing girls to imply that the Roaring Twenties and Prohibition is an era of decadence equal to that of pre-deluge excess. The moral lesson to be inferred is that the capitalist market of bust and boom and selfish greed has brought about a modern-day deluge in which 'brother wars with brother'. Later, a map of war-torn Europe that merges into deluge imagery affirms the apocalyptic pattern. And so, the next temporal shift takes us to the eve of the First World War and a scene on board the Orient Express train. A fellow passenger rebukes a pious minister, a Noah equivalent, and other passengers talk of either the impending war helping business, a godless world or science or 'military might' as the new God. The Bible-carrying minister speaks of 'God's eternal plan' and is again admonished: 'Faith is food for fools and invalids. If there is a God why doesn't he show himself.' At this point, a washed-out bridge collapses and the train is derailed and plummets into the onrushing river. God shows himself 'in wrath'. From underneath the wreckage, an unhand-cuffed prisoner joins Travis (George O'Brien) and his buddy Al (Guinn 'Big Boy' Williams) to help rescue Marie (Dolores Costello). They are later revealed to be mythical reincarnations of Noah's children.

Both Travis and Al enlist when America joins the war, but, when both are assigned to a trench squad to attack a German machine gun nest, Travis accidentally kills Al with a grenade. Fatally wounded, Al's last words are uttered: 'So long, old boy ... see you ... in heaven!' Later, when Marie and Travis (a married couple) and others are trapped under a demolished building, a minister compares the war and its 'deluge of blood' to the biblical story of Noah's Ark. The moral message is, again, that man's evil has provoked God's wrath. The film then reverts to the biblical time of Noah and the actors who played the roles of the prisoner, Travis and Al appear as Japheth, Ham and Shem, with Marie now as Noah's handmaid, Miriam ('beloved of Japheth'). King Nephilim (Noah Beery) has led his people from Jehovah to pay tribute to the 'false god Jaghuth' during the feast of gold. Noah's Ark on the mountainside is deemed the 'one altar [...] raised to Jehovah'. When Nephilim (a name alluding to creatures that lived before and after the Flood – Genesis 6:4) orders the sacrifice of the most beautiful virgin, Miriam is chosen. Japheth is blinded and set to labour on a stone-mill when he tries to save her. And Jehovah unleashes the apocalyptic deluge just as Miriam is to be slaughtered: 'From the four corners of the earth mighty tempests rose. God's wrath rode upon the winds.' With Miriam saved, Japheth's eyesight is miraculously restored, the Ark is afloat, and the 'fleeing multitudes' seek 'shelter' from 'the sundering floods'. And before returning to the First World War, an intertitle exclaims: 'That was the end of a world of lust and sin. God made His covenant and the rainbow appeared in the heavens.'

And when the entombed group emerge from the demolished building in 1918 and the Armistice is declared: 'Above this deluge of blood, and the graves of ten million, shall not the rainbow of a new covenant appear – the covenant of peace?' And the pious minister declares: 'Don't you understand? It is the beginning of the rainbow – the fulfilment of the sacrifice.' According to many social gospel thinkers, the war was a punishment for human decadence.

Released just one year before the Wall Street crash, the trans-historical apocalyptic pattern of greed appears prophetic, and yet the final intertitle, that is meant to reassure like 'God's monument of mercy', appears, in hindsight, a false prophecy: for the promise of a new beginning, as history tells us, turns again into another apocalyptic end. In fact, likening the bloodbath of the First World War to the biblical deluge during the inter-war period became a literary trope too: for example, Leonard Woolf's study of communal psychology was entitled *After the Deluge* (1931). The film is also remarkable for its use of 'the mythical method' that 'manipulates a continuous parallel between contemporaneity and antiquity', and that T. S. Eliot saw as a way of 'controlling, or ordering, of giving a shape and significance to the immense panorama of futility and anarchy which is contemporary history'.[17] Like *The Waste Land* (1922), *Noah's Ark* aims to recover a Christian grand narrative to give moral order to a post-war sense 'of futility and anarchy'.[18]

Feist's Pre-Code *Deluge*, a film rediscovered in 1987 when a version dubbed into Italian was found, translates 'Thomas Hobbes' State of Nature' to a post-apocalyptic return to the Wild West, a world of pagan debauchery and sinfulness, with a landscape that eerily mirrors the desiccated land of the Great Plains during the Dust Bowl storms of the 1930s.[19] Unexplained natural disasters destroy human civilization, and New York is hit by an earthquake and a tsunami causing a Manhattan skyline of skyscrapers to collapse and for people to be crushed by falling masonry. The film is very much in the vein of the Western, in which an order emerges based on physical power and primal urges of pre-civilized men. A symbolic conflict of two male types (the lawless man versus the lawyer) is played out between the caveman-like Jefferson and Martin, the sharply dressed lawyer from New York. The polarity of masculinity is visually distinguished via the stubble (in Martin's case: the lack of). Regression is also signified via the Bellamy gang, representing the Freudian male horde that hunts down women as sexual prey. They have already raped and killed a young female. And they are now on the hunt for Claire, the solitary female swimmer. The implication is that whilst the Wild West can be conquered and tamed, law and order needs to be maintained to keep the rogue male in check. Jefferson claims ownership over Claire: 'I told you she was mine!' – before strangling his rival. Martin (Sidney Blackmer), on the other hand, is a chivalric and well-spoken gentleman of family values. He is the homemaker, hence his ability to gather provisions in a tunnel (a place of safe accommodation), and not the cowboy.

While Wright's novel uses disaster to level out a British class system, Feist privileges noble patriarchy as a saving grace. In this survival film, Martin's fatherly embrace of his children is contrasted with shots of a marauding gang of male rapists. As scapegoated types, the film alluded to the rioting and the incipient signs of proletariat revolution that the New Dealers were hoping to head off. A local settlement of survivors (that is trying to build a town) is determined to 'wipe out' the Bellamy gang. The film symbolically returns the nation to a new Wild West beginning to present a new myth of creation (or nation rebuilding). *Deluge* ideally captures the post-1929 sense of a morally conflicted nation: one caught between religious piety (linked to the social values of order and decency) and rogue-like capitalist decadence.

Martin embodies the softening of capitalist excess through a return to small-town capitalism regulated by a softer vision of masculinity. In other words, the deluge is divine punishment for a society founded on the wrong social values. Before New York is struck by biblical apocalypticism, scientists are puzzled as to the inexplicable patterns of natural phenomenon. Nonetheless, an eclipse of the sun implies celestial intervention. And equating a post-apocalyptic wasteland to the Wild West underscores the vulnerability of a newly founded, supposedly modern civilization in which wealth and technology are a false macho-God. This is implied through the superimposition of sermonizing preachers over scenes of cascading skyscrapers (or Towers of Babel). One such preacher reads from Psalm 23: 'The Lord is My Shepherd'. The message, heard through scenes of apocalypticism that invoke fire and brimstone judgement, is one of elective reassurance – in that God's merciful stewardship will deliver the anointed into 'the house of the Lord forever'. It is therefore no coincidence that during the deluge, Martin's wife and children are seen praying arduously in a bedroom. And lo, out of the wasteland, Martin, the pious hero, emerges.

As a screen adaptation of Wright's novel, the altered gender politics in a reformed society reveals the ideological need to sustain the divine law of the father. As in the '70s' disaster films, a primitive order is reinstated to clear out radical politics. In the novel, Helen, first wife to Martin who was presumed killed by the deluge, invites Claire, the second wife who bears a child, to form a triadic relationship: 'They [Claire, Helen and Martin] went into the house together.'[20] This is in defiance of the established patriarchal law that insists upon a woman being allowed to select only one male partner. As Claire sees it: 'I suppose men will always try to make laws for women.'[21] Even though Wright's deluge fantasy does not permit a clean sweep of male control and is far removed from feminist utopian visions, the screen version sticks to the elective theology of the Noah story. In the film, Claire, the sporty survivalist, is the confused symbol of the liberated (rogue) New Woman. She can live without men. This is until she meets Martin, and then the lawless woman is deemed selfish and un-sisterly. When Martin is eventually reunited with his presumed dead wife, Helen, and two children in the village, Claire becomes belligerent with the lawfully married wife and her lawlessness is affirmed when in the final shots she is seen to swim away into the ocean (or God's deluge). Ultimately, the rogue male is to be violently removed, for the uncivilized rogue cannot be fully accommodated into the new creation. Wright's triadic experiment is rejected in the film, and Martin serves again the orthodox foundations of familial responsibilities. Children and a prior claim determine Claire's fate. Perhaps this signals a rejection of polygamy that is associated with a primitive society that is also aligned to the lawless Western genre. It is left unclear as to whether Claire is committing suicide or swimming to freedom, to escape the conditions set down that a single woman must marry a single man. The moral purge precludes the re-evaluation of sexual mores.

And even though Martin is a new man – liberal and chivalric – the puritan law of the American father must be sustained. Whereas the brutal man must be removed, Martin is good enough, along with his praying family, to be saved and to become the founders of a new society. He is elected by the villagers to be the leader of the community when he introduces a credit auction system to resolve the infighting over salvaged provisions that is the basis of a modern economy. In other words, the homemaker turns community-builder. And in bringing benign order to selfish capitalist urges, Martin is hailed as a protective patriarch (a Roosevelt nation-rebuilder) in a small town (which bears echoes of Johnstown of the 1889 flood). Martin is the social gospel deliverer: 'We're starting afresh [...] creating a cleaner civilisation [...] Let's pull together.' And so, the apocalyptic deluge affirms the process of purging and reformation: masculinity is cleansed of its predatory nature (sexual or capitalist) and out of ruination the American dream can start afresh with a stronger sense of its Christian foundational roots (one that is honoured by lawful women too).

The Last Days of Pompeii (1935)

As Arthur J. Pomeroy argues, RKO's remake of *The Last Days of Pompeii* (Merian C. Cooper and Ernest B. Schoedsack, 1935) is 'in many ways an answer to Cecil B. DeMille's epics, such as *The Sign of the Cross* (1932), since it offers unsubtle religious moralizing but without DeMille's spectacle of Roman orgies and sin'.[22] In this respect, this film is a continuation of the silent era that reinforces the 'message of the triumph of Christian virtue over pagan vice'.[23] The film is also in keeping with the purging ethos of the thirties that aligns pagan vice with unbridled capitalist greed. A humble blacksmith, Marcus (Preston Foster) is content with life but becomes a gladiator to acquire the money he needs to pay for a doctor and medicine to save (but in vain) his wife and son (run down by a chariot in the streets of Pompeii). There are powerful echoes of *Street Angel* (Frank Borzage, 1928) in which Angela (Janet Gaynor) tries to prostitute herself to pay for her seriously ill mother's medicine. The wider implication is that the poor, deprived of an affordable health service, are forced to abandon their better nature to merely survive. However, Marcus becomes enamoured by the wealth accrued from his gladiatorial victories and swaps a social world of virtuous poverty for that of state sponsored sinfulness. After killing one opponent in the arena, he adopts an orphaned boy, Flavius (David Holt), out of remorse. He then works for a slave dealer, Cleon (William V. Mong), and raids an African village for slaves. Here Marcus exhibits empathy for a noble bond between an African father and son who assert fellow humanity. He turns to trading instead, and eventually works for Pontius Pilate (Basil Rathbone), the Roman governor of Judea who reluctantly (as the film suggests) condemns Jesus who had miraculously healed Flavius. Marcus denies Christ when an apostle begs for his help during the agonizing journey to Calvary. When Marcus is head of the arena in Pompeii, the adult Flavius (John Wood) haunted by a childhood memory of Christ secretly rescues slaves condemned to fight in his father's arena. Flavius and the slaves are eventually caught and herded into the arena to fight against captured Britons, and then, on cue, Mount Vesuvius erupts. Fleeing panic-stricken Romans are crushed under falling masonry or engulfed by flowing streams of lava. Marcus repents and turns sacrificial Spartacus, liberator of the enslaved, and, whilst dying, is blessed by a ghostly vision of Christ.

Pomeroy sees the film as partly conforming to a gangster movie: 'the hero abandons any concern for other members of society in his desire for wealth'.[24]

This distortive ideology of American capitalism forces people to make a choice between Christian virtue and enslaving wealth. The parallel between the trans-Atlantic slave trade and the Great Depression is politically provocative and resonates with the nascent civil rights movement of the 1930s when the seeds of agitation and protest were planted.[25] However, the emancipatory and retributive purge does not contain a final image of the Black slaves, who had piqued Marcus's humanism, as saved, or rescued.

San Francisco (1936) and *In Old Chicago* (1938)

Both *San Francisco* (Woody Van Dyke) and *In Old Chicago* (Henry King) revisit actual disasters – the 1906 San Francisco earthquake and the Chicago fire of 1871 – according to the social gospel spirit of the thirties cycle. And in both films, bad capitalists repent. At the amoral heart of *San Francisco* is Blackie Norton (Clark Gable), a saloonkeeper and gambler, who owns the Paradise Club on Pacific Street. When the San Francisco Police later raid the club and destroy its gambling equipment, parallels to the decadence of the Prohibition era affirm the film as a moral inculcator vis-à-vis the excess and glitz of the Roaring Twenties before the Wall Street Crash (1929). Blackie is established as the alter ego of American capitalism, when in a sparring scene Father Tim Mullen (Spencer Tracy), a Roman Catholic priest and Blackie's childhood friend, knocks him out. The glamour of Hollywood musicals is invoked through Mary Blake (Jeanette MacDonald), a classically trained singer who is hired by Blackie and becomes a star attraction. Her signature song, 'San Francisco', is a big draw and becomes the city's anthem. Mary is eventually hired for the Tivoli Opera House run by Jack Burley (Jack Holt) where she can fulfil her classical potential. Significantly, Mary performs in a Faustian opera that, as a play-within-a-play, suggests her immortal soul is in danger when tempted by Blackie's amorous advances. She chooses to return to the Paradise but refuses to perform in front of a rowdy audience. Blackie's bullish masculinity forces Mary to accept Burley's proposal of marriage. This dramatic and moral tussle, as well as Blackie's exploitation of people, precipitates disaster. At 5.13 a.m. of 18 April 1906, the morning after Mary performed 'San Francisco' during the 'Chickens Ball' competition and publicly argued with Blackie, the city is struck by an earthquake. A montage spectacle of damnation recalls the renting of the earth in *The King of Kings*

(Cecil B. DeMille, 1927): statues of Greek gods look down in judgement; panic-stricken people are crushed by falling masonry or tumble into the abyss. Burley, Blackie's rival, is dead, and Mrs Burley's mansion is dynamited by US Army troops to form part of a firebreak.

Escorted by Father Tim to a makeshift camp in Golden Gate Park, Blackie hears Mary singing 'Nearer, My God, to Thee' – a hymn that also provides Christian closure to *Titanic* (Jean Negulesco, 1953) – to console the grieving and the homeless. It is an important scene in directing our sympathy for the necessity of the collective above individual wealth. The atheist Blackie falls to his knees in front of Father Tim and asks for God's grace and prays (Figure 1.1). Blackie joins a crowd marching arm in arm, singing 'The Battle Hymn of the Republic' that bears imagery of purification, and that John Steinbeck will subvert in *The Grapes of Wrath* (1939). The uplifting and sentimental Christian finale underscores the New Deal message of rebuilding and reformation during loss and disaster. An image of a modern built San Francisco is finally seen to strongly suggest a more blessed city and that the decadent city, a site of high capitalism in which women were objectified and exploited, has been morally cleansed. In

Figure 1.1 Blackie (Clark Gable) praying to, and thanking, God.

the tradition of biblical epics, disaster is an act of God. But interestingly, it is Burley who perishes and not Blackie. This is because as a Christian conversion narrative, the film's message is one of softening capitalist extremes and to convey a general concern about the nation's future direction and the kind of values that had been discarded prior to the corresponding disaster, the Wall Street Crash. In many respects, *San Francisco* exemplifies Hollywood's 'self-appointed role as public comforter' in a period of historical crisis and potential working-class revolution.[26]

In Old Chicago (1938) bears a closeness in plot and redemptive tropes to its parent film, with the title also referring to the main song – a jubilant celebration of the city. Chicago initially figures as a Promised Land before it dissolves into a version of Sodom and Gomorrah. Patrick, the father, dies racing his horses across the prairie against a train when nearing Chicago (in 1854) – 'a place of easy money'. The film's opening, while symbolic of the old moving into the new world, is an ominous sign of the capitalist death-drive that underwrites the American Dream. O'Leary, an Irish mother, sets up business as a washer woman, and her honest and decent work contrasts with that of son, Dion (Tyrone Powers), who establishes a saloon bar in 'The Patch'. Her other son, Jack (Don Ameche), is a principled lawyer and he is voted in as 'reformer' mayor of Chicago (in 1870) with the aim of cleaning up the Patch and to 'wipe out the mushroom growth' of licentious capitalism and activities of vice. Dion's ambitions are to build a bigger place, but his saloon bar, which is referred to as a 'tinder box', is a metonym for the precarious nature of America's rapid progress from the Wild West to the metropolis. And mirroring the sparring of Father Tim and Blackie, the sibling rivalry a stand-in for the conflict at the heart of the American dream: reforming ethics versus an unethical, profit motive.

Modelled on the reformist Roosevelt, Jack is fundamentally opposed to Chicago's rapid urban and financial growth at the expense of lawful decency. 'I see Chicago as a great city that people can be proud of. I'd wipe out all this mushroom growth ... start all over on a sound basis, with steel and stone.' Dion, on the other hand, epitomizes the rotten capitalism that Jack wishes to morally cleanse: '[Jack]: Everything that's rotten in Chicago comes out of the Patch. The whole thing is an atmosphere of vice and crime. It's getting out of control, and I'm gonna wipe it out.' Nonetheless, Dion is an exemplar of an American frontier spirit who needs to be rescued from the disaster, as well as from his corrupt ways: 'Dion's a great person. He can go anywhere, do anything ... if he only gets on the right track.' Dion operates his business interests like an unscrupulous Mafia protection racket and, echoing Jim Carter in *Dante's Inferno*, uses his newly married wife to avoid criminal justice. '[Dion:] And now, Mrs. O'Leary, suppose you go ahead and testify against me? [...] You didn't think I was gonna let you two get away with it, did you? [...] Go ahead with your grand jury investigation. She's my wife, and you know the law ... A wife cannot testify against her husband.' Therefore, the Chicago fire that destroys the old city arguably symbolizes the cleansing drive of New Deal reformation, with Jack positioned as a New Testament sacrificial saviour.

Set in 1870, the film invokes parallels with the Roaring Twenties and the 1929 Wall Street crash. The fire led to questions about industrial and urban development in the United States due to Chicago's rapid expansion at the time. For several decades, the city of Chicago was the fastest growing with a flourishing economy that brought residents from rural areas and immigrants from abroad. However, in the aftermath, poor building practices, with the use of thin wooden walls rather than brick, were seen to be the primary cause of the fire. Out of the ruins of the previous wooden structures arose more modern constructions of steel and stone, and the world's first skyscraper in 1885 – the Home Insurance Building in Chicago – was built using steel-skeleton construction. The film's final speech, spoken by Mother O'Leary (Alice Brady), celebrates Chicago's post-1871 rebirth as an allegorical endorsement of Roosevelt's financial and industrial reforms (Figure 1.2):

> But what he [my son] stood for will never die. It was a city of wood, and now it's ashes. But out of the fire will be coming steel. You didn't live to see it, my lad ... no more than your father did before you. God rest the two of you. But there's Dion left, and his children to come after. [...] Nothing can lick Chicago, any more than it could lick him. Aye. That's the truth. We O'Learys are a strange tribe. There's strength in us. There's strength in us. And what we set out to do, we finish.

The reformist mayor, who is shot dead by an unruly mob, is ennobled as a sacrificial endorsement of progressive and reformed capitalism. The decadent brother, Dion, is saved because the film, echoing *San Francisco*, symbolically redeems business. And again, as in *Deluge*, the treatment of women matters in the reformation of capitalism. But what truly matters is that the optimism of America's frontier myth has been restored. The last image is of a modern steel constructed Chicago, and from out of the ruins America will arise again.

Figure 1.2 Mother O'Leary (Alice Brady): 'It was a city of wood, and now it's ashes. But out of the fire will be coming steel.'

The River (1938)

Released before *The Wizard of Oz* (Victor Fleming, 1939), in which Dorothy escapes the Dust Bowl environmental disaster of Kansas and the American plains, Pare Lorentz's *The River* (1938) likewise marks the tail end of the Great Depression to convey the New Deal apocalyptic pattern of an end with a new beginning. Initially, the documentary film speaks of a destructive threat to the teleological drive of America's frontier history, brought on by 'extraction, exploitation of soil and raw materials, the inevitable side effects of settlement and cultivation, treated as though they were rapes of the land'.[27] But, *The River* fulfils the conventional closure of optimism and national rebuilding.

The River is probably the first eco-deluge film in which the Mississippi, once the creative source of commerce, the builder of a continent, is now the destroyer. The film blends poetic narration with Soviet-style montage and a dramatic score by Virgil Thomson to create an audio-visual poetic epic. The declamatory, anaphoric style of narration, with its lists of trees, cities and rivers, recalls the mellifluous verse of Walt Whitman's *The Leaves of Grass* (1855).[28] The documentary begins in a pioneering tone, yet soon shifts to one of apocalypticism: 'We built a new continent [...] But at what a cost? [...] We left the mountains slashed and burned, / And Moved on.'[29] Employing Thomas Chalmers's bellowing voice, the film reels out statistics from the Resettlement Administration on the numbers of flood victims.[30] At this stage, the message, 'planted and ploughed with no thought for the future', foreshadows the grimness and fatalism of John Steinbeck's *The Grapes of Wrath*.[31] Lorentz's poetic script for *The Plow that Broke the Plains* (1936) recalls too T. S. Eliot's 'What the Thunder Said' (*The Waste Land* 1922) in which images of aridity derived from the book of Exodus are divested of migratory optimism. And Lorentz also empties out the glorious promise of the frontier-biblical pilgrimage:

> On to the West!
> Once again they headed into the setting sun ...
> Once again they headed West
> out of the Great Plains and hit
> the highways for the Pacific
> Coast, the last border. Blown
> out – baked out – and broke ...
> Nothing to stay for ... nothing to hope for ... [32]

But while *The Plow* ends on a bleak view of an unforgiving natural order, with images of eco-refugees and a wasteland of topsoil erosion, the tone in *The River* dramatically changes to one of national pride: 'we have / the power to put it [the greatest river valley in the world] together again'.[33] The finale expresses faith in the industrial reforms of the New Deal, to regulate water flows and generate power: 'Power enough to make the river work!'[34] Commissioned by the Farm Security Administration, and 'approved' by Roosevelt, this is a New Deal disaster narrative of construction, destruction and reconstruction.[35] *The River*, in proving to be a useful tool for the policies of the Roosevelt administration and the US Farm Security Administration, envisages mankind as saving 'the land it destroyed'.[36] The key to the film's success was that it followed the 'fundamental form of an evangelical sermon', one which echoes the repentance and the faith in reconstruction voiced in *Deluge, San Francisco* and *In Old Chicago*.[37]

The Grapes of Wrath (1940)

Ending with a scene of flood, stillbirth and a dying man suckling on breast milk, John Steinbeck's 1939 novel, *The Grapes of Wrath*, contrasts with the era's apocalyptic pattern of symbolic cleansing.[38] As Robert DeMott puts it: '*The*

Grapes of Wrath is arguably the most significant indictment ever made of the myth of California as a Promised Land.'[39] Steinbeck twists the rallying cry of the 'Battle Hymn of the Republic' – 'He is trampling out the vintage where the grapes of wrath are stored' – to contaminate the purifying narrative as exemplified in the marching finale of *San Francisco*. For Steinbeck, who had witnessed the drought, the exodus and the floods that had blighted thousands of eco-refugees, the Great Depression was one of suffering without renewal, inducing an irredeemable anger amongst the migrant poor: 'in the eyes of the hungry there is growing wrath. In the souls of the people the grapes of wrath are filling and growing heavy, growing heavy for the vintage.'[40] Steinbeck presents a devastating account of exodus without the hope of a happy renewal.[41]

Given this, Pare Lorentz's film review of John's Ford's screen adaptation is tellingly misplaced:

> Whatever else it may be, *The Grapes of Wrath* is the first picture made in Hollywood since 1929 that deals with a current social problem, that has faithfully kept the intent of an author who stirred the country, that has reproduced the bloody violence that has accompanied an economic upheaval – a violence that has been reported in the press from many parts of the country besides California but never on film – a picture that records the story of a tragic American migration into slavery. It is quite a movie.[42]

Despite the parallels to *The Plow that Broke the Plains*, Lorentz overlooks the film's closing infidelity that re-invokes, instead, the ongoing myth of frontier migration. The film is more in keeping with the spirit of the New Deal, giving a view of the caring treatment of the Joad family in the welcoming Farmworkers' Wheat Patch Camp: a clean, modernized, camp run by the Department of Agriculture. In fact, the camp's caretaker (Grant Mitchell), fully dressed in luminous white, appears almost angelic – an equivalent to the spiritual father of a nation, F. D. Roosevelt. Tom's (Henry Fonda) surprised reaction to the caretaker's kindness and the first sight of a hospitable and sanitized camp, as well as the focus on the mother's optimism (that constitutes the female voice of renewal weaving through *San Francisco* and *In Old Chicago*) speaks of social gospel rebuilding. 'Ma's final affirmation ("We'll go on forever, Pa. We're the people.") is less an assertion of social consciousness than of the indomitability of the family', as well as the American dream (Figure 1.3).[43] The speech of Ma Joad (Jane Darwell) echoes that of Mother O'Leary's and is contrary to Steinbeck's closing image of a pitying Madonna substitute (without child)

Figure 1.3 Ma Joad (Jane Darwell): 'We'll go on forever, Pa. We're the people.'

breast-feeding a gaunt stranger (hungry for the 'vintage') in a barn pounded by rain. John Ford's screen adaptation expiates Steinbeck's wrath of the poor, the vision of people continually in exile, and is thus closer to Lorentz's *The River*: the biblical story of a people 'going out', overcoming and carrying forth towards a new promising horizon.

Conclusion

The restoration narratives of the 1930s aimed to re-establish American capitalism on an ethical basis and spoke of a social gospel ethos drawn from a broader movement. Even though the same Christian benchmark no longer existed, the 1970s owed much to the biblical apocalypticism of the 1930s, as evident in the Dantean symbolism of *The Poseidon Adventure* (Ronald Neame, 1972) and *The Towering Inferno* (John Guillermin, 1974).[44] The legacy of the deluge films is also evident in the made-for-TV movies of Irwin Allen, which invariably focused on re-establishing community bonds in a small town setting: *Flood!* (Earl Bellamy,

1976), *Fire!* (Earl Bellamy, 1977), *Hanging by a Thread* (Georg Fenady, 1979), *The Night the Bridge Fell Down* (Georg Fenady, produced 1979) and *Cave-In!* (Georg Fenady, produced 1979). The ethical message, recalling films of the thirties, is that the right balance between economics and moral responsibility must be struck. Similarly, Allen's narratives reaffirm the values of marriage and family as the bedrock of a healthy society. In *Fire!*, a widowed elderly lady, Martha Wagner (Vera Miles), is guilt-ridden for having not agreed to the marriage proposal of Sam Brisbane (Ernest Borgnine), who later dies saving a classroom of children. In the closing scene, Martha's inner torment is articulated by inferno flames. However, the critique of individualism is often aimed at materialist men who aspire to wealth above domestic duties. For instance, in *Hanging by a Thread*, which dramatizes a party of friends trapped in a disabled sightseeing cable-car dangling above a mountain gorge, male characters are ostracized or not according to how much they value familial ties. Confined to a small space, characters relive domestic disputes and traumas via flashback, and divine judgement is invoked when lightning strikes the suspended cable-car that functions more as a confession box for past sins. Disaster brings out the selfless and the selfish man. There is also a parallel to Allen's big-budget disaster films that critique a high lifestyle, with the 'Uptown Club' exposed as an exclusive society that conceals conspiracy and deceit. The continuities between the 1930s and 1970s strongly suggest that the social gospel message had not been heeded, hence the overarching theme of punishing irresponsible capitalists. But as George Seaton's melodrama of high modernity, *Airport* (1970), demonstrated, the relationship between work and domestic duties had been radically altered in a post-war America. The responsibility lay within a complex system, and men putting work before family and community come to the fore. The threat of potential disaster, instead, comes from a dysfunctional worker and sacrificial husband.

2

Melodrama in high modernity: *Airport* (1970)

Airport (George Seaton, 1970) is a curious anomaly in the disaster cycle of the 1970s, despite the persistent claim that the film is a 'trailblazer of the disaster epic'.[1] This is a retrospective evaluation, whereas at the time of its release, *Airport* was more likely to be deemed an 'epitaph to a by-gone era of film-making'.[2] For Stephen Keane, *Airport* inaugurates the classic phase (from 1970 to 1974) of the disaster cycle, providing a 'useful narrative template', but nonetheless its 'main catastrophic event' is a 'modest' affair.[3] Yet for Sheldon Hall, it did not 'produce any immediate successors in generic terms', except in terms of commercial aviation hijacking films.[4] The film that truly got the cycle going was *The Poseidon Adventure* (Ronald Neame), which was second-highest, rental-income earner (behind *The Godfather*, Francis Ford Coppola) in 1972.[5] For Vincent Canby, *Poseidon* put the 'Ark Movie' back 'in the water',[6] transposing the *Airport* formula of an 'all-star cast in jeopardy' into an ocean liner and exploiting a spectacular vision of doom.[7] *Airport*, strictly speaking, is a thwarted disaster movie. There is only one casualty: a jobless, suicide bomber – 'a defeated man in his fifties' – who dies a crappy death inside a trans-Atlantic Boeing 707 toilet.[8]

Airport was a huge commercial success for Universal Pictures and Ross Hunter Productions in 1970. Released on 5 March 1970, it was the highest-earning film in the calendar year, grossing $80,000,000 in the Canada and US market, above Robert Altman's *M*A*S*H*.[9] According to 'the all-time inflation-adjusted chart' (1967–76), *Airport* is ranked eighth, above *The Towering Inferno* (John Guillermin, 1974) and *Poseidon*.[10] However, Arthur Hiller's *Love Story*, which opened in December and continued to earn in the following year, would eventually become the highest grosser released in 1970.[11] The appeal of *Airport* owed much to the genre innovations of Arthur Hailey's best-selling 1968 novel: re-energizing melodrama by transposing a *Grand Hotel* narrative of multiple plotlines onto *the* site of high modernity: the airport.[12] Given the conflicting contexts of left-leaning New Hollywood and Richard Nixon's general election victory in 1968, *Airport* is reassuring, particularly as an endorsement of commercial aviation in the jet age. Nonetheless, *Airport* reflects the epidemic of skyjackings that occurred between 1968 and 1972 and opened a Pandora's box of disaster spin-offs. For instance, *Skyjacked* (John Guillermin, 1972) is reflective of the 'frenzied phase' of skyjackings in 1972, when hijackers, including lone 'frazzled veterans', disaffected by the end of America's idealism hoped to gain their fortune in a spectacular way.[13] The conservative nature of *Airport*, by contrast, has much to do with the way George Seaton's Oscar-nominated screen adaptation downplays the inherent dangers of a complex, big industry that was depicted in Arthur Hailey's novel. The commercial airliner becomes instead a vehicle for social melodrama, which was to become a feature of the cycle.

It is noteworthy that the examinations of the disaster movie by Stephen Keane, and Michael Ryan and Douglas Kellner, begin, because its commercial success spawned the cycle, with a study of *Airport* (as this book does).[14] For Keane, *Airport* is 'as leisurely as an airport lounge',[15] and for Ryan and Kellner, even though the airport is a 'conservative's nightmare', the film 'closes with images of rejuvenation. It is a golden moment for mid-American ideology. Corporations still look virtuous.'[16] *Airport* satisfactorily contains the threat – a suicide bomber – and rest assured the superstructures of high modernity have not yet been toppled. And given the emergence of New Hollywood, *Airport* is also a conservative filmic experience, a throwback to Hollywood multi-protagonist, all-star, ensemble, movies. Even the excessive use of the split-screen device – which was a modern trend – is deployed to sustain classical Hollywood coherence. Nonetheless, despite the script's corporate triumphalism, *Airport* is prophetic in terms of potential commercial airliner disasters. According to *The Disaster File: The 1970s* – 'a record of the major disasters of the 1970s' – the aviation death toll was particularly high.[17] *Airport* is not a film of Dionysian catastrophe – mass destruction, disease and death – but nonetheless the movie shows that the edifice of modernity was vulnerable and easily threatened, and is thus a significant benchmark of the disaster genre and as an aviation movie.

1968–70

As Mimi White puts it: 'While some historians and chroniclers identify 1968 as the start of the decade of the 1970s, others characterize 1970 as the last year of the 1960s.'[18] Released in 1970, *Airport* is a screen adaptation of Hailey's best-selling novel that was published in 1968, thus marking a shifting period of cultural conflicts and domestic tensions. In 1968, the Republican Richard Nixon narrowly won the presidential election and Martin Luther King was assassinated on 29 March in Memphis Tennessee. According to Terry Anderson, the year was 'one of the most significant years of the Twentieth Century'.[19] Both sides of the Atlantic witnessed a youth and student uprising, fomented by the first era of international televised news. The Tet Offensive 'ended all the heroic images of the World War II generation. [...] Tet killed John Wayne'.[20] The political fallout from Tet meant that President Johnson became 'the most notable casualty of the war'.[21] 1968 was also the year that 'white America killed Dr. King. [...] and the dream of racial equality'.[22] A few months later, following Tommie Smith's black glove salute, 'black power' was disseminated as a fashionable term.[23] To many older activists, 1968 also signified the end of the innocence and idealism embodied in the spirit of 'We Shall Overcome'.

Airport seemingly dispenses with the internal conflicts of the late-1960s. Hailey's novel and Seaton's film are very much in response to the Space Race and America's ascendancy in commercial airflights. On 24 July 1969, Apollo 11 landed on the moon (24 July 1969) and on 22 January 1970, the world's first jumbo-jet, the Boeing 747 made its first commercial passenger trip to London, carrying 332 passengers and 18 crew members. By transporting more passengers, this plane helped to control an ever-growing volume of air traffic. With 1970 a significant year for the expansionist goals of American commercial air flight, *Airport* expresses the optimism of America's post-war burgeoning economy and technological success. *Airport* is a safe film, spending more time 'grounded' than in the air, and focusing on 'professionals who actually work for the airport or the airline'.[24] Yet, the first theatrical release of *Airport* happened approximately six months prior to the Popular Front for the Liberation of Palestine (PFLP) hijack of four passenger airliners (including two Boeing 707s and one 747) bound for New York and London. Hijacking would become a regular feature of the disaster genre in 1970s, including *Skyjacked, The Taking of the Pelham One Two Three* (Joseph Sargent, 1974) and *Airport '77* (Jerry Jameson, 1977). Even though the depiction of a rogue bomber's attempt to bring down a 707 appears tame in comparison, *Airport* is nonetheless prescient according to the 'skyjacking crisis' when commercial airflights were 'ideal targets for [...] troubled souls' aggrieved by the failure of sixties idealism: the continued war in Vietnam, the civil rights assassinations.[25] The film may have fared differently at the box office had it opened following Apollo 13's near disaster on 11 April 1970, which was a reminder that America's frontier triumphs could be easily undone by technological failure. And in this respect, Hailey's novel voices an ominous premonition via Mel Bakersfield, the Airport Manager of Lincoln International Airport, who sees 'events moving towards some disastrous end'.[26]

The year in which *Airport* was released also marked a time of significant contrasts in terms of the continuing activism of countercultural sixties and the backlash of right-wing populism. The emergence of the Christian right was a repudiation of the Lyndon Johnson's 'great society'. In March of 1969, Nixon had launched 'Operation Menu' in which American B-52s carpet bombed the Eastern side of Cambodia. And in April 1970, a secret invasion of Cambodia was ordered. News of it fuelled anti-war sentiments, and on 4 May the Ohio National Guard killed four students during a protest at Kent State University. The three highest grossing films released in 1970 – *Love Story*, *Airport* and *M*A*S*H* – cross a range of contrasting genres: romance, disaster and black comedy, and are reflective of significant cultural contrasts and responses to wider events. Whereas the anti-genre *M*A*S*H* directed by Robert Altman articulated the dissenting mood of anti-Vietnam protests as a New Hollywood film representing 'the antiestablishment youth culture had emerged in the 1960s', *Love Story* constituted a retreat from wider politics of countercultural activism into a private space: the insularity of romance.[27] As Mimi Smith states, *Love Story* 'included a prominent university setting, but provided no inkling of the student unrest that was central to other films set on college campuses'.[28] And while the early 1970s was awash with apocalyptic and post-apocalyptic imaginings, prompted by *Planet of the Apes* (Franklin J. Schaffner, 1968) and Hal Lindsey's end-times blockbuster book, *The Late Great Planet Earth* (1970), *Airport* only hints at the emerging penchant for the dystopian and shows more affinity with *Love Story* than to the 'pumped up spectacle and sheer carnage' of *Earthquake* (Mark Robson, 1974).[29] Both films are good indicators of Hollywood's capitalization of best-selling genres appearing in the literary market.[30]

The way *Airport* shifts the issues of the changing times onto the level of the personal is evident too in *Love Story*. At the very end of *Love Story*, grief-stricken Oliver (Ryan O'Neal), while exiting the hospital in snowbound New York where Jenny (Ali MacGraw) had died, encounters his estranged father, Oliver Barratt III (Ray Milland), who says: 'I want to help Jenny.' And Oliver replies: 'Jenny's dead.' Remorseful, the father apologizes: 'I'm sorry.' Oliver's final words are: 'Love means never having to say you're sorry.' This advocacy of uncomplicated idealism amidst personal tragedy sums up the nature of romantic melodrama – its excessive pathos, and what Mimi Smith sees as the cross-generational 'bridge between Oliver and his father'.[31] This is in stark contrast to the hippie vigilante film *Joe* (Avildsen, 1970), where, under the right-wing tagline of 'Keep America Beautiful' the new generation is literally blown away by their disapproving parents. *Love Story*, instead, offers 'a completely unthreatening version of youth rebellion and generational reconciliation, ultimately proffering a reassuring image of youth culture and campus life in the familiar language of romantic melodrama'.[32] The two lovers also epitomized a new generation of actors (MacGraw was awarded the Golden Globe Award for 'Most Promising Newcomer' in 1969) that appealed to a new cinema demographic. Even in the period of downbeat New Hollywood, the biggest hits, such as the musical-comedy *Fiddler on the Roof* (Norman Jewison, 1971), attracted a more traditional and broader viewership, and after the success of *Star Wars* (1977) the focus of studio filmmaking was to replicate a family-friendly appeal.[33] *Airport* too is melodrama, but on a larger scale. So, while New Hollywood offered deconstructing genre, big audience cinema was re-energizing familiar genres.

Multi-protagonist films

This division between different kinds of cinema is reflected in the general response from film reviewers in 1970 who were almost unanimously contemptuous of *Airport*. Unsurprisingly, Pauline Kael, in *The New Yorker*, regarded the film as 'conventionally dull' and 'bland, predigested entertainment of the old school'.[34] *Airport* is a 'safe' money-spinning, dolefully cashing in on a commercially successful novel: 'There appears to be perfect harmony in the matching of his [Hailey's] businessman's approach with that of Ross Hunter, the producer, who bought a No. 1 best-seller that sold over four million copies, assembled a cast with twenty-three Oscars among them, and played everything safe'.[35] For Kael, 'trash cinema lay at the heart of cinema', so *Airport*, with its associations with the 'coarse and the common', was not to be taken too seriously.[36] Kael also sees *Airport* as appealing to an older audience, unlike the 'youth audience and the educated older audience' who is apparently entertained by Peter Bogdanovich's *The Last Picture Show* (1971).[37] New Hollywood films, inaugurated by Arthur Penn's *Bonnie and Clyde* and Mike Nichols's *The Graduate* in 1967, represent creative freedom. *Airport* was the worst kind of movie – a formulaic genre picture created by a Hollywood businessman.

Though old-fashioned storytelling was at the heart of *Airport*'s commercial appeal, for Roger Ebert the plotline of an in-flight bomber distracts from the main story: 'What Heflin does is undermine the structure of the whole movie with a sort of subversive overacting. Once the bomber becomes ridiculous, the movie does, too.'[38] Like subsequent films in the disaster cycle, *Airport* was compared to *Grand Hotel*, an MGM 1932 film directed by Edmund Goulding. For Vincent Canby, the resemblance to '*Grand Hotel* movies' means the film 'made in the space age' evokes 'nostalgic feelings'.[39] The comparison to *Grand Hotel* is indicative of *Airport*'s old-fashioned melodramatic approach to disaster that was subsequently imitated in the cycle. In her film reviews of *Poseidon*, Kael also invokes *Grand Hotel*: '[the] *Grand Hotel* approach to the romance of catastrophe',[40] '[a] waterlogged *Grand Hotel*'.[41] In terms of the *Grand Hotel* film itself, Kael regarded it as 'the best example' of 'what screen glamour used to be'.[42] And with an assembled cast and crew of Oscars winners, *Airport* appears nostalgic towards the glitz of classical Hollywood. The '*Grand Hotel* approach' is also a way of saying that *Airport* involved multiple unfolding stories in a single workplace setting, which was conveyed in the official film trailer: 'it has seven stories tied into one'. Any idea of potential disaster is only hinted at: 'for crisis authenticity, *Airport* has no equal'.[43]

It says something of 1970 that two films of contrasting cinematic styles, with both adopting a *Grand Hotel*-style narrative and yet garnering different critical responses, were commercial successes. *M*A*S*H* fares better in Kael's eyes, mainly because it subverts classical narrative norms to reflect the insanity of the Vietnam War: '*M*A*S*H* is a marvellously unstable comedy, a tough, funny and sophisticated burlesque of military attitudes that is at the time a tale of chivalry. […] the best American war comedy since sound came in, and the sanest movie of recent years.'[44] As Maria del Mar Azcona puts it, '*Grand Hotel* was conceived by its producer, Irving Thalberg, and MGM as a vehicle for the proud display of the studio's star power', and the current popularity of the multi-protagonist movie is inseparable from the works of Robert Altman.[45] This explains Kael's later likening of *Nashville* (Robert Altman, 1975) also to *Grand Hotel*: 'The picture is at once a *Grand Hotel*-style narrative, with twenty-four linked characters […]';[46] 'Altman uses a *Grand Hotel* mingling of characters without giving false importance to their unions and collisions […]'.[47] In fact, *Nashville* is responding to other features of the disaster cycle:

> the supreme example of the spiritual-intellectual disaster movie, with that multi-plot, multi-character structure essential to the genre, *Nashville* itself being, like

the ship of *The Poseidon Adventure*, the plane of *Airport 1975*, the skyscraper of *The Towering Inferno* or the Los Angeles of *Earthquake*, an image of America, though much more pessimistically conceived, with the notion of survival (as epitomized in the crowd's final mindless chanting of "It don't worry me") becoming bitterly ironic.[48]

While Altman's film, in response to collapsing studio system, conveys a cynical spirit that will influence post-Vietnam era filmmakers, *Airport* appeals by recycling 'tired genre formulae'.[49] And where New Hollywood, a group of Left-leaning, anti-establishment, young filmmakers, signalled the start of a less conventional mode of cinema in America, and critically responded to a series of events – the Vietnam War, the civil rights movement, the Kent State shootings (4 May 1970) and Nixon's election victory – *Airport* chimes with America's Space Age optimism.

Aviation film forerunners

In the wider context of Hollywood aviation movies, the *Airport* franchise belongs to the subgenre of aeronautical disaster films, revealing a general drift from the drama of a male pilot having to prove his worth by taking responsibility for aviation technology towards the social democratization of commercial airliners that is played out in Hailey's high modernity melodrama. As David A. Cook notes, Hailey's novel is indebted to antecedents in novels and films, such as *The High and the Mighty* (William Wellman, 1954), which established the 'formula of microcosmic melodrama combined with catastrophe-oriented adventure'.[50] The film is a far cry from pre-war aviation pioneering spirit captured in the 'knights in air' airmail sagas of the 1930s that epitomized a romance for high-flying masculine heroics. For instance, at the very end of *Night Flight* (Clarence Brown, 1933), a screen adaptation of Antoine de-Saint Exupery's novel, Errol Flynn is envisaged as an angel ascending into a celestial glory following a trail of pilots. The film dramatizes the conflict between the need to reach the destination on time (for instance, delivering serum to a hospital) and the dangers of night flying. Airmail operations pushed flying men to the maximum, but the sacrifice is deemed worthy and noble. Trials of masculinity are bound up with the advances of technology. Howard Hawk's *Ceiling Zero* (1936) centres on James Cagney, a maverick ex-war pilot who has lost his pilot's license but regains his masculine dignity via a self-sacrificial death for the sake of advancing aviation technology and the exploits of night mail service. Despite glimpses of psychology injury, fearful men are deemed weak. It is an industry that cannot afford any failure of pioneering masculinity. The message is clear: aviation heroes conquer the fear of death and become masters of the flying machine.

This theme of conquering fear and trauma and regaining mastery of the aviation machine is continued in wartime films, as in *Twelve O'Clock High* (Henry King, 1949) which depicts the gritty realism of daytime bombing combat. A much-respected station commanding officer, who over-identifies with his traumatized men in 918th bomb group, is replaced by General Frank Savage (Gregory Peck) who accuses some crew members of being 'yellow'. He hardens them through discipline and shock treatment: stop worrying about fear, consider themselves dead and take pride in the group. The 'maximum effort' means men are prohibited from admitting to pain and are taught to lock it all up. Consequently, Frank has a nervous breakdown. Although *Twelve O'Clock High* offers psychological insights of men pushed to the limit – 'it did something to his insides' – the film ultimately endorses stoic self-sacrifice.

The post-war period marked a transition from wartime to the saviour heroics of commercial airline pilots when the private space of the male *cock*pit is made public. In this respect, the literary-cinematic partnership of Ernest K. Gann and William Wellman is significant. William Wellman's *Island in the Sky* (1953), based on Ernest K. Gann's 1944 novel, very much conveys the idea that the cockpit is an exclusive, sacred space of existential drama. The pilot, John Wayne, takes on the heavy burden of a leader responsible for his male crew. 'Dooley is down!' becomes a rallying cry for other wartime transport pilots and, in this respect, the film is a celebration of the special male-aviation bond. Gann himself had been a wartime pilot who, like others, went on to become a commercial airline pilot. *The High and the Mighty* (1954) is, therefore, a pivotal American aviation disaster film, again adapted from an Ernest K. Gann novel (1953) and starring John Wayne as a traumatized flight officer. The film introduced a new thread to the aviation genre, translating the private inner torment of the pilot into the public melodramatic sphere of commercial airliners.

This paved the way for the thwarted disaster movies of the fifties, characterized by ex-war pilots forced to confront their inner demons by regaining control of a flying machine that is aligned to mastering fragile masculinity. The genre is a means of exorcising post-war male trauma. *Zero Hour!* (Hail Bartlett, 1957), scripted by Arthur Hailey and recycled for television as *Terror in the Sky* (Bernard L. Kowalski, 1971), is another example of disaster dramatized as therapy rather than as an ascending spiritual experience. No longer a private male space of locked-in feelings, the airplane is a dramatic space of shared feelings. Along with *The High and the Mighty*, this marks the beginning of aviation disaster as a melodrama of confession and trauma therapy. Passengers carry a personal baggage, and trapped in a confined space, confronting the imminent possibility of death, confess to their private matters and in turn resolve life issues, for example – a marital crisis or a tragic past.

Jet Storm (Cy Enfield, 1959), although a British film, is also a significant precursor. Here the shift from the crew to the passengers democratizes the genre and begins to de-gender the genre's thematic scope. The focus is less on existential masculinity and the theme of high modernity is signalled. A suicide bomber, Ernest Tilley (Richard Attenborough) is traumatized by the death of his daughter who was killed by a drunk driver in a hit-and-run accident. Seeking vengeance, he boards a transatlantic flight (London to New York) carrying the culprit, James Brock (George Rose). Ernest seeks retribution and the commercial airliner acts as an instrument of terror and a surrogate trial of justice. The film solicits a sympathetic view for the grieving father who invokes the language of absolutist moralism (i.e., we must pay for our sins), when he says: 'the whole world killed my little girl'. Hailey's innovation was to extend the airplane drama of melodrama, terror and trauma onto the larger commercial scale of aviation industry.

Arthur Hailey and big industry melodrama

'Few people who use a great modern AIRPORT think of the conflicting emotions … the personal and psychological problems […].'[51] As the opening to Arthur Hailey's novel demonstrates, which lists characters, including family members, who work in Lincoln Airport, the commercial success of *Airport* owed much to the way the author situated family melodrama within big industry. Detailed research lay the groundwork for Hailey's commercially successful books – *Hotel* (1965), *Airport* (1968) and *Wheels* (1971) – providing behind-the-scenes information about large-scale, complex organizations, 'typical of our day'.[52] Hailey's professional writing career began with a TV script, *Flight into Danger* (1956), for CBS, which was sold on to NBC and was filmed as *Zero Hour!* in 1957 for Paramount. It dramatizes a potential commercial airline disaster when the pilots fall victim to food poisoning. A traumatized Second World War spitfire pilot takes control of the flight and lands safely on a storm-hit Vancouver airport. Hailey's first big publishing success came in 1965 with *Hotel* and this established the blueprint for future novels 'in two respects': 'First there was his research. He spent about a year researching hotels (including reading 27 books about the industry), then six months reviewing his notes and, finally, about 18 months writing the book. Then there was the plot: at the core an ordinary person faced with a major crisis but surrounded by multiple plot-lines.'[53] *Hotel*, modelled on *Grand Hotel*, exhibits Hailey's incipient fascination with big industry melodrama and, in effect, *Airport* was the bringing together of *Hotel* and *Flight into Danger*.

The publication success of *Airport* that sold over 5 million copies, and that was bought by the producer Ross Hunter, had much to do with Hailey transposing the *Grand Hotel* multi-protagonist approach into a setting of high modernity. *Wheels* and *The Moneychangers* (1975) further demonstrate Hailey's skill for depicting the internal stresses of ordinary workers in big American industry: 'What I aim for in all my novels is a good page-turning story set against a real-life background, so the reader can learn something about hotels or airports or the police as he reads a good story.'[54] Given the everyday modern workplace settings and multiple unfolding plotlines, his novels lent themselves to TV serialization. *Hotel* was adapted into a primetime soap opera TV series which aired in ABC from 1983 to 1988, in a timeslot following *Dynasty* (1981–9). *Wheels*, directed by Jerry London and starring Rock Hudson, set in Detroit, is focused on the day-to-day operations of the automobile industry, and was also adapted into TV series in 1978. And *The Moneychangers*, set in a major bank, was adapted for television, aired by NBC for one season in 1976, starring Kirk Douglas and Christopher Plummer and produced by Ross Hunter (the producer also of *Airport* and *Pillow Talk*). Given the soap-opera potential of Hailey's big industry novels that somewhat anticipated the CBS television series, *Dallas* (1978–91), it is quite understandable that George Seaton would exploit the multi-protagonist narrative according to a classical narrative logic.

The jet age and the mid-air crisis

The success of *Airport* as a novel also had much to do with its publication at the end of the jet age that occurred between 1958 and 1968 and that had confirmed the global dominance of US commercial aviation. *Airport* was published a year before the spaceflight of Apollo 11 (16–24 July 1969) first landed humans on the orbiting moon. The live TV broadcast of Neil Armstrong's first step onto the lunar surface had effectively proved to a global audience that the United States had won the Space Race. According to Jenifer Van Vleck:

> In response to what President Eisenhower labeled the 'Sputnik Crisis', Congress passed the National Defense Education Act, which significantly increased federal funding for all levels of scientific education. In this context, achievements in jet aviation reassured the American public that their country had not lost its technological edge. Just two years after the *Clipper America*'s debut, the United States was producing and flying more passenger jets than any nation in the world.[55]

For Canby, the film is a cheery advert for the aviation success of the Boeing 707, an airliner passenger that had dominated passenger air transport in the 1960s and is credited for having established Boeing as a dominant airliner manufacturer: '[…] "Airport" eventually comes to look and sound like the world's first 137-minute, 70-millimeter television commercial, with short, regular interruptions for entertainment. The product being sold is the Boeing 707. "Take the wings off her," says the pitchman, "and you can use her as a tank."'[56] The invocation of the military warfare is an indicator of commercial airflight drama as a post-war legacy of the male-centred aviation films.

The final scene in George Seaton's 1969 screenplay draft conveys a celebratory endorsement of Boeing 707 as one of many aviation advances of the Jet Age:

> After a moment, SUPERIMPOSED, WE SEE the model of the airport of the future which we have established previously in the Commissioners' Board Room. Presently, when it is in the clear, we again have a SUPERIMPOSITION. WE SEE take-offs, landings or air-to-air miniatures of the aircraft of the future - - - the Boeing 747 and the S.S.T., the Concorde, the Douglas DC-10 and the Lockheed 1011.
>
> FADE OUT
>
> THE END[57]

The first flight of the Boeing 747 took place on 9 February 1969 and entered service with Pan Am on 22 January 1970. This larger, wide-bodied airliner was a means to democratize air travel by reducing seat costs. 'S.S.T.' refers to a civilian supersonic aircraft that can transport passengers at speeds greater than the speed of sound. For example, the Concorde, a supersonic passenger airliner, was first flown in 1969 and entered service in 1976 and reduced the transatlantic airliner flight time from New York to London to just under three hours. The McDonnell

Douglas DC-10 was first flown on 29 August 1970 and was commercially flown by American airliners from 5 August 1971. However, following the Flight 191 crash (25 May 1969) in which all 258 passengers and thirteen crew on board were killed, due to a design flaw, all DC-10s were grounded. The Lockheed L-1011, with a seating capacity of approximately 400 passengers, was the third wide-body airliner to enter commercial operations, after the 747 and DC-10.

The closing scene was excised in the final draft and the film itself. Nonetheless, George Seaton's screen adaptation glosses over the theme of urgency in the novel, the potential for a complex technological industry to bring about public disaster due to the internal stresses:

> Hailey attempts to demonstrate that the large modern airport is an immensely complicated combination of subsystems, many of which have technical components. Although in this novel the systems are tentatively under control, ultimately airports are subject to political, social and technological forces outside their control, and their integrity is constantly threatened by human weakness, selfishness, and, paradoxically, by the challenge of new aircraft designs.[58]

Unlike Seaton's screenplay, the novel instead closes with Mel's vision of an aviation industry that has not kept pace with the jet age: 'Either Lincoln International was in the jet age, or it wasn't; if it was, it must keep pace far better than it had. It was not, Mel thought, as if airports were an indulgence or some civic luxury. Almost all were self-sustaining, generating wealth and high employment.'[59] Mel is at the epicentre of the operations and his thoughts give a sense of the extent to which the romance of pioneering aviation had been replaced by concerns about an industry's deficiencies. The male is now responsible for a complex, technological industry. In other words, the focus is no longer on the flying heroics, for as Charles D. Bright states: 'The aviator as the subject of stories or as hero is notable by his absence.'[60] The novel, via the voice of Mel, contradicts Seaton's technological triumphalism:

> Less than a lustrum ago, the airport was considered among the world's finest and most modern. Civic politicians were given to pointing with pride and would huff and puff about 'air leadership' and 'a symbol of the jet age'. What most failed to realize was that Lincoln International, like a surprising number of other major airports, was close to becoming a white sepulchre.[61]

Seaton's screenplay treatment of the novel, by excising the character of Keith Bakersfield, points to a Hollywood containment of the potential hazards at the heart of the airport industry. Keith is the brother of Mel and an air traffic controller who is traumatized by the memory of a mid-air disaster. The novel paints a vivid picture of Keith's trauma: 'Keith's mind laboured on, self-torturing, sick with grief, recrimination.'[62] Keith is tormented by guilt and via flashbacks is haunted by the screams of the Redferns, Irving Redfern, his wife and their children – transmitted on the radio in the control room: "' … Mummy! Daddy! … Do something! I don't want to die … oh, Gentle Jesus, I've been good … Please, I don't want … "'.[63] The family were flying in a Beech Bonanza NC-403 that was struck by a diving National Guard T-33 jet. Lieutenant Neel ejected and safely parachuted to earth. Tragically, the tiny Beechcraft 'plummeted to earth'.[64] 'All three controllers involved in the tragedy – George Wallace, Keith Bakersfield, Perry Yount – were at once suspended from duty, pending investigation.'[65] Although Keith was exonerated, a 'young Negro supervisor, Perry Yount, was held wholly responsible'.[66]

The novel then presents an account of the racist backlash, with Yount being placed in psychiatric care following a nervous collapse. When seemingly recovering, he receives a printed bulletin from a 'California right-wing group opposing […] Negro civil rights', accusing '"bleeding heart liberals" [… of aiding] Negroes in attaining responsible positions for which they were not mentally equipped.'[67] By expurgating the plotline of the air traffic controllers, Seaton's screenplay overlooks the 'conflicting demands that can produce psychological stress and thereby threaten public safety'.[68] Seaton is also guilty of expunging the only time Hailey makes a direct reference to the American civil rights movement, racial discrimination, as well as the real dangers and traumatic risks of high modernity. The focus is more on a social melodrama within an American superstructure. The novel exposes the fault lines of modern technology and is more socially engaged in highlighting the theme of racism. In this respect, the film represents a corporate whitewashing of Hailey's novel.

The social drama cast

According to Peter Lev, *Airport* differs from some of popular films of 1969–70 because of a 'social universe […] that could have been staged in 1950', that is, 'a stable, middle-class, middle-aged social drama'.[69] However, *Airport* harnessed what Maurice Yacowar calls 'The ship of fools' disaster narrative in which disparate characters from a range of backgrounds are cast in a narrative of impending or potential doom.[70] This is reflected in the film's perspective of the democratization of commercial aviation which saw more middle-class passengers rather than businessmen travellers, as seen through the eyes of the flight attendant, Gwen:

GWEN'S POINT OF VIEW – MOVING SHOT

The CAMERA ADVANCES SLOWLY down the aisle, occasionally PANNING SLIGHTLY LEFT AND RIGHT to TAKE IN all the passengers. This affords us the chance to ESTABLISH the people we will come to know more intimately later – DR. CAMPAGNO, FATHER LONIGAN, Judy, the Italian family, SISTER CATHERINE GRACE, SISTER FELICE, etc. The passengers are a representative cross-section of travelers [...].[71]

For Ryan and Kellner, *Airport* affirms a new corporatism of America, which for Keane is 'markedly middle-aged, middle-level managerial, and mid-American' and 'firmly established in that decent, professional middle-ground of sympathetic manager Bakersfield and heroic captain Demerset'.[72] Yet, this ignores the demographic reality of airports towards the end of the sixties and *Airport*'s depiction of a countercultural threat to the traditional American family, with an emphasis on female workers too, such as Tanya Livingston (Head Customer Relations Agent) and Gwen Meighen (Chief Stewardess). The airport industry is depicted as a male-centred workplace, but women occupy key roles, and in turn the traditional role of wife is rejected for the romance of a working woman who is more attractive because she is economically individualistic. In the context of the decade's sexual politics and the continued struggle for equal rights, *Airport* anticipates the Equal Rights Amendment that was designed to guarantee protection against sexual discrimination for women under the law and passed both houses of Congress in 1972.

As a multi-protagonist film, unlike Robert Altman's casting of relatively unknown actors, *Airport* combines aging Hollywood stars and emerging, talented, actresses to create a cross-generational social drama. For instance, Mel, the airport manager, is played by Burt Lancaster who is amorously tied to Tanya Livingston, the Head Customer Relations agent, played by a much younger Jean Seberg, who came to prominence Jean-Luc Goddard's French New Wave film, *Breathless* (1960). She was thirty-two and Burt was fifty-seven. The casting of Seberg is indicative of Hollywood's keenness to redress declining cinema sales by attracting a younger audience. This said, as Nick Roddick rightly points out, the disparate collection of people in the cycle happened to be also 'topflight stars', 'overcoming apparently impossible odds in order to survive'.[73] The idea, though, that the 'stars survive' is part of a 'consistent ideological direction' in the cycle is questionable. The 'ship of fools' cast in *Airport* established a template for later disaster movies – the pairing of old stars with actors associated with non-mainstream cinema, including New Hollywood actors, such as Timothy Bottoms in *Rollercoaster* (James Goldstone, 1977) and Bruce Dern in *Black Sunday* (John Frankenheimer, 1977), as well as blaxploitation actors – notably Richard Roundtree in *Earthquake* (Mark Robson, 1974). Yet, *Airport* does not undergo the ritualistic purging of ageing Hollywood stars and the age differences is a reaction to the cross-generational clashes that characterized the countercultural sixties. Younger actresses are not cast at the expense of older actresses. The film's only Oscar, an Academy Award for 'Best Supporting Actress', went to Helen Hayes for the role of the little-old lady stowaway, Ada Quonsett. She was aged seventy and was the first person to have won the 'Triple Crown of Acting' in 1953. In *Airport*, the biggest threat to social stability comes in the form of extra-marital affairs, the result of changing work-lifestyle dynamics. And so, *Airport* does reflect a changing social universe, one that is in response to the sexual liberalism of the sixties – albeit for the benefit of a new kind of middle-aged, male employee (embodied in Mel).

By 1978, the disaster casting code guaranteed the survival of Michael Caine and Katherine Ross in *The Swarm* (Irwin Allen), who had played Elaine Robinson in Mike Nichol's New Hollywood film, *The Graduate* (1967) and for which she received Oscar and BAFTA nominations and the Golden Globe for the 'New Star of the Year'. The expectation is for a cinematic form of euthanasia that parallels *Logan's Run* (Michael Anderson, 1976): actors over a particular age will be terminated. The queen bee rival, Olivia de Havilland, and her male drones, Ben Johnson and Fred MacMurray, are a part of symbolic cull of old Hollywood stars.

Unlike subsequent, malfunctioning technology, disaster films, *Airport* does not jettison aging male stars, for the limelight is on a trio of professionals to save the day: Burt Lancaster – 'a powerhouse of energy',[74] Dean Martin – an adulterous 707 pilot, and George Kennedy – the 'cigar chomping, bull boss of the maintenance men', who is in a happy marriage, and is introduced boasting about his romantic-sex life.[75] As Keane points out, 'most of the characters are professionals who actually work for the [Lincoln International] airport and [TGA] airline. [...] *Airport* dramatizes the ways in which professionals can face up to, and ultimately succeed against, disaster'.[76] But for certain French film critics, the New Corporate male affirms the general view that disaster genre 'is in line with the reactionary ethics of "American liberalism", [...] exalt[ing] the values dear to the right, i.e., masculine values'.[77] Through the powerhouse of Lancaster, Martin and Kennedy, the film asserts the masculine control of aviation technology in safely landing the Boeing 707. *Airport* was also made during a period when airliners exploited overtly sexist imagery of 'unencumbered' stewardesses in their advertising and when a new phase of films about flight attendants, such as the soft-core 3D film, *The Stewardesses* (1969), *Stewardesses Report* (1971), *Fly Me* (1973), *The Naughty Stewardesses* (1974) and *Blazing Stewardesses* (1975), reinforced the prevailing sexualized image of the profession. At the time, flight attendants were coming more militant, challenging discriminatory employment policies based on gender, race, age, weight, pregnancy and marital status.[78] While *Airport* shows that the airport is a workplace for women too, via the depiction of Tanya, it also reinforces, to a degree, the image of the stewardess as 'Playboy Bunny' – 'available for sex and there to please' (Figure 2.1).[79] Aviation-cockpit masculinity and promiscuity go together, whereas male job-impotency is tied to old-fashioned, marital loyalty.

In a way, D. O. Guerrero (Van Heflin), a failed contractor and the suicide bomber on TGA Flight 2, a 'defeated man in his fifties', is a throwback to the stuffy fifties.[80] The film is, as Keane argues, about 'class wars', and despite the obvious differences in the way respective lifestyles are represented, Guerrero is given a degree of sympathetic treatment that offsets Ryan and Kellner's 'blanket ideological account'.[81] The social milieu of the working-class villain is 'a shabby living room' in a dank apartment that is 'only a notch above a tenement'.[82] His wife (Inez), played by Maureen Stapleton, has 'tired and dull eyes and a 'lifeless'

Figure 2.1 The adulterous 707 captain, Vernon Demerest (Dean Martin) envisaging the stewardess, Tanya (Jacqueline Bisset).

Figure 2.2 Inez (Maureen Stapleton), with 'tired and dull eyes', and Guerrero (Van Heflin), 'the defeated man in his fifties'.

voice, and works in a 'third-rate, short-order hash house'.[83] Guerrero subsists on '"hello-good-bye" jobs', and despite his flaws is devoted to his wife: 'Inez – I – I haven't been a very good provider – but I will be, you'll see. Goodbye Inez – I love you. Always remember that – I love you' (Figure 2.2).[84] He does not have a mistress. Both characters bear Hispanic names, Inez and Guerrero, suggesting that the class hierarchy of new corporatism is also based on ethnicity. The husband who cannot provide is dramatized as the racialized threat to vibrant world of high-flying modernity and sexual freedom.

The film does not celebrate monogamy and is an endorsement of the double lives of spunky, professional men. Vernon Demerest (Dean Martin) – the brother-in-law of Bakersfield (Burt Lancaster) – is having an affair with the stewardess, Gwen Meighan, played by Jacqueline Bisset and who came to screen prominence via 1968 films, *Bullitt* (Peter Yates) and *The Sweet Ride* (Harvey Hart), for which she received a Golden Globe nomination as 'Most Promising Newcomer'. Bisset during the making of the film was aged twenty-six, and Martin fifty-three. Seaton describes the pilot, Vernon, as having: 'a split personality', a bigamist on the ground (or in the words of Mel: 'an overaged juvenile delinquent'), and in the air, 'dedicated, extremely competent, trustworthy'.[85] The implication is that men who are good at high-pressured jobs attract younger women into bed. And men who are competent in the cockpit also know how to control the body of a stewardess. Vernon's objectification of Gwen in the terms of piloting a 707 reflects the prevailing cultural attitude that the stewardess of the jet age embodied an emerging type of American womanhood that was intimately connected to consumerism: 'Does he hold onto the controls too firmly? (he releases his hold and runs his finger-tips titillatingly up and down her torso).'[86] In other words, sexual liberalism amounts to a new freedom for men to exploit.

The film appears to also endorse the female sexual liberalism of the sixties via Vernon's extra-marital affair with Gwen. But when he discovers she is pregnant – Gwen is 'carrying someone who is part of us' – and initially considering abortion – 'it's not someone yet – it doesn't have life or breath or feeling' – Vernon, in a closing shot (from Sarah, his wife's point of view), is seen to have accepted the responsibility (at least) of fatherhood: 'Vernon's affection and attachment are obvious. [...] Sarah realizes she has lost.'[87] It is an ambiguous closure. The biggest fear for high-energy professional men is the emasculating domain of domestic life. Marital loyalty appears to be out of fashion. And sexual liberalism is not at the expense of older women. Cindy Bakersfield, the socialite wife, played Dana Wynter, whose previous best-known film was *Invasion of the Body Snatchers* (Don Siegel, 1956), has also been having a secret affair. The only collateral damage is a man who is loyal to a wife with tired and dull eyes. Their marriage is lacking in the virile energy of the sixties.

Split screen

The fractured relationship between the new corporate workplace and the traditional family is frequently framed via the film's dominating stylistic feature: '[Seaton] uses split-screens to the point when I feared I was becoming wall-eyed.'[88] The split-screen device had fallen out of favour by the mid-sixties in mainstream Hollywood cinema but re-emerged towards the end of the decade. Multi-frame sequences are evident in *Grand Prix* (John Frankenheimer, 1966), *The Thomas Crown Affair* (Norman Jewison, 1968), *The Boston Strangler* (Richard Fleischer, 1968) and *The Andromeda Strain* (Robert Wise, 1971). Split screen was also used in two films released in 1970 that signalled the alignment of New Hollywood experimentation with the countercultural sixties: *Woodstock* (Michael Wadleigh) and Brian de Palma's *Dionysus in '69*. A biography of the independent director is aptly titled, *Brian de Palma's Split-Screen: A Life in Film*, in which his early 'anarchic satires' are honoured for exploiting French New Wave influences.[89] Therefore, the extensive use of a resurgent cinematic technique gives *Airport* a fashionable appearance.

This said, the technique has a long film history in relation to Hollywood melodrama and narrative continuity, and, as De Palma realized, cinematic experimentation is invariably compromised for the sake of Hollywood's insistence on the market. De Palma's first studio movie in 1970, *Get to Know Your Rabbit*, was the start of a directorial career 'marked by the conflict between independence and Hollywood, between the desire for autonomy and the compulsion to conform', with the director refusing to 'compromise with the money men'.[90] In a post-war era, Hollywood was more open to trying out new formats (e.g., the use of three-lens Cinerama in *How the West Was Won*, 1962), and the split screen was partly connected to a commercial logic. Cinematic innovation rarely came at the expense of Hollywood storytelling, for as Todd Berliner puts it: 'Hollywood cinema generally makes the viewer's story construction process fairly easy.'[91] In this respect, the split-screen was a convenient means for fluent storytelling in *Airport*.

Therefore, it is no coincidence that the producer Ross Hunter had established a long film career associated with various melodramas, and in buying the rights for Hailey's commercially successful novel he most probably saw the potential for an all-star melodrama. Hunter had worked with Douglas Sirk on his 'women's pictures' of the 1950s, such as *All That Heaven Allows* (1955), *Imitation of Life* (1959), and *Pillow Talk* (Michael Gordon, 1959). One could say Hailey's novel belongs in the tradition of Sirk's *Written on the Wind* (1956) in terms of family melodrama and big industry, which is established in the opening sequence when Kyle Hadley (Robert Stack) is swigging from a bottle of raw corn and racing a 'yellow 1953 Allard J2X hot rod', accompanied by a 'doom-laden orchestral score' through a 'hellish landscape' of oil refinery drilling towers.[92] The innovative use of split-screen is particularly notable in the romantic comedy, *Pillow Talk*, when Jan (Doris Day) and Brad/Rex (Rock Hudson) have telephone conversations. The cinematic association of the split-screen technique and the telephone had been established in the American silent thriller, *Suspense* (1913), directed by Lois Weber and Phillips Smalley. In one memorable scene, the screen is split into three triangles, so all characters can be simultaneously seen: 'The Wife', alone with her baby in a remote house, phones her husband at his office, as 'The Tramp' ominously leans forward through a door. The house break-in reaches suspenseful fever pitch with the shot of a telephone wire being cut with a knife. As Tom Gunning notes, 'split-screen devices remain an alternative method of conveying phone conversations into the classical period [...]'.[93] But after 1913 the most frequent device for portraying a phone conversation was parallel editing – cutting from one end of the telephone line to the other.[94] While the split-screen technique is an overt signifier of cinematic technology, the telephone, according to Ned Schantz, is also an emblem of modern technology: 'Narrative film loves the telephone […] the phone is […] to the film what the letter is to the novel.'[95] In fact, the two modern technologies 'share a parallel history. Born in the late nineteenth century, each achieved a certain kind of stability in the first half of the twentieth century, and each has now entered a period of mutation and complex interconnection with other technologies.'[96] As Schantz sees it, *Pillow Talk* is 'obsessed with the telephone'.[97] And so is *Airport* – exhibiting the interconnections within the complex subsystems of the airport as well as being a device for bridging personal dramas.

In the 1969 script, the screenwriter, George Seaton, clearly marks out the moments when the split screen device is to be deployed. Multiple frames are often used to give a panoramic view of Lincoln International airport and its functioning unity: 'In MULTIPLE IMAGES WE SEE equipment on the move – trucks, busses, a flat bed with powerful searchlights and a jeep towing a rolling flight of stairs. They come from all directions, converging on the crippled 707 in the center of the screen.'[98] This scene is shortly followed with Tanya talking on the phone to Mel, using a two-way split screen:

> Now TANYA APPEARS at the other side of the SCREEN. She is seated at her desk and speaks into an ordinary phone. Tanya is in her middle thirties, slim, attractive, and completely feminine in spite of the fact she does a man's job.
>
> > TANYA
> > I just found something that —
> > MEL
> > (interrupting)
> > And I just <u>lost</u> something – runway two-nine.[99]

These two juxtaposed scenes are in keeping with Hailey's novel, conveying a sense of workplace teamwork and the growing animosity between the female sphere of domesticity and the male sphere of work. In the following example, Mel answers an urgent phone call from his socialite wife, Cindy:

> The portion of the SCREEN occupied by Tanya is REPLACED BY CINDY, Mel's wife. She is on the phone in her bedroom. Cindy, in her thirties, looks older for the simple reason that she constantly tries to look younger. For many reasons she has become bitter and resentful. When she is angry, she's venomous – which is the case at the moment.

CINDY
Where the hell are you?

MEL
Can't talk. I've got an emergency.

CINDY
You said you'd be home at six o'clock!
You promised me you wouldn't miss this dinner – you promised me a week ago!
Mel exhales heavily. Here we go again

MEL
A week ago I didn't know we were going to have the worst storm in six years.

CINDY
You've always got some damn excuse!

MEL
I'll call you back.
He hangs up. As he walks towards Tanya, a furious Cindy is WIPED OFF THE SCREEN, with the ORIGINAL SCENE REPLACING IT.[100]

The demands of work outweigh the callings of the family home, and Seaton economically conveys this through a split-screen wipe: 'Cindy is WIPED OFF THE SCREEN.' By the end of film, Tanya, the working woman, will have 'replaced' Cindy. The next heated phone conversation includes the children in separate panels, as Mel asserts his independent identity: 'The surest way to emasculate a man is have him work for wife's father. [...] I'll support my family my way on the income from my job' (Figure 2.3).[101] This time, Cindy hangs up.

Figure 2.3 The fractured relationship between work and the family.

Mel's masculinity is dramatically contrasted with the man defeated in his fifties, for he is tied to his job and is also depicted (more so in Seaton's script) as an industry expansionist. When Cindy later confronts Mel to say, 'The only answer is divorce', the encounter is face-to-face and in his office.[102] Domestic life is a side event and compressed into a split screen panel, and marital life is articulated via a fractured frame. The rare sighting of the two sharing the same frame is significantly interrupted by an urgent phone call: 'I've got a phone call.' Seaton adds the following description to announce the defeat of the feminine sphere: 'Knowing she can't compete with his job she crosses to the door and EXITS.'[103] In the first half of the film, prior to the intermission, the split screen invariably signifies the intrusion of high modernity into the domain of private romance. Desperate to move the 707, trapped in a snow blizzard, to safety, Mel needs Joe Patroni, the airplane maintenance engineer:

> Now, REPLACING the DASHBOARD on the other side of the SCREEN, WE SEE JOE PATRONI. He is half-sitting, half-lying in the corner of a couch, his left hand holding the phone, his right hand and arm around his wife, MARIE, who is snuggled up against him. Patroni is a powerfully built, uninhibited, good-natured bear. He's the best airplane engineer man in the business and he knows it. Except when he's eating or making love, which he has in mind at the moment, Joe is constantly smoking a cigar.[104]

Joe's opportunity to make love to his wife ('his favourite pastime') is disturbed by the calling of work.[105]

Following the intermission, split-screen underscores unity and teamwork across the subsystems of the airport. At one point, we see multiple images of security officers 'in various parts of the building [...] listening to Tanya's VOICE over the P.A. system'.[106] Seaton's original intention had been to exploit the split-screen effect to convey the chaos and panic that ensues when Guerrero escapes into the 707 lavatory:

> MULTIPLE IMAGES (SHOWING THREE THINGS THAT HAPPEN SIMULTANEOUSLY).
>
> In an ELONGATED PANEL RUNNING THE WIDTH OF THE SCREEN AT THE
>
> TOP – WE SEE Vernon start up the aisle toward the rear, Rathbone rises to go forward and get out of the danger zone – Thus blocking Vernon temporarily.

IN TWO VERTICAL PANELS BELOW, WE SEE:

(1) INT. LAVATORY

Guerrero slams the door shut and locks it.

(2) GWEN AT THE OTHER SIDE OF THE DOOR

[...]

THE ACTION CONTINUES IN THESE PANELS [...][107]

Seaton probably had in mind the multiple frame sequences in *Grand Prix* and *The Thomas Crown Affair*, but the fracturing spectacle is omitted and, instead, the scene conveys a reassuring image of the 707's crew in the way they handle potential disaster:

MUTIPLE IMAGES

In a HORIZONTAL PANEL OCCUPYING THE BOTTOM QUARTER OF THE

SCREEN – WE SEE the plane flying on a level course, although being buffeted. In the TOP THREE-QUARTERS, we are in ---

INT. FLIGHT DESK – SHOTTING BACK

Jordan is taking off his mask and checking the various indicators. In b. g. Vernon ENTERS. Through the open door WE SEE stewardesses and others are in the aisles, helping, reassuring.[108]

In sum, while allowing for smooth Hollywood storytelling, the split screen signifies working cohesion within a complex airport as well as the conflict between old-fashioned domesticity and a mainly male-occupied workplace. The use of split screen in *Airport* is also an early sign of how subsequent films in the cycle refashioned the stylistics of experimental cinema, albeit in a reduced form.

Conclusion

Whereas the disaster films of the 1930s were generally critical of decadent and irresponsible capitalism, *Airport* established a trend with a focus on the structural weaknesses of high modernity and the communal professional fixing of technical problems. But unlike the made-for-TV movies of Irwin Allen – *Flood!* (1976),

Fire! (1977), *Hanging by a Thread* (1979), *The Night the Bridge Fell Down* (1979) and *Cave-In!* (1979) – that reaffirm the bedrock values of marriage, family and small community living, *Airport* endorses the individualism of middle-aged men in an era of sexual permissiveness. The film's liberal ideology is conveyed through a cross-generational ensemble cast and sexually energized workforce at the expense of fraught domesticity and lifeless monogamy. The saviour is an adulterer, and the scapegoated villain is a devoted husband. The wild male, who had been purged in the deluge narratives of the thirties, re-emerges as a hero in a technocratic society. In *The Poseidon Adventure* (1972), the dramatic focus is on group jeopardy, and the moral question of who survives and who perishes is less clear-cut.

3

The dark carnivalesque: *The Poseidon Adventure* (1972)

Far more than *Airport* (George Seaton, 1970), *The Poseidon Adventure* (Ronald Neame, 1972), adapted from Paul Gallico's 1969 novel, captures the apocalyptic mood of the early 1970s. In the words of Nick Roddick, *Poseidon* 'cranked up the spectacular disaster and consequently provided much more peril and a massive death toll'.[1] It was the second highest grossing film in 1972, behind Francis Ford Coppola's *The Godfather*. Following on from the relative disappointment of Universal Pictures' *The Andromeda Strain* (Robert Wise, 1971) and its gruesome effects, the popularity of *Poseidon* owed much to its blend of the dark carnivalesque and survival-action drama that derives from two contrary strands: the *parodia sacra* of New Hollywood and the fantasy-adventure of Irwin Allen. Rather than dramatizing an ark movie allegory of redemption, the film is iconoclastic in the way it responds to the emergence of Christian evangelism via an 'upside-down' aesthetic that also undercuts the theme of Christian solace presented in preceding ocean liner disaster films.

The ark movie and *Parodia Sacra*

A review by Vincent Canby rightly positions *Poseidon* in the 'ark' subgenre of disaster movies: 'Ark movies are easy to describe: a group of assorted characters [...] are put aboard an ocean liner, in an airplane [...] the ocean starts sinking, or the airplane threatens to crash [...]. *The Poseidon Adventure* puts the Ark Movie back where God intended it to be, in the water.'[2] The 'ark movie' conjures up connections to the Genesis flood narrative and to Michael Curtiz's *Noah's Ark* (1928), which set the tone for a Great Depression cycle in which the American dream is purged of its capitalist sins in line with the social gospel of repentance and forgiveness. Roddick was the first to read the religious imagery of *Poseidon* as suggestive of a Dantean allegory: 'The submerged yet burning *Poseidon* is an image of hell. The trip upward is "a long journey of redemption," a journey filled with "purgatorial tests and trials".'³ Peter Lev positions *Poseidon* as part of an accommodating response to the immediate religious context in America:

> The Christian imagery [in this cinematic period] often remains at a very general level, so as not to offend portions of the audience. For example, the singing of 'Amazing Grace' at Thanksgiving in *Alice's Restaurant* subtly connects the hippie commune to Christian tradition, without specifying any doctrinal or denominational links. Another example would be *The Poseidon Adventure*'s Reverend Scott, whose group includes the Jewish Mr. and Mrs. Rosen. Indeed, Belle Rosen is one of the heroes of the film; with her underwater swimming she saves Scott and gives up her life for the greater good.⁴

The starring presence of Reverend Frank Scott (Gene Hackman) in *Poseidon* suggests an open and accommodating attitude towards religion, but his self-help confidence is ultimately dented, and the film conveys a critique of a resurgent conservative Protestant backlash that had helped Richard Nixon gain election victory in 1968. According to Daniel K. Williams:

> Evangelical Protestants began and ended the decade of the 1960s by campaigning for Richard Nixon. Sixty percent of evangelicals voted for Nixon in 1960, 69 percent did so in 1968, and 84 percent did in 1972. They considered him a 'man of destiny to lead the nation' and a man who was 'in God's place', as Billy Graham told Nixon on more than one occasion.⁵

The context was not simply one of 'orthodoxy versus progressivism', for, even though the Christian Right was based on its vocal opposition to the sixties, the movement also demonstrated an 'ability to copy, appropriate, co-opt, and pervert the decade's transformative impulses'.⁶ The mounting influence of evangelical Christianity at the start of the decade was also associated with blockbuster apocalypticism in the form of Hal Lindsey's *The Late, Great Planet Earth* (1970), which had outsold all other non-fiction books in the United States in 1970.

> [...] Lindsay offered a host of geopolitical predictions leading to the conclusion that 'some time in the future there will be a seven-year period climaxed by the visible return of Jesus Christ' – a seven-year period that 'couldn't begin until the Jewish people re-established their nation in their ancient homeland of Palestine'. Such fundamentalist belief has underpinned conservative American support for the defence of Israel consistently championed by such powerful American

evangelists as Pat Robertson, Jerry Falwell and Billy Graham, all of whom have claimed that Christians are better friends of the Jewish state than are most American Jews.[7]

Despite this context of religious revivalism, and that many films of the late 1960s and early 1970s have a religious dimension, it is surprising how few histories of films draw on Christian themes and imagery in this period.[8] The list of New Hollywood films exhibiting a religious (though not necessarily Christian) undercurrent is long: *The Graduate* (Mike Nichols, 1967), *Who's That Knocking at My Door* (Martin Scorsese, 1967), *2001: A Space Odyssey* (Stanley Kubrick, 1968), *Easy Rider* (Dennis Hopper, 1969), *Alice's Restaurant* (Arthur Penn, 1969), *M*A*S*H* (Robert Altman, 1970), *Catch-22* (Mike Nichols, 1970), *McCabe and Mrs. Miller* (Robert Altman, 1971) and *The Last Movie* (Dennis Hopper, 1971).

The seventies also witnessed numerous horror films, on both sides of the Atlantic, that dramatized the conflict between a Christian conception of metaphysical evil, such as: Roman Polanski's *Rosemary's Baby* (1968), *The Devil Rides Out* (Terence Fisher, 1968), Ken Russell's *The Devils* (1971), William Friedkin's *The Exorcist* (1973) and Robin Hardy's *The Wicker Man* (1973). Supernatural horror films, such as *The Omen* (Richard Donner, 1976), which draws on Hal Lindsey's end-times prophesies, can be read in general as a Christian reaction to the countercultural sixties. In sum, a more varied representation of religious themes in film culture was witnessed at the time *Poseidon* was released.

Even though Reverend Scott gives *Poseidon* a powerful religious dimension, the film should be viewed in the context of *parodia sacra* (a carnival or playful subversion of the sacred or dominant order) alongside, for instance, Stanley Kubrick's *Dr. Strangelove or: How I Stopped Worrying and Learned to Love the Bomb* (1964). Both films cope 'with existential fear through apocalyptic hilarity'.[9] *Poseidon* also elicits the pleasure of 'laughing at death' by transferring the spiritual to the 'material sphere of earth and the body'.[10] And the film abounds in grotesque imagery that irreverently mixes the profane and the sacred.[11] The film, in this respect, is concurrent with *The Godfather*, in particular the 'most elaborately orchestrated sequence' when the baptism of Michael's (Al Pacino) godson is intercut with a series of brutal executions by the Corleone family. Here Coppola 'correlates sacred ceremony with ritual murder', and Michael's renunciation of Satan is discredited, with the further suggestion that the grandson has been baptized into a fallen world.[12] Robert Altman's *M*A*S*H* (1970), in which 'The Last Supper' is desacralized, is another contemporaneous and notable example of *parodia sacra*.¹³ Harold E. Stine was the cinematographer for both *M*A*S*H* and *Poseidon*, with the latter officially promoted as 'hell, upside down', signalling the film's topsy-turvy approach to the ark movie and the generic expectation of salvation. In some respects, *Poseidon* foreshadows the mocking of prosperity theology in *The Day of the Locust* (John Schlesinger, 1975), when a holy roller preacher, Big Sister (Geraldine Page), performs public healings and proclaims: 'Jesus owns the oil wells, and the gasoline is prayer.' But more significantly, as an ark movie *Poseidon* is a secularized counterpoint to films that interpreted the mass death suffered during the sinking of the ocean liner, RMS *Titanic* (15 April 1912) in the ennobling terms of Christian faith.

Titanic (1953)

It is tempting to consider the sinking of the *Titanic* as a disaster model for *Poseidon*. In Paul Gallico's 1969 novel, the SS *Poseidon* is seen as a throwback to the trans-Atlantic era of luxury liners. It is:

> formerly the RMS Atlantis, the first of the giant transatlantic liners to become outmoded, sold and converted to a combination of cargo and cruise trade [...]. The SS Poseidon was as high as an apartment building, and as wide as a football field. Set down in New York she would have stretched from 42nd to 46th Street – four city blocks – or in London from Charing Cross Station to the Savoy. A third of her 81,000 gross tonnage was below the waterline, crammed with propulsion and refrigeration machinery, boilers, pumps, reduction gear, dynamos, oil, ballast tanks and cargo space.¹⁴

And the ship is also associated with the decadence of gaily opulence: '[...] she reeled drunkenly from side to side with the result that the motion combined with the motion combined with the hangover from the practically all-night, gala Christmas party and dance made the bulk of her five hundred odd, one-class Travel Consortium Limited passengers miserably and uncompromisingly ill'.¹⁵ In the film script (by Stirling Silliphant), as the survivors are confronted with a seemingly impassable obstacle, Mike Rogo (Ernest Borgnine) says: 'Tell them to open their hymn books and sing "Nearer My God to Thee"'.¹⁶ But the reference to the Christian hymn by Sarah Flower Adams and the allusion to the apocryphal last song the band played on RMS *Titanic* are delivered in an ironic manner.

The hymn was also sung by the remaining passengers stranded on the grounded SS *Valencia* (1906) and that was interpreted as 'looking death smilingly in the face'.[17] While the 1912 ocean liner disaster is commonly associated with the loss of traditional certainties, such as a belief in God, the hymn through the retelling of Jacob's dream invokes the 'ladder of ascent to God'.[18] *Poseidon*, on the other hand, is closer to Thomas Hardy's 'The Convergence of the Twain' (1912), published nine days after the sinking and that conveys the sense that the clash of human vanity and immutable nature is met with cosmic indifference:

And query: 'What does this vaingloriousness down here?'…

> Well: while was fashioning
> This creature of cleaving wing,
> The Immanent Will that stirs and urges everything
>
> Prepared a sinister mate
> For her – so gaily great –
> A Shape of Ice, for the time far and dissociate.[19]

The suggestion here is that a supernatural force, 'The Immanent Will', predestined *Titanic*'s fate, and yet the tone lacks tragic pathos. Rather than the act of divine retribution that calls for repentance, the 'convergence' is part of an intractable drive.

The hymn is pivotal to the moral conversion narrative of *Titanic*, for, as Paul Heyer points out, the film's primary course is 'personal rather than nautical', hence the focus on the Sturges family and a marital break-up.[20] The film at one stage was to be called *Nearer My God to Thee*, and it begins with footage of an iceberg breaking free from a glacier, thus echoing 'The Convergence of the Twain' and the creation of a 'sinister mate'. The film centres on the failed marriage between a wealthy expatriate in Europe, Richard Sturges (Clifton Webb), and his runaway wife, Julia (Barbara Stanwyck). Julia is trying to escape back to the simple life of the 'New World' to save their children, Norman and Annette, from the superficial trappings of a super-rich life. In this respect, the film is comparable to the Nazi propaganda film commissioned by Joseph Goebbels, *Titanic* (Herbert Selpin, 1943), that aimed to show that the forces of British and American capitalism had been responsible for the tragedy. The luxury North Atlantic liner, a symbol of wealth and decadence, was an easy target for anti-capitalist rhetoric. In the 1953 film, Richard and Julia are tearfully reconciled on the boat deck before Julia and the children are placed into a lifeboat. However,

Norman (the illegitimate son whom Richard had disowned) gives up his seat to an older woman to be with his nominal father. Meanwhile, a defrocked alcoholic priest, George Healey (Richard Basehart), heads down into the boiler rooms to comfort trapped crewmen and his last words uttered are: 'for the sake of God'. During the final moments, Norman and Richard find each other, and with the rest of the doomed passengers the crew sing 'Nearer, My God, to Thee', showing that adverse conditions are conducive for discovering a better self. In fact, Richard rediscovers a chivalric class-code and is better placed to meet his maker.

Irwin Allen: The master of disaster

While recalling the sinking of the RMS *Titanic*, *Poseidon*, the first disaster film that Irwin Allen produced (he also directed some of the action sequences), bears the hallmarks of Allen's preceding career in television and film. Allen also went on to produce, as well as direct, three other Hollywood disaster movies: *The Towering Inferno* (1974), *The Swarm* (1978) and *When Time Ran Out* (1980). The success of *Inferno*, coupled with his reputation established in the creation and production of popular television series, led to a string of made-for-TV disaster movies: *Flood* (Earl Bellamy, 1976), *Fire!* (Earl Bellamy, 1977), *Hanging by a Thread* (Georg Fenady, 1979), *The Night the Bridge Fell Down* (Georg Fenady, 1979) and *Cave-In!* (Georg Fenady, 1979). Hence the moniker of 'the master of disaster', and why to a large extent Allen's production style shaped the disaster spectacle in the 1970s. According to Paul Heyer, the high-budget British-made film, *A Night to Remember* (1958), directed by Ray Ward Baker and starring Kenneth More as the RMS *Titanic*'s Second Officer, Charles Lightoller, initiated a wave of disaster movies, including *Poseidon*.[21] But while *A Night to Remember* is credited for its docudrama nature, *Poseidon* exploits the fantastical drama of adventure as well as group jeopardy in a confined space.

In a 1977 interview, Allen pointed to the daily source of disaster: 'No, I'm not going to run out of disasters. Pick up the daily newspaper, which is my best source for crisis stories, and you'll find 10 or 15 every day. People chase fire engines, flock to car crashes. People thrive on tragedy. It's unfortunate, but in my case, it's fortunate. The bigger the tragedy, the bigger the audience.'[22] The idea that his production style is rooted in everyday realism is disingenuous, for it mainly derives from a specific genre exemplified in *The Lost World* (Irwin Allen, 1960) and that characterizes the sci-fi television serials of the 1960s: *Voyage to the*

Bottom of the Sea (1964–8), *Lost in Space* (1965–8), *The Time Tunnel* (1966–7) and *Land of the Giants* (1968–70). *The Lost World* showcased Allen's penchant for fantasy-adventure and was the first sound production of the 1925 silent screen adaptation of Sir Arthur Conan Doyle's 1915 novel. *The Lost World* concerns an expedition to a plateau in the Amazon basin of South America where prehistoric animals still exist, and as such belongs to a tradition of imperial adventure stories that fantasize about uncanny encounters with other worlds – or the marvellous in outposts of civilization. In Allen's film, the scientist hero, Professor George Edward Challenger, and a disparate group of travellers endure an assault course across a volcanic plateau, through a cave of volcanic lava. It is the kind of action sequence that is repeated in many of Allen's television dramatizations of adventure, as Jon Abbott notes:

> Irwin Allen was a showman, pure and simple, and *Lost in Space* (and his other hit TV series *The Time Tunnel, Land of the Giants*, and *Voyage to the Bottom of the Sea*) were intended as spectacle, adventure, and entertainment. The early *Lost in Space* was the equivalent of a high-budget Saturday morning serial, cliffhanger endings and all, and on that level it worked splendidly.[23]

The release of *Voyage to the Bottom of the Sea* (Irwin Allen, 1961) roughly coincided with MGM's 1960 production of H. G. Wells's *The Time Machine* (George Pal), and was part of a cycle that reflected 'drama's exploitation of science's New Frontiers of space, both cosmic and submarines'.[24]

The television series, *Voyage to the Bottom of the Sea* (1961), that was aired on ABC from 1964 to 1968, also exhibits Allen's knack for fantasy-adventure in the context of new frontiers. The pilot episode, 'Eleven Days to Zero', from Season one (1964), taking place in the then-future of the 1970s, is a staging for Allen's later disaster films. A series of global disasters (e.g., earthquakes and tidal waves), linked to a James Bond conspiracy plotline of world domination, must be averted by the nuclear submarine, 'Seaview': 'In exactly 11 days, a gigantic wall of water will smash and destroy the coastal regions of half the world. [...] Unless we act at once we face the greatest single disaster in the history of the earth.'

However, modern technology, this time, is the solution, with Admiral Nelson's plan to detonate a nuclear device near the North pole, according to a counterforce theory. Allen's forte for escapist adventure continued with *Land of the Giants*, that was last aired by ABC on 6 September 1970, and *The Swiss Family Robinson* that aired on ABC from 1975 to 1976. *Poseidon* is notable for framing disaster within the drama of fantasy-adventure. For Keane, 'the singular void left by disaster movies [in the late 1970s] would be filled by a wave of "action-adventure" films that went on to constitute a dominant trend in contemporary Hollywood cinema'.[25] However, it was the cross-genre of fantasy-adventure that shaped the commercial aesthetic of *Poseidon* and its spectacular escapism.

The Last Voyage (1960)

In terms of a more realistic portrayal of an ocean liner disaster, the primary antecedent is *The Last Voyage*, released in 1960 and directed by Andrew L. Stone. In fact, Paul Gallico's 1969 novel refers to the capsizing of SS *Andrea Doria*, a 1956 maritime disaster that is the historical inspiration for *The Last Voyage*. In the chapter, 'And Then There Were Twelve', Hubert 'Hubie' Muller – a wealthy playboy socialite – compares the overturning of SS *Poseidon* to the 1956 capsizing: 'A modern vessel with every safety appliance, rolling over like a canoe [...]. Look what happened to the Andrea Doria. Two ships with radar steaming into a head-on collision.'[26] Soon after the collision with *MS Stockholm*, which pierced the starboard side, *Andrea Doria* began to take on water and started to list severely to starboard. Forty-six people of the 1,706 passengers and crew died as a direct consequence of the collision, and the *Doria* eventually capsized and sank. The fatalities were mainly caused by *Stockholm*'s sharply raked ice breaking bow penetrating passenger cabins on various decks. *The Last Voyage* draws on the effects of the collision, when a huge explosion rips through the boiler room, and many decks above it, killing several passengers, and trapping Laurie Henderson (Dorothy Malone) under a steel beam. The ensuing drama involves her husband, Cliff (Robert Stack), trying to initially rescue the daughter, Jill (Tammy Marihugh), who is trapped on the other side of the cabin. The film begins with the voice-over of George Furness (who also plays Third Officer Osborne):

> The *S.S. Claridon*: a proud ship; a venerable ship; but as ships go, an old ship, a very old ship. For thirty-eight years she has weathered everything the elements could throw at her: typhoons, zero-zero fogs, the scorching heat of the tropics. Now she is scheduled for only five more crossings. Then a new ship, a plush, streamlined beauty, will take her place. It is then that the Claridon will fade into oblivion. She has an appointment with the scrap-yard – but it's an appointment she will never keep – for this is the last voyage ...

The striking parallels to *Poseidon* are the setting of an ageing ocean liner, a symbol of luxury travel before the jet age, and the escapades of survivors in an infernal environ. Cliff's perilous crossing of a giant hole that falls into the burning boiler room was appropriated for the action sequence when a group, led by Reverend Scott, climb up a ventilation shaft and Acres (Roddy McDowall) falls into the exploding shaft.

For its time, *The Last Voyage* was unrestrained in its depiction of relentless disaster, and it was praised by Bosley Crowther for its 'extraordinary feeling of the actuality being aboard a ship, the creeping terror of a disaster, the agony of a great vessel's death'.[27] The setting for the film was the condemned French luxury liner, SS *Île de France*, which had taken aboard 753 passengers from *Andrea Doria* and *Stockholm*. In 1959, she was sold to a Japanese breaker for scrappage, but before being used as a floating prop as the fictionally named SS *Claridon*. The final sequence, when the last remaining survivors (including the rescued Laurie and Cliff) rush to the stern, is noteworthy for its use of a low-level tracking shot to capture the real-time suspense of rising and churning seawater that is about to submerge the ship. A critic commented that the script took advantage of its fictional freedom, 'as the script of *A Night to Remember* could not', to create 'the most violently overstimulating experience of the new year in cinema'.[28] *The Last Voyage*, with its mix of explicit destruction and immersive realism in the confined space of a crippled ocean liner, is a model for the more adventurous *Poseidon*.

The comparison to *A Night to Remember* (1958) is relevant in terms of how class and stoical dignity are depicted differently. For Ken Ringle, the cataclysmic sinking of the *Titanic* perpetuated the 'class rigidity of 1912 [...] in that the greatest number of people aboard faced death or hardship with a stoic and selfless grace [...]'.[29] In other words, social restraint is reflected in a film that also restrains from the excesses of spectacle. In *The Last Voyage*, much of the drama focuses on the conflict between the dithering Captain Robert Adams (George Sanders), who is continually pressed by the second officers to evacuate the ship, and the Chief Engineer, Pringle (Jacob Kruschen), who refuses to abandon the crewmen in the boiler room. Open class warfare rages and turns physical, when Pringle accuses the captain of being a 'career-happy joke', telling him that 'if he did not bring the ship in, he would be through' – in other words, keeping the ship afloat maintains his promotion chances. Witnessed by officers on the bridge, Adams slaps the Chief Engineer and Pringle responds by saying 'if I ever put my hands on you, I'd kill … '. Shortly after looking at a letter promoting him to commodore, Captain Adams is crushed to death by a falling funnel. This contrasts with *A Night to Remember*, the crew's stoical heroism and Captain Edward J. Smith (Laurence Naismith) choosing to go back to the bridge and to go down with the *Titanic* as the makeshift band play 'Nearer, My God, to Thee'.

The Last Voyage is also notable for the supporting role of the American Black actor, Woody Strode, playing Hank, a heroic stoker who assists Cliff in carrying a cutting torch tank from the boiler room and for putting Jill in a lifeboat. The film was released in the middle of the civil rights movement – from the Montgomery bus boycott (1955) until Martin Luther King's assassination (1968).[30] It is a period when desegregation is going slowly or not at all, and when, in some places (e.g., Little Rock) there is resistance. 1960 is the year of the sit-ins at Greensboro, North Carolina. In the film, there is a suggestion of casual racism when a white passenger challenges Hank and sides with the distraught Jill who does not wish to be separated from her mother. But this is offset during the final scene, when Cliff lifts Hank on board a lifeboat and personally thanks him for his devotion in assisting Laurie's rescue: 'One I'd help aboard, personally.' The wider implication is that Black Americans are accommodated into a cinematic depiction of American society, when assisting privileged white families in their hour of need. Woody Strode's role follows on from that of the Ethiopian gladiator, Draba, in *Spartacus* (Stanley Kubrick, 1960), whose death, when attacking the Roman military commander, Marcus Glabrus (and sparing the life of the disarmed Spartacus – Kirk Douglas), sparks a gladiator rebellion. Strode's morally privileged role is significantly part and parcel of America's cinematic response to the *Titanic* disaster, in showing a more open society, despite the racial barriers, and one that is less bound by a rigid class hierarchy. In fact, the survival group in American disaster movies is often a microcosm of a more heterogenous society or reflective of a carnivalesque spirit.

The upending of the Christmas tree

Unlike *Dante's Inferno* (Harry Lachman, 1935), the Dantean symbolism in *Poseidon* is not used as a moral inculcator, and instead augments, in the Bakhtinian sense, a world turned upside down.[31] In *Rabelais and His World* (1965), Mikhail Bakhtin observes that in Rabelais's world the grotesque is not 'far removed from the primitive community's ritual laughter', which creates a 'suspension of all hierarchical precedence'.[32] The carnivalesque spirit 'celebrates the grotesque body of the world'.³³ This physical revelry is aligned with a spatial journey of descent into the lower stratum of society: 'The mighty thrust downward into the bowels of the earth, into the depths of the human body [...] the downward movement animates all [Rabelais'] images [...] directed toward the underworld, both earthly and bodily.'³⁴ In many respects, Bakhtin's theory is derivative of Friedrich Nietzsche's theme of the Dionysian dance of death that induces an intoxicating sensation of self-abandoning ecstasy as one merges with the dancing throng.³⁵ Yet, as Terry Eagleton points out in *Holy Terror*, the flipside to this is the frightful dance of death: 'It is a dark parody of carnival – a jubilant merging and exchange of bodies which like the carnival is never far away from the graveyard'.³⁶ The 'dark parody of the carnival', born out of pain and dismemberment, is a cathartic release that confronts and contains oblivion in a meaningless cosmos, but it also a 'folk disease' that threatens the 'sanity' of the civilized order. The drama at the very heart of *Poseidon* conveys what Eagleton calls the 'horrific jouissance' of Dionysus – the violence of the grotesque, the reviled malevolent force that reaps enjoyment in death-dealing and dismemberment, or the monster of the Id contained in carnival excess.³⁷

The harmonious revelry of the carnivalesque is established in the screenplay (third revised, final shooting, 24 March 1972) during the New Year's Eve celebrations that are taking place in the Poseidon dining salon. A 'twenty-foot, gaily decorated Christmas tree dominates one corner of the salon'.³⁸ The presence of a gigantic, 'gaily decorated' Christmas tree is a gesture towards a Dickensian carnival. And a 'banner reading "HAPPY NEW YEAR" stretches across the elegant old salon'.³⁹ The calm before the storm is also awash with festive food, jollity and drink: 'Dinner has come to an end. They've actually reached the dessert'.⁴⁰ A band is playing to underscore the intoxicating sensations. While the conflict between the captain (Leslie Nielson) and the new owner's representative, Linarcos (Fred Sadoff), represents the 'ship of fools' in Platonic allegorical terms – the problem of governance, the guests (including a prostitute, a preacher, and a policeman) on the captain's dining table constitute the carnivalesque in Bakhtinian terms: the temporary upending of social hierarchy. And the foreshadowing of horrific jouissance, the Id of carnival excess, is invoked when Linda Rogo (Stella Stevens) refers to a 'bas-relief of Poseidon against the bulkhead' above the dining table and the captain explains the mythological signification: 'In Greek mythology, the god of the seas [...] Also the god of storms, tempests, earth-quakes and other miscellaneous natural disasters. An ill-tempered fellow.'⁴¹ And right on cue, as though a portent, the captain sees the flashing light on a phone and is brought to the bridge to witness the mountainous wave heading their way: 'CAPTAIN (to group): "Would you all excuse me. Duty calls." (to Scott): "Reverend, would you mind taking over as host, until I get back?"'[42] The promotion of the reverend to dining table host foreshadows the later conflict with the 'authoritative' Pursuer, the 'hotel manager' when the god of storms has upended the ship's normal social hierarchy.[43]

The gregarious pleasures are a cue for Poseidon, 'an ill-tempered fellow', to spoil the party, as the staging of the dark parody of the carnivalesque occurs as soon as the party revellers toast the New Year: '[…] blowing their toy horns, throwing streamers, rattling their noisemakers, hugging, kissing. […] The singing of Auld Lang Syne and the holding of crossed arms is in full swing. The merrymakers carry on with a deafening and happy din.'[44] Traditionally, Auld Lang Syne is sung to bid farewell to the old year but was also often heard at funerals, implying that the carnival is never too far away from the graveyard. And when the ship is hit by the onrushing mountain of water, the carnival world rolls over and the metonymic items of Dickensian revelry are tossed into the air, joining the 'frightful dance of death': 'Dishes, cups, knives, forks are hurled off the tables, as the whip of the rollover progresses without letup.'[45] The tossed banquet objects invoke the carnivalesque spirit of tossing custard pies in slapstick comedy.[46] And at this juncture, the dark carnivalesque truly takes hold. According to the carnival as social allegory, Linarcos and other high-ranking officials above deck are killed first in the mode of a John Martin vision of doom: 'People tumbling over and over, falling and dropping, screaming, tumbled in upon each other.'[47]

And when the SS *Poseidon* turns turtle, the apocalyptic hilarity of *parodia sacra* is conveyed through an incongruous spectacle of carnage, upended festivity and an upside-down Christmas tree:

> Incongruously, yet spectacularly, the Christmas tree now hangs upside down from the ceiling, its tinsel loops drooping sadly. […]
>
> CLOSE ON SCOTT AND LINDA.
>
> He moves uncovering the person he has protected.
> LINDA
> (dazed)
> Jesus Christ! What happened?
>
> SCOTT
> We've turned over.[48]

Here the carnivalesque is at its darkly delicious, with the profane and sacred, including the priest and the former prostitute, being grotesquely mixed. Poseidon, a pagan deity of destruction, reveals the graveyard via the 'jubilant merging and exchange of bodies'. And 'Within carnival's *upside-down world*, implausible kings are enthroned in an atmosphere of contagious hilarity.'[49] So, it is poignant that Linda, the Bakhtinian unruly woman, should be the one, and not Scott, who utters the words: 'Jesus Christ!'

From here on, the pagan Christmas tree is seen by Scott as a means of escape, because: 'Life is up there'.[50] And what is left behind is a Dantean hell: '[...] the clusters of survivors remaining behind, most of them huddled / Around the Pursuer in a Dantean environment'.[51] The people he abandons, the weak and the meek, are likened to sheep in a 'Dantean environment'.[52] The Dantean drama, for Scott, is more than a physical, journey: 'Muller asked, 'Are you talking metaphysically, Frank?''[53] The journeying though Dantean infernal landscapes is a trial and a quest. But to what end? When the party make their way through the kitchens, it is described as a nauseating scene of horror and carnage, 'with flames coming out of the burners'.[54] In the novel, the Boiler Room is described as a monstrous underworld, recalling Harry Lachman's lurid spectacles of hell:

> Far above the catwalk hang the great, exploded boilers which once powered the ship. Two boilers are ripped and torn, their tubular insides bulging out in a chaos of ruptured parts. Smoke and steam still hiss from the broken piping. Scott leads them down through a labyrinth of twisted pipe and [...] Before a surface of oily water in which bubbles seethe.[55]

Echoing Hardy's poem, the vainglorious opulence of SS *Poseidon* is relegated to a grotesque body. And so, laughter in the face of death soon gives way to the holy terror of dismemberment.

Reverend Frank Scott

According to the ark movie conventions, Reverend Scott is meant to be a Noah figure, in the mould of Martin in *Deluge* (Felix E. Feist, 1933), leading the way and saving the elect from a damning deluge. Soon after being introduced to Scott, we overhear Belle and Manny Rosen (Shelley Winters and Jack Albertson), a Jewish couple, discussing their holiday plans in Israel: 'It says here there's a package tour to visit the mountain where Moses Received the Ten Commandments'. This is a compelling allusion to *The Ten Commandments* (Cecil B. DeMille, 1958) and to the associated idea of biblical epics as championing the patriarchal and militant leaders of the Jewish people, for instance: *Ben-Hur* (William Wyler, 1959) and *Samson and Delilah* (Cecil B. DeMille, 1949). Scott's pro-active form of saving grace, which is at odds with the passivity of prayer, endorses a fighting individualism that echoes the *übermensch* triumphalism of Samson, the strongman (Figure 3.1):

> You know, God is pretty busy.
> He's got a long-term plan for humanity that
> stretches far beyond our comprehension.
> So it's not reasonable to expect Him to
> concern Himself with the individual.
> The individual is important only to
> the extent that he's a creative link
> between the past and the future
> … in his children,
> or the contributions he makes to humanity.
> Oh, that doesn't mean God has forgotten us.
> On the contrary he has given to each
> And everyone one of us
> A great and infinite gift.
> A part of Himself – a spark from His eternal fire to be nurtured within us.
> To keep us warm and to strengthen our efforts.
> Therefore, don't pray to God
> to solve your problems.
> Pray to that part of God within you.
> Have the guts to fight for yourself. God wants brave souls.
> He wants winners, not quitters.
> If you can't win, at least try to win. God loves tryers.[56]

Figure 3.1 Reverend Frank Scott (Gene Hackman): 'God wants winners, not quitters.'

Scott preaches a particular brand of theology – one or 'rugged self-reliance' that is famously conveyed in William Ernest Henley's 'Invictus':[57] 'In the fell clutch of circumstance / I have not winced nor cried aloud. / Under the bludgeonings of chance / My head is bloody, but unbowed.' The theme of fearlessness, defiance and determination in the face of adversity is embodied in the character of Rev Scott, and Paul Gallico's novel foregrounds the muscular athleticism that fuels his manly preaching. We are told that 'no more than five years ago [he] had been Frank "Buzz" Scott, Princeton's All-American full-back, all-round athlete, two-time Olympic decathlon champion and mountain climber'.[58]

Scott is a projection of the American sportsmen whom Gallico had interviewed when working as a sports journalist at the start of his writing career: Jack Dempsey, Dizzy Dean and Bobby Jones *et al*. In his autobiography, *Confessions of a Story-Teller* (1961), Gallico states he retired in 1936 as 'one of the highest-paid sports-writers in the country'.[59] For Gallico, 'the American sports scene' provided dramatic material for his storytelling: 'Daily I was in contact with those necessary elements of drama, good against evil, suspense, frustration, climax and success. Every contest had its villain as well as its hero.'[60] In *Poseidon*, the sports hero is turned into the muscular evangelist, but Scott's religious identity can also be aligned to the concurrent prosperity theology of American televangelism. For Scott's abandoning of the meek and the weak and his rejection of 'quitters' concords with the demonization of weakness as failure, or in theological terms, as sin.

American prosperity theology first came to prominence during the Healing Revivals of the 1950s and took its lead from Russell Conwell's sermon 'Acres of Diamonds' that equated poverty with sin and this 'gospel of wealth' (anyone can become rich and so blessed through hard work) was an expression of muscular Christianity. The prosperity gospel was disseminated via televangelists, such as Jim and Tammy Faye Bakker, and as Kate Bowler puts it: 'The most controversial aspect of the movement was its radical claim to transform invisible faith into financial rewards'.[61] And by the 1970s, the prosperity gospel was widespread, and 'unhindered – and untested'.[62] The preaching of Granville Oral Roberts (1918–2009) typified the post-war emphasis on 'seed-faith' which appealed to the American dream: 'If you have faith as a mustard seed, you will say to this mountain, "Move from here to there", and it will move; and nothing will be impossible for you.'[63] In other words: 'You give a seed, you receive it back multiplied many times.'[64] And so overcoming and winning, in terms of material acquisition and well-being, is equated with God's approval.[65] Up until 1947,

Roberts had struggled as a part-time preacher in Oklahoma, but at the age of twenty-nine picked up the Bible and it fell open on 'I wish above all things that thou mayest prosper and be in health, even as thy soul prospereth' (3 John 1:2).[66] The underlying doctrine is that God wants to bless people, physically, economically, as well as spiritually. However, the 'prosperity' interpretation of health, wealth and well-being implicitly presents a discriminatory view of the poor, the weak-willed and disabled Christians.

At the very end of his autobiography, *The Call* (1952), Roberts gives an account of the founding of a university in 1965 which bears his name and likens the evangelistic mission to athleticism: 'Excellence is expected in all areas – intellectually, spiritually, and physically. Even in athletics. The world of sports is one of the greatest opportunities to witness a Christian has [...] to be competitive enough in athletics to win championships, reverent enough for each athlete to be a witness for Christ; to be strong enough in faith to expect a miracle.'[67] In Gallico's novel, Scott's preaching is seen as the by-product of a 'winning' athleticism: 'He was so young and his sports achievements still so recent that the American contingent was unable to see him as anything but Buzz Scott, Princeton's star full-back, two-time Olympic decathlon champion, skier, conquer of Andres Mountain Peaks and perpetual winner in the athletic lists.'[68] During a Sunday Sermon he tells the congregation that he keeps himself fit to 'score victories for God', and that

> God wants winners! God loves triers. He did not create you in His image to run second. He has no use for quitters, whiners or beggars. [...] Fight for yourselves and He will be fighting at your side uninvited. When you succeed, it is because you've accepted Him, and He is in you. When you dog it, you've denied Him.[69]

Beggars and the poor, who are dependent on the care of others, are aligned to the 'quitters' – individuals who lack courage and determination.

Yet, Scott's tragic hubris is to forget that nature is an implacable destroyer and part of a pagan, and amoral, cosmos: 'He [Poseidon] was the Greek God of earthquakes and water and only secondarily of the sea. One of his most significant titles in Greek was "Earthshaker". He was one of the Gods Scott forgot to curse before he did himself in.'[70] The novel, as well as the film, undoes any view of providence as rewarding the tryer who can master and overcome the forces of nature. The presence of Poseidon is a reminder that the world is not ordered according to human-centred needs and demands. Scott is not reliant on God's help, but he presumes a just reward, and his shaken faith is contrary to Charlton Heston's Moses who calls on God to command nature to act out divine retribution against the enemies of his people.

Holy terror

Scott's faith in a God who champions winners is brought into question by the violent death rate, echoing the view that divinity was 'no copilot' in disaster films.[71] Stephen Keane's reading of *Poseidon* is that 'the film is not afraid to question blind faith in the orthodox or the unorthodox'.[72] Nonetheless, Keane still assumes the presence of providence, albeit a vengeful one:

> the ideological focus of the film is provided by religion [...] with the modern-day commercial travellers [...] tested, and even punished, by an act of God. [...] In the central disaster of the film, the image of a benevolent God is completely overturned by the act of a vengeful God and the passive belief in salvation completely taken to task.[73]

The conflict lies between a passive orthodoxy and an assertive unorthodoxy, as well as the symbolic conflict between Greek (Poseidon) mythology and Christian (active/passive) faith. Scott's enraged sermon, as he hangs from a hissing valve above a fiery pit in a Christ-like manner, resonates with the book of Job and the problem of evil: how to reconcile the benign notion of divinity with pointless and excessive suffering? As Scott rails against a cruel and unjust God, there is no Mount Sinai human-to-God call and response. God is either silent, temporarily absent or dead. Scott's death certainly raises questions about the nature and even the existence of God. Scott's death enables some of the remaining survivors to escape the Dantean hell. But at what human cost? Why should Belle die? A noble sacrifice or a senseless death? And what about the injured waiter, played by Roddy McDowall? These are the neophytes who embraced Scott's spirit of overcoming. Their deaths are arbitrary and contrary to Scott's winning logic. Scott's trial of ascension does not prove the existence of a benign or rewarding Christian god but more likely a deity (if any exists) that affirms the dark carnivalesque of the film.

In *The Birth of Tragedy*, Nietzsche identifies pre-Socratic, Euripidean tragedy as upholding a worldview that resonated with the nihilistic spirit of a modern, godless world. Pagan gods were indifferent to the sufferings of humanity.

Tragedy reveals an inexpressible horror, for the Dionysian state exposes humanity to the terror and absurdity of existence. But tragic art contains its aesthetic panacea as well as the revelation of tragic suffering. And the Dionysian dimension of tragic art eschews an illusory form of metaphysical relief that is played out in the religious version of the Fall and that translates man's search for knowledge into the theme of the defiance of God's law. Greek tragedy, instead, conveys a view of man as an instinctive overreacher, whose Promethean active search for knowledge is his undoing. The death of Scott dramatizes the tragic undoing of Promethean virtue, the belief that willpower alone is sufficient for ascending through hell. The revelation is that pagan horror is at the heart of the natural order.

The final film scene foregrounds the infernal landscape of a Dantean environment, but nonetheless tones down the graphic violence and the religious torment that is dramatized in Paul Gallico's novel. The climax of the physical ascent is staged via two preceding chapters when the survivors reach the engine room of the ocean liner. The chapter 'Mount Poseidon', with a title that echoes Mount Sinai – the mountain on which the Ten Commandments were given to Moses by God, dallies with the allegory of Scott leading the elect to a resurrection that is a mountain 'ascent'[74]: 'Don't think of it as you're seeing it, but simply as a mountain to be climbed. It's everything you find on a mountainside: crevices, projections, buttresses, pinnacles, clefts, foot and handholds. There's hardly a single peak left in the world that someone hasn't managed to climb!'[75] Scott calls on his followers to move a mountain, mirroring the 'seed-faith' interpretation of Matthew 17:20. But the title to the subsequent chapter, 'And Then There Were Twelve', as a play on Agatha Christie's *And Then There Were None* (1939), implies the staging for the inevitable climax of modern nihilism.

The eventual defeat of Scott's muscular-mountaineering evangelism occurs in 'You Can't Win 'Em All', when very close to the escape exit and situated next to the propellor shaft, Linda Rogo falls to a grusome death: 'She hit the triangular steel spearpoint thrust out from the side, it pierced her through the back, and emerged from her chest. She gave a long drawn out, "ahhhhhhhhhhhhh" of pain, first high-pitched, then trailing off. Thereafter her voice echoed through the dark cavern, she cried out, "Rogo, you son-of-a-bitch".'[76] Belle sees her impaled death as '*God's punishment*'[77] and Linda's surviving husband, a Catholic, asks Scott to say a prayer: 'He waited for the Minister to make the sign of the cross over her, but Scott did not do so. Instead, his face even more darkly suffused, he shouted aloft, "What did You have to do that for? Why? [...] What am I supposed to pray?" cried Scott. "God save a soul snatched from her in another senseless killing?"[78] It is 'another senseless killing', and even Rogo's faith in God and the ascent to resurrection promised by Scott are challenged by the witnessed carnage, echoing Ezekiel's vision of unredeemed death: 'He had looked down at the bodies sprawled on their backs upon the pavement and the clay-grey faces unstained [...] and thought to himself: *Dead is dead*. And it could have been the other way around with curious spectators gaping at the remains of Rogo, and that would have been that and no resurrection.'[79] And when the rest of the survivors think the ship is about to sink, thinking that 'death was at hand for all of them and the Poseidon [was] poised for her final plunge', Scott cries out, angrily, against God (Figure 3.2):[80]

> What more do you want? I made you a promise. We've kept it. We haven't quit. We've never stopped trying, have we? [...] Why do you let us come so far, you bastard, if you're going to take us now? It's us who invented you. If it weren't for us, you wouldn't be! Jaweh! Marduk! Baal! Moloch! You're still the same old killer with the smell of blood in your nostrils! [...] Eater of babies!' He shrieked. 'Butcher of women! Slaughterer of men! You've had the boy and the girl. What is it you want – another sacrifice? More blood? Another life? [...] Spare them! Take me!' bawled the Reverend Frank 'Buzz' Scott and threw himself into the pit below. [...] The waters of Hell Lake had risen higher, swallowing up the slope of what had been the approach to Mount Poseidon.[81]

Figure 3.2 Reverend Frank Scott (Gene Hackman): 'What is it you want – another sacrifice? More blood?'

This scene of *parodia sacra* profanes the encounter of Moses with God when he had ascended to the top of Mount Sinai in the book of Exodus (19:2–7):

> Then Moses went up to God, and the Lord called to him from the mountain and said: 'This is what you are to say to the descendants of Jacob and what you are to tell the people of Israel: "You yourselves have seen what I did to Egypt, and how I carried you on eagles' wings and brought you to myself. Now if you obey me fully and keep my covenant, then out of all nations you will be my treasured possession. Although the whole earth is mine, you will be for me a kingdom of priests and a holy nation." These are the words you are to speak to the Israelites.

The cited passage introduces the first major account of the Law in Exodus, and, from an Orthodox Jewish perspective, this established the Israelites as the People of God. From a New Testament perspective, '"Israel" is more than just the biological descendants of Abraham, Isaac and Jacob, and for St. Paul the "New Israel" is constituted by the "children of the promise".'[82] It is worth recalling that Scott was introduced to the audience soon after the Jewish couple spoke of a package tour to visit the mountain where Moses received the Ten Commandments. The blessing of salvation through faith has not been borne out and Scott re-enacts the lore of ritual blood sacrifice that exists in the Old Testament as well as the fertility mythologies of Baal *et al*. Scott throws himself into the 'waters of Hell'.

In the film, Scott's torment and pagan sacrifice takes centre stage and is dramatized as the final death, following the deaths of Mrs Belle Rosen and Linda Rogo. In the novel, Belle dies of a heart attack when the remaining survivors are about to be saved by rescuers and one of the characters unconsciously paraphrases the deceased Reverend: 'Dear God, if you want any more of us, take me.'[83] Having led the survivors to the propeller shaft room's watertight door, explosions rupture a pipe releasing hissing steam geysers, spraying scalding torrent against the closed hatch. Their escape is blocked. This initially appears to be an insurmountable obstacle, or the 'final frustration' that breaks Scott's control.[84] The deaths of Linda, Belle and Acres fuel his impassioned indictment of a Christian god:

> He turns his eyes toward the steel deck above him.
>
> SCOTT
>
> What <u>more</u> do you want of us?
> CLOSER SHOT ON SCOTT

SCOTT
(a burst of rage
against God –
now he shouts out)

[He leaps and grabs onto the burning-hot valve wheel to shut off the steam.]

We've come all this way! No thanks
to You. We did it on our own. No
help from You! We didn't ask You
to fight for us – but, damn it, don't
fight against us. Leave us alone!
What more do You want? How many
More sacrifices? How much more
Blood? How many more lives?
Acres wasn't enough? Belle wasn't?
Now this girl? You want another
life? Then take me![85]

Even though the film tones down the blasphemous language, it remains evident that Scott has submitted to the holy terror of pagan lore. Scott manages to close the steam valve for the ruptured pipe to clear the escape route. He turns on the valve to face the survivors to tell Rogo to lead the group out. He lets go of the valve and falls into the flaming water below – providing the blood sacrifice. As stated in the screenplay: '[...] he plunges down into the fiery water below. The sacrifice has been made'.[86] Scott's death enables the remaining survivors to reach the propellor shaft, and it constitutes a male act of self-sacrifice that is typical to American patterns of Christian redemption. Nonetheless, Scott invokes the universal deity of a pagan cosmos that is equivalent to a modern nihilistic view, in that the innocent suffer in a senseless and violent world.

Conclusion

The dark carnivalesque is an aesthetic means of confronting and containing the horror of disaster, and it is what makes *Poseidon*, in the words of Canby, 'fun'. In fact, the film was once a staple of festive film programming on UK television, and *Die Hard* (John McTiernan, 1988) owes much to *Poseidon* for establishing a festive template of anarchic violence and macabre comedy. The destructive orgy of *Poseidon* also paved the way for 'event' films, such as *The Towering Inferno* (1974) that, likewise, was released in December (in the United States) to capitalize on the Christmas season. However, while a quintessential superstructure disaster movie, *Inferno* largely entertains via a primal fear – death by fire – and its infernal realism, for some, is too close to the bone.

4

Skyscraper apocalypticism: *The Towering Inferno* (1974)

The Towering Inferno (John Guillermin), with its all-star cast, countless extras, hundreds of stunt men, state-of-the-art special effects, realized Irwin Allen's vision: the bigger the tragedy, the bigger the audience.[1] Hollywood went bigger, with a big budget production set in the superstructure of American high modernity: the skyscraper. And because of the theme of capitalist greed, *Inferno* struck a chord with audiences in a time of economic slump, for both the Hollywood studio system and America at large. The spectacle of destruction, the biblical fall of a towering construction, chimed with the times too, mirroring the fall of Richard Nixon's presidential reign in August 1974. For Stephen Keane, *Inferno* 'is quite possibly one of the most impressive' and the 'most reassuring disaster movies of the 1970s'.[2] More so than its predecessors, *Inferno* helped to establish a superstructure blockbuster tradition by reducing the disaster epic to a genre formula: multiple stories, superficial types and a cataclysmic event in a single, enclosed setting. As a big-screen event, it also broke new ground with the collaboration of two major studios and modern marketing techniques that continued into the Reaganite eighties and later with franchise conglomerates. *Inferno* established a template for *Die Hard* (John McTiernan, 1988) that is set in a Los Angeles skyscraper on Christmas Eve, and also for *Skyscraper* (Rawson Marshall, 2018), a film that self-referentially blends its film forerunners. In other words, *Inferno* is impressive, 'not only in terms of the 1970s but also in comparison with more recent standards'.[3] Nonetheless, it also signalled the limits of a genre in terms of the delicate balance between a fantasy spectacle, realism and tragic catharsis. *Inferno* is probably difficult viewing for a post-9/11 and post-Grenfell Tower audience. This is because it was intended as a message film; one may even go so far as to say that it is an apocalyptic revelation.[4]

For Thomas Stubblefield, when the passenger airliners struck the Twin Towers, the 'busy streets of Manhattan turned disaster movie'.[5] In other words, it was a public spectacle that competed with a long cinematic tradition of skyscraper inferno films, especially *Inferno*. Stubblefield also argues that in the post-spectacle aftermath the absence of horror is evident in 9/11 visual culture, and the falling man photograph is part of an 'absence of impact' (the fall of a figure without the visual image of impact) in cinematic history.[6] He refers to a photograph of the Triangle Shirtwaist disaster that 'presents the fall as an entirely offscreen event'.[7] Corpses of the factory jumpers are seen on the streets of Manhattan. While the public spectacle of disaster can rupture symbolic space, the cinematic aftermath of the Triangle Factory Fire of 1911 demonstrates a long absence of visible horror, thus affirming the paradox of a public spectacle that immediately calls for visual containment or effacement. Like 9/11, the abiding question is raised: how can cinema represent the violent reality of mass destruction when revisiting an historical disaster?[8] Keane's view that *Inferno*, notwithstanding the violence, is ultimately reassuring is contradicted by Pauline Kael who found its realism 'very offensive', suggesting that reality, weighted by history, can also break through the blockbuster spectacle.[9] *Inferno*, a cipher of cinematic tropes and forerunners, is revealing in terms of Hollywood's fascination with the spectacle of inferno disasters that is borne out of America's urban history.

Inferno disasters and cinematic forebears

At the turn of the twentieth century, city infernos were a recurring disaster, for as American towns grew quickly into densely populated cities, many of wooden constructions, a single fire could cause a lot of material and human loss. The Great Fire of 1901 that occurred in Jacksonville (Florida) killed seven people, destroyed 2,368 buildings and left almost 10,000 residents homeless. The 1906 San Francisco fire, the after-effect of an earthquake, burned out of control for four days and nights and destroyed 25,000 buildings. The Great Baltimore Fire of 1904 destroyed more than 1,500 buildings. And there was too: The Great Conflagration of 1902, Paterson (New Jersey), and the Great Chelsea Fire of 1908 that destroyed nearly half of the city in Massachusetts. And prior to this, the Great Chicago Fire of 1871 destroyed much of central Chicago, killing approximately 300 people, leaving more than 100,000 people homeless. In the 1910s alone there was: The Great Fire of 1911, Bangor (Maine); Houston's largest fire in 1912; the Great Salem fire of 1914; the Paris, Texas fire of 1916; and The Great Atlanta Fire of 1917. The modern-day Fire Department of New York City, that went into service in 1865, has tackled numerous inferno disasters, including two notable tragedies: The Triangle Shirtwaist Factory fire in 1911 that killed 146 garment workers and The World Trade Center 9/11 holocaust that involved approximately 2,600 deaths (including 343 firefighters and seventy-one law enforcement officers).

The inferno spectacle in an urban setting was established as an attraction in early cinema, which often combined the melodramatic sensation of a firemen rescue with a redemptive closure. The heroic elevation of firemen, who in the line of duty put the lives of others before their own, also bears a long tradition of cinematic expectation. The only real heroes are the fire fighters in *Inferno*, which is dedicated to them, as stated in the opening credits: 'TO THOSE WHO GIVE THEIR LIVES SO THAT OTHERS MIGHT LIVE – TO THE FIRE FIGHTERS OF THE WORLD – THIS PICTURE IS GRATEFULLY DEDICATED.' The tendency to heroize firemen was established in *The Life of an American Fireman* (1903), directed by Edwin S. Porter and made for the Edison Manufacturing Company, which in the form of a dreamlike portent anticipates the supernatural visions of the Christ-saviour in *World Trade Center* (Oliver Stone, 2006). Porter's film depicts firemen rescuing a woman and a child from a burning building, and is notable for the opening shot, 'The Fireman's Vision of an Imperiled Woman and Child', in which a seated fireman is juxtaposed against a bubbled split-screen image of a mother and a praying child in a bedroom. The fireman appears troubled when he gets up and moves about in an agitated manner. From the second shot, 'A Close View of a New York Fire Alarm Box', the viewer is meant to infer the same fireman has set off the alarm, with the subsequent shots showing firemen stirred in their sleeping quarters and leaving the engine house on fire engines. The innovative use of editing and the shots of the firemen rescuing the woman and child from the thick smoke are an early cinematic example of spectacle integrated within a complex narrative structure.[10] The film is also seen as an exemplar of early cinema melodrama: 'Edison's *Life of an American Fireman* (1901), directed by Edwin S. Porter, was built around two sensation scenes – a thrilling race of fire trucks and a treacherous rescue of a woman and child trapped in a burning building.'[11] The thrilling spectacle of the racing fire trucks is amplified by on-screen spectators lining the streets of New York. The film establishes a template in combining melodrama with the spectacle of potential disaster. Furthermore, the opening shot of the fireman's vision and the fact that, at this stage in the story, there is no sign of danger implies a portent or a calling that is immediately answered. Coupled with the title, '*The Life of* […]', the suggestion is that this is a regular occurrence, and that the fireman is blessed with telepathic insight.

The blending of melodrama and death-defying heroism, whilst exonerating the corrupt, is also a narrative trend in inferno-disaster films. In *The Fireman* (1916), Charlie Chaplin – despite his initial clownish reluctance – heroically scales the outside of a building to save the daughter of a father who deliberately set fire to the house to collect the insurance money. The couple kiss and walk off screen, implying that romance is the just reward for such heroism. The father is not seen punished. In a way, the narrative outcome is, in part, reflective of Chaplin, the little, working-class/homeless/immigrant man who was not one for 'overthrowing authority, but […] kick[ing] it in the pants'.[12] Comedy can afford to absorb the lack of moral redemption. And in the case of Chaplin's comedy, the focus is on the pathos of oppression (and not the tragic dwelling on suffering) in which pity is experienced without fear. Chapin invariably mocks the structures and leaves the power be – hence the limitations, or ultimately the lack, of the heroic.

In Old Chicago (Henry King, 1938) helped establish the urban inferno as a symbol of purification vis-à-vis capitalist corruption and decadence. The film revisits the Chicago fire of 1871, and as the blazing fire spreads across the city from one wooden building to the next, firemen tackle the flames on rooftops, scaling ladders and racing horse-driven fire apparatus through panic-stricken streets. In the meantime, Dion O'Leary (Tyrone Powers), who runs a fiery saloon via dishonest practices, is convinced that his brother, Jack (Don Ameche), deliberately started the fire and sets out with his cronies to seek revenge. In this Cain and Abel story, Jack (the political reformer) is killed trying to create a firebreak, and Dion, in a scene of holocaust devastation, is reunited with his Irish, Catholic, immigrant mother (Mrs O'Leary) and reconciled with his wife, Belle (Alice Faye). As the city burns to the ground, Mrs. O'Leary predicts that the city will be rebuilt and flourish after her son's sacrifice: 'It's gone and boy's gone with it, but what he stood for will never die. It was a city of wood, and now it's ashes. But out of the fire will come the steel.' The surviving members of the O'Leary 'tribe' look upon, as spectators standing in a boat upon the river, a city in flames. Fire, a symbol of purifying capitalist decadence, would have resonated with audiences with a strong Christian outlook in the Great Depression. In the Bible, fire can be a symbol of divine judgement, the destruction of the wicked, God's protection, divine presence, enlightenment and miraculous purification. The idea that out of the ashes, the American dream is rebuilt bears a Christian redemptive closure, one that ennobles the tragic suffering. The sacrificial death of a reformer (Jack) was for a grander design. Echoing *The Fireman*, the wicked are forgiven and not punished, but instead rehabilitated into post-disaster reconstruction, with the implication that reformed capitalists are needed for the future of America.

The Triangle Factory Fire (1911)

Hollywood reveals a prevailing narrative of heroizing firemen and exonerating wicked capitalists, but, when the cinematic fantasy space is ruptured by the reality of inferno tragedy, the moral redemption becomes problematic. On 25 March 1911, at 4.40 pm, as employees were preparing to leave a shirtwaist factory in the Greenwich Village neighbourhood of New York's Manhattan, a fire broke out, soon consuming the upper three stories (8th–10th) of the Asch building, 23–29 Washington Place. 146 workers, mainly Jewish or Italian immigrant women (aged fourteen to twenty-three), perished.

> In all, the fire killed 146 people, some 62 of whom jumped to their deaths on (and sometimes through) the pavement below. A dozen or so crowded onto the fire escape, which collapsed when the panicked workers could not make their way around the outward-opening window shutters. Firefighters found 30 corpses in the elevator shafts. The rest burned to death inside the factory. Some 40 or 50 bodies were piled up against the ninth-floor doorways.[13]

One onlooker, Louis Waldman, describes the sensation of witnessing the deaths of workers:

> Horrified and helpless, the crowds – I among them – looked up at the burning building, saw girl after girl appear at the reddened windows, pause for a terrified moment, and then leap to the pavement below, to land as mangled, bloody pulp. This went on for what seemed a ghastly eternity. Occasionally a girl who had hesitated too long was licked by pursuing flames and, screaming with clothing and hair ablaze, plunged like a living torch to the street. Life nets held by the firemen were torn by the impact of the falling bodies.[14]

It was the worst workplace disaster in American history prior to the 9/11 tragedy. As David Von Drehle points out, the 146 deaths provoked sensational headlines – because it was a visible and spectated disaster that had taken the lives of young women: 'Death was an almost routine workplace hazard in those days. By one estimate, one hundred or more Americans died on the job every day in the booming years around 1911. [...] Disaster followed disaster, but little changed. Then came the Triangle fire.'[15] The Triangle Waist Company factory was a sweatshop, employing 500 workers who worked 52-hour weeks in cramp and unsafe conditions, earning very low wages. During the 1911 trail, a key piece of evidence was the locked door to the Washington Place stairway on the ninth floor. Survivors gave their testimonies, 'and told versions of the same story: As the flames entered the crowded loft, the workers ran to the door. They pushed and pulled, twisted the knob this way and that. The door would not budge.'[16] Isaac Harris and Max Blanck (the factory owners, who had escaped onto the building's roof) were eventually acquitted of manslaughter. Two years later, the 1913 lawsuit found them liable of wrongful murder.

Leon Stein's book, *The Triangle Fire* (1962), gives a vivid account of the tragic fire, which, according to William Greider is told in a 'brilliant cinema fashion'.[17] The Triangle disaster was a public spectacle, which Michael Hirsch notes was 'witnessed by scores of New Yorkers' – like the World Trade Center attack – as many 'stood frozen with horror'.[18] Because the deaths were so graphic, the systematic causes could no longer remain hidden. As Arthur F. McEvoy puts it: 'Crucial to its impact was the fact the Triangle disaster was exceedingly public; the deaths at Triangle made manifest essential aspects of U.S. labor relations that had hitherto remained hidden.'[19] Each of Stein's chapter is headed with an epigraph from Dante's *Inferno* to frame the realism with a sense of apocalyptic doom that took place on the ninth floor. For example, Chapter 1. 'Fire: I intend to show Hell – Dante, *Inferno*, Canto XXIX: 96.'[20] Here, Stein gives a visual description of the garment workers who jumped:

> Down came the bodies in a shower, burning, smoking, flaming bodies, with disheveled hair trailing upward. These torches, suffering ones, fell inertly. [...] At 4:57 a body in burning clothes dropped from the ninth floor ledge, caught on a twisted iron hook protruding at the sixth floor. For a minute it hung there, burning. Then it dropped to the sidewalk. No more fell.[21]

For the contemporary poet Chris Llewellyn, it was the 'day it rained children' – caused by the privileging of products over people.[22] The Dantean apocalyptic frame is also a means of passing judgement on the architects of the disaster, the owners who made their fortune in selling the feminine apparel of shirtwaists, which were advertised as symbolizing American women's newfound freedom.

The cinematic response to this holocaust horror is revealing in terms of how visual culture confronts and contains tragedy and trauma. In the immediate aftermath, two films were made by the Thomas Edison Company (that had produced *The Life of an American Fireman*) in cooperation with the National Association of Manufacturers: *The Workman's Lesson* and *The Crime of Carelessness*. Both were made in 1912, one year following the acquittal of the Triangle factory owners, and in siding with American manufacturers they constitute propaganda:

> By the early 1910s, several corporations were using movies to promote their interests. Especially aggressive was the National Association of Manufacturers (NAM), which, after the disastrous 1911 Triangle fire (which killed more than a hundred female garment workers), produced two films depicting employers' heightened concern for workplace safety: *The Workman's Lesson* and *The Crime of Carelessness* (both 1912). Provoked by these propaganda efforts, labor activists countered with their own films. [...] More successful were those films that presented their political messages in the guise of popular sensational melodrama stories.[23]

One of the first intertitles in *The Workman's Lesson* states: 'The older workmen do not like to bother with newfangled safety devices', and the boss appears on the factory floor, next to an inspector, rebuking workmen for removing safety devices on machinery. When a workman, as it initially seems, has his arm amputated – the result of removing a safety device from a machine, another intertitle states, 'the result of disregarding the safety device'. The accident is depicted as a threat to any potential romance. There is no direct reference to the Triangle tragedy, but the message of this moral lesson is clear: the disaster was the result of the workers disregarding safety regulations.

The Crime of Carelessness (directed by James Oppenheim) further exemplifies the use of melodrama to indirectly apportion blame onto the garment workers. In response to public outrage over the Triangle shirtwaist fire, the anti-union National Association of Manufacturers financed an Edison-made silent film. The first intertitle states: 'Fire Laws Disregarded / Mill Owner – Bigelow Cooper/ Inspector – Austin Conroy.' And in the shot, fire exit for floor 8 is seen blocked, with the owner negotiating with an inspector. For the second intertitle, we are given the names of the melodramatic lovers: 'Lovers / Hilda / Tom Watts, a machinist.' And their engagement is announced in a later intertitle. It is Tom who is shown to be 'careless', persistently smoking cigarettes at the workplace, despite being reprimanded by both Hilda and the owner, who points to a 'Positively No Smoking' sign. In the meantime, the engaged couple fantasize about the 'little cottage' they wish to buy, and Hilda shows her wedding dress to her parents. The factory fire begins when Tom discards a smouldering match. Following the intertitle, 'Fire!', a group of workers try to break through blocked Exit 8, with Exit 14 also impassable. Tom, though, with an axe, breaks through a wall and the workers escape. But Hilda, overcome by smoke, is still trapped inside. Tom rushes in and rescues her from the smoke-engulfed factory and is outside greeted as a hero by an onlooking crowd, including the owner. But as soon as he confesses to having caused the fire, Tom is ostracized and shunned by the community. And the result of Tom's carelessness: 'No employment. The workers are the sufferers.' Hilda too, bearing crutches, cannot work. Her dreams appear to be dashed as her wedding dress is put away. Tom, unemployed too, is guilt stricken. He writes a letter to Hilda bearing his guilt. An intertitle declares: 'Her reasoning', and we are shown a frozen image of the inspector, the owner and Tom pointing the finger of blame at each other. Empowered, Hilda visits the owner and reasons with him to give Tom a job again – and shows him the letter in which Tom confesses to his guilt. A visually animated Hilda remonstrates and points the finger of blame at the owner, who appears mortified and writes a letter to Thomas Watts: 'We are both to blame; I for not making the factory safe, you, for smoking. Come back to your job at the new factory. I am sure we have both learned our lesson. Henry Waters.' Grateful, Hilda kisses the hand of the owner and two weeks later finds Tom in a ghetto. Tom is jubilant when he is shown the letter by Henry and the couple embrace and seem to look ahead to the future.

It is telling that in neither film is the inferno horror depicted and that the factory owners are exonerated of manslaughter while workmen are adjudged to have been the cause of accidents in the workplace. By castigating Tom, who is the cause of misery on the domestic front and in the wider community, *The Crime of Carelessness* demonizes the workman. In the immediate aftermath of the disaster, it was perhaps easier to demonize men rather than the women who had perished. The focus on melodrama that dramatizes the happy harmony between work and romance, with the avoidance of social realism and an inferno spectacle, is reassuring in terms of also promoting the American dream.

As Richard A. Greenwald states: 'the [Triangle] fire has come to represent the triumph of progressive/liberal reform over the excesses of industrial capitalism: victory snatched from tragedy'.[24] This is certainly reflected in *With These Hands* (Jack Arnold 1950), a film that marked the fiftieth anniversary of the birth of the International Ladies' Garment Workers' Union and that redressed the message of preceding propaganda films. The film depicts, through docudrama flashbacks, the struggles and accomplishments of the ladies' garment workers (and the labour movement). It takes viewers back to scenes of ghetto poverty in New York at the turn of the century. In the Triangle factory, we see bullying bosses or foremen who insist on keeping the doors and the windows closed and barring the workers from seeing Union organizers. A caricatured boss is seen locking the door, entrapping the female workers and the narrator informs us that this is: 'March 25th, 1911.' Just before the first signs of the fire are spotted, two women are seen sharing a joke. Women are heard screaming and seen running to the locked door, as smoke envelops the frame. Some women, in the general panic, collapse on the floor or try to break open the windows. As the blazing fire engulfs the factory floor, the hands (that once worked the sewing machines) are banging the locked metal door and this image merges into flames. This scene (as the screams reach the fever pitch of terror) cuts to one of mourning – a line of coffins, as the narrator says '146 dead – dead immigrants and the dead children of immigrants. There are the dead martyrs and the martyrs not yet dead.' Their names are immortalized, and the flames are symbolic of a collective sacrifice for the good of future garment workers. Graphic scenes of inferno terror and death are absent, and the emphasis is on tragic suffering as ennobling because it is sacrificial.

The aftermath of 9/11 has shown how difficult it is for art in any form to address a traumatic event of such magnitude. The made-for-TV-film, *The Triangle Factory Fire Scandal* (Mel Stuart), first aired on NBC at 9 pm in 1979, is a rare example that, at the end of a decade in which films such as *Inferno* had experimented with a horror spectacle, contextualizes an historical disaster whilst not eschewing scenes of inferno death and suffering. That said, certain disaster conventions remain intact. According to Tom Buckley, the scandal is framed by unconvincing 'soap-opera situations': 'Immigrant seamstresses are sweated and seduced by their bosses, bring home their pay packets unopened to obtuse old-world parents and dream of marrying millionaires. [...] Their grinding poverty is talked about but not seen.'[25] However, the backstories allow for a degree of social realism, with the opening shots establishing the historical setting in New York, the locale for Jewish and Italian immigrant communities. Echoing *With These Hands*, Morris Feldman (Tom Bosley) is depicted as a bullying, factory floor manager, who is accused of having paid off the fire inspector. In one scene, he threatens to sack a 38-year-old lady for not completing her daily quota of garments. A cigar-smoking boss also admits to having bribed police. Women are treated like criminals and the head machinist, Vinnie (Ted Wass), sexually preys on vulnerable young women (he molests Gina, played by Stacey Nelkin), whilst proudly stating that this is America and here things are done differently (implying that the land of the free means loose morals). The lady garment workers are fixated on courting with young men and Connie, who initially rejects the union man, shows a passing interest in a rich factory owner. So, generally, men are depicted as sexual predators, womanizers, bullying bosses or oppressive fathers. Sonya (Lauren Frost) is slapped in public when seen dancing with a man at a street party by her orthodox Jewish father – she had lied to her mother at the synagogue service, saying she was ill. Nonetheless, the immigrant women remain enrapt by the American dream.

In the factory fire sequence, the union man (who had repeatedly said, 'In unity is strength') perishes with his girlfriend, Gina jumps and survives, the bosses crawl across a ladder suspended from the rooftop to an adjacent building, and the Catholic Connie (who says it is a 'mortal sin' to jump and commit suicide) is rescued by firemen. Florence is the first person seen to jump. There are no shots of women engulfed in flames, because television was not permitted to be as graphic as cinema in this period. Onlooking spectators on the streets look away as the bodies fall. Feldman is treated as a hero for carrying his daughter across the ladder. And in one of the final scenes, Sonya's mother, believing her daughter has died, cries out 'Why?!' for Sonya then to appear, crying 'mama' and is embraced by relieved members of the family. The film cuts to a low angled shot of the factory, followed by a series of frozen shots of women running through a fire-consumed factory floor or jumping to their deaths, as we hear the narrator passing judgement on the disaster: 'The sweatshop conditions with blocked exits and inadequate fire escapes caused much of the tragedy.' And the resolving scene moves forward in time, with the narrator stating: 'From the Triangle factory ashes, the infant International Ladies' Garment Workers' Union gained support and strength. For the survivors, there was solace in the credo carried from other troubled lands. Life must go on.' This is a cue for the redemptive closure. Feldman (who too was given a soap opera backstory, making it known that his wife had died) and his daughter, Ruth, are enjoying a leisurely day off, strolling through the streets of New York. The father corrects the formalities of her grammar and buys her a 2 cents raspberry ice. And they walk off to watch the Easter parade. As Tom Buckley sees it, the depiction of Feldman is ambiguous: 'Tom Bosley seems confused as one of the factory managers. It's understandable, because it's not clear whether he's supposed to be a tough but fair boss or a bloodsucker.' This scene cuts to one of the three surviving garment ladies (Sonya, Gina and

Connie) holding hands, wearing white gloves, dressed in fashionable garments and hats, and promenading a bustling street: 'When we go to the dance tonight, Gina, remember, to dance with a boy all you have to do is smile.' And the three, right on cue, deliver brim-full smiles. Sonya's words recall the establishing scene, 'Friday 24 March 1911', when Florence, walking to work, speaks to Sonya about a hat she covets: 'After we get paid, I'm gonna own that hat. Sonya: real ostrich feathers.' Florence was the first person seen to jump out of a factory window.

To cast Bosley, who had a loveable persona from the sitcom, *Happy Days* (then in its prime), helps to humanize Feldman and to redress the caricaturing of the factory owners as monstrous, and recalls the moral relativism of films that exonerated the brutal factory owners. Feldman's stoical acceptance of his wife's death, and his courage in saving the factory bosses and his daughter, is meant to offset his inhumane treatment of the garment workers as well as the charge of manslaughter and the lawsuit of wrongful murder brought against the factory owners. The resolving image of Feldman with his motherless daughter normalizes him. In other words: 'To understand all is to forgive all.'[26] His moral rehabilitation is conveniently juxtaposed with the aftermath image of the surviving garment workers who, as if on a catwalk, parade the fashionable items that Florence had once coveted. Given that the shirtwaists made in the Triangle factory were advertised as a symbol of Women's newfound freedom in America, the closing image endorses the logic of the American dream, which is reborn (from out of the ashes). The two class groups are not reconciled, in the two separate closing scenes, but they are symbolically united. The message is that the survivors can carry on enjoying the pleasures of the American dream that had originally inspired the immigrants who worked and perished in sweatshops. And in the grand scheme of human tragedy, the Triangle factory disaster is a small sacrifice to pay. The garment workers who died horrific deaths are not martyred, and the survivors who appear in the final shot are stitched into an American way of life that 'must go on'.

The technological sublime

The Triangle Shirtwaist Factory fire in 1911 was a tragedy that foreshadows 9/11: victims perishing with no means of escape from a tall building inferno. While *Inferno* anticipates 9/11 in a case of life imitating art, it is also a film that confronts the threat of terrors in an immediate domestic setting, unlike films such as *Krakatoa, East of Java* (Bernard L. Kowalski, 1969), that are served up in exotic situations. Centre stage of the *Inferno* tragedy is 'the glass tower', the tallest skyscraper in the world, an iconic superstructure of American high modernity and a recurring feature of cinematic skylines, symbolically charged with multiple associations. Elevated architectural constructs inevitably invite symbolic readings, as Roland Barthes noted: 'The Tower is also present to the entire world. First of all as a universal symbol of Paris, it is everywhere on the globe where Paris is to be stated as an image [...] its simple, primary shape confers upon it the vocation of an infinite cipher [...]'.[27] And as Martin Parker argues, in 'Vertical Capitalism', the skyscraper is also an 'infinite cipher' – a symbol of modernism, technological sublime, economic aspiration, advertisements for the ego, greed on an inhuman scale, hierarchy and exclusion.

In American cinematic culture, the skyscraper is often associated with the romance and modernist aspirations of New York. At the turn of the century, when film footage showed the construction of skyscrapers and work crews seemingly defying gravity, the New York skyscraper skyline has been the ideal setting for dramas about crime and greed. For instance, a 1906 melodrama, filmed during the actual construction of a skyscraper in New York City that includes several scenes of real work crews, takes advantage of the vertiginous backdrop to depict the intrigues of robbery and the thrills of physical action that somewhat anticipate Harold Lloyd's skyscraper exploits. The final scene is of 'a hand-to-hand fight between the foreman and the villain that takes place on the unprotected ledge of the steel framework of the building'.[28] The cinematic skyscraper is a dramatic structure for visual thrill and the spectacle of violence that was translated during the decade of the Great Depression into visions of mass destruction. In *Deluge* (Felix E. Feist, 1933), New York is hit by a tsunami caused by earthquakes that destroys the city's symbols of 'vertical capitalism'. City destruction and reconstruction is a familiar narrative pattern in the 1930s' output of disaster movies. The iconic closure to *King Kong* (1933) in which the mighty monster, free from captivity, climbs The Empire State Building, has also been read as a symbolic attack on the once imperious, but now fallen state of, America's vertical capitalism. Merrill Schleier argues, King Kong's fall from what was then the tallest building in world is symbolically concomitant with the skyscraper's 'fall from grace during the Depression'.[29] Tall buildings were, at the time, regarded as 'tombstones of capitalism'.[30]

The fallen tower bears too mythical and biblical significations. The Tower of Babel story is a biblical apocalyptic warning of vertiginous aspiration above mortal lot. And 'The Tower' Tarot card (XVI) symbolizes the fall from grace. It follows immediately after 'the Devil' and 'is associated with sudden, disruptive revelation, and potentially destructive change'. Imagining the ruination of civilization via falling towers is a common trope in early cinema and high modernism. The 1927 Berlin premiere of *Metropolis* exploited the symbolism of the book of Revelation and its connection to the Tower of Babel.[31] The apocalypticism of T. S. Eliot's *The Waste Land* (1922) draws parallels between a collapsed modernity and the hellish symbolism of Dante's *Inferno*:

> What is the city over the mountains
> Cracks and reforms and bursts in the violet
>   air
> Falling towers
> Jerusalem Athens Alexandria
> Vienna London
>   Unreal[32]

The destruction of towers, representing metropolitan decadence and its tragic hubris, by the elemental force of fire bears a mythological dimension that is particularly connected to Dante's vision of punishment. As Geoff King says, it is a force that breaks into 'the paved, built-up and "civilised", "over-civilised", or "decadent" and "artificial" worlds […]'.[33] The Holocaust – mass inferno death on an industrial scale – increased the imagining of Hell as a living hell.[34] Falling towers and their visualized infernal landscapes are also a reminder of the living horror that always potentially exists in a technological modernity from where there is no escape.

    Undoubtedly, the apocalypticism of *Inferno* is borne out of an 'infinite cipher' of cultural and cinematic tropes and associations, including a dystopian tower of modernist disintegration. *The Glass Inferno* (1974), by Thomas N. Scortia and Frank M. Robinson, is set in a modern high rise that was deemed a 'fire trap in the sky' and immediately establishes the holocaust spectacle via a horror trope: 'Every beast has a time and place of birth.' The 'Glass House' is first perceived by locals as a sublime symbol of the city but by the end of the novel is a sign of inevitable destruction: 'It's like death and taxes […] It's inevitable.'[35] And even in death, the Glass Tower is a figure of sublime terror: 'The spark flares, touches a splintered piece of wood, and for a moment the pale ghost of the beast is outlined against the cold morning air.'[36] Richard Martin Stern's *The Tower* (1973) further exploits the Dantean and gothic dimensions of the fallen tower: 'The building breathed, manipulated its internal systems, slept only as the human body sleeps: heart, lungs, cleansing organs functioning as automatic control, encephalic waves pulsing ceaselessly.'[37] The two novels are united by a common theme: the construction and destruction of the building bears an inevitable agency of its own or a 'character of its own'.[38] In this sense, Stern plays more on the trans-historical and cine-intertextual themes of disaster to underscore the idea that the fallen tower is one of high modernity tragedy. There is a jocular reference to *King Kong* which is read as a story (documentary like) on 'how civilization overreaches itself'.[39] The novel, at this stage, tragically foreshadows the 9/11 disaster: 'We know how to build the tallest building in the world, but we're having trouble figuring out how to get people out of it.'[40] The inevitable disaster of the World Tower is also likened to the Titanic and the Hindenburg: 'Never again a *Titanic* blundering in the ice lanes. Never again a *Hindenburg* filled with explosive hydrogen gas.'[41]

'The Glass Tower', in *Inferno*, is frequently referred to as 'The Tower' and the opening scenes establish it as a wonder of technology. During the opening gala evening, when The Tower is illuminated in the San Francisco skyline it is viewed with awe by luminaries, government officials and stars of screen and television: 'Oh, it's absolutely unbelievable. It's astonishing.' With the public opening and the lush red carpet invoking Oscar night, there are powerful echoes of the opening scene in *Singin' in The Rain* (Gene Kelly & Stanley Donen, 1952) when 'The Royal Rascal' is premiered and Don (Gene Kelly) tells the gathered crowd a false version of his life story, which is contradicted by flashbacks that reveal the undignified truth behind the Hollywood dreamworld. And as Senator Gary Parker (Robert Vaughn), chairman of the Federal Urban Renewal Commission, speaks through a microphone to the gathered crowds of the 'magnificent building' representing 'yet another landmark in a long succession of landmarks for this great city', James Duncan (William Holden) confronts his son-in-law (with parading handshakes and smiles): 'Where were you all day? I wasn't aware the leash was tight. When I get the time, I want to ask you a few questions, and I expect some straight answers.' In the behind-the-scenes style of Arthur Hailey's big industry novels, it is a scene of intra-familial tension, as well as dramatic irony that punctures the technological sublime. The scene is also reminiscent of the carnival atmosphere that characterized the opening day of The Empire State Building when its erection seen as a symbol of hope during depression.[42] David E. Nye sees skyscrapers as being used as 'landmarks and icons of progress'.[43] The modernist romance of the skyscraper was cemented by John A. Roebling who saw mankind as becoming "'the lords of creation" as they multiplied production to create a new technological Eden'.⁴⁴ The skyscraper also provided 'an Olympian sense of perspective that could be immediately translated into a sense of power over nature'.⁴⁵

While *Inferno* is a skyscraper tragedy, the Glass Tower is also a synecdoche for other historical disasters of high modernity. When James Duncan first greets Doug, the building's architect (Paul Newman), he speaks as an optimist who has embraced the modernist romance of the skyscraper: 'Well, what I wanted to tell you is that, uh, Senator Parker's flying in for the dedication tonight, and he's almost guaranteed the urban renewal contract. Now, do you know what that means? Skyscrapers like this all over the country.' At the same time, a sign above an elevator reads: 'We Build for Life.' It is meant to be ironic and points to, as does his optimism, a hubristic faith in technology and design. The touchstone for the architectural hubris on display in *Inferno* is probably Howard Roark (Gary Cooper, the architect and visionary egotist in *The Fountainhead* (King Vidor, 1949), an adaptation of Ayn Rand's 1943 novel, for he is the link between skyscraper modernism and capitalist individualism. There is also a foreshadowing of Ballard's *High-Rise* that denudes Le Corbusier's egalitarian urban planning into a social hierarchical dystopia. In the Glass Tower, the floors above the Promenade Room are exclusively residential. *Inferno* is also a disaster homage to the sinking of the SS *Titanic* which occurred on its debut Atlantic crossing. The Promenade Room party smacks of luxury and an indifference to oblivion as well as to the underbelly of workers who maintain the tower. Vincent Canby referred to *Inferno* as 'an-end-of-the-world movie', and like *Poseidon* it is also an end of the world party – a continuity underscored by the singer at the party being Maureen McGovern who had recorded a no. 1 single version of 'The Morning After' (1973) from the 1972 film (and won Best Original Song at the Oscars).⁴⁶

Death by fire

One could say all forms of screened disaster served to armchair spectators are symbolic fantasies, filtering and containing tragic suffering: 'If tragedy ennobles sufferings, then it edifies only at the cost of the truth, since most real-life suffering is not in fact ennobling.'⁴⁷ Here, Eagleton echoes Žižek in the sense of the cinematic spectacle exceeding the cause – it is at the expense of painful truth.⁴⁸ The spectacle is also 'closely tied up with assertions of authenticity'.⁴⁹

While reviewers lauded the film's epic visual spectacle, Kael was repulsed by the violent realism that was predicated on the primal fear of death by fire.[50] The 'hero' is, as Sterling Silliphant (the film's screenwriter) intended, the raging fire, the cause of mass death and destruction.[51] The body count is quite high, and violent death is meted out indiscriminately. Let us count the ways: falling down a shaft or a stairwell – and set alight too (alas anonymous fireman); out of an external, glassed elevator (alas Lisolette Mueller played by Jennifer Jones). crushed by a million gallons of water or forced out of the Promenade Room on the 135rd floor (alas tuxedo partygoers), crushed by a falling statue (alas Carlos, the bartender – Gregory Sierra), falling in a breeches buoy (alas Roger, played by Richard Chamberlain), forced out of a broken window by a fire backdraft and falling alight (alas Lorrie played by Susan Flannery), dying in an exploding helicopter, or burnt alive.

This is the body count. But death by fire is often dramatized in the style of documentary realism that offsets escapist fantasy typical of Hollywood spectacle. The first victim to be engulfed by flames occurs when Doug Roberts (the Glass Tower architect) and the electrical engineer, Will Giddings (Norman Burton), go to the eighty-first floor to inspect a possible fire caused by an electrical fault. Giddings is hit by a fireball, when pushing a guard from a door. He screams in agony, and drapes are used to smother his enflamed body. A close-up of Newman reveals a facial expression of shocked horror as he perceives Gidding's first-degree burns and charred flesh. This is followed by the sight of enflamed ceilings crushing firemen crews as the fire spreads through corridors. The first scene of mass death happens when a descending express elevator, loaded with a group of partygoers from the Promenade Room, opens onto the eighty-first floor where the fire is out of control. Screams are heard, as Steve McQueen looks on in horror. The lift returns to the Promenade Room and an enflamed man stumbles out of a lift with this terrifying death witnessed by partygoers. It is one of many deaths by fire that are diegetically spectated. Screams of hysteria ring out, women either faint or are comforted by men in tuxedos, and Harlee Claiborne (Fred Astaire) takes off his dining jacket to cover the charred corpse. The rest look on, paralyzed with fear.

Perhaps the most brutal, nasty and vindictive pyrotechnical scene of retribution is when death by fire invades a post-coital scene in the Duncan Enterprises offices on the sixty-fifth floor. Dan Bigelow, *the Public Relations Officer* (Richard Wagner) is having a secret affair with his secretary, Lorrie (Susan Flannery). She is wearing only a shirt and a pair of knickers. Perhaps sins of the flesh in the corporate tower of Babel warrant such violent punishment? As the flames and smoke encroach on the isolated and entrapped couple, Bigelow makes a desperate attempt to get help by running through a holocaust obstacle course. The action sequence is filmed in slow motion, with John Williams's score reaching fever pitch when Bigelow lights up like a Roman candle. The film cuts to his mistress screaming in horror (Figure 4.1).

The sublime terror is further amplified by close-ups of Lorrie desperately grasping for air. She breaks open a window with a chair, is consumed by a fire backdraft, screams, crashes through the broken glass and there is a cut to an external shot to follow the enflamed, plummeting body. It is an edifying and detailed depiction of death by fire, one that is in the spirit of an in-vogue horror spectacle, exemplified by the brutal and realist, *The Last House on the Left* (Wes Craven, 1972), as well as splatter and exploitation films.

The reassuring reading rests on the *schadenfreude* effect of watching Roger, the scapegoated capitalist villain, falling to his death from a buoy. The film sets Roger up to be the fall guy from his stage entrance. Roger is not a self-made man, but the spoilt and callow son-in-law of the builder. He is a throwback to a Victorian melodramatic type. Whereas the architect, Doug, enjoys the wilderness (and perhaps used to 'wrestle grizzly bears in Montana'), Roger revels in luxury and being the flirtatious playboy. His marriage with Patty Duncan Simmons (Susan Blakely) is on the rocks. As he says to Doug: 'Buddy, you are in the dreamworld. I deal in realities.' Doug's strict ethical standards on electrical specifications do not match the corrupt realities of corporate business. It is a familiar theme of profit and 'kickbacks' at the expense of safety. The film also delivers the expected comeuppance to nepotism and to anyone who would mess with 'Daddy's

Figure 4.1 Death by fire.

Building': 'Patty: Roger, if you've done anything to Dad's building, God help you. Roger: Baby, I don't need God's help. Or your old man's. Not anymore. So don't expect me to shake every time daddy barks.' The implication is that defying the Tower of Babel, or the law of the father, will provoke God's wrath. Roger is the overreacher, and when death by fire encroaches the Promenade Room Roger is also typed as a Titanic bruiser who only wants to save himself. But the scapegoating of one capitalist villain does not compensate for the holocaust carnage.

The moral heart of the film is Lisolette Mueller (Jennifer Jones). She tolerates and forgives the conman, Harlee. She rushes to the eighty-seventh floor to help save a deaf mother and her two children. She is patient and not hysterical. And when it seems that she may have found a man to be a partner in her old age, she dies a horrible death: falling out of the external, glassed elevator. There is no obvious religious theme or figure in the film. Roger defies the patriarchal God of the Tower of Babel. There is a passing glimpse of a priest giving last rites to the dying – but he plays no active, speaking role. For a second, there is the sight of a waiter praying in the Promenade Room. There is a brief panning shot of firemen in body bags. No solace is given to Harlee (except to be handed Mueller's cat): 'Harlee: Excuse me. She was in the elevator with you. The fine-looking lady. Mrs. Mueller. Have you seen her? Fireman: I'm sorry. She's dead.' The father's words of comfort to Patty when she sees the remains of her husband's body are equally unsparing and pitiless: 'You know there's nothing that any of us can do to bring back the dead. All I can do now is pray to God that … I can stop this from ever happening again. I don't know.' Some of the partying tuxedo men – the *crème de la crème* – die, but also the deferential and kindly faced bar waiter, Carlos. Firemen are heroized but firemen also fall or burn to their deaths. The spreadsheet of death is meant to look expansive. Stars perish but William Holden who plays James Duncan, the builder, who is accused by Roger of shaving costs, survives: 'Where did you save the other $4 million in Doug's original budget?' The multiplication of violent and senseless deaths points to a scale of pessimism that is disturbing. *Inferno* does not close on a triumphant, and resounding, note in the way *Jaws* and *Star Wars* do by obliterating the monster (i.e., a big killer shark and the Death Star) and is closer instead to the downbeat or tragic ending of New Hollywood films: *Midnight Cowboy* (1969), *Easy Rider* (1969), *The Last Picture Show* (1971) and *Chinatown* (1974). For Richard Neubert, the open-ended closure of Mike Nichols' *The Graduate* (1967), with the suggestion of an uncertain future for the eloping couple (played by Dustin Hoffman and Katherine Ross), is both 'complete and incomplete'.[52]

Apocalyptic revelation

Inferno indulges in sublime terror, but it is also a cautionary narrative of high modernity, which suggests an uncertain future – as spoken by Michael O'Halloran, the Chief of the San Francisco Fire Department (played by Steve McQueen): 'You know, we were lucky tonight. Body count's less than 200. You know, one of these days, they're gonna kill 10,000 in one of these firetraps. And I'm gonna keep eatin' smoke and bringin' out bodies, until somebody asks us how to build 'em' (Figure 4.2). Doug, the architect, responds with the possibility of dialogue and compromise between skyscraper architects and fire safety experts: 'Okay, I'm asking. You know where to reach me. O'Halloran: So long, architect.' For Keane, the finale implies repentance. Two of the biggest movie stars at the time survive and are given hopeful, reconciliatory lines to finish the film. But the SFFD Chief bears a message of apocalyptic revelation; for one day, the tragedy could be bigger and one that was recounted in newspapers.

In 1988, Stirling Silliphant wrote a piece for the *Los Angeles Times* (10 May) entitled, '"Towering Inferno": A Bit of Art Too Often Imitated by Life and Death', in which he quotes the film's closing dialogue.[53] Silliphant was prompted by Thomas Kelsey's famous photo of the First Interstate Bank building: 'a devilish mouth of fire eating its way upward from the 12th floor'. The skyscraper inferno image brought back to the scriptwriter the 'genesis of the film', and he recalls that his first film consultant had been a fire marshal in San Francisco, who saw property owners, and some builders and architects as the 'enemy' of building safety codes. So, Silliphant in his script,

Figure 4.2 Michael O'Halloran (Steve McQueen): 'You know, one of these days, they're gonna kill 10,000 in one of these firetraps.'

came down hard on builder apathy and subcontractor shortcuts. [...] We had no idea how ominous a presage our film would be. Shortly after its release, high-rise fires began killing people all over the world – in San Paulo, in New York – and the critics [spokesmen of the building industries] were silenced. But we felt no sense of triumph or vindication.[54]

Like critics who labelled *Inferno* as 'ridiculous', a critical reviewer of Richard Martin Stern's *The Tower* (1973) also dismissed the plausibility of a skyscraper inferno disaster at the time of its publication: '[...] if this newly completed Manhattan superstructure is indeed the biggest and most modern office building in the world, then how the devil could a mere fire seriously threaten all those luminaries who have gathered on the 125th floor to celebrate its opening? A steel and aluminium skyscraper couldn't turn into a raging inferno, could it?'[55] The recurrence of historical disasters is part of a tragic cycle when alarmists and prophets of doom are unheeded.

On 26 February 1993, a truck filled with explosives detonated in the underground garage of the North Tower of the World Trade Center. Six people were killed and 1,042 people injured, some from smoke inhalation. According to a prosecutor, during the trial of Ramzi Yousef, the chief aim of the attack was to 'make one of the twin towers collapse into the other'.[56] This terrorist attack can be deemed a dress rehearsal for 9/11. At the time, it was much reported that the explosion had exposed flaws in the emergency systems. In an article for *The New York Times*, headed 'Tougher Code May Not Have Helped' (27 February 1993), Josh Barnabel reported on the WTC being exempt from New York's stringent fire codes:

> To Amy Herz Juviler, a former Criminal Court judge, the image of smoke snaking down the emergency stairwells of the World Trade Center yesterday recalled safety concerns raised two decades ago about the flagship project of the Port Authority of New York and New Jersey.
>
> Back then the building was caught in a jurisdictional tug-of-war between the Port Authority and the Fire Department, which wanted to impose the city's stringent high-rise fire-safety rules.
>
> In the early 1970s, Ms. Juviler, then an assistant attorney general who had just moved into the state's newly finished offices on the 47th floor of 2 World Trade Center, was startled to see smoke from small construction fires in the basement curl up through the emergency stairwells for at least 50 stories and she was worried.

'I called the Fire Department at the request of the Attorney General, and the Fire Department assured me that this was not the world's safest building', she recalled yesterday. 'Those stairwells, not some but all of them, were flues. There was no break to keep the smoke out.'

[...]

But Ms. Juviler and state legislators who fought for years to put the Trade Center and other Port Authority structures under the New York City code remain concerned that some of the mishaps and mayhem could have been avoided.

The picture painted by the Fire Department was so bleak, Ms. Juviler said, that the issue was dropped. 'We chose not to further alarm our people', she said. 'In the case of a real fire like "The Towering Inferno" we knew there was no escape.'[57]

Juviler was referring to the fire that broke on the eleventh floor of the North Tower on 13 February 1975, and that spread to the ninth and fourteenth floors after igniting cable insulation in a utility shaft. There was no fire sprinkler system at the time in place. In an article published the next day in *The New York Times* (28 February 1993), with the headline of 'Explosion at the Twin Towers: Proud Landmark, Vulnerability Exposed', James Bennett reported on the Port Authority's repeated defence of the emergency system.[58]

It is telling that, prior to 9/11, *Inferno* was a portentous reference point for the death-trap skyscraper in the event of a raging fire. Amy Juviler's account of the 9/11 terrorist rehearsal in 1993 is an affirmation of *Inferno* as a revelation. For the revelation of apocalypticism is to 'reveal what is hidden' and what is yet 'unfulfilled'.[59] *Inferno* is neither a divinely inspired, nor a literal, prophecy revealing the future course of events. Yet, as an imagining of the fall of high modernity, *Inferno* is a symbolic portent that makes visible the fault lines of technological modernity.

Conclusion

The Towering Inferno is a modern tragedy that exceeds reassuring spectacle. The blood sacrifice of Roger Simmons – the dodgy electrical engineer and frustrated son-in-law in the oedipal drama of a falling tower – is insufficient catharsis to assuage the cumulative terror. The film lacks the dark carnivalesque of *The Poseidon Adventure* (1972), and its death by fire realism is harrowing. Nonetheless, in not quite striking the right balance between fear and pity, *Inferno* is the most powerful film in the cycle. Today, it makes for uncomfortable viewing, because *Inferno* is a vision of hegemonic destruction that Hollywood consistently disseminates and, at the same time, denies.

5

Los Angeles – a 'convicted' city: *Earthquake* (1974), *The Day of the Locust* (1975), *Smash-Up on Interstate 5* (1976)

Los Angeles, a final American frontier city and famous for the Hollywood sign situated on Mount Lee, is the setting for many cinematic imaginations of dystopian annihilation.[1] Commenting on *Earthquake* (Mark Robson, 1974), Pauline Kael said there was no point in imagining the devastation of Los Angeles: for many, the city already stood 'convicted'.[2] Because of its proximity to the San Andreas Fault, the city is a site of seismic hazards. Hollywood is situated in a notorious earthquake zone. This partly explains Hollywood's fascination with natural disaster as dramatic material for the spectacular, and why many films have foregrounded 'an image of Los Angeles as a disaster zone'. In fact, since the release of *Earthquake*, the city's reputation for 'hosting the Apocalypse' has increased.[3] It is also because California is 'the terminus of the American Dreamscape', where the migratory exodus and the coeval drive of modernity meet their final destination on the western sphere.[4]

The two big hits of 1974, *Earthquake* and *The Towering Inferno* (John Guillermin), are both set in the two major cities of the Californian state – Los Angeles and San Francisco – and are a far cry from the triumphant finale of *How the West was Won* (1962):

> The west that was won by its pioneers, settlers, adventurers is long gone now. Yet it is theirs's forever, for they left tracks in history that will never be eroded by wind or rain – never plowed under by tractors, never buried in compost of events. Out of the hard simplicity of their lives, out of their vitality, of their hopes and sorrows grew legends of courage and pride to inspire their children and their children's children. From soil enriched by their blood, out of their fever to explore and be, came lakes where once there were burning deserts – came the goods of the earth; mine and wheat fields, orchards and great lumber mills. All

the sinews of a growing country. Out of their rude settlements, their trading posts came cities to rank among the great ones of the world. All the heritage of a people free to dream, free to act, free to mould their own destiny.

While Spencer Tracy narrates, Cinerama captures the achievements of modern construction: the Hoover Dam (constructed between 1931 and 1936), the Golden Gate suspension Bridge in San Francisco (completed in 1937) and the Four Level Interchange (opened in 1953) in Los Angeles. Yet, if one US city epitomizes the tragic hubris of modernity or 'what men [the builders of bridges and the city dwellers] choose to forget', it is Los Angeles.[5] Or to echo Mike Davies, 'Los Angeles has deliberately put itself in harm's way'.[6] Two films discussed in this chapter, *Earthquake* and *The Day of the Locust* (John Schlesinger, 1975), illustrate Hollywood's preoccupation with apocalypticism and its denial of disaster. The final example, a 1976 made-for-television film, *Smash-Up on Interstate 5* (John Lewellyn Moxley), dramatizes the modern reality of disaster in the 'Dream State' of California.

Earthquake (1974)

In the words of Jack Matthews: 'Natural disasters have provided Hollywood with dramatic material from the earliest days, but the film community, perhaps because it was situated on the San Andreas Fault and didn't want to tempt fate, resisted using earthquakes as subject matter for decades'.[7] *Earthquake* was the first disaster movie to depict the full magnitude of an earthquake striking Los Angeles. Following the success of *The Poseidon Adventure* in 1972, Jennings Lang, Universal Pictures and George Fox (the co-screen writer) were persuaded to produce a super-spectacular of 'awesome violence'.[8] The earthquake is ideal material for an all-encompassing 'event' film, one that upstages the confined drama of SS *Poseidon*. As David M. Anderson puts it: 'an earthquake is an awesome event, primeval in its effect, and enormous in its effect on the human psyche'.[9] The earthquake – the shaking of the earth – with the possible secondary effects of ground rupture, landslides, floods, fires and tsunamis (plus the human impact of mass destruction of buildings and infrastructure, death, famine and disease) is the most violent and disturbing form of natural disaster. In the Bible, earthquakes can wipe out whole cities, and, given their apocalyptic potential, lend themselves to cinematic imaginings of cataclysmic purging. In *The King of Kings* (Cecil B. DeMille, 1927), the renting of the earth occurs during the crucifixion scene and is depicted in the style of John Martin's *The Great Day of his Wrath* (1951–3): the infidels who mocked Christ are crushed by falling rocks or thrown into the abyss, including Judas – hanging from a tree. A Jerusalem temple is torn in two when struck by lightning, and a Jewish priest pleads: 'Lord God Jehovah, visit not thy wrath of Thy people Israel – I alone am guilty!' The earthquake is witnessed as a punitive act of God, and as a warning that no city, nor civilization, is invulnerable to such devastating effects. The earthquake also taps into anxieties concerning modernity and rapid urbanization, and in this respect the 1906 earthquake of San Francisco, the deadliest earthquake in the history of the United States, is an abiding reference point. 3,000 people died and 80 per cent of the city was destroyed, with the devastation and fatalities mainly due to a dense population residing in wooden constructions or the result of what H. G. Wells saw as America's obsession with the 'limitless bigness' of its cities and its concomitant 'ultra-human force'.[10]

Following the 1971 Sylmar earthquake, which had caused the partial collapse of several major freeway interchanges in Los Angeles, the intention of *Earthquake*, according to Mark Robson, was to awaken a sense of imminent peril: 'Superficially, I felt that [John J.] Fried (author of *Life Along the San Andreas Fault*) is right. Californians *have* shoved their never-ending peril into the backs of their minds [...] Nevertheless, the awareness of danger is an ingrained part of Californians' minds.'[11] And the intention was also to produce a spectacle that competed with reality: 'Let us assume [...] that between now and the film's release in November, there is a major earthquake in Los Angeles and a million people are killed. This may keep people away from the film. But who knows, maybe more people will go. Sometimes catastrophes add to the excitement.'[12] As Davies sees it, what is bad news in the region can be good news for 'Hollywood [that] fattens on the spectacle of natural catastrophe'.[13] And yet, despite the marathon of destruction effects, *Earthquake* does not treat the subject matter with a sense of sublime awe. In the words of Kael, it is a 'jokey form of destruction' in which 'we [...] take a campy pleasure in seeing the big-name actors and the old plot situations – and the motion-picture capital itself – totaled'.[14] For Kael, the disaster film was 'a death wish for the film art' – and 1974 was the peak year for 'processed schlock' and morbidity in terms of seeing how 'old favorites have aged'.[15] *Airport 1975* (Jack Smight, 1974) fared no better: 'a campy joke – a box of rotten candy for movie junkies and TV dispos'.[16] In her essay, 'Notes on "Camp"' (1964), Susan Sontag construes 'camp' as a style that dethrones 'the serious'.[17] In this sense, watching outmoded, glamorous stars (symbols of a stale Hollywood) perish as disaster fodder is a form of campy industry cleansing. It is also a distancing effect from the potential reality of an earthquake. In effect, delivered in the similar spirit of *Sunset Boulevard* (Billy Wilder, 1950), an 'insider's' end-of-the empire film, *Earthquake* is a 'confused piece of self-adulation' and self-mockery.[18]

From the onset, the self-referential setting is pronounced. The establishing aerial shot, which sweeps across the Hollywood Hills to the Mulholland dam, greets Stewart Graff (Charlton Heston) jogging in front of the 'Hollywood Sign'. Much of the film's exterior locations are close to Universal Studios. The first interior cut is to the domestic scene of a bickering couple, with Ava Gardner (as Remy) wearing exuberant eye lashes – she's a washed-out femme fatale, who fakes suicides to keep her man. The deranged performance of Gardner recalls Gloria Swanson's dramatics as Norma Desmond, the delusional Hollywood star in *Sunset*. And when Graff visits his mistress, Denise (a young, braless, aspiring actress), the Hollywood Sign looms ominously in the horizon, bridging and framing a melodramatic backstory. In the next scene, a Los Angeles squad car, driven by Patrolman Lou Slade (George Kennedy), is involved in a high-speed chase. The pursued sports car ends up in a 'luxurious' hedge owned by Zsa Zsa Gabor (aged fifty-seven in 1974), next to a mansion seen in *Rebel Without a Cause* (Nicholas Ray, 1955). The barbed cynicism in this peripheral scene is that Los Angeles is an extravagant nest for Hollywood has-beens. At least, Walter Matthau (aged fifty-four), bearing no hallucinations of bygone grandeur, plays a washed-out, 'imperturbable drunk' straight.[19] This is a film at the expense of a washed-out Hollywood.

The most in-joke scene occurs when Denise Marshall, played by Geneviève Bujold (aged thirty-two), in her small, rented home below the dam, asks Graff to read out the lines for an auditioning scene of seduction in which he plays the 'big movie star' and she plays the 'nymphomaniac'.[20] Heston has been upstaged by an emerging, talented, actress, implying he is no longer the 'big movie star'. The role of Denise was Bujold's first Hollywood role, and she received a Best Actress Oscar nomination in 1969 for her performance as Anne Boleyn in *Anne of the Thousand Days* (Charles Jarrott).[21] Denise represents the sexual vitality lacking in Graff's marital life: "'Don't worry," she murmurs, "I'm not a nymphomaniac. I'm not Mary Poppins, but I'm far from a nympho."'[22] Unlike Gardner, Bujold is not a sexless, movie throwback. Other ironic allusions include Richard Roundtree, famous as the Black action hero, John Shaft, playing a daredevil stunt rider and being mistaken by a man in a bar with a pool cue for Peter Fonda (Wyatt, 'Captain America') from *Easy Rider* (Dennis Hopper, 1969).

The suggestion is that Hollywood is only good at refashioning anti-heroes from competing cinematic trends: New Hollywood and blaxploitation. And when Rosa Amici (Victoria Principal) refuses to ride on the back of Quade's stunt bike, her declared preference is to go to see a movie: 'The Clint Eastwood at the Royale'.[23] Perhaps Rosa prefers a white masculine hero from an established film genre, because she goes to see *High Plains Drifter* (1973), an American Western, in which Eastwood plays a mysterious stranger who metes out retributive justice in a corrupt frontier mining town. Eastwood's shootout eventually becomes the cue for the erupting earthquake and the ensuing panic amongst the fleeing auditorium members. This time, L.A. Hollywood is the corrupt town that is going to be wiped out.

Prior to the self-destructive purge is a fermenting melodrama, for which each actor was carefully selected to play a particular role. Claire Jenkins makes the claim the 'family has taken centre stage in [...] two recent cycles in a way it had not in previous disaster film cycles (most notably that of the 1970s)'.[24] In films, such as *Independence Day* (Roland Emmerich, 1997), *Armageddon* (Michael Bay, 1998), *Deep Impact* (Mimi Leder, 1998), *The Day After Tomorrow* (Roland Emmerich, 2004) and *War of the Worlds* (Steven Spielberg, 2005), 'the threat to mankind is clearly aligned with a threat to the traditional American family'.[25] In the group jeopardy films of the 1970s, the focus is to some extent on 'non-familial groups' and Jenkins is right to point out that one exception is the Bakersfield 'dysfunctional family' in *Airport* – who are also reflective of a changing dynamic between domestic and workplace spheres.[26] However, Jenkins neglects to consider the non-traditional, familial melodrama that precipitates the disaster in *Earthquake*.

In response to *Poseidon*, Mark Robson felt a need to marry melodramatic backstories with catastrophe:

> An earthquake is a release of seismic energy. Our people ought to be as pent-up and ready for release as the ground under their feet. Without slamming them over the head with the fact, we ought to make the audience feel – unconsciously, their nerve ends – that the quake is somehow generated by the characters they're watching, not the San Andreas fault alone.[27]

At the epicentre of the melodramatic storm are the 'pent-up' roles played by Charlton Heston and Ava Gardner, two principal stars chosen to 'be the in joke of an industry that enjoys the idea of self-destructing'.[28] Their loveless, childless marriage, with Graff pursuing an extra-marital affair, takes centre stage for the 'mounting-doom' half of the film. Graff is on the edge of leaving his wife and Remy is struggling to hold on to him at whatever cost.[29] And 'their problems reach the boiling point at the exact instant the cataclysm hits'.[30] Graff has discovered that his boss and father-in-law, Sam Royce, had offered him promotion on a proviso: 'Graff: "You've got yourself a new president." Remy: "And you'll stay away from Denise Marshall?"' For Graff, this is one of many bribes: 'Our whole marriage has been a series of bribes!'[31] And Graff's fury is matched by nature's fury: 'With incredible speed, the city of Los Angeles virtually disintegrates. The earth tilts and is torn apart, creating crevasses that swallow hundreds of screaming men and women. High buildings crumble into rubble and dust. Elevated freeways collapse, dropping cars and trucks to destruction below … '[32] The earthquake is the shaking of marital tempers and a phallic manifestation of Heston's rekindled libido: 'Denise: "You made love with such … anger. Why?" "Don't be hurt," Graff says. "I learned something today. It made me furious – at my wife. Not at you."'[33] Disaster is clearly aligned to a family, but one that is not worth saving, for it is metonymic of a financially, and oedipally, fraught Hollywood system.

The soap-opera triangle is energized by Gardner, who was chosen because her feature-film career had recently been inactive: '"You know why I want her?" Robson said. "That perfect WASP wife quality, It's a great mask for bitchery."'[34] For Kael, Gardner is 'cast as a tiresome bitch whose husband (Heston) is fed up with her' and she is 'just one more old star to beef up a picture's star power'.[35] And to complete the Oedipal drama, Lorne Greene was given the role of Royce, the paternal owner of a major construction company. He also fulfils 'the picture's quota of TV personalities'.[36] At the time, Greene was a household name because of his television role as the benign patriarch, Ben 'Pa' Cartwright in *Bonanza* – a Western NBC series that ran from 1959 to 1973. Sam is aware of Graff's engineering talents and that his daughter clings on to an impoverished image of a university football star: 'When you met Stewart, he was a dirt-poor kid on an athletic scholarship. You *still* half see him that way. But now he doesn't need you, and he doesn't need me. Not a firm in town won't take him on his own terms.'[37] Again, the in-joke is that Heston is a fading talent, or a talent trapped in a nepotistic film industry. But Gardner was also cast in the role of WASP wife because of her impoverished star status.

The symbolic purging of old Hollywood presupposes the scapegoating of a patriarchal figure who represents the biblical underwriting of cinematic apocalypticism. The death of Heston-Graff, as well as the manner of his death, as Heston himself acknowledged, was an on-screen sacrifice that gratified a zeitgeist bloodlust: 'Our death scene was one of my more spectacular screen demises. [...] The ending did what I predicted: it stunned the audience into shocked silence. *Earthquake* was a monster success.'³⁸ According to Heston's account, if the script writers had had their way, Gardner would have been swept away, to drown alone in a flooded storm drain, and Heston, in the classic tradition of male stars, would have survived. But instead:

> I never approved the original ending where my character survived the earthquake. They agreed to a change to accommodate my death in a futile, doomed effort to save my bitchy wife, which seems to me to lend some credibility to a basically implausible story. (An earthquake destroys the whole city, this guy with the mean wife and the neat girl friend escapes scot-free, wife killed, neat girl left alive for him while he rebuilds Los Angeles?) [...] *Against great pressure, I succeeded in dying in the film.*³⁹

Though lacking the death-rattle of Reverend Frank Scott, the drowning of Heston is the most iconoclastic death scene in the disaster cycle. That said, the watery sacrifice does not, as Nora Sayre notes, make up for the gender politics of *Airport '75*: '[...] it would be nice to see the Charlton Heston and Karen Black roles reversed, so that an experienced woman pilot would guide a sobbing male steward at the controls: "Take a left turn, honey." "Oh God I can't." "Now, now"' (Figure 5.1).⁴⁰

The filmic death of Heston speaks volumes in terms of the shifting codes of apocalypticism in post-war American cinema, for it marks a significant fall from grace for the Episcopalian, classical actor who had played numerous epic religious roles: Moses in *The Ten Commandments* (Cecil B. DeMille, 1956),

Figure 5.1 The ubiquitous Charlton Heston reclaims the *cock*pit from Karen Black in *Airport 1975*.

Judah in *Ben-Hur* (William Wyler, 1959), the Christian Castilian knight in *El-Cid* (Anthony Mann, 1961), God twice as well as John the Baptist in *The Greatest Story Ever Told* (George Stevens, 1965). For Kael, the casting of Heston as Graff was an obvious choice, because 'the all-time king of prestige epics' was now 'a dependable heroic joke'.[41] The 'fatigued heroism' of America's 'Adam' represented a seismic shift in Heston's film career (from 1956 to 1974), from biblical epics to lead roles in disaster and post-apocalyptic films, such as *The Omega Man* (Boris Sagal, 1971) and *Soylent Green* (Richard Fleischer, 1973).[42] His role as George Taylor in *Planet of the Apes* (Franklin J. Shaffner, 1968) was pivotal. It is telling that Heston was playing to biblical type in the iconoclastic finale:

> The half-buried Statue of Liberty shows him at last that he's home on Earth. On his knees, despairing, he condemns his fellow man: 'You did it, didn't you ... you really did it. Goddamn you all to *hell!*' [...] 'But he's not *swearing*', I said, 'He's literally calling on God to damn the people who destroyed the world.'[43]

Heston invokes the retributive voice as heard at the top of Mount Sinai in *The Ten Commandments*, when he played both God and Moses, and it is unsurprising given his symbolic reading of the biblical exodus to the promised land: 'The words Moses spoke as he watched his people cross over Jordan, free at last, are cut in the rim of our Liberty Bell, They define this country: "Go, proclaim liberty throughout all the lands, unto all the inhabitants thereof [...]"'[44] In cultural and cinematic terms, Heston's ignominious drowning eclipses the totemic fall of the Statue of Liberty, for in the secular scheme of disaster the righteous are not protected by the laws of nature.

When another aftershock strikes, the Hollywood dam, damaged by an earlier tremor, bursts open and the reservoir floods Hollywood, drowning hundreds. People have reached the clear section of a storm drain and are being hauled up a manhole shaft by medics. Denise reaches the surface. When an ominous rumble is heard,

> the storm drain fills with swift-running water, carrying off dozens, and Remy is halfway up the ladder when a man steps on her hand. She loses her grip, plunges twenty feet into the drain. Graff and Slade, fighting the current, have almost reached the ladder. Graff sees Remy's thrashing body swirl past. He glances up the shaft, spots Denise far above. Everything in him wants to follow her. But he pushes himself away from the ladder, swims after his wife. He reaches Remy, struggles to keep her afloat. A section of the weakened drain roof gives way right above them. They disappear in the churning water.[45]

In the film, Remy calls out her husband's name, and Graff's glance at Denise on the ladder instantly intimates the conflicted loyalties and the ultimate sense of moral duty. Graff chooses an archetypal noble form of sacrifice – remaining loyal to his wife.

However, death by water is a symbolic redress for the punitive drowning of the pursuing Egyptians in the Red Sea – the spectacular centrepiece of Cecil B. DeMille's 1956 film. It is also a significant counterpoint to Moses's mastering of nature's destructive forces for retributive ends that affirmed to a post-Holocaust audience the Exodus deliverance of the Jewish people, the consolidation of modern Israel and the Law of Moses over heathens. 'Fear ye not, stand still, and see the salvation of the Lord.'[46] However, Heston's sacrificial death can also be read as recompense for adultery. After all, Graff's angry sex is matched by nature's fury. So, in a way, the apocalyptic tropes of biblical epics still feed into *Earthquake*: 'The writers and directors of "Earthquake" have still managed to make two points essential to our enjoyment of disaster movies: (1) that the people caught in the disaster have somehow flaunted God's physical laws, and (2) that God is punishing the victims for sexually misbehaving.'[47] Or perhaps their marriage is being judged according to conservative values – for the privileging of individualistic careerism above the reproduction of children. Either way, Heston's decision to die demonstrates the actor's awareness of the extent to which his career's trajectory was an indicator of America's standing in the world: 'The Arab successes in the Yom Kippur war, coupled with their subsequent oil embargo, have transformed the West's economy of abundance. Standing in the gas lines to fill our tanks, we've realized there's a bottom to the cup.'[48] When playing Moses, the cup runneth over.

Another in-joke casting, to parallel the fall of Moses, is that of Marjoe Gortner, 'the former child evangelist', in the role of a 'righteous psychotic' – Jody Joad, the grocery store manager.[49] Marjoe, a contraction of Mary and Joseph, was the son of professional evangelists who began preaching at three years old, and at the age of twenty-eight he retired from the 'Jesus business' – tent revivals in the American South. *Marjoe*, directed by Howard Smith and Sarah Kernochan, which won the 1972 Academy Award for 'Best Documentary Feature', shows Gortner as, in the words of Stephen Holden, 'an unsavory, if fascinating, cultural product of the Jesus-hippie connection that flourished in the early 1970s'.[50] It depicts Gortner's final weeks on the Pentecostal church-and-tent circuit, and then in cities, such as Los Angeles, footage shows Gortner 'gleefully' exposing the tricks of his trade and demonstrating 'how his grown-up style incorporates moves garnered from rock stars like Mick Jagger'.⁵¹ *Earthquake* was Gortner's first film role and there is an ironic nod to his past when he asks Lou Slade to remove chanting Hare Krishnas from the front of the store: 'Officer, can you order these freaks out of here? They've been scaring my customers away [...]. Slade: You got something against religion?' The Hare Krishna movement had been founded in 1966 in New York, and the conversion of George Harrison, following the Beatles visit to Rishikesh in North India to study meditation with the Maharishi Mahesh Yogi, affirmed in the song, 'My Sweet Lord' (1970), helped to popularize the faith as part of the non-violent, hippie culture of protest. So, the dialogue may be alluding to the tension between the peace movements of the sixties and the backlash of religious evangelism.

The affront is made doubly ironic when Joad, called up by the National Guard, becomes aligned to violent subjugation. He leaves work, and at home when changing into his NCO uniform is teased by housemates for having posters of male bodybuilders. Later, he executes the group of men for the homophobic ridiculing (the reference to 'fag' still rankles): 'Maybe they didn't steal these necklaces and things. Maybe they're fags that like to dress up in women's jewels.' Now fully regressed to a primal type, Jody also tries to take ownership of, and to force himself upon, Rosa Amici inside a secluded store: 'Nobody left but me to take care of you.' Slade (who had sided with the peace-loving Krishnas) saves Rosa from possible rape and Jody's hard (or fragile) masculinity is once again pricked: 'Nuts am I, huh? You got your nerve. Only a whore would wear that.' As the folksy copper, Slade, says, 'Earthquakes bring out the worst in some guys.' Perhaps Gortner is paying for the capitalist sins of his past evangelism, and so is typed as a vile homophobe and misogynist and also reduced to a Hobbesian state of nature. In the carnivalesque spirit of the disaster movie, both actors (Heston and Gortner) associated with religious orthodoxy are demoted from the spiritual to the material sphere.

While the symbolic demise of Heston and Gortner may have appealed to a post-countercultural audience, the casting of Richard Roundtree, who had reached stardom in the *Shaft* films, as 'a black, second-string Evel Knievel' is an indicator of Hollywood's then cynical exploitation of blaxploitation trends to appeal to a wider demographic (Figure 5.2).⁵² While historically African American actors and actresses are scarce in blockbuster movies – yet James Earl James is the voice of Darth Vader – some actors starred alongside Heston: Rosalind Cash (as Lisa) in *The Omega Man* (1971), Rosey Grier (as Gary Brown) in *Skyjacked* (1972) and Paula Kelly (as Martha) and Brick Peters (as Hatcher)

Figure 5.2 Richard Roundtree as 'a black, second-string Evel Knievel', alongside Rosa Amici (Victoria Principal).

in *Soylent Green* (1973). O. J. Simpson plays the chief security officer in *The Towering Inferno*, which was directed by John Guillermin and scripted by Stirling Silliphant, both of whom also worked on *Shaft in Africa* (1973). The casting of Black actors in disaster movies was not new – for example, Woody Strode as Hank Lawson, the stoker, in *The Last Voyage* (Andrew L. Stone, 1960).

As Jans Wager argues, 'a handsome male model [...] provided an alternative image to the integrationist roles often portrayed by Sidney Poitier that Hollywood had favored throughout the 1960s'.[53] Shaft relies upon a group of Black militant nationalists who are identified with the Black Power movement. A Black advertising firm was also hired by MGM to popularize '*Shaft* by using the rhetoric of black power'.[54] As David Walker sees it, Black heroes, such as John Shaft, were a welcome respite 'from characters like James Bond and cinematic icons like John Wayne'.[55] Nonetheless, for William Lyne, while Roundtree's Shaft provided audiences with an assertive, self-confident Black male hero, blaxploitation consistently undermines the potential threat of Black revolutionary groups such as the Black Panther Party.[56] Black revolutionaries appear only in the first film of the *Shaft* sequence, which does everything to disempower the movement's potential. It portrays the group as unable to hold a successful secret meeting and shows its leader Buford both saved and emasculated by Shaft. *Super Fly* (Gordon Parks Jr., 1972) portrays revolutionaries in a similar way; they are poorly organized and unthreatening in the face of the main character's rugged individualism. As in *Shaft*, Black power is reworked, revised and eventually rendered invisible.

Similarly, the casting of Roundtree as a Black imitation of Knievel implies a devaluing of Black politics, even though Quade is heroically elevated above the likes of Gardner, Gortner, Greene and Heston. Miles: 'Come on, Lou. This is really important to me. This big Vegas hotel guy is coming to see this act. There's never been anything like this. If that hotel sponsors us, I could wind up on ABC's *Wide World of Sports*. After that, you could forget about Evel Knievel. It would be just the Miles Quade story.' Here Quade believes he can outdo Knievel's failed attempt to rocket 1,600 feet across Snake River Canyon in the steam-powered Sky-Cycle X-2, on 8 September 1974, which ABC's *Wide World of Sports* was unwilling to finance. As Andy Webster notes, there was 'something fundamentally American about the stunt motorcyclist', who performed his feats 'in a spangled outfit evoking Liberace and Elvis Presley'.[57] The biopic, *Evel Knievel* (Marvin J. Chomsky, 1971), contextualizes 'Knievel as a hero inspiring the country after Vietnam-Watergate disillusionment. He was simply an all-American self-promoter'.[58] At the close of the film, George Hamilton delivers a voice-over monologue in the character of Knievel:

> Important people in this country, celebrities like myself – Elvis, Frank Sinatra, John Wayne – we have a responsibility. [...] I am the last gladiator in the new Rome. I go into the arena and I compete against destruction and I win. And next

week, I go out there and I do it again. And this time – civilization being what it is and all – we have very little choice about our life. The only thing really left to us is a choice about our death. And mine will be – glorious.

Knievel likens himself to white American celebrities – Elvis, Sinatra and John Wayne – as well as the 'last gladiator' who competes 'against destruction', thus envisaging himself as a death-defying superhero. However, Quade's stunt ride, an in-joke reference to Hollywood returning to its fairground origins, is an indicator of Hollywood's reductionism of blaxploitation. During the first practice run he falls off the 360-degree loop. Shaft cannot compete with Knievel's gladiatorial triumphs. Quade's talents shine though in the rescuing of Denise's son, thus echoing that of Woody Strode as the rescuing stoker. The implication is that the value of Black power lies in the servitude of white folk in times of distress.

Roundtree in playing a saviour figure for white folk follows a pattern of rendering the cultural image of Black masculinity as 'powerless':

> What happens to Roundtree in the seventies parallels what happens to the representations of black masculinity and militancy in U.S. popular culture: all are rendered powerless. [...] John Shaft, much like the Black Panthers and the Black Power movement, loses his cultural significance even as blaxploitation wanes and the Hollywood production companies return to business as usual. Roundtree epitomizes what Hollywood and mainstream television do to potentially dangerous and profitable properties, as well as cultural movements. Just as the state marginalized the ability of the Black Panthers and the Black Power movement to effect social change by the mid-seventies, Hollywood film and television successfully marginalized black masculinity, showing it as ineffectual.[59]

Roundtree reprises his role as rescuer, but in the guise of a mock superhero, and this racial re-identification is contrary to William Marshall seeing the African identity of Mamuwalde in *Blacula* (William Crain, 1972) as a means of conveying a measure of self-respect.[60]

The Day of the Locust (1975)

While *Earthquake* 'fattens on the spectacle of natural catastrophe' via a jokey form of destruction, John Schlesinger's 1975 screen adaptation of Nathanael West's novel, *The Day of the Locust* (1939), satirically exposes the poisonous effect of apocalypticism on the collective imagination.[61] In the film, Tod Hackett

(William Atherton) arrives in 1930s Hollywood to work as an artist for a major studio. He rents an apartment, with walls that exhibit minor earthquake cracks. Faye Greener (Karen Black) – an aspiring actress – later escapes injury during the studio shooting of a Waterloo battle scene in which the set (that Tod had illustrated) violently collapses. When *The Buccaneer* (Cecil B. DeMille, 1938) is premiered at the Grauman's Chinese Theatre, Homer Simpson (Donald Sutherland) violently kills a child, Adore Loomis (Jack Earl Haley) in a parking lot. Homer is subsequently pursued and attacked by a baying mob and a full-blown riot breaks out, while Tod witnesses Goyaesque apparitions that had figured in his paintings. In some respects, the narrative reflects West's own working experience with many studios – RKO, Universal and Columbia and starting with Republic Productions in 1936 as a screenwriter. West soon became disillusioned with Hollywood and was pessimistic about pitching good writing to a wider audience: 'mass man by his very nature preferred trash to art'.[62] And in a similar and timely spirit, the film trashes the trash by transforming the disaster genre into a 'grotesque farce'.[63]

Unfortunately, it is a film that has lived under the shadow of Robert Altman's *Nashville* (1975), which for James Hoberman deconstructs the 'multi-star, mounting-doom, intersecting-narrative format' of the disaster genre.[64] Country performers converge at a fundraising gala concert for a candidate's presidential election campaign and a loner (David Hayward) produces a gun from a violin case and shoots at the stage, seriously injuring Barbara Jean (Ronee Blakley) – the sweetheart of Nashville. But in a way that Hoberman sees *Nashville* as contrary to *Jaws*, *Locust* should be considered as a critical riposte to *Earthquake*'s 'Cecil B. DeMille approach to disaster'.[65] *Locust* has been compared to, though not always favourably, to *Nashville*. Edward T. Jones saw Altman's film as a 'more genuine tribute to Nathanael West' – the author of 1939 novel, *The Day of the Locust* – for unlike the Schlesinger film, *Nashville* eschews an indulgence in the apocalyptic of 'outsized films like *Earthquake*'.[66] That said, Robert Mazzocco compared *Nashville* unfavourably to the *Locust* novel, noting that while West contrasted his loser world against the 'dream dump', in *Nashville* the dream dump is all there is.[67] Though *Locust* is not explicitly anti-genre, its importance rests as a self-reflexive backlash to Hollywood's specularization of disaster in the earthquake zone of Los Angeles.

For Mark Shiel, the locale and its close association with Hollywood often means that the landscape of Los Angeles is, by extension, a part of the 'specularization' of Hollywood.[68] This is typified in *Singin' in the Rain*

(Stanley Donen, 1952), a backstage musical that deconstructs the genre by demythologizing the Hollywood story of stardom and glamour. Nonetheless, the allure of the musical spectacle remains intact. *Sunset Boulevard* (1950) is another prime example of the deconstructive film, and in fact Wilder's film is integral to the Hollywood web of self-referentiality in *Locust*. The crowds in the apocalyptic finale are attending the premiere of Cecil B. DeMille's *The Buccaneer* (1938), which is a nod towards DeMille playing himself in *Sunset* during a film-in-film studio production of *Samson and Delilah* (1949) – both Paramount productions. This is because DeMille (1881–1959), who converted 'an obscure Californian orange grove into an international movie centre', is synonymous with an Old Testament moralism and a primary target in Schlesinger's film.[69] As Vincent Canby perceptively observed, *Locust* is an attack on the film industry's apocalypticism that is found in 'gimcracky' biblical epics.[70] It is revealing that in West's novel there is no reference to DeMille's 1938 theatrical release premiering at 'Kahn's Persian Palace Theatre'.[71]

Locust is not a disaster movie, though it shares one conventional characteristic: a mounting-doom format. And the apocalyptic finale is a realization of the disaster imagination. Even though *Locust* does not deconstruct the disaster genre in the way *Nashville* does, it presents instead a psychological study of Hollywood's dalliance with catastrophes in what Claude Estee (Richard Dysart) calls, when discussing the Goyaesque production sketches of Tod Hackett (William Atherton) for a Waterloo film: 'a disaster area'. *Locust* is a critique of Hollywood's exploitation of apocalypticism (as symbolic) and indifference to disaster (as real), with 'the interplay between audience and entertainment-illusion' one dimension of the film's self-reflectiveness.[72] In this respect, the film is a throwback to *Singin'*, realized in the gala premiere scene, but one that aims ultimately to reveal the horror at the heart of the spectacle.

Tod's painting as a prefiguring of the film's apocalyptic ending, with his sketches merging into phantasmagoria, is tragic prolepsis – a staging of what's to come. When Tod is checking out a rental room, Tod notices a crack in the wall:

– It isn't as flashy as some of the places, but we pride ourselves on being a little classier.
Tod: the crack's real?
– Oh, yes. We call this our 'earthquake cottage'. Mrs. Porter had occupancy then. During the big one in '33? Property damage ran into the millions.
Tod: Would you fix it if I stayed for a while?
– Oh, no. No, this is our showplace.

Tod plants a red flower into the crack and pins his Goyaesque sketches onto the wall where once a sign read: 'Thank God for calamities now and then to remind us HE is greater than men.' For the landlady, natural disasters are an act of God, reminders of HIS omnipotent power. Tod, though, replaces the sign with images of earthly horror caused by human acts of barbarity. The suggestion is that the two realms mirror each other; to riff off John Lennon's song, 'God' (1970): 'God is a concept by which we measure our pain', but God is also an affirmation of the human propensity for violent retribution.[73] The scene is expressive of the pervasive imperviousness towards disaster that is linked to the politics of concealment and everyday indifference. For Davis, the 'social construction of "natural" disaster is largely hidden [in Los Angeles] from view by a way of thinking that simultaneously imposes false expectations on the environment and then explains the inevitable disappointments as proof of a malign and hostile nature'.[74] The 'earthquake cottage' is a metonym of this perspective, but it is also Hollywood in miniature: a 'showplace' for translating natural disasters into artistic renderings of apocalypticism. The concealment of the earthquake damage, either via religious cant or tragic art, amounts to the same psychological need to mask a painful truth. Hollywood's complicity in a culture of denial in an earthquake zone it cohabits is voiced by Claude when he questions whether posted warning signs would have 'made any difference' regarding the construction of a Waterloo film studio-set. The danger signs are best forgotten or concealed, for Hollywood would prefer to be party to grand illusions of destruction.

Tod's painting, that 'contains elements of his paranoid drawings', prefigures the apocalyptic conclusion because it is 'Tod's subjective elaboration of the riot'.[75] As critics have already pointed out, *Locust* is a postmodern film, and, with echoes of *Westworld* (Michael Crichton, 1973), the Los Angeles dreamland is like a Disneyland that translates the American history of trauma into a theme park. In effect, the apocalyptic riot is the result of Tod's poisoned imagination. Following the studio-set collapse, he says to Faye Greener (Karen Black): 'I had visions of you mangled, and just when I've found you again.' Faye is a pursued object of desire and a projection of Tod's apocalyptic mind. Visions of violence are inseparable from the ideal. And so, what he imagines returns as a grotesque haunting. Tod theatrically mouths the inexpressible horror of the Waterloo soldiers in his sketches, which turns into an expressionistic scream, echoing the ghostly figure in Edvard Munch's *The Scream* (1893), and a visual grotesquery of the riotous violence. Discussing his sketches with Claude, Tod says: 'I concentrated on faces.' The sketches are Dantean perversions of the classical Hollywood close-up.

Tod's horror scream also mimics the hellmouth (the jaws of hell), the entrance to hell that is often envisaged as the gaping mouth of a monster. In Albrecht Durer's woodcut, *Four Horsemen of the Apocalypse* (1498), the grisly figure of Death wields a pitchfork, sits on an emaciated horse, adjacent to a hellmouth that devours the damned.[76] The earthquake, too, is associated with Revelation (16:18): 'No earthquake like it has ever occurred since mankind has been on earth, so tremendous was the quake.' Meanwhile, as though a mute Greek chorus, the faceless Goyaesque figures appear as observant apparitions. It is a scene of uncanny horror that supports W. H. Auden's view that *Locust* is a cautionary parable about 'a Kingdom of Hell whose ruler is not so much the Father of Lies as the Father of Wishes'.[77] Unfulfilled fantasies turn into hellish nightmares. For when the real object of fascination is reached, rather than expressing awe at the grandeur of the Hollywood dream, what is experienced, in Lacanian terms, is the emptiness at the heart of the real. This is conveyed in West's novel as boredom and betrayal:

> Their boredom becomes more and more terrible. They realize that they've been tricked and burn with resentment. Every day of their lives they read the newspapers and went to the movies. Both fed them on lynchings, murder, sex crimes, explosions, wrecks, love nests, fires, miracles, revolutions, war. This daily diet made sophisticates of them. The sun is a joke. Oranges can't titillate their jaded palates. Nothing can ever be violent enough to make taut their slack minds and bodies. They have been cheated and betrayed. They have slaved and slaved for nothing.[78]

The cinema of attractions creates false beliefs, ideals and promises. The Hollywood star-gazing crowd turn into vicious, vengeful, rioters. For James F. Light, the characters in West's novel are 'grotesques'.[79] In the film, Tod is a grotesque who mouths the ineffable terror at the heart of the spectacle.

But the more sinister suggestion is that Hollywood poisons the collective imagination via industrially churned out apocalypticism. The riot that takes place in front of the gala opening of DeMille's film is an apt testament to the gargoyle of holy terror. The imbrication of biblical epics and religious showmanship is conveyed in a holy roller church gathering led by the preacher, Big Sister (Geraldine Page), who performs public healings through the influence of the Holy Spirit. The backing choir sing, 'There is power in the blood', and she boisterously proclaims: 'Jesus owns the oil wells, and the gasoline is prayer.' The scene is a realization of what James F. Light sees as the production of grotesque 'farce' portrayed in West's novel.[80] It is the kind of protestant evangelism that Flannery O'Connor satirizes in *Wise Blood* (1952) and that Marjoe Gortner exposed in *Marjoe* (1972) as a fraudulent and lucrative form of Pentecostal preaching that modelled itself on rock stars, such as Mick Jagger.

Yet, according to Jay Cocks: 'This is a movie turned out by the sort of mentality that West was mocking.'[81] It is a criticism voiced too by Roger Ebert: 'And yet there's something fundamentally wrong with "The Day of the Locust," and that's made most clear in the violent, spectacular riot near the film's end. A world premiere at Grauman's Chinese Theater has drawn all of the locusts, who strain against the police lines, hungry for sustenance from the stars hurrying inside.'[82] The star-gawping crowds are a stand-in for the plague of locusts, who hunger for devastation, and yet Schlesinger feeds his audience with the sustenance that the film mocks. But, in the spirit of New Hollywood, the director invites critical distance, meaning the spectacle of violence is distinct from the thrill ride of *Earthquake*. According to Hoberman: 'Two kinds of filmmaking passed each other in June 1975. *Nashville* was intellectual, *Jaws* visceral; *Nashville* looked back to the 1960s, *Jaws* ahead to the 1980s.'[83]

The same can be said of *Locust* and *Earthquake*. Yet, whereas *Nashville*, according to Hoberman, had predicted 'the rise of a politics as meretricious and authoritarian as the mass culture industry', *Locust* predicts the irresistible rise of apocalyptic fantasies that hollow out the horror in a bigger, showy, thrill ride.[84]

Smash-Up on Interstate 5 (1976)

The car is synonymous with the 'Dream State' of California, and, as R. C. Lutz argues, while films revel in the glamour of the car, dystopian assaults on Californian car culture also exist (though less frequently). *The Graduate* (Mike Nichols, 1967) 'hauntingly foreshadows the "running out of gas" of car culture' that happened in the first oil crisis of 1973, and this presaged Cynthia Kadohata's novel, *In the Heart of the Valley of Love* (1992), in which an apocalyptic future of collapsed freeways departs from the 'Golden Era' of California freeways as seen at the end of *How the West was Won*.[85] J. G. Ballard's *Crash* (1973), a pornographic novel about car technology and carnage, is linked to the eroticization and adulation of cars in California: Dr Robert Vaughan recreates the car crash that killed James Dean, who starred in *Rebel Without a Cause* (Nicholas Ray, 1955), a film set in Los Angeles and notable for the 'Chicken Run' car crash. James Dean's car crash death at the age of twenty-four, near Cholame, California, in 1955, immortalized a cultural image of eternal youth and fast and dangerous driving. West also died in a car crash at an intersection near El Centro, California, with his wife, Eileen, in 1940, when returning to Hollywood.[86] His death can be added to a long list of Hollywood car crash fatalities, such as Jayne Mansfield in 1967. Despite the death toll, the car remains the 'golden calf' of California, and such idolatry was satirized in West's *Locust*:

> [...] in its most exuberant incarnation, the luxury car, is wheeled before the faithful on Oscar night. Crowds gape, in person and later, before television screens, when the celebrated High Priests of popular culture, the movie stars, starlets, and moguls, wheel out their most expensive vehicles to minister to the age-old mass craving for glamor and spectacle.[87]

The imbrication of luxury cars and Hollywood in a novel that critiques the film industry's specularization of disaster is telling.

But perhaps the most telling artistic statement on car-death culture is Andy Warhol's *Green Car Crash* (1963), inspired by a magazine photo of a crash, the outcome of a police pursuit in Seattle:

> Warhol's repetitions of car crashes, suicides and electric chairs are not like the repetition of similar and yet different terrible scenes day in and day out in the tabloids. These paintings mute what is present in the single front page each day, and emphasize what is present persistently day after day in slightly different variations. Looking at the papers, we do not consciously make the connection between today's, yesterday's, and tomorrow's "repetitions" which are not repetitions.[88]

Warhol freeze-frames the scene of death, and with garish colours and repeated images anticipates the experimentations of New Hollywood vis-à-vis spectacles of violence. He also paves the way for Ballard's exploration of car crash fetishism. It is a reminder too that while the car occupies centre space in the American dream, it is also integral to an endemic, yet unspoken, disaster phenomenon. In the United States, deaths by motor vehicle-related injuries were at their highest in the 1970s, with road fatalities in California peaking at the end of the decade.

According to the 'National Highway Traffic Safety Administration', injury caused by road traffic crashes is the largest public health problem in the United States: 'Annually, more than 30,000 Americans are killed on our roads.'[89] Warhol's freeze-framing of a car crash death is not too dissimilar to Tod's hellmouth – a theatrical gesture of modern tragedy that exposes the horror at the heart of the dream.

The romance of the liberated automobile on the open road is also contrary to the everyday reality of traffic congestion in ever-expanding suburbs, and, in this respect, *Smash-Up on Interstate 5* was a standout made-for-TV movie in the 1970s. *Smash-Up* was aired 12 March 1976 on ABC, and was loosely based on *Expressway*, a 1973 novel by Trevor Dudley-Smith. It is set on Interstate 5 in California, a major highway that links the major cities of San Diego, Santa Ana, Los Angeles, Stockton, Sacramento and Redding. The date is 4 July, 24 hours before the summer vacation officially starts. During the opening credits, aerial shots show 4 and 5 lane congested freeways and a maze of criss-crossing junctions. On the ground, close-ups show streams of traffic, stationary or grinding to a stop. Panning shots show highway patrol police cautioning drivers. This is California car reality. The film cuts to a close-up of patrol sergeant Sam Marcum (Robert Conrad), and a voice-over the car radio is heard: all units are pursuing a possible suspect vehicle involved in homicide, reported going north bound. The 'pursuit' genre, a cycle identified by Tico Romoa as starting from 1968, in which a lengthy car chase(s) feature, is seemingly signalled through a shot of a pursuing line of patrol vehicles merging onto the freeway and then the sight of an overhead helicopter.[90] Sergeant Marcum's patrol vehicle races ahead, weaving through the traffic.

But generic expectations are soon undercut, when the sergeant announces in a voice-over that a 39-vehicle crash is about to take place. The film intercuts to a series of close-ups of people involved in the story:

> Sunday, July 4th, 11:05 am. In a few moments some of these people will become holiday weekend safety statistics, participants in a major smash up on California's Interstate 5. 39 vehicles will be involved. 62 people will be injured. 14 will die. Officially, it will be listed as 1179 accident, caused by mechanical failure. Nothing in the record will appear about: fear, anger, love, frustration, about the human factor. This story is about that human factor. About some of those holiday statistics: who they were, what they did in the 48 odd hours that brought them all, complete strangers, together to face their destiny on Interstate 5. I'm Sam Marcum, Sergeant of California Highway Patrol. I'm one of those statistics.

When the smash-up occurs, there are multiple close-ups of terrified faces, slow-motion action shots and freeze-frames of cars colliding, spinning, skidding, swerving, spinning over, vehicle explosions, a motorcyclist passenger flung onto the highway, a rider flung over a car roof, a van careening onto its side, a truck smashing into stationary vehicles. It is a sequence equal to Sam Peckinpah's climatic gun battle in *The Wild Bunch* (1969). The effect also resembles Warhol's *Green Car Crash* with the sequence capturing the totality of destruction as simultaneously muted and emphasized. And by inverting the mounting-doom format, the film takes its anti-genre cue from *Nashville*. Altman de-sensationalizes a vehicle pile-up to dramatize the emergence of an organic community out of the commotion. In a similar vein, *Smash-Up* focuses on the relationships that form by chance in a reconstruction narrative. The rest of the film is dedicated to the multi-protagonist backstories that lead up to the 39-vehicle smash-up. An intertitle states: 'Friday Afternoon. 48 Hours Before Smash-Up.'

In portraying the 'human factor' behind the dehumanizing statistics, the film imitates the multi-protagonist storytelling of the disaster genre. But the aim is to re-humanize rather than to sensationalize – to put a human face on what would otherwise be a muted fact. By exploiting avant-garde aesthetics of violence, it counters the affectless effects of news reportage, thus exposing the everyday crash trauma that is part and parcel of living in high modernity. But perhaps more significantly the film counterpoints the spectacle of vehicular mayhem in the pursuit film that dominated the first half of the decade, and in turn deromanticizes a car culture enshrined in American modernity. The pursuit film was a low-budget equivalent to the blockbuster in terms of muscular action, with men showcasing their driving skills. Even though *Bullitt* (Peter Yates, 1968) initiated the pursuit trend, *Grand Prix* (John Frankenheimer, 1966), which uses montage sequences by Saul Bass to capture the high-octane glamour of high-speed racing was instrumental in a muscle-car aesthetic. *Bullitt* demonstrated 'the impact a great chase scene can have on the overall success of a film'.[91] To invoke a male-centred exaltation in machine eroticism, Steve McQueen's high-performance duel is augmented by the hard diegetic sounds of the revving engine and the shifting gears of a Mustang GT, and is cued by Lalo Schifrin's rumbling, modal score. Steve McQueen went on to make *Le Mans* in 1971, and in the same year *The French Connection* (William Friedkin) was released and in the style of a gritty urban realism that is evident in *The Seven-Ups* (1973), directed by Philip D'Antoni (the producer of *Bullitt* and *The French Connection*). Both give glimpses of urban wastelands, including automobile graveyards – smashed-up car scrapyards that are reflective of America's vehicle industry recession as well as metaphoric of post-industrial gloom. Whilst honouring what Jesse Crosse sees as 'the primitive' thrill 'of the hunter closing in on its quarry', they also deglamourize American modernity.[92]

Smash-Up shadows a fad for automobile demolition via a multi-vehicle pile-up, but its stark television realism, while a far cry from the countercultural nihilism of *Vanishing Point* (Richard C. Sarafian, 1971), captures the congested 'terminus of the American Dreamscape'. With a focus on multiple-death tragedies, the film does not displace the cause onto a secondary, fantasy level or a bad capitalist. Instead, the disaster focus is on a superstructural site, and the cause is identified as 'mechanical failure'. Unlike Irwin Allen's television disaster movies, the setting is not a confined space (the ideal dramatic TV format) that constricts perspective, nor, as in group jeopardy films, is the focus on a microcosmic group of survivors. Disaster does not bring people together. And it is not a scenario to survive. The lack of mounting-doom drama in the opening sequence means the car carnage is instantaneous and is thus more horrific. There is no sense of fantasy escapism. It is an everyday occurrence that is inherently part of high modernity. The bigger the superstructure (e.g., the skyscraper and the multiple-laned freeway), the more likely the diminishing of human agency.

At the end of the film, *Smash-Up* retells the opening car carnage in real time and with a focus on the bloody aftermath, including burning automobiles, public grieving and corpses. Sergeant Marcum, with a cut above the left eye is treated by a nurse, Laureen (Donna Mills), who has feelings for him, and shaking his head in dismay utters the question: 'How did it all happen?' With lovers reconciled, the closure gestures towards a conventional disaster denouement. But death comes indiscriminately, and Sam's question of causality sticks. Sam tells Laureen to go back to work, implying that attending car crash casualties is routine and inevitable (like a tragic cycle). This is not *Earthquake*. Human sin does not precipitate disaster. The cause is modernity, which is not without sin.

Conclusion

Smash Up on Interstate 5 tests what passes as worthy material for the disaster movie. By definition, a disaster is a singular and calamitous event that causes great damage or loss of life. Even though car crash fatalities are an endemic part of modern living, a car crash is only disastrous when a deadly pile up. Currently, more than 46,000 people die in crashes on US roadways every year. This is in stark contrast to the number of civil aviation deaths: approximately 350. The spectacle of aviation disaster lends itself better to the melodrama of the disaster genre: an eclectic bunch of strangers, confined in a small space, have sufficient time to reflect on past glories and miseries before meeting their deaths. A car crash death is relatively instantaneous. *Smash Up* also arrests the acceptance of car crash films, such as *Gone in 60 Seconds* (H. B. Halicki, 1974) that was shot in Los Angeles, which normalize violence in daily modern life. Ordinary carnage is the flipside of 'carchitecture' (an urban landscape that is built for automobile travel). The low-key realism of *Smash-Up* is also distinctive from menacing automobile shockers or petrol-hedonistic, horror films, such as *The Cars That Ate Paris* (Paul Weir, 1974) and *Death Race 2000* (Paul Bartel, 1975). In *Death Race 2000*, Frankenstein (David Carradine) kills with his winning car Mr. President (Sandy McCallum), the dictator who believed that the Transcontinental Road Race satisfied the public's need for performances of violence. Yet, the revolutionary weapon derives from a modern arena of pleasure and violence. So, challenging the cinematic gaze of horror in the disaster spectacle is the key to altering a naturalized perception of modernity vis-à-vis disaster.

6

Modern arenas of pleasure and violence: *Rollercoaster* (1977), *Two-Minute Warning* (1976), *Black Sunday* (1977)

By 1976, the cycle was increasingly moving towards a spectacle of event terrorism that implicated the viewing subject into the violence of American society.[1] This was in marked contrast to the Manichean drama of *Star Wars* (George Lucas, 1977) that, like the hyperreality of Disneyland, shielded the spectator from the horrors of history. Pauline Kael had likened the destruction orgies to a 'Roman-circus mentality', a throwback to the colosseum spectacles of biblical epics, implying that the cinematic ritual of bloodletting was a depraved form of amusement.[2] For instance, Cecil Be DeMille's *The Sign of the Cross* (1932) is notable for turning the Roman amphitheatre into a Coney Island freak show of impaled pygmies, killer animals and naked Christians. However, the grotesque spectacle is framed by shots of a diegetic audience exhibiting contrary emotive and moral responses, thus suggesting a critical view of the blood-lusting revelry and its mass appeal. And rather than interpellating the verisimilitude of destruction, as in *The Day After Tomorrow* (Roland Emmerich, 2004), *War of the Worlds* (Steven Spielberg, 2005) and *Greenland* (Ric Roman Waugh, 2020), the presence of the diegetic spectator sometimes offers a counter perspective, as exemplified in John Guillermin's ecohorror version of *King Kong* (1976) when Jessica Lange's emphatic facial expressions are a moral rebuke to the vulture press's objectification of the fallen, magnificent creature. In fact, the critique of the Roman-circus mentality existed in a series of seventies films in which spectators in modern arenas become the targets of terrorism. They capitalized on the thrill ride and uncanny horror to equate immersive spectacles of pleasure and violence with public atrocities, such as the Munich massacre of 1972, that exploited the big spectacle. *Rollercoaster* (James Goldstone, 1977), as a Universal Pictures follow-on to *Earthquake* (Mark Robson, 1974), affirms the cycle's return to the fairground origins of Hollywood's spectacular cataclysms. *Two-Minute Warning* (Larry Peerce, 1976) and *Black Sunday* (John Frankenheimer, 1977), both set in sporting stadia (Los Angeles Memorial Colosseum and Miami Orange Bowl), return the cinematic gaze of horror.

Post-Code violence and blockbuster fantasies

In its commercial peak year, 1974, the cycle had dramatically shifted from the high modernity melodrama of *Airport* (George Seaton, 1970) to visions of 'massive doom' that characterized the large-scale, and spectacular, 'event' movies.[3] Kael viewed the destruction orgies as a sign of money-making desperation for a ruined Hollywood industry, and as a means of satisfying reactionary voyeurism, singling out *Earthquake*, set in the city of Los Angeles, for its 'marathon of destruction effects'.[4] And Kael also likens the producer, Jennings Lang, to an infamous depraved voyeur: 'Nero was considered crazy, but if he'd sold tickets and made money out of his pyromaniac spectacle, would he be considered smart, like Jennings Lang and the other executives who make profits out of financing bowdlerizations of old movies while refusing to finance new ideas?'[5] Lang had produced numerous disaster movies: *Earthquake* (1974), *Airport '75* (1974), *Airport '77* (1977), *Rollercoaster* (1977), *The Concorde ... Airport '79* (1979), and was primarily responsible for turning Universal productions into 'event' movies. Kael was disparaging too of *Inferno*: 'this thing is like some junky fairground show – a chamber of horrors with skeletons that jump up'.[6] In other words, the disaster cycle solicited uncomplicated primal pleasures, and a low state of tragic purgation comparable to the cheap thrills of non-cinematic spectacles.

But the cycle was also increasingly imitating trends in screened violence, following the final dissolution of the Production Code and its replacement with the ratings system in 1968 that had allowed for a new freedom. As Jim Kendrick notes, 'entire genres and subgenres built around violence', during the 1970s, included the most popular, such as disaster movies.[7] For Amy Rust, the rise of graphic violence via avant-garde technologies – multiple-camera montage, squibs and artificial blood, freeze-frames, and zooms – was reflective of a changing violent climate in America. Assassinations, gun homicides, the Vietnam War and increasing public violence were mediated through television news, in response to an increasing demand across the political spectrum for 'authentic' realities.[8] *Earthquake* mimics the horror spectacle using artificial blood in the falling elevator scene to create a splat effect on the camera. *Inferno* echoes the balletic style of Sam Peckinpah, via the use of slow motion to create an eerie or lyrical effect, when Dan Bigelow (Richard Wagner) and his mistress, Lorrie (Susan Flannery), are consumed by a raging fire.

By 1976–7, though, the cycle's popularity was waning and three films, in particular *Two-Minute Warning*, *Rollercoaster* and *Black Sunday*, were a major disappointment for the studios who had expected bigger box office returns. They were eclipsed by the sporting drama, *Rocky* (John G. Avidsen, 1976), and the space opera, *Star Wars*. While the darker visions of the disaster genre had chimed with a jaded Nixon generation, the fantasy filter had also allowed for a comfortable experience. *The Hindenburg* (Robert Wise, 1975) had shown that revisiting a historical event, the 1937 German Zeppelin disaster, and the sights and sounds of tragic suffering by using actual newsreel footage and the radio coverage by Herbert Morrison, was uncomfortable viewing. As Cook points out, it was the first major disaster film 'based on a real event' and the 'first to lose a significant amount of money, indicating the cycle had run its course'.[9] For Roger Ebert, watching people race about in flames and fall to their death 'isn't fun. We go to disaster movies for fun'.[10] Here the diegetic spectator is the *in-media res* news reporter, who is so horrified by what is being witnessed that he stops watching: 'I … I'm going to step inside, where I cannot see it. Charlie, that's terrible. Ah, ah … I can't, I … Listen, folks; I … I'm gonna have to stop for a minute because I've lost my voice. This is the worst thing I've ever witnessed.'[11] And yet, the cinematic audience is meant to watch and listen as 'authentic' reality breaks through the spectacle.

Black Sunday, a terrorist film that dealt with unpalatable truths, also upsets the delicate balance between realism and spectacle. Paramount thought it would be a successor to *Jaws*, and for Robert Evans (the producer) the post-Vietnam theme was a 'turnoff':

> […] I must say that *Black Sunday* was a real downer for me; it was a minor success but a major disappointment. Paramount thought that it was going to be their "*Jaws*" and so did I. I guess the subject of terrorism was a turnoff: it was too close to home. People are not interested in going to the movies to see what's happening in headlines and my personal feeling is that the movies dealing with Vietnam will not do very well either. Vietnam is like cancer – people don't want to be reminded of it. They want catharsis, escape.[12]

In fact, *The Deer Hunter* (Michael Cimino) and *Coming Home* (Hal Ashby), two films that deal with the trauma of the Vietnam War, were successes the following year in 1978. Nevertheless, in 1977, escapism came in the form of *Star Wars* that, as Roy Scranton sees it, two years after the fall of Saigon (30 April 1975) had 'managed a remarkable trick'.¹³ It recast violence into a fantasy that united the nation: 'It's a story about how violence makes us American. It's a story about how violence makes us good.'¹⁴ The 'trick' is for an audience to lose one's sense of reality in another reality, as Murray Pomerance recounts:

> When things look real at the movies, one can be so enthralled as to lose a sense of reality in the 'reality' of the experience. I sat in an audience far below Times Square to watch *Star Wars* in the summer of 1977, and at the moment – that glorious and epoch-marking moment – when Han Solo and Chewbacca threw the *Millennium Falcon* into hyperdrive, the twelve hundred or so captivated souls all leaned back and shouted 'Wohhhh!!!' in one single, gargantuan breath. It was an embodied experience of 'reality', not reality, we were having together down in that darkness, as no such acceleration existed in the real world any of us knew or had imagined looking like this. Surely at the same moment that we fell for it, we were aware that this was a trick. But the 'truc', or 'trick', was an agency of the marvelous, a harbinger of delight and wonder, not a mechanism for manipulative and immoral deception. To be deceived here was to see the light.¹⁵

Star Wars was part of, as Paula J. Massood argues, Hollywood's return to familiar genres (science fiction, the musical and the melodrama) and nostalgic and uplifting film narratives as a counterblast to the years of crisis. 1977 saw the inauguration of a new president and: 'Jimmy Carter struck a chord with a nation still reeling from the horrors of Vietnam, the lies and deceptions of Watergate, the cutbacks and shortages of the oil-induced recession of 1974–75, and a rising inflation rate.'¹⁶

Star Wars fitted the bill that marked a key shift from a 70s' cinematic trend characterized in Peckinpah's *The Wild Bunch* (1969) and *Straw Dogs* (1972) that had both attempted to undermine the viewer's conventional vantage point when watching movie violence. The violence in *Star Wars*, on the other hand, bolstered by special effects technology, is innocuous and 'emptied of [...] anti-establishment tenor'.¹⁷ Unlike the *Black Sunday*, it is devoid of contemporary realism in terms of direct references to Vietnam, domestic or transnational terrorism. When Luke Skywalker obliterates the Death Star, the ensuing explosive flash resembles the pyrotechnics of a firework display and is met with John Williams's triumphant score, Han Solo's line 'Great shot kid – that was one-in-a-million!', and the supernatural voice of a Jedi mentor: 'Remember, the force will be with you ... always.' There are no graphic images, screams of terror nor shots of panic-stricken faces. As soon as 'the force' guides the proton torpedoes into the exhaust port, mass destruction is reaped, yet the horror of death is hollowed out in the void of space.

The cataclysmic closure of *Star Wars* parallels the killing of a shark 'elevated to the stuff of myth' by Brody in *Jaws*.[18] As Ethan Alter explains, the author of the novel, Peter Benchley, had penned a different ending and had complained to Spielberg. But Benchley

> changed his tune when he saw how audiences leapt to their feet after the shark was blown to smithereens. (The creature's fate, by the way, is more than a little reminiscent of the Death Star explosion that closes out the original Star Wars – which arrived in theaters two summers later – right down to Brody having to score a direct hit at the exact right angle in order to blow his target up. Perhaps Spielberg's buddy George Lucas made a mental note of how that finale wowed the crowd.)[19]

Jaws and *Star Wars* share similar 'Wohhhh!!!' moments, with one former affirming eco-sadism, which, as Andrew Britton points out, also involves the restoration of ideological confidence:

> The film is inconceivable without an enormous audience, without that exhilarating, jubilant explosion of cheers and hosannas which greet the annihilation of the shark and which transform the cinema, momentarily, into a temple. Annihilation is the operative word. It is not enough for the shark to be killed, as it is in the book, only two feet from a helpless, hopeless hero whose two companions have already been devoured, and who has, himself, been implicated too disturbingly in the tensions which the shark has released. The film monster has to be, literally, obliterated. Evil must vanish from the face of the earth.[20]

The official trailer confirms that the shark is framed by a demonizing, horror spectacle, reminiscent of *The Exorcist* (1973), and the creature features of the 1950s that are 'obliterated': 'There is a creature alive today who has survived millions of years of evolution without change without passion and without logic. It lives to kill. A mindless, eating machine. It will attack and devour, anything. It is as if God created the devil and gave him jaws.'[21] *Jaws* positions the viewer as 'potential victims' as well as 'helpless observers' via numerous water-level shots.[22] Nonetheless, the shark, in a way that is typical of 'revenge of nature' films, is framed as the terrorizing 'It'.

Star Wars, as well as *Close Encounters of the Third Kind* (Steven Spielberg, 1977), 'represented a turning point in American cinema, simultaneously confirming the potential profitability of a new style of effects-driven, crossmarketed, heavily merchandized, saturation-booked blockbuster [...] and the ability of such fundamentally juvenile narratives to appeal to a global audience'.[23] They take on a level of fantasy that departs from the cycle's fantasy filter and 'ostensible realism'.[24] However, by lifting the 'protective shield', the cycle was confronting an unpalatable home truth: 'We are a violent society in a violent world!'[25]

Dirty Harry

Violence assumes a myriad of cinematic forms and is also represented via different perceived threats as a means of displacing social and ideological anxieties. The monstrous shark, an invisible threat to the micro-capitalist order of a beach town, metaphorizes anxieties in relation to the Vietnam War and Hollywood's financial situation. In vigilante films, in particular the *Dirty Harry* film series – *Dirty Harry* (Don Siegel, 1971), *Magnum Force* (Ted Post, 1973) and *The Enforcer* (James Fargo, 1976) – starring Clint Eastwood as Inspector 'Dirty' Harry Callahan of the San Francisco Police Department, the monstrous takes on a human form. Kael was highly critical of the 'unreal' killing that was 'dissociated from pain'.[26] The scenes of carnage that the audience are meant to 'gasp at in surprise and pleasure' appear comparable to the 'big blowouts' in the disaster movie. But as Kael rightly points out, Clint Eastwood makes action melodrama 'an almost abstract exercise in brutalisation'.[27] He is a stalwart hero of a conservative fantasy of retributive justice, overcoming any potential disaster in the form of domestic terrorism and hijackings. In *Dirty Harry*, Scorpio (Andy Robinson) is a proto-terrorist and serial killer, holding the city of San Francisco to ransom and who also hijacks a school bus. In *Magnum Force*, Callahan violently tackles two hijackers on a commercial plane in an airport. And in *The Enforcer*, Callahan, again via an excessive use of unregulated force, deals with a criminal gang posing as a terrorist group called the 'People's Revolutionary Strike Force'. These libertarian fantasies of law enforcement are reflective of an increase in political violence:

> During the 1970s, a time of particularly extensive political violence, 60 to 70 terrorist events took place in the United States every year – 15–20 times greater than the decade after 9/11. Moreover, terrorism was considerably more lethal

during the 1970s, when 72 people died during terrorist incidents – roughly five times the number who were killed on U.S. soil in the post-9/11 period.²⁸

The Weather Underground Organisation and the Symbionese Liberation Army represented two well-known violent domestic groups of the radical left, but, as L. Stampnitzky points out, terrorism took on a 'transnational' character, following the Munich Massacre in 1972:

> Although there had been a number of hijackings and other serious incidents of political violence from 1968 to 1972, it was the massacre at the 1972 Munich Olympics that took on central symbolic significance in the history of terrorism. The events at Munich have been inscribed in popular and expert histories of the problem alike as the spectacular event that inaugurated the era of modern terrorism. […] Not long after the events at Munich, President Nixon established the first official US government body charged with focusing on the terrorism problem, the Cabinet Committee to Combat Terrorism.²⁹

In ruthlessly containing the terrorist problem, Callahan also becomes the cheerfully 'sadistic', 'double' of the nihilist killer:

> He [Scorpio] is presented as pure evil with no redeeming features, a pure outsider, with no backstory, outside of society and its rules, present only as threat to the social order. To the extent that Harry is like Scorpio, he too is to be repudiated, as sharing in the latter's villainy. This is not to say, however, that Harry is simply Scorpio's double or alter ego. Harry may have Scorpio-like aspects but he is not presented as a pure outsider.³⁰

As Christopher Falzon also points out, the sadism of Scorpio is established in the opening scene through a 'threatening gaze':

> It consists of a longish meditation, through Scorpio's gun sight, on the young woman swimming in a rooftop pool, as he delays the moment before finally shooting her. The delay turns Scorpio's predatory targeting of his victim into an episode of sexual voyeurism, and thus, from the start, sexual voyeurism is linked with criminality and violence. That police are also potential objects for Scorpio's gaze, and so vulnerable to violence, is indicated because the film actually begins with a list of names, the 'Tribute to the police officers of San Francisco who gave their lives in the line of duty', which then dissolves to the muzzle of Scorpio's gun.³¹

With the camera framing Scorpio's eyesight, this depiction of psychopathic violence does not directly challenge the audience's complicity in the sadistic gaze of voyeurism. This is because, even though the 'dirty' methods of Callahan mirrored the increased violence of America as depicted in a Post-Code era, the lack of avant-garde experimentation results in a conservative co-opting:

> It is not as formally significant as *Bonnie and Clyde* (Penn, 1967); it does not challenge the genre of the cop thriller as stylishly as *Point Blank* (Boorman, 1967); it is not as experimental as *M*A*S*H* (Altman, 1970); nor is it as challenging in its social criticism as *Midnight Cowboy* (Schlesinger, 1969) or *Medium Cool* (Wexler, 1969). Its plot and structure are decidedly traditional, conservative even.[32]

New Hollywood

The flipside of the movie's 'moral position', which Roger Ebert referred to as 'fascist', is New Hollywood's more artful and liberal perspective.[33] The disaster cycle, too, was 'not as experimental', although it did absorb countercultural violent aesthetics which had become a norm in mainstream cinema – albeit 'in a somewhat diluted form'.[34] *The Andromeda Strain* (Robert Wise, 1971), with its use of freeze frame, close-ups, rapid editing and multiple split-screen takes its cue from Peckinpah's multiple-camera montage and slow motion in *The Wild Bunch* (1969), that stylishly breaks with classical Hollywood's bloodless realism: 'We watch our wars and see men die, really die, every day on television, but it doesn't seem real. We don't believe those real people are dying on that screen. We've been anesthetized by the media.'[35] Peckinpah's stylish mode of conveying the horrors of violence was to challenge what he saw as the previous screen traditions that treated violence 'like fun and games'.[36] And to a large extent, the destruction orgies of the cycle also represented the horror of violence 'like fun and games'.

Irwin Allen's call to magnify the vicarious thrill of disaster is far removed from the defamiliarizing methods of New Hollywood: 'People thrive on tragedy. It's unfortunate, but in my case, it's fortunate. The bigger the tragedy, the bigger the audience.'[37] Allen's idea of recycling onto the big screen the daily consumption of tragedy is in stark contrast to Andy Warhol's view that the repetitive mediation of disaster becomes affectless. In 1963, Warhol gave an interview to Gene Swenson, speaking of the *Death and Disaster* series of screen-printed canvases that had been prompted by a 'big plane crash picture, the front page of a newspaper: 129 DIE'.[38] Warhol's *Green Car Crash* (1963) imitates media repetitions but also freeze-frames human tragedies that are ordinarily muted banalities. In 1964, Warhol also created the *Electric Chair*, but notably in contrast to 'the images that depicted the tragedies of its human subjects, [it] is devoid of all human presence'.[39]

In many respects, Pop art is a counterpoint to the cinema of attractions whose origins lie in a violent spectacle that involved more of a disinterested subject. As Bennett Capers argues: 'By depicting an empty execution chamber, Warhol [...] subtly [...] shifts the focus from the painting as object to the viewer as subject. He thus foregrounds the space the viewer occupies as a spectator and a witness.'[40] Warhol's anti-spectacle recalls the electrocution on an elephant at Coney Island, which affirms Tom Gunning's concept of the cinema of attractions and its relation to the shock of the modern. In 1903, Thomas Edison released a seventy-four-second actuality film, *Electrocuting an Elephant*, in which 'an elephant is led through a crowd by its handler, shackled with electrodes attached to its feet, and then electrocuted. Smoke rises from its feet, and its body goes stiff and then falls over, lifeless, to the ground.'[41] This grotesque public spectacle foreshadows the 'Roman-circus mentality' exhibited in *The Sign of the Cross*, but there was more of an immediate historical link between the moving image and torture and execution: 'Edison was instrumental in the development of the electric chair's use of AC current as a means of state execution [...] Thus, there was a strange parallel between the invention of motion pictures and the invention of the electric chair [...].'[42] From its 'first flickerings of moving images', cinema was 'fascinated by images of brutality', including electrocutions and natural disasters.[43]

Even though the disaster cycle shared, broadly speaking, the period when New Hollywood also commercially thrived, from *Bonnie and Clyde* (Arthur Penn, 1967) and *The Graduate* (Mike Nichols, 1967) to *One Flew Over the Cuckoo's Nest* (Miloš Forman, 1975), *Dog Day Afternoon* (Sidney Lumet, 1975) and *Shampoo* (Hal Ashby, 1975), and shared too similarities in conveying darker visions of American society, the primary focus on mass destruction was to create a thrilling form of entertainment. New Hollywood was more interested in directly addressing the immediate crisis, such as the Watergate scandal, for instance: *All the President's Men* (1976), whilst other films were reflective of: *The Conversation* (1974), *Shampoo* (1975), *Three Days of the Condor* (1975), *Chinatown* (1974), *Nashville* (1975) and *Taxi Driver* (1976). Disaster movies, on the other hand, displaced anti-establishment sentiments via threatening physical objects, such as a man-eating shark or other destructive forces of nature.

The cycle belongs also to the schema that Elsaesser has dubbed 'the affirmative-consequential model of narrative', which was inverted by New Hollywood, according to the dramaturgy of suspense, spectacle and violence.[44] Rather than heroes with a clear goal who resolve the spectacular crisis, the anti-heroes in New Hollywood films are caught up in a modernist tragedy of 'indeterminacy', as in *The Last Picture Show* or *Easy Rider*: 'The tragedy of the protagonists of the post-traumatic cycle is [...] that they fail to see this state of affairs that everyone else seems to ignore or already take for granted'.[45] However, as we shall see, the affirmative model of spectacle was not so determinedly asserted in *Two-Minute Warning* and *Black Sunday*.

Rollercoaster (1977)

In the classic phase (1970–4), the cycle was more intent on returning to the fairground origins by 'offering audiences the treat of spectacular cataclysms'.[46] In doing so, the cycle was refashioning symbiotic connections between the early cinema spectatorship and the amusement park, both of which 'aggressively subjected the spectator to sensual and psychological impact'.[47] It is no coincidence, therefore, that the decade of the 1970s simultaneously witnessed the resurgence of the amusement park and the emergence of the blockbuster and the studio theme park. Universal Studios had a particular vested interest in promoting an immersive, media convergence of the thrill ride and the disaster blockbuster. According to Gemma Blackwood, studio tourism at Universal was a 'new economic strategy [that] contributed to the rise of blockbuster cinema in the 1970s, a genre that is well known for providing spectacular virtual "rides" [...]'.[48] Initially, Universal working with the executive producer, Jennings Lang, was buoyed by the success of *Earthquake* that had been promoted as an 'event' movie, one that capitalized on the biblical apocalypticism of John Martin paintings that had shaped the scale and spectacle of Cecil B. DeMille's films, while imitating the thrill sensations of the fairground ride via Sensurround (low-frequency speakers created a rumbling effect) and a Panavision camera (called the 'Shaker' to create a rocking effect). Mary Murphy likened the experience of seats rattling to also that of a 'rock concert or a sports event'.[49] Nora Sayre viewed the virtual experience as to be competing with the 'feelies' in *Brave New World*.[50] The synergy of the amusement park and the disaster blockbuster was affirmed when Universal Studios turned *Earthquake* into an attraction that simulated a large earthquake, rated at 8.3 on the Richter scale – the size of the one that devastated San Francisco in 1906. *Earthquake: The Big One* was one of Universal Studio Florida's original attractions and opened on 7 June 1990, and it closed twice due to real earthquakes (19 October 1989 and 28 June 1992). *Jaws* had also been refashioned into a small attraction, involving an animatronic shark, as part of the Studio Tour at Universal Studios Hollywood in 1976. The primary aim of Universal was to compete with Disney and the fantasy of 'living inside the movies'.[51] The cinematic thrill ride that stimulated physical sensation was also integral to the immersive realism of the disaster spectacle.

Rollercoaster (1977) was another Jennings Lang production that used Sensurround and Panaflex cameras to replace subjective sensations with a physical experience. On its release, the film was reviewed as 'effective pop entertainment [...] like an amusement-park ride'.[52] In fact, *Rollercoaster* married the mediation of disaster closely to the amusement park as a 'commodification of risk', in creating the sensation of 'being on the brink of grave bodily harm'.[53] One official film poster that stated, 'Somewhere in the crowd is a killer who can turn their smiles into screams', invokes the trope of uncanny horror which is enacted by the male antagonist (played by Timothy Bottoms). Screams of joy turn into screams of horror when a bomb on a wooden rollercoaster at Southern California's Ocean View Amusement Park is detonated via remote control, and 'The Rocket' flies off its track, killing many of its riders (Figure 6.1). *Rollercoaster* was promoted as one you 'ride' and its virtual realism was enhanced by point-of-view shots at the head of the coaster's cars. The storyline of an anonymous blackmailer threatening popular American institutions links *Rollercoaster* to

Figure 6.1 The synergy of the disaster spectacle and the amusement park is affirmed in *Rollercoaster*.

Two-Minute Warning and other films, such as *The Taking of Pelham 1-2-3* (1974), that are reflective of domestic terrorism and 'potential for mass casualties'.[54] Yet, even though the serial bomber, who is trying to extort $1 million from the executives of amusement park companies, is typed as the abuser of simple family pleasures, and, in effect, is akin to the monster shark in *Jaws* that preys on holiday makers on the beach town of Amity Island, the film is ultimately a celebration of the sensory excitements that the modernized amusement park had to offer. 'The Rocket' which featured in the film's opening horror sequence was a wooden coaster which was destroyed in the making of *The Death of Ocean View Park* (1979). It is telling that the final target, the steel coaster, 'Revolution', is unscathed, and was in fact 'The New Revolution' which opened to the public on 8 May 1976, at Six Flags Magic Mountain theme park (California) and that was the world's first to feature a vertical loop. The amusement park industry underwent resurgence in the 1970s, following a slow decline during the Depression.[55] It is unsurprising, given Universal's investment in studio parks, the film is a celebration of the technological advancements of the amusement park from the wooden to steel construction, and that poetic justice is delivered when the party pooper is killed by a coaster named after the American Revolution during July 4th celebrations.

Despite the triumphalism, the film belongs to a cinematic tradition that associates the amusement park, given its epithet of cheap thrills and the commodification of danger, with decadence, murder and damnation: *The Lady from Shanghai* (Orson Welles 1947), *Brighton Rock* (John Boulting 1948) and *The Third Man* (Carol Reed 1949). *Rollercoaster* was described at the time as 'a suspense melodrama of the sort that Alfred Hitchcock does best and most wittily (and sometimes most cruelly)', thus aligning it to Hitchcock's *Strangers on a Train* (1951) and the closing scene when Bruno and Guy fight on the amusement park's carousel.[56] The operator is mistakenly killed by a pursuing police officer, causing the carousel to spin out of control. As Lee Edelman notes, the climax when the merry-go-round jumps its tracks offers 'for the audience's amusement the scene of destruction it has craved all along'.[57] And for Joseph Litvak, the scene also presents the 'quintessentially Hitchcockian coupling of comedy and horror'.[58] *Rollercoaster* is in keeping with the spirit of Hitchcock's macabre humour with the combination of Lalo Schifrin's funfair score, amplified by 'Magic Carousel' – the End Title, shots of a bomb located under the crotch of a male rider, and the post-Watergate wit of the pursuing Insurance inspector, Harry Calder (George Segal).

Dante's Inferno (1935)

Dante's Inferno (Harry Lachman, 1935) is probably the first American film to turn the amusement park into a hellish space and to translate the spectacle of risky fun into an uncanny conceit that plays on Mircea Eliade's notion of the carnival as when 'all barriers between the dead and the living are broken'.[59] As Amilcare A. Iannucci argues, the film 'is a modern morality story which follows the life of the ruthlessly ambitious Jim Carter (Spencer Tracy)'.[60] In the opening scenes, Carter is a ship stoker and the ship's bowels plus the coal-fuelled flames of the steam engines are visually likened to Dante's *Inferno* from *Divine Comedy*. Carter takes over a fairground show, appositely called 'Dante's Inferno', run by 'Pop' who believes Dante's book bears a true message of vice and ineluctable punishment that we should heed. Carter, instead, appears to identify with a picture of Alexander the Great, the conqueror who cuts through the Gordian knot, and in like spirit adopts the hard-line capitalist principles of the American dream. Carter marries Pop's niece, Betty, and they have a son, called Alexander. The show becomes a great success, with Carter turning it into a more lurid spectacle. However, a distraught fairground owner, who has lost his wife and life savings, commits suicide by throwing himself into the lower depths of the 'Inferno' show.

The symbolic message is that Hell is a living reality. Later, an inspector declares the fair unsafe and Carter bribes his silence. But when there is a partial collapse (due to safety shortcuts), Pop is injured. Recovering in hospital, Pop admonishes Carter, and a post-impressionistic, 'terror-inducing', depiction of Dante's hell is shown, exhibited the spectacle of divine punishment.[61] The complicit inspector then commits suicide and confesses to the conspiracy that incriminates Carter. Betty commits perjury in court to prevent Alexander's father from going to penitentiary. With his marriage broken, Carter turns his attention to establishing an unsafe gambling cruise ship, called the SS *Paradise*, 'a floating pleasure palace, laden with sin and shameless revelry'.

This is a retelling of SS *Morro Castle* (*en route* from Havana to New York), when in September 1934 fire broke out in a storage locker and high winds fanned the flames through the ornate wooden interiors as the inexperienced and disorganized crew struggled to extinguish the blaze and to transmit an SOS signal. Many of the crew abandoned ship. 137 passengers and crewmembers died. The ship eventually beached itself near Asbury Park, New Jersey. In the film, when the pleasure palace catches fire, Carter heroically redeems himself by keeping the steam engines going to steer SS *Paradise* towards the coastline where the survivors could be rescued. Carter's son is rescued, and Carter is reunited with his wife, promising to lead a virtuous life with the realization that money isn't everything. As Iannucci argues, Lachman essentially exploits Dantean material mainly as a 'moral inculcator'.[62]

Carter's 'Inferno' show, a volcanic underworld of decadent thrills, somewhat foreshadows the 'junky fairground ride – a chamber of horror with skeletons' that for Kael characterizes the destruction orgies of the seventies (e.g., *Earthquake* and *Inferno*).[63] But it also sets down a marker for the dark carnivalesque of American horror films set in amusement parks, such as *Carnival of Souls* (Herk Harvey, 1962) and *Malatesta's Carnival of Blood* (Christopher Speeth, 1973). And while Universal productions capitalized on the thrill ride and uncanny horror experience to enhance the immersive spectacle, a series of seventies films presented dystopic visions of the theme park as outlets of hedonism, hyperreality and violence: *Westworld* (Michael Crichton, 1973) and *Futureworld* (Richard T. Heffron, 1976), *The Stepford Wives* (Bryan Forbes, 1975). *Rollerball* (Norman Jewison, 1975), *Death Race 2000* (Paul Bartel, 1975) and *Logan's Run* (Michael Anderson, 1976). In *Rollerball*, *Death Race 2000* and *Logan's Run*, the carnival environments of the everyday are means of maintaining 'the true mechanics of power'.[64] And '*The Stepford Wives* makes domestic space into a kind of patriarchal theme park'.[65] *Westworld* started the seventies trend in transforming the Disney Park fantasy of living inside the movies into a place of uncanny horror. Michael Crichton was inspired by the hyper-realistic animatronic figures in Disney Park and the original film grounded 'the story in the very notion of kitsch consumerism and heteronomous commodification'.[66] For A. M. Butler, the dreamworld is a space for 'tourists to escape from the contemporary horrors of the Vietnam War, economic crises and the emerging Watergate conspiracies'.[67] In a telling scene, when the Gunslinger (Yul Bryner) challenges John Blane (James Brolin) and Peter Martin (Richard Benjamin) to a Western showdown, Blane treats it as theme park fun (Figure 6.2).

> Blane: 'Your move.'
> (Shot rings out.)
> Blane: 'I'm shot.'
> Martin: 'What?!'
> Blane: 'I'm shot.'
> Peter Martin: 'O my God!'

Figure 6.2 John Blane (James Brolin) is shot, and the reality of death disturbs the theme park fun.

Martin sees blood flowing out of Blane's dead body and the shock revelation is that the game that allows for the pleasure-seeking spectator to be a modern gladiator is checked by the reality of death. In exemplifying the dark carnivalesque of the studio park the scene represents a critique of Disney-hyperreality that for Jean Baudrillard shielded the United States as a nation from its violent history.[68] But two post-*Jaws* disaster films also used modern arenas of pleasure in which to violently target the American consumer of the big spectacle and to, in turn, implicate the otherwise disinterested subject into the violence of American society.

Two-Minute Warning (1976)

Two-Minute Warning (1976) is set in the Los Angeles Memorial Coliseum football stadium, and, as the wording on an official poster suggests – '91,000 people / 33 Exit Gates / 1 Sniper' – the film plays on the claustrophobic terror of a confined space. The film also deploys the horror trope of the invisible man with a gun, this time set loose in a stadium. The opening sequence, when the anonymous killer occupies a position on a tall building and shoots a cyclist, visually quotes 'the longish meditation, through Scorpio's gun sight' in *Dirty Harry*.[69] The serial murderer appears to be in the mould of Scorpio but is more of a nihilistic variation, without motivation and a criminal identity. The focus is on the voyeurism of a violent spectacle and the spectators inside a football stadium. With a camera shot framing the eyesight of the killer's rifle to show the reality of sight coming to the lens, the opening self-reflexive motif of murderous voyeurism echoes Michael Powell's *Peeping Tom* (1960) in which the audience are also framed as violent voyeurs. This is underscored by the anonymity of the killer, who is given no backstory and is generally perceived via fractured body parts (hands, feet and eyeball) or via the multiple screens in the TV control room that is relaying the live footage of the football game. Roger Ebert found the film 'disturbing', with the killer 'an agent of violence, so that we can be entertained by his victims'.[70] And by unashamedly exploiting 'two of our great national preoccupations, pro football and guns', the film foregrounds the parallels between 'a Roman-circus mentality' of the cycle and thrill ride by turning the eyesight of the indiscriminate killer onto the diegetic spectator.[71]

The uncanny blurring of institutional violence and the spectacle of a destructive orgy occurs when the sniper shoots randomly into the crowd, killing selected spectators (who have worn their hearts on their sleeves and have confessed to their sins). The first hit is Steve (David Janssen) who has walked through a tunnel from the concourse having just proposed to Janet (Gena Rowlands) (Figure 6.3). His death is instant, bloody and unnoticed by cheering crowds as his dead body rolls down the concrete aisle. The scene of indifference is a barbed comment on the reality of violence that is shielded by spectacle. This is counterpointed by the interior shots of the control room producers, whose facial expressions of horror echo the colosseum spectators of DeMille's *Sign of the Cross*. The sporting spectacle is eventually ruptured when cheers of elation turn to screams of panic and terror and the stadium crowd stampede,

Figure 6.3 The spectator (David Janssen as Steve) is the target of violence in the big spectacle.

whipped into a frantic, herd mentality by the gunman's indiscriminate shooting. The close-ups of panic-stricken faces uncannily echo the preceding expressions of elation and triumph. The closing scenes of police identifying bodies and Sam McKeever (Martin Balsam) tearfully looking towards an empty football stadium affirm the nihilism embodied in a killer who, for Richard Eder, constitutes an 'an abstract threat'.[72] As Charlton Heston recalls: 'Universal was positive it would out-gross *Earthquake*. It was a flop. We had struck a nerve; the public didn't want anything to do with terror in a Super Bowl.'[73] Heston also believes the film struggled commercially because 'no sympathy was created [...] for any of the characters'.[74] Despite the backstories, the spectacle of death appears brutal and clinical.

No sympathy is given to the sniper, too. In refusing to humanize the indiscriminate killer, the film appears to be akin to the reactionary politics of the vigilante film and its generic opposition to 'bleeding heart' liberals. The sniper is evil Other, and undeserving of a backstory. This is the view voiced through Sergeant Chris Button (John Cassavetes) who speaks of the news-media's obsession for biographical details. But the killer's amoral nihilism and lack of political affiliation in the act of violence cut across the decade's entrenched ideological wars. He is an abstract threat in the sense of being a terrorist who targets spectators in the big spectacle arena for sadistic pleasure.

Black Sunday (1977)

Directed by John Frankenheimer for Paramount Pictures, *Black Sunday* (1977) was released soon after *Two-Minute Warning* and shares a similar story of a violent attack at a championship football match. 'To show how great minds operate in parallel channels, there is the recently published "Two Minute Warning" by George La Fountaine. In that, a malcontent ensconces himself atop the stadium in a Super Bowl game determined to shoot down some prominent Americans. [...] "Black Sunday" has the added fillip of being topical [...]'.[75] It is based on Thomas Harris's 1975 novel, which was inspired by the Munich massacre at the 1972 summer Olympics when a Palestinian terrorist group, Black September, took eleven members of the Israeli wrestling team hostage in the Olympic village before killing them.

The Munich massacre had proven that big sporting events were possible targets for disseminating a terrorist cause to a global audience.[76] And '*Black*

Sunday is one of the first films to acknowledge terrorist acts as spectacles carefully staged for the greatest possible mass media exposure [...] terrorism is an assault on the world's screens as much as an attack on human beings, who are viciously reduced to "collateral damage" when terrorism finds its actual targets.'[77] *Black Sunday* brings the big spectacle of international terrorism to America's domestic scene.

The film is also striking for relativizing the politics of the Arab Israeli conflict, by focusing on Michael Leander (Bruce Dern), a psychologically damaged Vietnam veteran, who sides with the Black September group and the operative, Dahlia Iyad (Marthe Keller), in conspiring to launch a suicide-bomb attack over the Miami Orange Bowl during Super Bowl X as a means of punishing the United States for supporting Israel. In the words of Bruce Dern:

> It's another triangular situation. I play a Goodyear blimp pilot, Marthe Keller plays a Palestinian terrorist who enlists me to perpetrate a disaster in America, and Robert Shaw plays an Israeli agent. We're all on gr[e]y horses in this movie, no blacks and no whites, and by the end the audience will be rooting for both sides, because of the terrible things that have happened to us in life.[78]

Dern is right in saying that the film challenges conventional melodramatic moralism, by allowing the Palestinian voice to be heard via Dahlia. She is also depicted as a terrorist by-product of Israel's mistreatment of the Palestinians, for in the words of Colonel Riat (Walter Gotell), an Egyptian contact:

> Her name is Dahlia Iyad. Of Arab-German extraction. Born on a farm near Haifa, formerly Palestine, in 1948. Her father, brother killed by Israeli commandos in war of same year. She, sister, mother expelled, '49. Lived in a tent in desert refugee camp, Gaza, '49. '57, her mother died of typhus, '51. Sister raped in war of '56. Refugee camp, Jordan, '57. Sent by Arab League to Beirut University, '66. Geneva, '70. Black September: joined in 1973. Here is her face. Look at it. After all, in a way, she's your creation, Major Kabakov.

Giving Dahlia a backstory affirms Stephen Prince's view that unlike most other popular depictions of terrorism as simply evil or 'crazy', *Black Sunday* acknowledges terrorist violence as often deriving from 'the unintended consequences of foreign policy', including in this case US support for Israel and anti-Palestinian policies.[79] And in coupling Dahlia with Lander, the film further collapses the ideological boundaries. The enemy within is the legacy of Vietnam and American society's failure to rehabilitate traumatized soldiers. This is made clear in the opening scene, when Dahlia and other members of the Black September group are shown film footage of Lander confessing as a Viet Cong POW to the atrocities he committed:

> I am Michael J. Lander, Lieutenant Commander, United States Navy. I was captured on February 10, 1967, while firebombing a civilian hospital near Ninh Binh. I am guilty of my war crimes, and although I'm guilty of my war crimes, the Democratic Republic of Vietnam hasn't punished me. They have, uh, showed me the suffering that I have caused by my crimes. I'm sorry for what I've done. I am sorry that we killed children and I call upon the American people to stop the war. The Democratic Republic of Vietnam has no animosity toward the American people. It's the warmongers who are making the war. What about Vietnam? Forgive me.

The focus on a four-time decorated war veteran, who has sided with an anti-American terrorist cell, invokes the kind of cynicism akin to a New Hollywood perspective on morally ambiguous, anti-heroes. Significantly, John Frankenheimer had made contributions to New Hollywood via *French Connection II* (1975), and its 'pessimistic fatalism' is characteristic of Frankenheimer's 70s' oeuvre.[80] Lander shares parallels with Jimmy 'Popeye' Doyle (Gene Hackman), who is blinded by his obsession to track down the elusive drug kingpin Alain Charnier (Fernando Rey). He is used as a bait by the French police in Marseille, and when captured by the drug ring is injected with heroin in a secluded hotel. The scenes of addiction and drug withdrawal relates to what Daniel Varndell terms a 'little death', or a moment of 'existential ambiguity'.[81] Popeye is revealed to be the uncanny double of an evil twin in the criminal underworld.

Lander's anti-American zeal also puts *Black Sunday* in what has been termed the 'post-traumatic cycle' (1970–6) that exhibited the breakdown of ideological confidence in American culture and values: '[…] the trauma suffered by soldiers in Vietnam, then by the nation as a whole, was reflected in this second cycle of films whose heroes, like the heroes of Vietnam, are manipulated, exploited, and left paralysed by the realization of their powerlessness in the face of a corrupt system.'[82] Lander, too, is depicted as unhinged and paranoid, or in a 'catatonic' state, disconnected from his surroundings.[83] There are echoes of Travis Bickle (Robert De Niro), who suffers from post-traumatic stress disorder in Martin Scorsese's *Taxi Driver* (1976). A traumatized Vietnam veteran also featured in *Skyjacked* (John Guillermin, 1972), in which Jerome K. Weber (James

Brolin) hijacks a Boeing 707 to defect to Moscow. Furthermore, *Black Sunday* anticipates the 'revenge fantasy' of an abused victim in *First Blood* (1982), which dramatizes, according to Frank Sweeney, post-Vietnam disillusionment and the collapsing of ideological binaries in terms of American soldiers becoming the enemy.[84] The deputies are 'pursuing a "war"' against John Rambo (Sylvester Stallone) who represents the Viet Cong, and the destruction and capture of the sheriff's department is equivalent to the fall of Saigon.[85] Lander is one more monstrocized exemplar of unstable masculinity, fulfilling the Vietnam trope of 'sado-masochistic fantasy/experience', whereby the physical and psychological trauma unleashes a wild killer.[86] Lander's revenge fantasy against his 'homeland' is also reflective of America's domestic terrorism, the 'potential danger lurking at home'.[87] Despite Dern's claims of political ambiguity, ultimately the film leans towards the politics of *The Enforcer*. Kabalov is the victorious action hero in the mode of a vigilante, tough male type, who fights crime by any means necessary.[88] The FBI agent, Sam Corley (Fritz Weaver), initially distances himself from Mossad's counter-terrorist tactics, but a 'dirty' code of violence is eventually legitimatized. The film, in a cursory way, when Robert Moshevsky (Steven Keats) says he sees both sides of the Arab Israeli question, foreshadows Steven Spielberg's *Munich* (2005) in equating 'Operation Wrath of God' (Mossad's retaliatory assassinations against Black September) with the Munich terrorists. But this is quickly checked when Dahlia, disguised as a nun, kills the Israeli agent in hospital. Kabalov's counter-terrorist attitude hardens and his nickname, 'The Final Solution', implies he is also willing to fight an unethical war. He forces precious information out of Muzi (Michael V. Gazzo) by sticking a gun into his mouth. The ruthless Mohammed Fasil (Bekim Fehmiu), who organized the Munich massacre, is gunned down by Kabalov, and his killing is symbolic compensation for the Munich massacre and an indirect endorsement of Mossad's retributive vengeance. It is a killing that is not depicted in Harris's novel. The audience is meant to be rooting for one side. This may explain why the film scored badly internationally, with its release coinciding with two television films, *Victory at Entebbe* (Marvin J. Chomsky, 1976) and *Raid on Entebbe* (Irvin Kershner, 1977), that celebrated the Israeli military rescue of hostages in Uganda ('Operation Entebbe').

Nonetheless, the spectacular finale, set in Miami Orange Bowl stadium, parallels the nihilism of *Two-Minute Warning*, not only via images of crowd panic, but also by juxtaposing the violence committed on the football pitch in the name of sport and the gunfire exchange between the *Jaws*-like dirigible and the pursuing helicopter. Lander's motives of vengeance against the spectators resonate with the Munich massacre as a terrorist publicity event:

> Do you understand what I went through? Huh? Do you know that I was months a prisoner of war? Do you know that I was months in solitary confinement, in a little 4 × 4 bamboo cell? 367 days, six years they held me! As a prisoner of war! And then I came back here, and my life was hell back here because she took it away from me, they ... every single one of them took it away from me. All those guys, too. Yeah, I see them every Sunday. I see them from up there, down in the mass. Their little upturned faces and their two little weenies and a Coke, watching the big game, cheering the big game, because they cheer all the good things. They cheer the big game, and they cheer court-martials, and they love the big event because it makes them feel big, and I was going to give it to them big! They'd have been talking about that goddamned game for the next 5,000 years!

The implication is that the big spectacle spectators are also complicit in an unthinking love of both state militarism and Lander's downfall. Vengeance is attempted through the return of the cinematic gaze of horror to bring the spectated violence of Vietnam and Munich into American lives. Lander's poignant monologue echoes the lines delivered by ABC's anchor-man, Jim McKay, in the immediate aftermath of the 1972 Munich Olympics hostage massacre: 'Our greatest hopes and our worst fears are seldom realized. Our worst fears have been realized tonight. They've now said that there were eleven hostages; two were killed in their rooms.'[89] As David Scott Diffrient argues, McKay's rhetorical blending of global news and sports reporting implies that tragedy is played out like the human drama of Athletic competition.[90] By importing international terrorism into a domestic sporting sphere, the Freudian reality principle of the external world is rudely introduced, one that disrupts the mediating role of violence in the hedonic culture of modern games.

As in *Westworld*, there is an awakening to the reality of violence and a disturbance of the spectator-spectacle dynamic, one that echoes Peckinpah's views on watching the Super Bowl as a socially sanctioned violent spectacle: 'I'm a great believer in catharsis. Do you think people watch the Super Bowl because they think football is a beautiful sport? Bullshit! They're committing violence vicariously. Look, the old basis of catharsis was a purging of the emotions through pity and fear.'[91] Peckinpah's words recall the critical view of Kael, in that cinematic bloodletting satisfies a Roman circus mentality. However, *Black Sunday* constitutes more of a psychological affront to the comfortable gaze of the spectator (diegetic and non-diegetic), especially by representing the aggressors as brutalized victims of recent historical wars. And in making Lander a casualty of the Vietnam War as well as an instrument of Black September terrorism, the convenient ideological binary of monstrous threat and victim collapses. Lander is a by-product of America's foreign policies and international terrorism. Lander is a home-grown threat, bringing America's exported terror back home.

Nonetheless, the staging of a terrorist spectacle is ambiguous, for, in the words of Corey K. Creekmur, the film also

> acknowledges its own losing battle as a widescreen major motion picture against the pervasive power of broadcast television as the dominant medium of the postwar era (a cultural status to which Frankenheimer himself of course contributed significantly): the television broadcast of the Super Bowl obtains an audience that only the few, newly defined 'blockbuster' films could dream of addressing, so terrorism is staged for television coverage, with whatever representation it finds in cinema increasingly irrelevant to its aims.[92]

In the 1970s, terrorism was often staged as a television event and the blockbuster competed with mediated realities of mass killings. The disaster movie was responsible for the rise of a blockbuster spectacle that was to deliver a more reassuring display of violence.

Conclusion

Rather than an end-of-the-decade exhausted formula, the disaster movie was conceptually maturing by dramatizing parallels between event terrorism and spectated violence. One should see the cycle's fading popularity as concomitant with Hollywood's recasting of post-Vietnam trauma and violence into cinematic fantasies that neither belonged in the realm of probability nor challenged the viewer's interpellating gaze.

7

Bee ecohorror: *The Swarm* (1978)

The Swarm (Irwin Allen, 1978), a screen adaptation of Arthur Herzog's 1974 novel, is exemplar of Hollywood ecohorror (ecologically themed horror) that constituted a distinctive subgenre of the disaster cycle. Unlike disaster movies that mostly involved elemental forces wreaking large-scale havoc on humanity (quakes, fires, tidal waves etc.), ecohorror entails revenging nature in the form of collectively acting insects/animals. Films such as *The Food of the Gods* (Bert I. Gordon, 1976), *Orca* (Michael Anderson, 1977), and *Day of the Animals* (William Girdler, 1977) implicate humanity as the *prima causa* in an escalating chain of events that showcases nature's potential, destructive horror. Even though the horror spectacle supersedes the eco-premise – the abuse of non-human nature – *The Swarm* is more than a monster movie, for the film was responding (albeit belatedly) to the 'African bee scare' in the 1970s and an associated set of racial and gender tropes.

The 1978 film marked the end of the disaster cycle, and, until now, it has not received any critical attention. This is probably because the 'killer-bee farrago' has been described as 'the worst film ever made'.[1] And, like *Piranha* (Joe Dante, 1978), is judged to be one more revenge of nature film inspired by *Jaws* (Steven Spielberg, 1975), which 'is at once a landmark and an aberration in the disaster movie cycle [...] in which Vietnam and Watergate were real-life disasters'.[2] Vincent Canby's review adequately sums up why Irwin Allen's big-budget film fared so badly vis-à-vis Hollywood's move to more profitable genres:

> Three of the most successful films of the last 12 months share these [spectacular melodrama] roots with 'The Swarm' – George Lucas's 'Star Wars', Steven Spielberg's 'Close Encounters of The Third Kind' and the screen version of 'Grease'. Yet as Lucas, Spielberg and the people who put 'Grease' together transcended the tacky, B-picture genres they recall with affection and imagination, Allen merely reproduces the tacky genre while spending a great deal of money doing it. There's not a frame of film, not a twist of plot, not a line

of dialogue, not a performance in 'The Swarm' that suggests real appreciation for film history, only a slavish desire to imitate It. That's not enough.³

Canby was also right to say the film was the 'apotheosis of yesterday's B-movie', such as the big-bug feature, *Them!* (Gordon Douglas, 1954), that influenced the ecohorror output of the 1970s. *The Swarm*, as ecohorror, could not compete with 'popcorn-friendly blockbusters'.⁴ Nonetheless, the 'farrago' – a confused mixture of eco-tropes – in an era that was challenging male destructive influences on nature, is significant as both a variation of the bee movie, such as *Invasion of the Bee Girls* (Denis Sanders, 1973), *Killer Bees* (Curtis Harrington, 1974) and *The Savage Bees* (Bruce Geller, 1976), and as a Hollywood dramatization of environmentalist concerns, via the Africanized bee and its associated racial and gender politics.

The African bee scare

The production of *The Swarm* was announced in 1974 at the height of the disaster cycle, but was postponed, with Allen leaving 20th Century Fox for Warner Bros. due to the cancellation of three planned disaster movies.⁵ The delay in the theatrical release meant that the supposed threat of killer bees sweeping north from Brazil and invading the United States had not been borne out by 1978. Herzog's prophesized swarm, seemingly authenticated by the insertion of a historical account of the species mutation in the novel, appeared stingless:

> In 1956 a Brazilian entomologist had imported African bees with the idea of crossbreeding them with Brazilian bees and creating a family as industrious as the Africans but as docile as the European bee. [...] Before the crossbreeding experiments were completed an unbelievable series of errors resulted in the escape of twenty-six swarms headed by African queens. [...] The bee – *Apis mellifera adansonii* – proved biologically cunning as well as irascible. It was an invader. [...] Because of its vitality, skill at robbing other bees of their honey stores, and most of all its genetic dominance, *adansonii* had accomplished a biological miracle. Like the Huns, it swept forward.⁶

It is true that the crossbred Africanized bees were accidentally released in 1957 from hives operated by the geneticist and entomologist Warwick E. Kerr, who was attempting to breed a strain of bees that would produce more honey. Herzog is guilty, though, of adding to the media scare, in likening the bees to invading 'Huns'. Herzog's eco-fiction belongs to a post-Carson tradition of American environmentalism that used apocalyptic rhetoric to frame a potential ecological crisis. So, while contributing to the racialization of the bee scare, Herzog nonetheless introduced ecological themes too.

In the style of Rachel Carson's *Silent Spring*, which brought environmental concerns to the American public in 1962, the bee scare is a sign of cosmic disturbance in the natural order: '[The bee] had voluntarily escaped from the garden of Eden with poor fallen man for the purpose of sweetening his bitter lot.'[7] Herzog cites William Morton Wheeler's *Social Life Among the Insects* (1923) to frame the bee in lost-pastoral terms. The bee was once a sacred creature of Eden and a friend of man. But Herzog soon shifts to news-media alarmism: '"There seems to be no natural barrier to block the bees, and they could be in North America within four to six years, says a study financed by the Agriculture Department. The most alarming, and best-known characteristic of Brazilian bees is their aggressiveness, according to the report." [*Chicago Daily News*, 24 August 1972].'[8] The angry swarm is a Frankenstein monster, a scientific violation of the bee's divine genesis, but Herzog also exploits the invasion trajectory to underpin the cautionary tale.

The extent to which a racialized, invasion hysteria was being projected onto the Africanized swarm is evidenced by 'The Killer Bee' skit on *Saturday Night Live* (11 October 1975). In the sketch (season 1, episode 9), husband (Chevy Chase) and wife (Gilda Radner) are sitting in the lounge listening to the radio: 'We interrupt this program to bring you this bulletin from the newsroom. Swarms of South American killer bees have been spotted crossing the border into California.' At this point, Killer Bee Juan (John Belushi) enters through the window, and crosses behind the sofa and puts a knife to Wife's neck. A radio announcer voices the scare story: 'Eyewitnesses say that the bees are yellow and black, and dress much the way Eli Wallach did in the movie *The Magnificent Seven*. The bees are also overweight.' The killer bees demand the whereabouts of the pollen, and their leader (Elliott Gould) regales, with a faux Mexican accent, a tale of agrarian woe:

> We have reached the end of our journey. If we are to go back to the village, we will go back empty-handed. Señor, my people are poor people. For many years they have worked hard. The harvest is so small for so long. I knew we had to leave, to search elsewhere to feed our young. We started to move north last April.[9]

The sketch foregrounds the racist link between bee invasion hysteria and migration fears, by parodying the convention of the besieged town in the Western genre and that the swarming bees are marauding, poverty-stricken, Mexicans. *The Swarm* also racialized the swarm, and the repeated references to 'the Africans are coming' were seen by Canby as to 'take on a hilarious ominous meaning'.[10]

Ecohorror

Herzog's novel typifies the way ecofiction, at the time, dramatized an ecological theme via the horror of 'nature strikes back'. The predatory creature genre was big business in the 1970s, and this also came in the form of the avenging monstrous insect.[11] The American film, *Willard* (Daniel Mann, 1971), had spawned killer bee, killer shark and killer whale films, such as *Jaws* and *Orca* – an adaptation of Herzog's 1977 novel. According to John Sutherland, they often move from an 'initial eco-OK position to frank, Darwinian delight in the struggle to death'.[12] In other words, the eco-premise – for instance, the pollution of a food chain – is eventually superseded by a horror spectacle. Herzog's bee is more than an anthropomorphic symbol, for the Africanized bee constitutes, in his eyes, humanity's incursion on nature, and the novel is 'a wake-up call to the dangers facing these miraculous insects and, by extension, humankind'.[13] Humans depend on the survival of the bee, because this species is essential to a bio-diverse ecosystem. However, Herzog's narrative of a man-made ecological crisis is compromised by Hollywood apocalypticism, or the foregrounding of nature-avenging horror.

Derivative of Carson's scientific realism, Herzog heightens the bee scare by presenting a composite of newspaper clippings, scientific charts and maps, footnotes to bona-fide journals, and a glossary of entomological bee terms. The novel also uses an anti-pastoral mode to prefigure the apocalyptic. The opening chapter, 'A Picnic', intimates that excessive human consumerism, in particular a dependency on sweet goods, and intolerance towards bees (that are meant to sweeten the 'bitter lot' of 'fallen man') underlie the culture-nature conflict.[14] A family is picnicking near Maryville, New York: 'whose provisions included sugar in various forms; as it turned out, too much sugar for their own good'.[15] Wild bees are also taking full advantage of the weather, 'frantically gathering nectar and pollen'.[16] The bees soon congregate around a 'honey jar' and 'scrape at the

Styrofoam cups', and the mother, Mary, violently attacks the honey creators: 'She dared to snatch the insecticide can from the table, jabbed the button and held it down until her thumb was white from the pressure.'[17] The child's hunger for all things sweet is matched by the bee's hunger: 'Those bees are pigs, just like us kids.'[18] The revenge of nature is an Ovidian form of poetic justice: 'She open her mouth to scream but received on her tongue a swab of pain.'[19] The picnic attack is metonymic of the grander eco-disturbance: the excessive human demand for sugar correlates to the scientific production of a mutant bee species.

The novel constitutes a critique of America's exploitation of natural resources, techno-scientific modernity and the inter-related effects of capitalism, consumerism and pollution. Herzog was a prolific writer of ecologically oriented fiction that conveyed the adverse human impact on nature, and his seventies oeuvre – *The Swarm* (1974), *Earthsound* (1975), *Orca* (1977) and *Heat* (1977) – is prescient. The novels are concerned with the themes of earthquakes, global warming, sea-life depletion and a bee eco-system. Herzog often exploits apocalyptic terror to forewarn of a potential ecological crisis, and this is especially illustrated in *Heat* that uses a Dantean inferno vision of an overheated planet to dramatize the greenhouse effect, which is brought on by a high level of carbon dioxide in the atmosphere due to the overuse of energy resources.[20] *Orca* is notable in drawing on aspects of contemporaneous ecofeminism.[21] Dr Rachel Bedford, a whale expert, articulates a sense of female affinity with the sacred otherness of a hunted species and Captain Nolan is deeply affected when he mistakenly harpoons a pregnant orca that miscarries on his boat. Unfortunately, the film adaptation distorts Herzog's green ethos (empathy for the sacred otherness of the non-human) by dramatizing a climax of completed revenge: having followed the grieving orca to the Strait of Belle Isle, Nolan (Richard Harris) is thrown to his death by the killer whale. The narrative is a man-versus-beast plot (echoing Ovidian myths of human transgression and hunter-hunted role reversals). A revenge instinct is attributed to the whale, yet vengeance is not the primary objective in Herzog's novel, for the orca does not kill Nolan, who survives to ruminate on the 'sin' he has inflicted upon 'mother nature'.[22] Nonetheless, the film is distinctive as an eco-riposte to *Jaws* that was marketed according to a horror spectacle predicated on the dissemination of shark phobia.

The Swarm exhibits recognizable features of in-vogue ecohorror. Rather than a nature-reverential representation of bees as a force of living abundance and fertility, bees are envisaged in the mode of biblical plague (e.g., the plagues of Egypt in the book of Exodus – e.g., frogs, lice, wild animals and locusts – sent by

God to punish the unrighteous). The hive mind (insect collective intelligence) is a cipher for collective revenge, and not a social model for communal living or matriarchal utopia, as in Charlotte Perkins Gilman's short story 'Bee Wise' (1913). Swarming, a spring phenomenon, is crucial to the honeybee's reproduction, but, as John Schlesinger's *The Day of the Locust* (1975) showed, Hollywood is addicted to male-centred apocalypticism. And in this respect, the film is a continuation of films that monstrocized the beehive as a feminine force.

The Swarm also chimes with a concurrent end-time discourse that was popularized by Hal Lindsey's *The Late Great Planet Earth* (1970), which was adapted into a 1978 film narrated by Orson Welles. Lindsey's prophesies drew on biblical apocalypticism, while citing the frequency of famines, earthquakes, wars (e.g., the Six-Day War of 1967) and the Oil Crisis of 1973 as signs of Christ's second coming. The book, which outsold all other non-fiction books in 1970, the year when the first Earth Day (peaceful demonstrations across the United States calling for environmental reform) occurred, points to the Janus-nature of American environmentalism that also drew on plague rhetoric to create eco-cautionary narratives. The uneasy alliance of eschatological Christianity, geopolitical science and ecohorror is underscored by the brief appearance of Dr Paul Ehrlich in Lindsey's 1978 film. Ehrlich reiterates the neo-Malthusian logic of *The Population Bomb* (1968) – in that unchecked human population growth will have an inevitable consequence. Ehrlich's cursory endorsement of Lindsey's prophetic pattern is indicative of the blurring of environmentalist science and science fiction. Ehrlich's envisaged post-apocalyptic scenario, which drew on Cold War nuclear terror, was played out in the sci-fi film, *Soylent Green* (Richard Fleischer, 1973): global overpopulation, climate catastrophe and food shortages. *The Swarm* also exhibits the dissonance that existed between science, insects and culture, by squarely linking religious symbolism with ecological sentiments.[23]

Whilst exploiting biblical imagery, Herzog also draws on the mythology of the bee and its mythologized social identity. The tiny creature was venerated in ancient mythology as the industrious producer of sweet honey and was sometimes aligned with divine femininity, yet equally feared because of its suicidal 'sting of death' – hence the associations with 'fallen man'.[24] The bee symbolically embodies a sacred-demonic duality, thus appealing to ecofeminists (the beehive polis is a model for matriarchal utopia) and, on the other hand, lending itself to a set of bee movie tropes (such as the monstrocized queen bee and its compliant colony). Various feminists, such as Gilman, have employed the 'community' of bees as a model of society. However, the 'absolute attachment and devotion that the workers display towards their queen' can be deemed troublesome.[25] The gendering of the bee is particularly significant for appreciating how Hollywood transposes eco-tropes into a cinematic spectacle. The avenging nature narratives of the 1970s are a response to 1950s' sci-fi movies, such as *It Came from Outer Space* (Jack Arnold, 1953) and *The Thing from Another World* (Christian Nyby, 1951), that exploited the non-human threat as a stand-in for a range of ideological terrors, for instance: post-war women who had 'evolved' from a domesticated position in society and had gained agency on male terms – hence the poisoning of the 'natural' social order. The 1977 film, *Empire of the Ants* (Bert I. Gordon), is illustrative of how ecohorror resorted to the monstrocizes of the queen insect (ant/bee) as a symbolic means of punishing pushy, careerist matriarchs. A land developer, Marilyn Fryser (Joan Collins), whose matriarchal power is mirrored in the ant colony that has taken over an island, dies in the throes of her uncanny double: the queen ant.

The female power of the bee

Prior to the disaster cycle, the bee had been used pervasively in film as an anthropomorphic symbol of female power, a precursor to the ecological symbolism of *The Swarm*. Joan Collins's performance echoes that of Joan Crawford as the southern belle matriarch in *Queen Bee* (1955), in which the queen bee is a metaphoric means of demonizing incipient feminism in the 1950s. Directed by Ronald MacDougall, who had been the screenwriter for the male anxiety-driven *Mildred Pierce* (1945) that also starred Joan Crawford (as a careerist mother), *Queen Bee* is underwritten by the gender politics that typified American film noir in which female power means troubled masculinity and psychological terror. The misogynistic expectations that need to be satisfied were conveyed in Bosley Crowther's film review: 'Five minutes after Miss Crawford appears on the luxurious scene, acting the queen bee like a buzz saw and oozing her unctuous poison from every cell, it is evident – no, it is mandatory – that she should be taken out and shot or run off a cliff in an automobile, which is how it is finally done.'[26] From the very start, Eva Phillips (Crawford) exerts an indomitable will of domination over her Georgia mansion, the matriarchal polis of the hive. Eva exploits her southern belle charms to manipulate the helplessly obedient male drones: for instance, her husband Avery (Barry Sullivan), an alcoholic mill owner, bears a deeply cut Z-shaped facial scar to signify the emasculated status of the drone that bears no deadly stinger and whose primary role is to mate with the fertile queen. Avery's disfigurement is an initial psycho-dramatic sign of the hive's status quo. Judson Prentiss (John Ireland), who is engaged to marry Avery's sister Carol (Betsy Palmer), is a symbolic drone too. The extended metaphor of the all-powerful beehive is brought to the fore when Carol warns Jennifer Stewart (Lucy Marlow), a family cousin, of Eva's hidden queen bee ways. Jennifer has been won over by Eva's 'sweetness' – the mythical and magical allure of sacred honey that is the queen's feminine essence – and as if under a pheromone spell, she has become Eva's personal assistant. This provokes the need for Carol to demythologize the romance of the queen bee:

> Carol: 'You know I used to wonder about Eva until I read a book about bees. [...] We used to keep bees for the orchard – there's a whole chapter devoted to the queen, the ruler of the hive, the queen bee who stings all her rivals to death. [...] Your turn will come – she'll sting you one day ... oh, ever so gently so you hardly feel it until you fall dead.'

Carol is soon a witness to the monstrous and sexual influence of Eva when she espies the rendezvous of Eva and Jud in a darkened room. Jud rejects Eva's femme fatale advances and insists on marrying her sister, Carol. The piqued and wronged queen, in response, hints at ultimate revenge: 'you'll be sorry'.

In a later scene that takes place in Carol's bedroom, Eva reveals to Jennifer a psychotic and paranoid side that hints at the vulnerability and inner terror that come with an ageing queen who is having to fend off her rivals: 'You don't know the things they've made me do trying to protect myself. And how ashamed I've been because of them. You don't know how they are, but you'll find out as I have. [...] I wish I could get rid of them as easily as this trash.' With increasing manic despair, Eva twists Carol's horse-riding whip (a device to exert control over animals through pain compliance) between her hands and smashes from a shelf a row of sporting memorabilia and trophies (symbols of youthful vigour). Eva's jealousy and hatred towards the male drones and the younger females are revealed in the Georgia hive; in 'getting away from her' the power base of her matriarchal status is undermined. The queen bee is left vulnerable without the structure of the hive, hence the defensive mechanism of complete control. At this point, Avery's disfigurement can be seen as a scar of pain compliance. Matriarchal autocracy turns into a reign of terror when Carol learns of Eva's affair with Jud, and she hangs herself in the barn – thus mirroring the suicidal drive of the bee colony at the bidding of the queen.

Eva has also hired a nanny, Miss Breen (Katherine Anderson), who terrorizes the children. Ted, her son (Tim Hovey), is frequently woken up by a nightmare in which he is driving a speeding car towards a mountain with Eva as the passenger. Psychological terror is a sign of the oppressive bind that Avery realizes can only be overthrown by committing an act of murder-suicide. Jud, though, can pre-empt the drone revolt of Avery, and drives a speeding car, with Eva as the passenger, over a cliff. And as the car rolls over, there is a sound match-cut from Eva's scream to the scream of Ted who is disturbed again by the recurring nightmare. Comforted by Jennifer, Ted's affirms the prophecy of his disturbed sleep: 'It happened! It happened!' The nightmare affirms the male anxieties of the genre, for the hatred of the mother and the queen bee is a projection of vulnerable masculinity towards the independent female. The finale literalizes the film's enforced allegory: the matriarchal beehive is a nightmare of female empowerment and male obedience. In doing so, *Queen Bee* defined a queen bee prototype that reflected an immediate postwar anxiety of incipient feminism that was to shape subsequent ecohorror depictions.

Following on from the matriarchal terror of *Queen Bee*, Daniel Petrie's *Sting of Death* is a forerunner of the killer bee films in the 1970s by monstrocizing the female force of the apiary. First adapted for the ABC TV series, *The Elgin Hour*, it is based on H. F. Heard's *A Taste for Honey* (1941), with the title alluding to 1 Corinthians 15:55–6: 'O death, where *is* thy sting? O grave, where *is* thy victory? The sting of death *is* sin; and the strength of sin *is* the law.' The implication is that the matriarchal beehive is an extension of sin with the power of the law over sin lying in the male domain. Heard's story is a reworking of Arthur Conan Doyle's short story, 'His Last Bow' (1917), when Holmes is living as a hermit in the Downs. The famous sleuth confesses to Dr Watson that the 'magnum opus' of his latter years is *The Practical Handbook of Bee Culture, with some Observations upon the Segregation of the Queen*: 'Behold the fruit of pensive nights and laborious days when I watched the little working gangs as once I watched the criminal world of London.'[27] In associating the industrious bee with the criminal world, Holmes criminalizes the apiary. Heard further weaponizes the bee by transforming the 'benign' apiarist type into a sadist who breeds a 'homicidal hive'.[28] In fact, Mycroft (played by Boris Karloff) suspects that Mr Hargrove (Martyn Great) will stop at nothing in using the evil mutation to satisfy his sadistic cravings. This is another modern, dystopian bee trope: the male beekeeper who masters the single-mindedness of the swarm. This is contrast to the bumbling Silchester (Robert

Hermyn) who fetishicizes the sweet honey that must be served fastidiously for breakfast every morning by his housekeeper.

The drama foregrounds the theme of male ownership over the honey-producing hive and the mythical duality of the bee: a sweetness that is consumed, capitalized and controlled for a sting that is deadly. As Maurice Maeterlinck states: 'Man may believe, if he chooses, that possessing the queen he holds in his hands the destiny and soul of the hive.'[29] It is a curious morality that men deploy the 'homicidal hive' against the female. Hargrove's first victim is his long-suffering, off-camera wife. In the 1966 British horror, *Deadly Bees* (Freddie Francis), which is loosely based on H. F. Heard's novel, the primal feminine force of the apiary is used to subjugate and terrorize women. As we shall see, the Africanized bee, too, is the monstrous result of a male desire to control the production levels of honey. However, Heard also hints towards a reversal of power in the gendering the bee, by alluding to the Actaeon myth and with reference to the death of the bee breeder: 'his bees caught him – like Actaeon [...] and his hounds'.[30] The suggestion is that the feminine social order of bees can turn against male ownership, and so the bee becomes a symbol of female vengeance.

If 1950s' sci-fi movies tended to monstrocize the queen insect and her social-organism, Sylvia Plath used the bee as a feminist symbol. Her 'bee poems' in *Ariel* (1962) – 'The Bee Meeting', 'The Arrival of the Bee Box', 'Stings' and 'Wintering' – can be seen as belonging to a tradition, starting with Gilman in the early 1900s, in which the queen bee is liberated from the discourse of male ownership. The implicit environmental concerns of Plath's poetry coincided with the 1960s' nascent eco-consciousness of Rachel Carson. And her 'bee poems' certainly, like Gilman's 'Bee-Wise' (1913) that presents 'swarming' as a gendered eco-model to be expanded, formed a general counter-narrative to a reactionary set of bee tropes that later crept into ecohorror films. Plath's bee poems, to some extent, are in response to her father's (Otto Plath's) entomological and invasive objectification of bee life, as recorded in his 1934 book *Bumblebees and Their Ways*. Otto frequently describes digging up nests or colonies of bees or experimentations that involved capturing and confining queen bees for the satisfaction of his entomological curiosity whilst bemoaning the 'vindictive' sting.[31] Together, Plath's six bee poems dramatize the transition, on the poet's part, from one of beekeeping initiation to that of psychological identification with the separatist, female polis of the beehive. It is in 'Stings' that Plath envisages the cosmic terror that can be potentially unleashed by the manhandled queen bee: 'Now she is flying / More terrible than she ever was, red / Scar in the sky, red comet / Over the engine that killed her – / The mausoleum, the wax house.'[32] The poem completes Plath's psychological transformation, in seeking total female liberation from the male drones and, by extension, the male keepers of bees.

Whereas *Queen Bee* established the femme fatale prototype of matriarchal bee terror, Plath's 'bee poems' foreshadowed the politics of ecofeminism that equated the liberation of women with the unleashed queen bee and her beehive. Perhaps the only American film of the 1970s that gets close to imagining a possible separatist dominion modelled on the bee polis is *Invasion of the Bee Girls* (1973). The film is a sharp parody of invasion hysteria, with allusions to *Invasion of the Body Snatchers* (Don Siegel, 1956) and its charged allegory of McCarthy Communist paranoia and dehumanizing, cloning conformity. A closer allusive context is Ira Levin's satirical novel, *The Stepford Wives* (1972), in which submissive and docile housewives in an idyllic Connecticut neighbourhood are cloned automatons of a Pygmalion dystopia: women embody the impossible ideal of male fantasy (sexualized and sanitized). *Invasion of the Bee Girls* also plays on the Frankenstein myth, with Dr Susan Harris (Anitra Ford) the equivalent to the real-life entomologist Warwick E. Kerr whose genetic experiment (crossbreeding honeybees from Europe and South Africa) led to the Africanized bee scare. Dr Susan Harris also reverses the power roles of Pygmalion and Galatea, and in turn the gender politics of the suburban community in *The Stepford Wives*, by metamorphosing ordinary housewives into a swarm of aggressively sexualized queen bees, who trapped in the insect's maternal cycle kill men through sexual exhaustion. Men, victims of predatory queen bees, play the role of drones that die when having mated with a fertile queen. The film ambiguously envisages the erotic fantasy of female promiscuity as well as the systematic assassination of the male species. The film ultimately conforms to a misogynistic allegory of ecohorror, in monstrocizing the gendered insect that by necessity must be destroyed.

But the film is also a throwback to the Pre-Code Hollywood films of sexually empowered and liberated women, whilst exploiting the gothic dimensions of the queen bee in the mould of the vampiress. Inverting the politics of the hunted queen bee is commensurate with the rape-revenge subgenre of 1970s' exploitation films. In one scene, a gang of men sexually assaults Julie Zorn (Victoria Vetri), the head librarian at the laboratory of the government-sponsored Brandt Research, and the local Sheriff Captain Peters comes to her rescue. The Sherriff also discovers that many of the firm's male leading scientists have reputations as 'sexual players'. Dr Harris when engaging in sexual intercourse kills Herb

Kline, who is disloyal to his devoted wife. In imitating the mating patterns of insects that kill the male, Dr Harris and the mutated women subvert the sexist logic of a patriarchal dominion. The insect social world offers an alternative order in which women can redress the predatory nature of the male species. The film inverts too the misogyny of the Pygmalion myth that, according to Irwin's *The Stepford Wives*, underwrites the domestic conformism of post-war America, by reworking the beekeeping procedure of 'supersedure'. As the queen ages, her pheromone output diminishes. The film interprets this to mean sexless housewives. A queen bee that becomes old will be replaced by the workers, which is forced by the beekeeper clipping one of the queen's middle or posterior legs. Unable to properly place her eggs at the bottom of the brood cells, the workers will kill the 'reigning' queen by 'balling' her: clustering tightly around her. The film frequently refers to the death of a male drone-scientist as 'balling' to imply a power reversal in the roles of beekeeper and queen bee. In one scene, Dr Harris transforms Kline's wife Nora into a Bee Girl through a controlled process of mutation through which she is cocooned in a chamber and enveloped by 'balling' bees. She emerges from the 'pupal' stage of metamorphosis to be bombarded with radiation before appearing with the black compound eyes of a mutated bee. In this respect, Dr Harris ambiguously plays the role of Plath's 'sweet God' that liberates the sanitized women, and 'balling', rather than meaning the demise of the aging queen (that Plath interpreted as a state of vulnerability in a male beekeeping culture), signals a process of gender radicalization.[33]

The film is a carnivalesque fantasy that temporarily empowers women at the expense of men, yet as such must give way to the status quo. Captain Peters rescues Julie just in time from being turned into a vamp-bee in the laboratory and Dr Harris's mutating machine is destroyed along with the feminist avenging bee. And to underscore the reversion to male mastery, the film closes with Captain Peters exerting sexual dominance in bed over the 'talkative' Julie as the camera moves to an erect and fecund flower. The final image asserts the message that Dr Harris and her matriarchal sci-fi beehive had messed with the natural order of sexual reproduction. And yet in a Bakhtinian sense, *Invasion of the Bee Girls* is a filmic example of dialogic literature, for we are left with the tantalizing sensation that the male dystopian canon of bee movies has failed to obliterate the alien voice of feminism.

The imagined haunting of a terrorizing bee is a recurring trope and is frequently conveyed via a sexual fantasy that is sometimes likened to the ecstasy of a male drone fertilizing the queen bee. In Herzog's *The Swarm*, the interweaving narrative thread of Henry David, a male beekeeper who reveres his bee stock, carries an implicit ecofeminist critique of the male apiarist type that is central to *A Taste for Honey*, and that also recalls the entomological colonialism of Plath's father, Otto Plath. Henry initially presumes that the bees 'were his slaves'. But unlike many beekeepers, Henry does not kill off his stock in the 'fall' to buy new bees in the spring. He also attributes a superior intelligence to the bee species: 'Bees were the exact opposite of people, David thought. People seemed to have no sense of the future of their race, but cared only for themselves and their immediate wants. Bees, on the other hand, cared for the future and nothing for themselves. Even stinging was altruistic: for a bee, to sting was to die.'[34] Henry comments too on the perishing of the male drone when mating with the queen as well as the bees' 'inbred respect for royalty' that forbade the individual act of stinging the aging queen: 'Instead, they chose a means of execution in which no single individual could be held responsible, like a firing squad. They balled her, clustering around her in such numbers that she was crushed or suffocated. She didn't fight to live; it was her job to die.'[35] Eventually, Henry takes the place of the 'balled' queen and is resigned to the fate that befalls the reigning queen: 'Henry David felt honoured, not betrayed. The bees reserved this rite for royalty. They were balling him, as they balled a queen.'[36] Significantly, the erotic-enwombing death wish of the beekeeper echoes the sadomasochism dramatized in *The Invasion of the Bee Girls*. And rather than the monstrous-feminine, that is symbolized as the *vagina-dentata* of the beehive in which the desired sweet honey is viciously protected, Henry adopts a female-centred identification with the hunted old queen.[37] Henry's point of view and ritual initiation into the social ways of the beehive somewhat mirror the deconstruction of the anthropocentric perspective in Plath's bee poems.

While *Invasion of the Bee Girls* had only threatened the overturning of a 'natural sexual order', *Killer Bees* (1974) is the first bee film in which the queen bee is not symbolically punished, thus echoing Gilman's 'Bee-Wise' in which a self-sufficient agrarian community is modelled on the matriarchal order of the beehive. *Killer Bees* is a made-for-TV film and directed by Curtis Harrington, famed for 'Batty Dame' films and who was a forerunner of 'New Queer Cinema' (queer-themed independent filmmaking of the late-1980s and-1990s). It is also co-written by Joyce and John Carrington who co-wrote, too, *The Omega Man* (1971). Gloria Swanson (the so-called Batty Dame) plays Madame Van Bohlen, a strong-willed grandmother-matriarch of a California family that operates a successful vineyard. Entirely filmed on location in California's Napa Valley, the camera frequently dwells on Van Bohlen's antebellum mansion to underscore the antiquated decadence of the Southern gothic. Swanson's matriarchal control over the males of the family and her wintering and nocturnally active bees clearly parallels the pheromone power of the queen bee and, in this respect, the film is a continuation of *Queen Bee*. The bees terrorize the local villagers and kill any unsuspecting male trespassers. The film's gothic horror owes much also to Alfred Hitchcock's *The Birds* (1963) and *Psycho* (1960), hence the Bernard Herrmann style score and more importantly the Oedipal complex theme that is signalled with the introduction of the pregnant Victoria Wells (Kate Jackson) into the household. The Oedipal drama reaches its climax when Madame Van Bohlen perishes following a heated verbal exchange with Victoria, the new fertile queen, who insists on a status of independence outside of the oppressive collectivism of the Bohlen family estate. The end of the ageing Dame/Queen is symbolically confirmed when it is revealed that her once loyal bees stung her, and the rival queen bee during Swanson's funeral is forced into the attic that contains brood cells. Victoria's initiation into the matriarchal beehive is a witty inversion of the vertical spatiality of the motel in *Psycho* – when the corpse of Norman's mother is discovered in the basement where, in Freudian terms, the primal Id resides. Victoria is now the head of the family, and this is affirmed when the fertilizing father (drone and once errant grandson of Madame) of the new fertile queen, after sipping from a glass of honey-based Bohlen wine, agrees to remain at the estate.

Killer Bees marries together aspects of the gothic and queer thinking, in suggesting that the beehive is a social model for an alternative productive household (or ecosystem), constructed in opposition to the 'straight' ideology of male agrarian stewardship. The title to the film, *Killer Bees*, is a misnomer in gesturing towards the killer bee genre of the 1970s, because rather than taming the primal threat that is in the hunted old queen bee, the film endorses the matriarchy of the bee polis. The success of the Bohlen's Californian wine industry is based on the special ingredient of sweet honey, and the bee's mythical 'sting of death' is harnessed for the benefit of female power. The film's eco-politics resonates with Plath's 'Wintering': 'The bees are all women, / Maids and the long royal lady. / They have got rid of the men, / The blunt, clumsy stumblers, the boors.'[38]

The racialization of the bee and eco-sadism

While previous bee movies had primarily exploited the gendered idea of the bee as female, Irwin Allen's *The Swarm* is more focused on the racialization of the bee. For rather than championing the feminist polis of the beehive, the film is more in keeping with the television film, *The Savage Bees* (Bruce Geller, 1976), and its 1978 sequel, *Terror Out of the Sky* (Lee H. Katzin), that make an explicit reference to Africanized bees, which are transported on a Brazilian banana boat to the shores of the United States. The film only touches on an ecological dilemma: destroying the invasive bees through the indiscriminate use of pesticides will disturb the delicate food chain that is dependent on bee pollination. This soon gives way to the emphasis on the bees as 'savage' and murderous, thus burying the ecological cautionary warning. The film plays on an Ovidian grotesquery in that the consumption of bees via balling is totemic revenge for excessive human consumption of food. It is discovered, during an autopsy, that a farmer's stomach contains bees. The story happens during the 'Mardi Gras' festival of New Orleans, a carnival also known as 'Fat Tuesday' which occurs before the ritual fasting of the Lenten season. The bees act out the dark carnivalesque when the festival revellers are attacked by the swarm. But any possibility of feminist liberation is suppressed in the finale, when Jeannie Devereux (Gretchen Corbett) is trapped in a red Volkswagen Beetle by an engulfing swarm. She is allied with the male beekeeping fraternity and balling is a means of enwombing her back into the matriarchal fold of the beehive. However, the bees are immobilized in an operation performed by men who occupy a position equivalent to that of Otto Emil Plath – the 'surgeon' of beehives.[39] In the sequel, *Terror Out of the Sky*, Jeannie (Tovah Feldshuh), a principal entomologist, is still haunted by the memory of the bees. Liberation from the discourse of androcentric dualism that underwrites the persecution of the queen bee is overturned by the combined might of military power and male-centric entomological manipulation. In other words, the gender-symbol potential of the bee is violently suppressed.

Similarly, *The Swarm* stages an archetypal Darwinian face-off (a competition between evolving species) with the invading swarm deemed a super-organism (obedient to a collective will) as well as a supra-rational force that exceeds the destructive power of modern warfare: 'It's damn hard to believe that insects have accomplished what nothing in the world could've done, except germ warfare or a neutron bomb: neutralize an ICBM site.' The film rekindles the science-military duel of big bug features through the bee annihilator, General Thaddeus Slater (Richard Widmark) and the sunflower seed-eating Dr Bradford Crane (Michael Caine). Whereas the sentimental Crane recognizes the worth of the honeybee, the military-minded Slater attributes mind-like intentionality, thus echoing the social-colonial dimensions of H. G. Wells' 'Empire of the Ants' (1905) – for the bees are also an evolved collective intelligence.

Herzog had lived in the shadow of nuclear war and his support for nuclear disarmament is reflected in the publication of *The War Peace Establishment* (1969). Generally, in nuclear holocaust films, for example, *Panic in Year Zero!* (Ray Milland, 1962), that dramatize a social breakdown to a Hobbesian 'state of nature', the gender binaries of the Western genre are reinstated: women carry out the domestic duties of the cave-man habitat and men revert to the rough law of the gun to protect the sexual honour of their female folk. But in *The Swarm*, nuclear holocaust is replaced by the avenging feminine force of nature and the full armature of the American military is emasculated by what Crane eventually identifies as a hive mind led by a 'young queen'. In this sense, the swarming bees echo the apocalyptic imagery of Plath's liberated honey-machine. Existential grief is writ large in the film, and towering figures of American masculinity are, through human loss, reduced to pitiful figures. In a poignant scene, Jud Hawkins (Slim Pickens), a country bumpkin, angrily demands to see the body of his son killed by the bees in the missile base: 'Hawkins: "Oh, God! No!" Military personnel: "I'm afraid you can't take him, Mr. Hawkins." Hawkins: "The only way you can stop me is to shoot me, and I'd thank you if you would."' Hawkins's determination to embrace a toxic body and to take charge of the burial echoes the attempts of Antigone (the daughter of Oedipus) to secure a respectable burial for her dead brother, Polynice, in Sophocles's *Antigone*. Putting the father in this role is a way of highlighting the relationship between human loss and the male domination of nature as well as dramatizes the feminization of male attitudes. This scene parallels that of Helena Anderson (Katharine Ross), who is grief-stricken by the death of a boy, Paul, the only survivor of the Durant family attacked by bees. Before dying, Paul lies delirious in a hospital bed, terrorized by a nightmarish giant bee. Helena's existential questioning speaks of a painful human condition: 'Why this one? In the whole damn world, why this boy? My God, Brad. What good is all that science? All that equipment at the base? All those doctors?' The giant bee that terrorizes the human psyche, while derivative of B-movie gigantism, is a symbol of a Darwinian fight to the death that causes innocent suffering. Grief is anthropocentric and the film does not promote inherent worth of all living beings regardless of their instrumental utility.[40] Unlike the film *Orca* that depicts animal pain and suffering, the bee swarm is a homogenous plague. Any suggestion of environmental ethics is only voiced through a perpetually angry, Michael Caine.

While the use of animals as social symbols undermines the status of actual animalness, and hence removes environmental considerations, the pollution or abuse of nature is often used as a synecdoche assuming a wider social struggle between genders, class or ethnic groups. By 1978, the association of the bee scare with migratory hysteria had become a source for mockery. 'The Killer Bee' skit turns the bees into Mexicans. In Herzog's novel, the media-driven, invasion scare story is undercut via a national mood of racial guilt: 'They say the bees were sent by God, who's black, to punish America for its selfishness.'[41] Ecohorror often uses a non-human threat as a stand-in for ideological terror, as exemplified in *Them!* that was released during the McCarthy 'Second Red Scare' era. *Them!* is very much dependent on the insect tropes inherited from H. G. Wells's short story, 'Empire of the Ants' (1905), which speaks of the precarious dominion of *Homo sapiens* on Earth as well as colonial anxieties: 'an alien threat lurking with Europe's colonized, supposedly domesticated nature.'[42] As Charlotte Sleigh points out, the 'machine-like qualities' of ants have meant that they are often seen as 'close relatives' of bees.[43] The beehive is a stand-in for an industrialized workforce. Given the racialization of the bees and that the setting of the film is Texas, a state that had witnessed slavery on an industrial scale, the 'killer-bee farrago' can be read according to 'reverse colonialism' that was being played out in an era of race-conscious films.

Early examples of reverse colonialist narratives came in the form of late-Victorian invasion literature, such as H. G. Wells's *War of the Worlds* (1898), which was adapted into an American science fiction film in 1953, one that projected anti-communist paranoia. While certain narratives of reverse colonization can be seen as paranoid texts through the brutal suppression of the avenging creature, other narratives, such as *Planet of the Apes* (Franklin J. Schaffner, 1968), defamiliarize notions of speciesism by imagining what it is like to be the hunted prey (analogous to the colonized or dehumanized slave) rather than the colonizer (i.e., the hunter or slave owner). According to Stephen D. Arata, 'reverse colonialism' is exemplified also in Bram Stoker's 1897 novel, *Dracula*, in which the racial Other in a monstrous form invades the colonial nation, and, in effect, reflects a sense of racial guilt and anxiety.[44] In the pioneering blaxploitation film, *Blacula* (William Crain, 1972), vampirism is an extended metaphor of slavery's legacy. Prince Mamuwalde, who in 1780 appealed to Count Dracula to help in the suppressing of the slave trade, was once the ruler of the Albani African nation. Dracula, a white racist, transforms Mamuwalde into the vampire, Blacula, and in 1972, when the coffin of Blacula is unwittingly purchased and transported to the modern city of Los Angeles, he is freed. However, the curse of the undead means that Blacula will forever thirst for blood, and he indiscriminately preys upon the citizens of L.A., thus further spreading the curse of Dracula. Arata argues that reverse colonization holds a mirror up to the monstrosity of a culture's imperial ideology, and, in this sense, the Dracula curse is for Black Americans to be continually enslaved by racial stereotypes: creatures of the night (i.e., bats) and the dark arts/the occult. The sequel, *Scream, Blacula, Scream!* (Bob Kelljan, 1973), expands upon the film's subtext, and this time Blacula hates being a vampire for he recognizes that the curse means to enslave others.[45] The curse of vampirism also constitutes a double identity (the undead: neither living nor dead), and by analogy Prince Mamuwalde has lost his original indigenous identity and is now a crossbreed of white racist and African prince.

The Swarm was produced in the mould of reverse colonialism, invoking parallels to the Cold war paranoia of sci-fi movies, while also responding to the Africanized bee scare as a racialized invasion narrative. On first contact with the swarm, which has attacked a military complex, a helicopter pilot identifies, at first, what appears to be: 'A black mass. A moving black mass!' (Figure 7.1). Sylvia Plath had likened the boxed African bees to a maniacal 'Roman mob', suggesting repressed anger and a potential uprising.[46] She also describes the African bee in racial terms: 'Black on black, angrily clambering.'[47] Given the racial synecdoche of the 'Africanized' bee, 'black mass' invokes the idea of Pan African nationalism

Figure 7.1 The helicopter pilot (Steve Marlo) identifies 'a moving black mass'.

that was associated with blaxploitation cinema and the Black power movement. Of course, homogenizing a continent of people as a Black swarm is problematic, but it is in keeping with the allegorical nature of ecohorror. The invading bees are never referred to as 'Africanized' but according to either the singular, 'African', or the plural, 'Africans'. Crane also insists on 'Africans' rather than 'Brazilians', and he gives a distorted entomological account of the species, neglecting to mention the European strain: 'a mutant species of the original African killer bee'. Reverse colonialism is further implied when he states that the African attack is the 'first alien force' to invade America. The Southern state setting of Texas also gives credence to the analogy of avenging Black slaves and the 'black mass' of invading bees. African slaves were shipped to the Southern states – approximately 4 million before the abolition of slavery – and this figure was invoked in terms of the mass size of the swarm. 'Swarming bees' also referred to fleeing black slaves.[48] Slavery greatly contributed to the agrarian economy of Texas, and, following the Texas Revolution that ended in 1836, the state became an independent republic protecting the right to own slaves. In antebellum Texas, slavery grew even more rapidly. 'The census of 1850 reported 58,161 slaves, 27.4 percent of the 212,592 people in Texas, and the census of 1860 enumerated 182,566 slaves, 30.2 percent of the total population. Slaves were increasing faster than the population as a whole.'[49] The parallel between the bees as industrious pollinators of the crops (the honey-machine) and Black slaves as sustaining the antebellum agriculture is later depicted in the novel by Sue Monk Kidd, *The Secret Lives of Bees* (2001), that is set against the backdrop of the Civil Rights Movement and the legacy of slavery and segregation in the South – the label on the jars of honey bears the image of the Black Madonna.[50]

The location of Marysville (a small town 3 miles from the Texas-Oklahoma border), associated with the Old West pastoralism and the Western theme of the besieged small town, is the ideal setting to capture the 'black providential vengeance' of Herzog's novel. *Buck and the Preacher*, directed by the so-called integrationist Sidney Poitier and released in the same year as *Blacula* (the apex of blaxploitation craze) and the 'soul Western', *The Legend of Nigger Charley* (Martin Goldman), dramatized the retributive justice of Black action heroes against the continued violence of plantation owners in a post-Civil War period. When Marysville is attacked by the swarm, a news reporter (Lee Grant) invokes the language of guerilla warfare: 'I'm reporting from Marysville. The swarm left a devastated community. The town is reeling from the vicious raid that left many of their friends dead. The town was preparing for its Flower Festival.' It is perhaps, therefore, no coincidence that many of the all-white cast share an affinity with the Western genre: Richard Widmark had had various support roles in Western films; Ben Johnson was once a world champion rodeo cowboy; Slims Perkens had been an American rodeo performer; Henry Fonda was famed for starring in John Ford films; and Olivia de Havilland once played Mrs Custer in *They Died with their Boots on* (Raoul Walsh, 1941) that depicts General Custer's 'last stand'. One could read the death of Maureen (Olivia de Havilland), along with her two suitors (Ben Johnson and Fred MacMurray), as the purging of an ageing Hollywood system. Cameron Mitchell (the actor who played General Thompson) saw them as forming 'the geriatric love story'.[51] The death of de Havilland is on a par with Charlton Heston's fall from grace in *Earthquake* (1974). But the melodrama of two elderly bachelors (retiree Felix Austin and town Mayor Clarence Tuttle) vying for the marital status of a maternal schoolmistress (childless, Maureen who nonetheless adores her school children) mirrors the beehive polis: male drones vying for fertility rites with an ageing queen. The presence of de Havilland, a surviving star from the Golden Age of Hollywood, recalls that of Gloria Swanson as the 'batty Dame' in *Killer Bees*. And in the blaxploitation crime comedy, *Dolemite* (D'Urville Martin, 1975) and the sequel, *The Human Tornado* (Cliff Roquemore, 1976), 'Queen Bee' is the character name for Lady Reed, signifying the repositioning of the 'mammy' figure. Maureen, therefore, is marked prey, because as a surrogate mother she is the white mammy rival to the queen bee, the mother of a 'black mass' of bees (Figure 7.2). Maureen is also the worshipped matriarchal figurehead in the *classicus locus* of white supremacy, and a misrecognised symbol of infertility in a town that is about to celebrate a flower festival.

Figure 7.2 Maureen (Olivia de Havilland) looks on in horror at her school children who have been killed by a swarm of bees during a flower festival.

Another apposite setting for the staging of reverse colonialism is Houston, which becomes the apocalyptic terminus in the film. In the novel, New York is the climatic site for the final Darwinian face-off but is dethroned by Houston, the setting for three earlier '70s' dystopian sci-fi films: *Rollerball* (Norman Jewison, 1975), *Logan's Run* (Michael Anderson, 1976) and *Futureworld* (Richard T, Heffron, 1976). In 1973, the Arab oil embargo had caused the demand for Texas oil to boom and for people from the 'Rust Belt' states to migrate to Houston for jobs. Mexicans during this period also migrated to areas of petrochemical industries – in particular, Houston. From 1963 to 1980, a sky-scraping boom occurred in Houston and thirty-eight of its tallest buildings were built in the 1970s, such as One Shell Plaza. The Nuclear Generating Station began to be constructed from 1975 and NASA's Johnson Space Center and Mission Control Center are in Houston. As the industrial powerbase of Texas and the 'Space City', Houston heightens the dramatic battle between the modern forces of scientific industry and avenging nature. Given its established associations with economic migration and might, and dystopian futurism, Houston lends itself to the return of the repressed in terms of 'alienated labour'.[52] The beehive is the monstrous other, 'untamed and unfettered' nature revolting against the enslaving creator and oppressor signified through the film's colonial settings and white cast.[53]

According to John Sutherland, the narrative of ecohorror invariably leads to the closure of what he termed 'eco-sadism', when audiences take gratification from the 'justified slaughter of wild things'.[54] In this respect, ecohorror is deemed harmful in re-articulating the 'inherent violence of western thought' and by necessitating the suffering of animals to reimpose Anthropocene domination.[55] This is certainly the case in the film version of Herzog's novel. After dropping eco-friendly bombs on the bees, the invasive threat is officially handled as a military matter. General Slater: 'I've been authorized by the president to close down your operation. From now on, the war against the bees will be under military direction the way it should've been from the first.' After destroying a nuclear power plant, the gathering black mass of bees engulfs the city of Houston. Military personnel with flame-throwers conflagrate the bees and Houston becomes a firestorm. Crane then analyses tapes from the original bee invasion and concludes that their alarm system attracted the swarm into the base:

> Crane: What you are hearing is the African bee's mating sound. But listen. This was made by the alarm system, not the bees. But they sound alike. The alarm system at the missile base drew them in. The similarity confused them. When it

stopped, they left. [...] The sonic alarm system happens to be an exact duplicate of the duet between the queen and the young queen challenging her.'

It is only at this point that an explicit reference is made to the matriarchal order of the bee polis. But the identification of a matriarchal social order is the means towards reasserting the anthropocentric order. Sound floats, which imitate the mating call of a rival queen bee, lure the swarm of bees to an oil slick that has been spread across the Gulf of Mexico. The air force is called in to set alight the oil slick and to annihilate the bees by an all-consuming ball of fire (Figure 7.3). The bees are destroyed according to a symbolic punishment that reaffirms the petrochemical industrial might of Texas: the oil slick spread across the Gulf of Mexico is a pollution trace. The ending points back towards *Them!* when the queen ant and her hatchlings in the vast storm-drain system under Los Angeles are destroyed by flamethrowers. In this sense, the violent destruction of a feminine force of nature resonates with other films released in 1978, such as Randal Kleiser's *Grease*, in which women are a 'throwback to the 1950s, preceding the arrival of feminism in the later 1960s'.[56] Given its mandatory closure, *The Swarm* is a throwback to *Queen Bee*, preceding the arrival of ecofeminism in literary utopias.

However, the obliteration of the swarm and the restoration of a social order, which also recalls *Jaws*, are contrary, as in the screen adaptation of *Orca*, to Herzog's intended closure. In the novel, a carpet of bees has descended upon New York and the human populace await its tragic fate: 'The first change noted by John Wood, covered with sweat and sitting morosely in the dark, unbearably hot living room, was the silence. He had become accustomed to the constant

Figure 7.3 Eco-sadism.

rattle of bees striking the windowpanes that the sudden quiet startled him.'[57] The scene of impending doom echoes *The War of the Worlds* (Byron Haskin, 1953), when global Martian victory appears nigh and praying survivors take refuge in the deserted city of Los Angeles. Yet, unexpectedly, the swarm of bees ascends, overflies the Empire State Building and the World Trade Center and flies out into the ocean where they drown themselves. During the next annual meeting of the American Entomological Association there are various speculative theories as to the suicidal 'fate of the enemy'.[58] But the main body of opinion holds that the bees were suffering from a 'virus-induced genetic defect' that had been planted in factory-bred queens who had mated with African drones: 'this gene, carrying its message to the Africans, dictated negative survival, meaning death. It had affected the African elite, which had led the bees to race suicide'.[59] This overt race language is not so evident in the film. Nonetheless, Herzog leaves the reader with a note of mystery that conveys eco-respect for the non-human otherness of the bees: 'People demand answers, and Krim's answer was the best they had. But, Wood said, smiling grimly in the darkness, perhaps science had no answer.'[60] The Hollywood closure reveals a regressive ideology, one that encloses 'nature'. The open-ended closure of Herzog's novel, on the other hand, underlines a more meaningful understanding of the ontological gap between the human and the natural order.[61] Herzog's eco-tragedy could be that the blind suicidal will of the bee super-organism is a metaphor for a destructive drive of human history.[62] The swarm symbolizes human monstrosity and an instrumentalist treatment of the non-human. After all, the Africanized bee was a Frankenstein monster, the product of a foolhardy scientific experiment that hoped to bypass the intractable laws of nature. Herzog suggest that the bees may one day return, and so the novel is a wake-up call to future eco-disasters. For the bee is vital to an ecosystem and human self-preservation.

Conclusion

Although the film clearly draws on the novel's set of inherited gendered and racial bee-tropes, *The Swarm* neither coheres as an ecofeminist nor as a reverse colonial allegory. Herzog's concern for humanity's meddling in the natural order is side-lined and the film reverts to the militaristic apocalypticism established in the big bug features of the fifties, with the maniacal bee returned to the beekeeper's box. Ecohorror, in ultimately gratifying a lust for destruction, is rarely a balanced hybridic genre and is generally a flawed expression of post-Carson environmentalism. Counter-examples include *Phase IV* (Saul Bass, 1974), which concludes with a vision of inter-species regeneration, and *Silent Running* (Douglas Trumbull, 1972), in which a forest greenhouse in deep space is saved at the expense of the crewmen, including Freeman Lowell (Bruce Dern). Both imply that humanity and non-human nature, as it is, cannot harmoniously co-exist. *The Swarm* also affirms the inherent violence of mankind and modernity by not imaginatively transcending anthropocentric apocalypticism. It goes without saying, the film is at odds with the ecofeminism of the 1970s that 'paired the liberation of women with the restoration of the natural environment'.[63] Potential disaster, as Herzog's novel suggests, looms on the horizon. Perhaps this is because the agency of disaster lies elsewhere and within?

8

The destructive gaze: *The Medusa Touch* (1978)

It might appear odd to end with a film that has been classified as British horror.¹ Released in 1978, directed by Jack Gold (a British director) and based on a 1973 novel by Peter Van Greenaway (a British author), *The Medusa Touch*, though, was distributed by Warner Brothers Pictures, with the screenplay by the American writer, Richard John Briley, and co-starred the American actress Lee Remick, as the psychiatrist Dr Zonfeld, who also appeared in the American-British supernatural horror, *The Omen* (Richard Donner, 1976). *The Medusa Touch* is a trans-Atlantic, end-of-the-decade subgenre (merging horror and disaster) response to the cycle. The American connection is signalled during the opening when the reclusive novelist, John Morlar (Richard Burton), is watching a television news broadcast concerning American astronauts trapped in orbit around the moon (Achilles Six – a mission to inaugurate man's first permanent station on the moon). It is an allusion to Space Race disasters, such as Apollo 1 (27 January 1967) in which the three crew members were killed, and it later becomes apparent that Morlar had psychologically willed the disaster of Achilles Six along with other disasters, such as the downing of a Boeing 747 that crashes into a London office tower. Morlar forces Zonfeld to witness the event to demonstrate the destructive powers of his psychokinetic abilities. He insists that during his childhood he willed, too, the sudden deaths of people he disliked: bickering parents and a boorish Schoolmaster. As Morlar says: 'I have a gift for disaster.' Morlar appears to be modelled on Damien Thorn, the anti-Christ child, but he is not 'an evil man'.²

This is despite Morlar taking revenge against God-spouting persecutors. Morlar, bed-ridden with measles and terrorized by a 'priest ridden' Irish nanny, prays: 'Dear Lucifer, let her burn in hellfire as you're burning me.' But the nanny also invokes fire and brimstone wrath: 'But Lucifer did not triumph for the Lord is mighty and terrible and, in his wrath, he poured his fury out like fire, tormenting

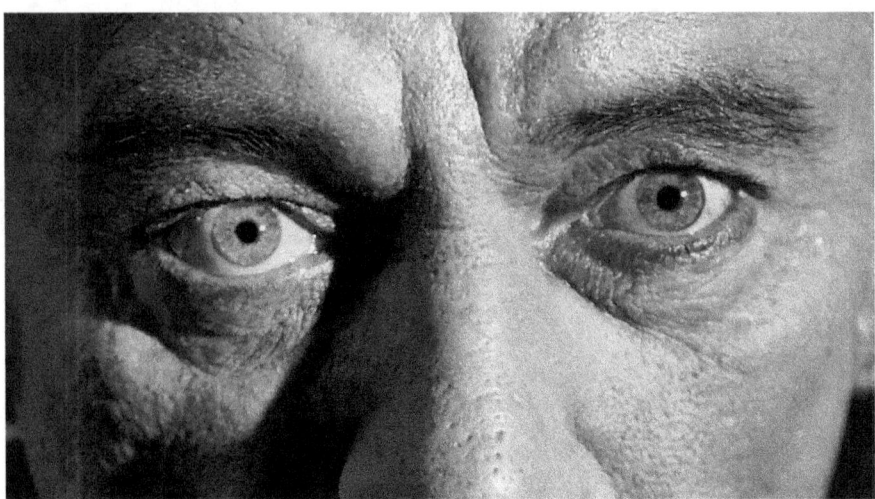

Figure 8.1 Richard Burton as Dr Morlar.

the wanton, searing the flesh of those who dwelled in iniquity.' Morlar appears to harness Satanic powers, but in adulthood confesses to not believing in the existence of Lucifer, let alone God. Nonetheless, Morlar's gift for disaster as an act of vengeance is fuelled by a moral disgust that echoes the divine retribution of social justice prophets, such as Amos: '[…] let justice roll down like waters, / and righteousness like an ever-flowing stream.'[3] Practising as a Barrister, Morlar expresses a hatred of the British establishment, and in a courtroom defence speech he pours scorn upon institutions (such as the Imperial War Museum) that revel in a history of warfare and mass destruction:

> We are supposed to be civilised, yet we do shove innocence into that chamber of horrors, stuffed with pain, mutilation and death and say: 'This is what put the great in England'. But where in that asylum of grotesques do we find framed the armament manufacturer's cheque book, together with Grandpa's pathetic medal and his artificial leg? […] It is not the Defendant who should be on trial here, but a besotted establishment who can cheerfully send a generation to slaughter in the name of war.

Later, Morlar also condemns the Space Race that diverts wealth from good causes, such as helping the poor and the destitute. Zonfeld is initially convinced Morlar is 'deluded', and Morlar's novels reveal a preoccupation with divine revelations of disaster that are simultaneously psychological manifestations: 'The walls of Jericho fell to the power of thought.'

Eventually, Zonfeld realizes that Morlar possesses destructive mental powers, and she bludgeons him (seemingly) to death with a statue of Napoleon. Morlar's mind, though, is indestructible. From his hospital bed he brings down a cathedral on the 'unworthy heads' of a VIP congregation attending a fundraising event for the crumbling building's restoration. Man is serving the wrong kind of divinity. When a detective, Monsieur Brunel (Lino Ventura), discovers a scrapbook of newspaper cuttings, Morlar's motives are tied to a preoccupation with modern disaster of various kinds: 'Floods, tornadoes, earthquakes, massacres, riots, killings, air crashes, famine ... nothing but disaster.' Brunel recognizes that Morlar's morbid fixation is a revelation of the continual excess of disaster: 'when you see them collected like this, you realize how much disaster we live with. [...] there's no end to disaster'. Humanity abides in disaster. Humanity is defined by disaster.

Zonfeld now believes Morlar is to blame for the disasters. But pathology and telekinesis are red herrings. The film's title, *The Medusa Touch*, a play on two Ovidian tales – the Midas touch and the Medusa gaze – implies that the agency of destruction lies in a mytheme that runs across time. Morlar condemns institutional religion because it simultaneously conceals and co-opts what is consistently told in Ovidian tales. When King Midas is granted a choice of anything he wants from Bacchus, everything he touches is transformed into gold: 'A happy man, / He watched his servants set a table before him / With bread and meat. He touched the gift of Ceres / And found it stiff and hard; he tried to bite / The meat with hungry teeth, and where the teeth / Touched food they seemed to touch on golden ingots.'[4] The gift was a bane. Humanity is cursed by its own selfish desires. Morlar's gift is a curse that surpasses Medusa's destructive weapon of terror, and he is the disaster man because he acts out the Freudian flipside of Eros – Thanatos – that drives human evolution, as Morlar explains to Zonfeld in the novel: 'Civilisation [...] is an artifice devised to cover up unpalatable truths.'[5] The unpalatable truth is that humanity is given to destruction in various forms (war, the Holocaust, the crucifixion of Christ etc.), and Morlar turns this tragic view into an agenda. He is a more horrific variation on Tod in *The Day of the Locust* (John Schlesinger, 1975), for, rather than embodying the poisoned imagination of cinematic apocalypticism, Morlar embodies the death drive that is inscribed into high modernity and its superstructural fault lines. Morlar is a throwback to the retributive logic of biblical epics yet upholds a mythico-religious interpretation of humanity's standing in the world. For Medusa is a 'metaphor for humanity's fear of encountering its own dark deeds'.[6] Morlar reverses the demonized gaze, like the camera that turns against the diegetic spectator in the big arena spectacles of *Two-minute Warning* (Larry Peerce, 1976) and *Black Sunday* (John Frankenheimer, 1977). So, Morlar is only evil in being the diabolical mirror image of what is deeply set inside the human psyche, which is also both indestructible and destructive.

The Fury (1978)

The Medusa Touch was released in the year that horror or supernatural films about telekinesis came to the fore, including *The Fury* (Brian De Palma, 1978) and *The Initiation of Sarah* (Robert Day, 1978) – a made-for-TV movie (aired 2 February on ABC). All three films are derivative of *Carrie* (Brian De Palma, 1976) in which Carrie White (Sissy Spacek), a persecuted social outcast, uses telekinesis to exact revenge. *The Fury* is exemplary in terms of the return of the Lacanian gaze when in the final scene Gillian (Amy Irving), who embodies the mythological fury of Medusa, turns Childress (John Cassavetes) into a cursed tragic figure (*à la* Oedipus Rex or King Lear) with blinded, bleeding eyes. The alluring, abusive law of the father is dispossessed of its possessive look:

> Childress: You'll begin by putting all the tragedies behind you. I think that'll be easier if you accept my help. All the bad things you heard about me aren't true. I'm not a bad man. All I want is for you to trust me. Time will take care of the hurting. That's the simple truth. Tears are good. Don't be afraid of crying. Tears are just what we need right now. I'll be a good father to you, Gillian. You can depend on that.

The sightless Childress shouts, 'Where are you?!', and Gillian damns him, 'You go to hell!', and Childress explodes.

The Fury is not a disaster movie, but like *Medusa* it comments on the political state's misappropriation of the sacred for destructive means. In one telling scene when Dr Jim McKeever (Charles Dunning) and Dr Ellen Lindstrom (Carol Eve Rossen) converse on the possibilities of research into telekinetic powers, McKeever acknowledges the inability of a modern society to assimilate the potential benefits of a mythico-religious force:

> Ellie, even the most backward tribes, the most primitive cultures on earth would welcome the birth of a Robin Sandza. And in time, he'd become their magician,

their prophet, their great healer. But there is no place for these kids in our culture. Because they're so superior to what we hold sacred. And what a culture can't assimilate it destroys.

Instead, the objective of the government is to exploit both Robin (Andrew Stevens) and Gillian as a state weapon: 'Childress: "How's our boy wonder?" Doctor: "Those films of his father's death have an unleashed an incredible emotional force. Why he's developing the power of an atomic reactor". Dr Susan Charles (Fiona Lewis): "Or an atomic bomb". Disaster movies convey the horror at the heart of modern superstructures, and horror movies depict the horror inherent in human nature. However, when Robin causes mass murder at an indoor amusement park, the two genres blur.

It is telling that Gillian gently kisses the eyes of Childress, before unleashing the retributive power of telekinesis. She plays the mother to a man who desperately seeks, but ultimately lacks, control of a person who he treats as a child (hence 'Childress'). Echoing Sigmund Freud's essay, 'The Uncanny' (1919), and its interpretation of E. T. A. Hoffmann's short story, *The Sandman* (1816), in which a bogey man causes the eyes of sleeping children to bleed, Childress's eyes can be read as part of the psychodrama of male-oedipal mastery. Robin also rejects his biological father when he scratches the face of Peter Sandza (Kirk Douglas) before falling to his death. To covet the power of telekinesis is to desire the destructive power of human nature. In Freudian and Lacanian analysis, the eyes and the phallus are linked – an 'anxiety about one's eyes, the fear of going blind, is often enough a substitute for the dread of being castrated'.[7] Through bodily mutilation, Gillian castrates Childress and he is dispossessed of oedipal mastery. What makes *Medusa* so poignant is that Morlar possesses a Medusa fury that is aligned to the vengeful female gaze, thus complicating the male-centred spectacle of apocalypticism. It is a gaze that stares directly back into the camera and into the viewer's eyes. Morlar returns the cinematic gaze of horror. As film critics have acknowledged, Laura Mulvey's critique of the objectifying camera draws on Jacque Lacan's concept of the gaze – when the object of our look 'reflects our own nothingness'.[8] Lacan refers to this as the 'evil eye of the gaze' which has the 'effect of arresting movement, and, literally, of killing life'.[9] In other words, Morlar acts out the destructive gaze of the audience who *will* disaster via the spectacular.

This relates to what Susan Sontag regards as 'the unassimilable terrors', which is a significant caveat to what Nick Roddick sees as the purging function of the genre. The restorative closure of the disaster movie does not necessarily mean a 'getting back to normal'.[10] Like the terrors that infect the psyche, there are also terrors of modernity, to echo Ryan and Kellner, that cannot be closed off and that will inevitably be reopened.[11] While *Airport* (1970) contained the potential threat in the form of domestic and international skyjackings, *Skyjacked* (1972) re-enacted the cautionary tale: 'unless something is done *now*, disaster will ensue'.[12] *The Towering Inferno* (John Guillermin, 1974) and *Black Sunday* are cinematic rehearsals of 9/11, when the real – either the precarity of superstructures and international terrorism – breaks through the 'protective shield' of the spectacle.[13] Unlike fantasy spectacles, disaster movies remind us that 'history, far from being one of steady progress, is in fact an incremental accumulation of crashes' and disasters.[14] They expose the hubristic faith in the technology of high modernity, when 'the advances of civilisation are found to be fragile and dangerous'.[15] But they also convey the cyclical nature of disaster that is written into human nature – for Morlar's gaze is suggestive of a timeless mythico-religious force that we choose to forget.

The disaster movie is an essentially earthbound form, operating within the realm of the possible, though it would be foolhardy to bifurcate in terms of a secular or religious perspective.[16] Biblical tropes consistently feed into the symbolic fall of high modernity and its multiple sites. Cecil Be DeMille's *The Ten Commandments* (1956) is exemplary of Hollywood's ideological invocation of Old Testament divine terror to defend the righteous (the Hebrews and the Christian democratic-West) and to punish the ungodly (the Egyptians and the Communist atheist East). In *The Poseidon Adventure* (Ronald Neame, 1972), the ocean liner and the righteous logic of retribution is turned upside down. Yet despite the iconoclasm of the cycle, *The Swarm* (Irwin Allen, 1978) invokes plagues of locusts and *Inferno* invokes the Tower of Babel to frame a schema of damnation. John Martin's *The Great Day of His Wrath* (1851) informs the epic-scale of destruction in *Earthquake* (Mark Robson, 1974): 'The scenes of carnage are big blowouts dissociated from pain – spectacles for the audience to gasp in awe (as if we are staring into a John Martin painting).'[17] Apocalypticism has underwritten cinematic moralism for decades. In *The King of Kings* (Cecil B. DeMille, 1927), the mockers of Christ tumble into the abyss when Matthew 27:51 is cited in the intertitle: 'And the earth quaked – and the rocks were rent.' In the 1923 version of *The Ten Commandments* (Cecil B. DeMille), Danny (the wayward son and architect), ignores the 'Ten Commandments' and uses cheap materials to build a towering church that collapses onto his mother. His brother, the Christ-like carpenter, instead follows the social gospel of forgiveness and even aids a Mary Magdalene type. The symbolic punishment of Danny (the irresponsible capitalist) very much foreshadows *Inferno*.

The didactic point is no matter how modern one is, the reckoning is in the present tense. In *Deluge* (Felix E. Feist, 1933), the metropolis of New York is hit by a huge tidal wave (of biblical proportions) cleansing America of decadent high capitalism. The subsequent wasteland regression visually parallels the Dustbowl disaster. The symbolic fall of high modernity has been played out in numerous films, reflecting the ephemeral nature and dark romance of America's power: 'Look on my Works, ye Mighty, and despair! / Nothing beside remains. Round the decay / Of that colossal Wreck, boundless and bare / The lone and level sands stretch far away.'[18] And yet, the blind spot remains in a way that relates to Andy Warhol's *Death and Disaster* series (1962–4): modern tragedy is high-impact banality.[19] And the *schadenfreude* effect gained in watching bad capitalists being ritually damned is integral to the symbolic order. Hence the existential paralysis (or the sense of deterministic fate) at the heart of high modernity and its 'hyper-rational organizations'.[20] Disaster movies are a counter to optimistic humanism by exulting in the darker visions of high capitalism. And yet, contemporary disaster movies in a delusional way salvage human agency by recycling the elective theology of biblical epics in which WASP families are saved from earth-shattering apocalypticism. There are no indigenous people of Greenland in the nuclear bunker built in Greenland in the film called *Greenland* (Ric Roman Waugh, 2020). Who is saved is still predicated on ideas of the family, to imply the promise of continued human existence. Some films, such as *Elysium* (Neill Blomkamp, 2013), address the geopolitics of Neo-Malthusian predictions, and *2012* (Roland Emmerich, 2009) questions the selection process (via dramatic asides), though the ark is ultimately reserved for a fleeing American family. To echo Fredric Jameson, Slavoj Žižek, and Mark Fisher: it is easier to imagine humanity's oblivion but not your own.[21] The Medusa gaze is a poignant reminder that disaster is about us, within us and is happening NOW!

Conclusion

The Medusa Touch brings disaster within the purview of the individual psyche, implicating the Lacanian gaze in terms of cinematic spectatorship. In this respect, the film is a continuation of *Black Sunday* and Michael Lander's desire to return the cinematic gaze of horror, thus bringing the spectated violence of the 1970s into people's cosy lives. The indictment is that the spectator is not a mere passive witness to disaster. John Morlar, who is seen at the start of the movie glued to the television, interpellates morbid curiosity as a ritualized activity. The destructive threat does not derive from a disgruntled outsider (a defeated man in his fifties) nor modernity itself, for instance: a nuclear power plant – see *The China Syndrome* (Jeff Bridges, 1979), or a super machine-gone-rogue – see *Colossus: The Forbin Project* (Joseph Sargent, 1970). Neither is it a deadly organism of extra-terrestrial origin nor other non-human life forms as depicted in *The Andromeda Strain* (Robert Wise, 1971) and *Invasion of the Body Snatchers* (Philip Kaufman, 1978). The destructive source is unfamiliar and all too familiar. *The Medusa Touch* also indirectly comments on the cycle's sacrificial figures. Morlar cannot be sacrificed, for he embodies the indestructible force within the cyclical drama of disaster. He is not evil – Morlar is a Nietzschean anti-Christ who mocks the pious platitudes of civilization and the institutions built on the foundations of destruction. Modernity cannot contain nor confront the true source of disaster: mankind, the Behemoth, the chaos-monster, or what H. G. Wells would see as 'the round Palaeolithic savage in the square hole of the civilized state'.[22] In other words, modernity is neither an assured sign of progress nor an evolving humanity. Modernity masks what men choose to forget: intractable human nature. And this is evident, no more so, than in Morlar's self-blaming, which points to a form of toxic masculinity that is not too dissimilar to the vigilante heroes in *Joe* (John G. Avildsen, 1970) and *Death Wish* (Michael Winner, 1974). In a time of interpersonal chaos (i.e., sexual permissiveness, women asserting their rights) and social chaos wrought by post-Watergate cynicism and post-industrial economic turbulence, male dominance is reasserted via violent means. Man has a gift for disaster.

9

Aftermath

By examining the disaster cycle in terms of subgenres that accord to sites or contexts of modernity, this book has shown that the disaster movie is multi-directional. One of the cinematic legacies of the disaster movie has been the Hollywood blockbuster. *Jaws* (Steven Spielberg, 1975) can be seen as a disaster cycle spin-off, and the superstructure spectacle of *The Towering Inferno* (John Guillermin, 1974) paved the way for *Star Wars* (George Lucas, 1977). However, in following Roger Ebert's edict that the disaster movie should be fun and not too close to harrowing reality, *Jaws* and *Star Wars* constitute fantasy expressions of disaster. The former, with the unseen creature causing mass terror, can be read as conveying anxieties about the Vietnam War, and *Star Wars*, after the Fall of Saigon (April 1975), recasts the American hero through a fantasy of violence. But both therapeutic narratives are dependent on metaphoric displacements of current disaster, and while *Jaws* marked the beginning of the end for the cycle, *Star Wars* exemplified the blockbuster supersession of mass terror via mythic, unreal, violence and, in turn, the direct critique of high modernity capitalism. The supernatural horror genre has also exploited the disaster spectacle, as exemplified by David Cronenberg's *Dead Zone* (1983) and the *Final Destination* film series (2000–present) that use prophesies of disaster as a macabre device. More than the genre itself, the disaster spectacle has endured, but its dispersal into other cinematic forms poses questions with regard to its intended effects or cultural impact.

Superman (1978): Comic Book Disaster

For Ryan and Kellner, the transition from 'super humans to super-cops and superheroes', in a wave of cross-generic, action-adventure films, was the 'perfect antidote to disaster'.[1] The transformation represents a 'principal ideological move', turning 'anxiety' into 'affirmation'.[2]

In many respects, it was the comic-book fantasy of *Superman* (Richard Donner, 1978) that kick-started the repackaging of the disaster spectacle in the form of the superhero blockbuster. Its box office success – the highest grossing film of 1978 in the United States, just above *Grease* (Randal Kleiser, 1978) – had much to do with the way the film strikes an epic tone of American optimism at the end of a bleak decade. *Superman* is an upbeat, and transcendental, riposte to the earth-shattering carnage of the disaster movie, as well as the urban decadence of films set in a morally bankrupt New York City, such as *The French Connection* (William Friedkin, 1971) and *Taxi Driver* (Martin Scorsese, 1976). Like Woody Allen's *Manhattan* (1979), *Superman* closes the decade as 'a nostalgia for another city' that is beyond urban American vice.³ Christopher Reeve plays a mild-mannered superhero, who, contrary to the vigilante film, turns crime fighting into a harmless affair and a throwback to bloodless, classical Hollywood. And as the unregulated crime-buster gracefully flies through the illuminated skyscraper scape of New York – passing landmarks such as the World Trade Center and the Statue of Liberty – the once crime-infested metropolis is safely protected by an 'overgrown-boy-scout' (in the words of Lex Luther), who preaches humility and non-violence. For *Superman* is a New York film, and the benign *übermensch*, delivered from outer of space, is a kind of divine deliverance, recalling the illumined figure of Moses (Charlton Heston) in *The Ten Commandments* (Cecil B. DeMille, 1956), as well as other child-like, gravity-defying, interventionists, such as Mary Poppins (Julie Andrews).

Superman is a moral and manly compensation for the urban decay of modernity, and this is reflected in the comic book origins of the superhero, his dual identity and the two authors' identity as Jewish immigrants: '[Jerry] Siegel's and [Joe] Shuster's personal experiences also shaped their creation. Both were second-generation Jewish immigrants. Both were socially awkward. Urban violence had touched Siegel's life at the age of fourteen when his father was killed in a robbery.'⁴ Superman is also reflective of the reconstruction of the masculine frontier adventure hero in the comic books of the late-1930s and-1940s, for the '1938 Superman relocated the dynamics of frontier confrontation to the modern city, allowing a benign superman amidst human civilization'.⁵ Superman's superstrength can be likened to the figure of Samson, celebrated as Jewish hero in Zeev Jabotinsky's published novel, *Samson The Nazarite* (1927), which served as the basis for Cecil B. DeMille's biblical epic, *Samson and Delilah* (1949). Interestingly, Superman's weakness, a vulnerability to kryptonite, parallels Samson losing his strength – 'if my head were shaved'.⁶ Chambliss and Svitavsky argue that the key to Superman's success was his dual identity, which they read as reflective of an internalized Jewish stereotype, even though 'his apparent weakness belied the Kryptonian immigrant's true self. The costumed Superman is the revelation of that self.'[7] Superman's metamorphosis, in the movie, is also a legacy of the divine intervention witnessed in *The Ten Commandments* when Moses rescues his people by bringing disaster down upon their persecutors. In other words, *Superman* is a thinly veiled return to biblical epics via a refashioned disaster movie.

The genesis of the superman mythology, in the film, establishes the symbolic birth of the quasi-religious hero and sets the tone of mass death and destruction. On the planet Krypton, the biological parents, Jor-El (Marlon Brando) and Lara (Susannah York), send their infant son to Earth in a small spaceship, reminiscent of the biblical story of baby Moses being placed in an ark on the river Nile. Meanwhile, Krypton is being destroyed by its red supergiant sun, and the populace, in scenes visually recalling the depiction of sinners and infidels tumbling into a chasm in John Martin's *The Great Day of His Wrath* (1851), is violently dying – *en masse*. The ship lands near Smallville, Kansas, and immediately the child shows off his Samson-like strength to his adoptive parents, Jonathan and Martha Kent (Glenn Ford and Phyllis Thaxter), when he lifts their truck. Raised in a Puritan homestead in a Midwestern state, he is taught to be unassuming by Earth parents, who, like Joseph and Mary, have been blessed with a God-like child not born of an earthbound woman. Also, like Christ, Superman is both seemingly Son of God and Man, who disguises his true metaphysical identity while behaving as a humble servant via Clark Kent, an awkward reporter for the *Daily Planet*. In perhaps the most religiously inflected scene, Superman learns from his numinous father, who appears as a hologram in the Fortress of Solitude, of his reason for being sent to Earth: to bring out humanity's capacity to do good. Dressed as the caped wonder, muscular Christianity is unleashed.

On the big screen, Superman's reassuring mission is to avert disaster and its after-effects. The film is a hypertext of disasters and disaster films. The appearance of Gene Hackman as Lex Luther, the criminal genius, is an ironic invocation of Reverend Frank Scott in *The Poseidon Adventure* (Ronald Neame, 1972). One of the screenwriters involved in adapting the comic strip was Mario Puzo, who had also worked on *Earthquake*, and the destruction of planet Krypton visually paraphrases the official promotion poster for the same film. John Williams, who composed the triumphalist film score, is the bridge between the monster-horror, *Jaws* and the space opera, *Star Wars*. When Superman is revealed to the world, he saves Lois Lane (Margot Kidder), who falls from a helicopter that then falls from the top of a skyscraper. Momentarily, she is a falling body, echoing the Triangle Shirtwaist Factory fire in the Greenwich Village of Manhattan, New York (1911). The scene of a gawping and astonished crowd gathered below recalls *Inferno* and *King Kong* (John Guillermin, 1976). Soon after, Superman saves Air Force One from crashing after a lightning strikes an outboard engine. Superman averts disaster and mass death.

This is a mini-rehearsal for the movie's climax that is dedicated to multiple, potential disasters, which Garrett Martin has described as 'pure disaster turf'.[8] Lex Luther diverts two nuclear missiles during a military test, hoping that at least one will detonate in the San Andreas Fault, causing a California earthquake. The 1974 film springs to mind. While Superman diverts one missile into outer-space, the other strikes its intended target. The Golden Gate Bridge and the Hoover Dam are damaged. Superman seals the fault line to mitigate the after-effects, saves a busload of children and prevents a flood disaster. He also restores to life (Lazarus-like) a dead Lois, buried underground. In fact, the only gruesome death occurs when Lois's car falls into a crevice and she is suffocated by falling earth (Figure 9.1). Her screams of terror are genuine, unlike the previous screams *à la mode de* comic book. Her death prompts Superman, for the only time, to exhibit the wrath of a demi-god. He defies his father's message to not intervene in human history and reverses disaster and time, by rotating planet Earth – backwards.[9] It is unclear as to the exact time, but Superman's personal grief is cured, and Lois miraculously overcomes the ineluctable forces of time and death. History is rewritten and redeemed. *Superman* 'blocks out the past'

Figure 9.1 Superman (Christopher Reeve) retrieves the dead body of Lois Lane (Margot Kidder), though her life is soon restored *à la* Lazarus.

for Lois, and thus retreats from history, like *Star Wars*.[10] For Geoff King, *Star Wars* was a conscious effort by George Lucas to revivify the frontier myth damaged by the repercussions of the Vietnam War.[11] *Superman* revivifies the frontier crusader, as well as the disaster spectacle, via the *deus ex machina* of a miracle saviour. When he delivers Luthor and Otis (Ned Beatty) to a prison, the warden thanks Superman: 'This country is safe again, thanks to you, Superman.' And Superman replies: 'No sir. Don't thank me. We're all part of the same team.' Superman brought justice, saved the masses from disaster, unified the country and in doing so also symbolically healed the trauma of the seventies that had been played out in the disaster cycle.

Superman does not conform to the '70s' conventions of the disaster genre (only in the sense of an enormous cast of bygone actors and a prolonged spectacular climax), yet nonetheless it established a superhero trajectory of disaster prevention. Richard Lester's *Superman II* (1980) and *Superman III* (1983) continue in a similar vein of miracle-trauma therapy: a detonated bomb inside an Eiffel Tower elevator is pushed into space; a chemical plant fire is extinguished with a giant block of ice; and a global oil crisis is resolved by the destruction of a supercomputer. When Superman attends to the problems, the disastrous decade is vanquished – as signified by a car pulling up at the gas pumps. Attendant: 'Regular or premium?' Driver: 'What the hell, she hasn't had a drink in so long, let's give her a tankful of the good stuff.' The good times are back. Even Lois's chronic lovesickness is cured through a lingering amnesiac kiss.

While the *Superman* film series (1978–87) continued the camp style tradition of the cycle, especially in the directorial hands of Richard Lester, the devastation caused by General Zod (Terence Stamp), Ursa (Sarah Douglas) and Non (Jack O'Halloran) – three archfiend Kryptonians – propelled comic book (including Marvel) adaptations in another direction. Post-9/11 films have reassured through increased destructive revelry and a neoconservative agenda of victors and warrior fantasies.[12] To quote Reverend Frank Scott: 'God likes winners.' In *Superman Returns* (Bryan Singer, 2006), an airplane is prevented from hitting a baseball arena and the diegetic spectators triumphantly greet Superman as a returning god. In *Man of Steel* (Zack Snyder, 2013), the soft power of Superman, encapsulated by Christopher Reeve's performances, is replaced by a humourless, ego-driven tale of landmass devastation, with General Zod (Michael Shannon) and Superman (Henry Cavill) engaging in a cataclysmic battle across Metropolis and destroying much of it in the process.[13] The vision of global citizenship (albeit rooted in American imperialism), the assimilationist fantasy of the immigrant story in response to fascism in the 1930s, and the mythico-religious epic have long receded.[14]

The superhero film also continues Hollywood's preoccupation with an amnesiac form of narrative therapy that underwrites a prevalent Hollywood spectacle of disaster. This is exemplified in *Black Panther* (Ryan Coogler, 2018) and *Black Panther: Wakanda Forever* (Ryan Coogler, 2022) that are meant to empower a subjugated people through the alternative history of 'Afrofuturism'. In the words of Delip Menon: 'The film Black Panther is watched within a visual and political terrain in which the black body is presented no longer only within histories of previous abjection – slavery and apartheid – but in visions of future reconstitution.'[15] The superpower derives from a breaking free of a history that repeats itself: 'Africa needs to tell its own stories and think its own thoughts. There can be no looking homeward across the ocean for the African American; there can indeed be no telling the story of Africa only in terms of loss.'[16] However, *Black Panther* constitutes a repetitive filmic experience in being reliant on fantasy and a warrior aesthetic that shield the United States as a nation from its violent history. In the cinematic space of alternative history, the transatlantic slave trade is forgotten, and yet, in *Wakanda Forever*, a repressed political unconscious is represented via Talokan, whose ancestors, the Aztecs, were colonized by the conquistadors and who war with the inhabitants of Wakanda (future Africa).

The disaster spectacle in superhero has also increasingly become the manifestation of imperial vigilantism. For Tom Pollard, as the superhero movies became more violent, villains 'resembled terrorists', and the heroes 'grew vastly more powerful'.[17] 9/11 unleashed powerful emotions, and vengeance was one of them. Pacificism and non-violence do exist in certain characters who are willing to compromise.[18] But, by and large, super heroism co-exists with super destruction, privileged political symbolism and justifiers of vigilantism.[19] According to Monika Philips, cultural icons of unrestricted heroic violence have recently been adopted to privilege white male aggrievance and vigilantism.[20] It is a legacy of white vigilantism in the form of Dirty Harry *et al.* that persisted in the 1970s, when at the same time the Black action hero films, created in response to the intransigence of liberal progressives and as cinematic expressions of Black vigilantism – for example, *Buck and the Preacher* (Sidney Poitier, 1972), were not distributed widely via mainstream cinema. In other words, the disaster spectacle persists as a skewed means of articulating regressive, and ideologically coded, retribution.

Aviation disasters

Most contemporary straight disaster movies are processed schlock, destined to be television or B-movie carnage-fodder. Melodrama is quickly bypassed to achieve the gratification of a high-impact spectacle and survival scenario. With the focus increasingly on action-oriented plot, state-of-the-art special effects and large-scale productions, the genre has lost sight of the social melodrama of *Airport* (George Seaton,1970) and its kitsch charm. Instead, Arthur Hailey's genre innovations – with an emphasis on the structural workings (the internal politics and pressures of working conditions and personal dramas) – crossed over into made-for-TV movies. Hailey's 1968 novel showed that potential disasters are likely to be the consequence of a convoluted, high-stake system. The story of Keith Bakersfield and the stresses of an Air Traffic Controller foreshadow *Crisis in Mid-Air* (Walter Grauman, 1979) that was aired on CBS. In this made-for-television film, Nick Culver (George Peppard) suffers from recurring nightmares of an air collision caused by a military jet performing aerobatics. His accumulated anxiety results in a family break-up. But he is eventually reconciled with his wife, Betsy, when he prevents Flight 802 (a disabled airliner) from hitting a bus (driven by a former airport worker who has lost his mind after a cab driver killed his child) that was crashed onto the runway. Nick is cleared of the mid-air disaster and promises to leave his job. Unlike George Seaton's screenplay, *Crisis in Mid-Air* depicts the very real correlations between trauma and a risky environment typical of modernity.

Aviation disaster movies have traditionally dramatized the trial of masculinity, and the camp aesthetic of the *Airport* franchise allowed (to some degree) for an alternate drama of male trauma. Nonetheless, despite the democratic opening up of a typically male space, subsequent films have invariably suggested that a queer-coded presence constitutes a symbolic threat to masculine authority in the fight for group survival.[21] This was exemplified in *Skyjacked* (John Guillermin, 1972), based on the 1970 novel, *Hijacked*, by David Harper, in which Jerry Weber (the skyjacker), a traumatized Vietnam War veteran, is clearly going through a crisis of masculinity – he is not the army type but fantasizes about military reward and bears a father complex. In the film, the cockpit pilot, Captain Henry 'Hank' O'Hara (the ubiquitous Charlton Heston) is defined by his job, and his erotic-fantasy predictably involves an air hostess. Weber (James Brolin) transcends gender and ideological boundaries: the message of a bomb threat is written with lipstick on a first-class bathroom mirror; he befriends Gary

'Boo' Brown (Roosevelt Grier), a Black jazz cellist, and he tries to defect to the Soviet Union. Heston reasserts the exclusive gender politics of the 'island in the sky' when he cries out 'Get off my plane!'. Like the shark in *Jaws*, the skyjacker is wiped out.

In *Airport '75* (Jack Smight, 1974), the sexual politics is yet again sustained when First Stewardess, Nancy (Karen Black), takes control of a Boeing 747 flight deck after the first officer is ejected from the jet, the flight engineer killed and the captain is blinded (following a mid-air collision). Only by accident can a stewardess occupy the male *cock*pit. This is a rare example of female elevation, one that is resolved when Murdock (that indomitable Heston), after being lowered from a helicopter through the hole of the cockpit, lands the plane safely at Salt Lake City International Airport. Pauline Kael describes Black as 'archaically helpless' and someone who is 'treated like a puppy'.[22] Masculine control of the flying machine is reinstated when Heston switches off the autopilot to reach a necessary altitude. Yet, though lacking in training, Nancy appears calm in a crisis and her cockpit performance is a small symbolic victory.

In her essay, 'Notes on "Camp"' (1964), Susan Sontag construes middle-class kitsch as a camp aesthetic, with an emphasis on artifice and social levelling. 'The hallmark of Camp is the spirit of extravagance.' She also refers to the camp style as a bad, but enjoyable, movie and as 'out-of-date'.[23] In many ways, the comedy of *Airplane!* (Jim Abrahams, David Zucker & Jerry Zucker, 1980) foregrounds the camp style of the cycle by mocking 'outmoded' tough-guys, the male stars who had appeared in aviation disaster films or television dramas/films: Lloyd Bridges – *San Francisco International Airport* (1970–1), Peter Graves – *SST Death Flight* (David Lowell Rich, 1977), Robert Stack – *The High and the Mighty* (William A. Wellman, 1954). The camp, surreal humour is largely voiced via Stephen Stucker, who plays an air traffic controller and whose phallic jokes deflate the machismo of the aviation movie.

The legacy of fragile aviation masculinity is witnessed in post-9/11 films, such as *Sully: Miracle on the Hudson* (Clint Eastwood, 2016), starring Tom Hanks, and *Flight* (Robert Zemeckis, 2012), starring Denzel Washington. Whereas the latter deconstructs the public image of the cockpit, *Sully*, released to coincide with the 9/11 anniversary, restores the saintly image of a pilot responsible for the lives of passengers. The film is a tribute to Chesley Sullenberger, who as captain of US Airways Flight 1549 safely ditched in the Hudson River in 2008. Tom Hanks, as a reassuring figure, is a consoling presence for a post-9/11 generation: 'You know, it's been a while since New York had news this good – especially with an airplane in it.' *Flight*, though, in depicting Denzel Washington as an alcoholic pilot (with echoes of *Crisis in Mid-Air*), unmasks the free-spirited persona of the pilot. Death has given Captain Whip Whitaker a new perspective on life, and now it is the male pilot who needs to be saved – from a trashy, promiscuous lifestyle that was partly endorsed in *Airport*.

Both *Flight 93* (Peter Markle, 2006) and *United 93* (Paul Greengrass, 2006) are consoling 9/11 eulogies that focus on the passenger's moral victory when a commercial airliner is used as a political weapon of retributive terror. United Airlines Flight 93 was hijacked during the 9/11 attacks with the suspected target either the White House or the US Capitol Building. As docudramas, they exploit the intense drama of a confined, terrorized space. *United 93* partly takes its cue from *Crisis in Mid-Air*, in suggesting that the disaster was also the result of busy, uncontrollable, air traffic. *Flight 93*, in extending the drama out via phone exchanges into the homes of relatives, underscores the 9/11 drama as a unifying victory of resistance: 'with courage and resolve the passengers of Flight 93 prevented their plane from reaching its likely target'. In both, the passenger's revolt is mythologized into the rallying cry of 'Are you ready? Okay, Let's roll', the last cell phone words of Todd Beamer, who also recited the Lord's Prayer and the 23rd Psalm. Whereas other recent hijack or air terror films, such as *Passenger 57* (Kevin Hooks, 1992), *Air Force One* (Wolfgang Peterson, 1997) and *Snakes on a Plane* (David R. Ellis, 2006), recycle familiar ingredients, taking the aviation disaster genre into the realms of exploitation thrills, political and action thriller, *Flight 93* and *United 93* constitute aerial arks of salvation.

As the film title suggests, *Aftermath* (Elliott Lester, 2017) pays little attention to an actual aviation disaster, the 2002 Überlingen mid-air collision, and is focused on two individuals who are deeply affected by a mid-air collision. Roman (Arnold Schwarzenegger) is based on Vitaly Kaloyev who had lost his wife and two children on board Bashkirian Airlines Flight 2937, and who murdered Peter Nielsen (Scott McNairy), the air traffic controller believed to be responsible for the collision. The film presents a parallel, sympathetic perspective of an aggrieved father and husband and an air traffic controller suffering from traumatic stress. The film is also a redemptive redress to the retributive crime of Kaloyev who had tracked down and stabbed to death Peter in the presence of his wife and three children. When Roman does not receive an apology from the airliner company, he confronts Jacob at the door of his apartment, who also does not offer an apology (saying instead the disaster was an accident), and he stabs Jacob – who bleeds to death in the presence of his sobbing wife (Christina) and son (Samuel). Roman is convicted of murder and is released early on parole, and while visiting his family grave he is confronted by Samuel who also seeks revenge. However, unlike Kaloyev who was treated as a hero in Russia for punishing a person responsible for the aviation deaths, Roman apologizes and Samuel is moved by Roman's contrition. The overall suggestion is that Roman-Kaloyev was wrong to apportion blame, and that if he had had an intimate view of the breakdown and remorse of Jacob-Peter, then forgiveness may have been the alternate outcome. In this respect, *Aftermath* partly redresses the excision of the Keith and Perry plotline in George Seaton's *Airport* screenplay as well as the exclusion of Hailey's novelistic perspective of the interconnected pressures of a highly complex industry.

Ark movies

The immediate and obvious successors to *Poseidon* are *Beyond the Poseidon Adventure* (Irwin Allen, 1979), *The Poseidon Adventure* (John Putch, 2005) – a made-for-television disaster film – and *Poseidon* (Wolfgang Peterson, 2006). But it is Roland Emmerich's *2012* (2009), billed as 'the Mother of all disaster movies', that continues the cinematic vogue for the 'prophecy phenomenon' in the form of a Noah's Ark story.[24] Despite Emmerich presenting himself as an 'apolitical maker of "popcorn movies"', the global geopolitics of the film is troubling.[25] For while the film is based on the eschatological belief that cataclysmic events would occur in 2012, it is climate fiction inflected by the elective theology of deluge movies. The focus is on a white fleeing family being saved on one of the nine arks built by China and G8 nations. Billions of people die by either earthquake or mega-tsunamis, and when the Curtis family reach Ark 4 it is revealed that mostly wealthy people, such as the Russian billionaire Yuri (Zlatko Burić) and his sons, are boarding the arks – they were sold tickets to pay for the cost of construction. Perhaps the most disturbing scene in terms of geopolitical survival is when Satnam Tsurutani (Jimi Mistry), an astrophysicist who discovered the neutrinos that are the heating the Earth's core, is killed along with his family and panic-stricken thousands by a tsunami that strikes the coastline of a South Asian country (India) that has been singled out (in reality) as highly vulnerable (like its neighbour, Pakistan) to climate change. While I write this, recent floods in Pakistan have 'plunged around one-third of its land mass into water'. Pakistan contributes less than 1 per cent of global carbon dioxide emissions. 'Despite being a poor country, it has always been vociferous about climate change and global warming, urging leaders of richer countries to act before it's too late.'[26] But this is not a film about a poor country saving itself, and, to underscore the chosen family theme, one of the children of Jackson Curtis (John Cusack) is called Noah (Liam James).

To be fair, though, like other movies such as *Children of Men* (Alfonso Cuarón, 2006), *Elysium* (Neill Blomkamp, 2013) and *Greenland* (Ric Roman Waugh, 2020), *2012* does comment on the issue of ecological refugees, though mainly displaced through the scapegoating demise of Yuri, who falls into a deep canyon as the loaded gates of Ark 4 are opened; and his sons are caricatured as obese and obnoxious. The stereotyping of the 'filthy' rich as fatuous Russians (the ideological enemy) is on a par with the representation of the screaming hordes fleeing the gigantic tidal wave, a scene of the sublime apocalypticism. And when the waters recede and Africa has risen above the waters, the final image is of Jackson Curtis and Kate Curtis (Amanda Peet) rekindling their romance and their family reunited. However, there is a brutal honesty about eco-salvation prophesies that recall the predictions of ecological collapse in neo-Malthusian publications, such as Paul R. Ehrlich's *The Population Bomb* (1968). Survival is predicated on one's wealth and demographic situation. The people who perish are poor, thus fulfilling too the message of the prosperity gospel. Salvation in God's superyacht is for the elect few.

The Towering Inferno: Post 9/11

If one film constitutes a vision of hegemonic destruction, then it is *The Towering Inferno*, for it harrows in the way it 'anticipat[es] several homages to the World Trade Center tragedy in a case of life imitating art'.[27] In the immediate aftermath of 9/11, references to the Hollywood disaster movie and the rhetoric of the apocalyptic sublime reverberated: 'The collision of the jet passenger planes with the Twin Towers, their subsequent collapse into nothingness, the ominous absence within the smoke-filled skyline, the busy streets of Manhattan turned disaster movie – these scenes were images as much or more than actual events.'[28] A debate was conducted via the *London Review of Books* letters page.[29] Neal Ascherson referred to the event as 'the most open atrocity of all time, a simple demonstration written on the sky which everyone in the world was invited to watch. This is how much we hate you. [...] Now, [...] leaders are writing

"Retribution" on the clouds.'³⁰ For Mary Beard: 'The horror of the tragedy was enormously intensified by the ringside seats [...]'.³¹ In his essay on 9/11, 'The Spirit of Terrorism' (2nd November, 2001), Jean Baudrillard writes: 'The fact that we have dreamt of this event, that everybody without exception has dreamt of it – because no one can avoid dreaming of the destruction of any power that has become hegemonic to that degree – is unacceptable to the Western moral conscience.'³² However, the claim that the Twin Towers were destroyed 'by the utter nihilism inherent in capitalism itself' for Bruno Latour needed to be checked by 'the cultivation of a *stubbornly realist attitude*'.³³ It was a view shared by Hal Foster: 'These events are unspeakable, but they shouldn't be left in the oppressive space of the Sublime.'³⁴ Yet, rather than 'an oppressive space', the sublime, for Slavoj Žižek, is something that harrows the mind, going way beyond mere entertainment: 'Its citizens were introduced to the "desert of the real" – to us, corrupted by Hollywood, the landscape and the shots we saw of the collapsing towers could not but remind us of the most breathtaking scenes in the catastrophe's big productions.'³⁵

Oliver Stone's 2006 cinematic memorial, *World Trade Center*, draws on various disaster genre conventions and the heroic elevation of firefighters reaches a metaphysical level. It is also a film that plays out the apocalyptic-retributive rhetoric of George W. Bush: 'I'm not sure which is more frightening: the horror that engulfed New York City or the apocalyptic rhetoric emanating daily from the White House. "We will rid the world of evil-doers," President Bush announces as he embarks on an open-ended "crusade" (does he understand the historical freight this word carries?) against people who "hate us because we are free"'.³⁶ It affirms Žižek's view that 9/11 was sold to the world as a 'clash of civilizations' with the 'innocent gaze confronting [an] unspeakable Evil which struck from the Outside.'³⁷ As Karen Randall sees it, the *WTC* re-creates 'the events of that day as if it were already a disaster movie.'³⁸ D. M. Kellner has also argued that the film 'draws on generic features of the disaster film, showing people on the street reacting to the horror and TV images of the event' and by focusing also on the heroism of ordinary people.³⁹ The film carries forth a disaster convention via an overt religious framing of the trapped members of the Port Authority Police which extends triumphantly to all the rescuers, including the Ground Zero firefighters. The participants, therefore, enact a ritual drama of cosmic war, between the divinely inspired rescuers and the evil-doers.⁴⁰

During an interview, Oliver Stone acknowledged his debt to the films of Robert Bresson and Carl Theodor Dreyer when shooting the rescue of two surviving

Port Authority Officers – Sgt. John McLoughlin (Nicolas Cage) and Will Jimeno (Michael Peña) – trapped in a hole as 'each scene in the "hole" gets lighter'.[41] For Stone, these scenes are a 'meditation on death'. He then speaks of preparing Nicholas Cage for the acting role: 'I was reading to him from the *Tibetan Book of the Dead*, trying to take the actors to the edges, the edges of death, based on philosophy and the little that I know of having sometimes felt like I had died. I mean, what is death? Something to pass through but also something larger than we are.'[42] Stone sees the important message of the film as 'regeneration out of the cataclysm'.[43] This theme of regeneration is predicated on the vision of a Christ-saviour figure that is closely aligned to a Christian fundamentalist and former Marine, Sergeant Dave Karnes (Michael Shannon), who seeks God-inspired vengeance. Karnes was the first to discover the two officers trapped under the ruins of a fallen Tower, cued by Will Jimeno's dream of an illuminated Christ bearing a bottle of water. Before Karnes sets off on his solitary rescue mission, he is seen praying in a chapel above a Bible, with the pages turned to the book of Revelation. In other words, Stone's cinematic memorial of America's skyscraper holocaust is an Armageddon revelation. Henceforth, the tragic cycle. For *World Trade Center* does not recognize that: 'Evil resides (also) in the innocent gaze itself which perceives Evil all around itself.'[44] Where now the theme of forgiveness and rehabilitation?

9/11 (Martin Guigui, 2017) takes its cue from a made-for-television film, *The Elevator* (Jerry Jameson, 1974), in which a diverse group of people are trapped inside a high-rise elevator. Jerry Jameson (the director of *Airport '77*) had also directed the Irwin Allen-inspired *Terror on the 40th Floor* that was first aired on NBC2 (14 September 1974) in which a secret Christmas Eve office party is ruined by a creeping fire. The homage in *9/11* to the seventies cycle is emphasized by the appearance of Jacqueline Bisset, who played Gwen Meighen, the chief stewardess on TGA Flight 2 in *Airport*, as Diane. Like Stone's film, *9/11* exploits the group jeopardy formula of death-confronting confessionals in a confined space to endorse the American dream that is enshrined in corporate skyscrapers and in Jeffrey Cage (Charlie Sheen), a multi-millionaire businessman who owns an office in the North Tower. In a heated exchange with Jeffrey, Michael (Wood Harris) – a Black delivery man – raises the issue of structural racism:

> Michael: Not everybody has their own private plane.
> Jeffrey: Do you know why I have my own jet, Michael?
> Michael: White rich guy.

Eve Cage: For your information, this guy doesn't come from money. His dad worked in a factory. His mom died when he was 12. He went to public school, and when he barely graduated, he went to work alongside his father and all of his brothers, and that was it, that was decided. But you know what he did? He refused to accept that story because he imagined something bigger for himself.

Prior to Airlines Flight 11 crashing into the building, Eve (Gina Gershon) had hoped Jeffrey would sign divorce papers. Jeffrey puts his work before his family. But disasters bring out the best and worst in people. The implication is that Michael is the worst of America's salad bowl (represented in the elevator) because he accepted his 'story' and lot in life, and the principle of envy distorts his racial prejudices. Michael, though, had 'imagined something bigger' embodied in the North Tower. The inversion of *Inferno*'s theme of class warfare is emphatically affirmed with the heroizing of Jeffrey, who is aligned to the firefighter (Ian Fisher), in putting the lives of others before his own. The North Tower collapses and the fate of Jeffrey and the fireman in the elevator shaft is left unknown – possibly going the way of Sgt. John McLoughlin and Will Jimeno. The Tower has fallen but the spirit lives on.

Earthquakes: Hollywood apocalypticism

Even though disaster movies carry forth a serious cautionary message, in the seventies the genre invited an immediate parodic response (e.g., *The Big Bus*, James Frawley, 1976) to all-too-familiar genre expectations. However, intertextual satires do expose Hollywood's recycling of the apocalyptic.[45] *Drive-In* (Rod Amateau, 1976), which perhaps takes its cue from Robert Altman's anti-genre film, *Nashville* (1975), is also a satire of potential, multiple sites of disaster in the cycle. The latest disaster film, *Disaster '76*, is premiered at the 'Alamo' theatre, in a small Texas town. *Drive-In* is a retrospective, albeit satirical, construction of the 1950s' drive-in experience, and by making *Disaster '76* the centrepiece for a film-in-a-film comedy, the cycle is implicated in the trash associations of the drive-in culture. Likewise, the disaster movie supposedly appeals to an unsophisticated but knowing audience, and the spoof underscores the idea that the cycle was commercially driven by a need to outdo its predecessors in terms of low culture sensationalism and an ever-increasing catastrophe scale – hence the pulping. On board a Boeing 747, the pilot asks that the champagne bottles be cracked open to celebrate New Year's Eve. Inside a toilet, a disgruntled ex-employee of the commercial airline is placing a ticking bomb in a suitcase. Cut to a carload of male teens sharing a bottle of hard liquor, and cut back to the drive-in movie, *Disaster '76*: a German bomber has hit the cockpit and a ship's captain is conversing with an Air Stewardess. (Meanwhile, a couple are attempting uncomfortable sex in the backseat of a steamed-up automobile.) In a skyscraper, there is a heated office debate: 'Cheap cuts to construction – for instance, no stairs. Stairs are old fashioned – what idiot is gonna walk up 196 floors? Look guys, my ladder only goes up to the 2nd floor.' And inside the damaged cockpit: 'You've done a great job, Margo. Prepare for landing.' The plane hits the tower and there are scenes of fire engines rushing to the inferno. Later, due to 'inclement weather', the drive-in movie is stopped, but when resumed, a ship is sinking, and a shark is dangerously prowling. The ship's captain accidentally harpoons an inflatable dinghy. Chased by a shark fin, the captain emerges from out of the sea onto a post-apocalyptic beach and addresses the camera: 'Someone's got to rebuild Rio.' And as the vehicles depart from the drive-in theatre, the lyrics of a country song (like a Greek chorus) interject: 'God's gonna get you for that. God's gonna get you for that. There's no place to run and hide. He knows where you're at.' After parodying the hybridic regurgitation of disaster movies, *Drive-In* ends by invoking the cycle's refashioning of biblical epics that were popular when drive-in cinemas also flourished in the late fifties. The film is perhaps making an obscure allusion to *The Ten Commandments* being released in 1958 at some drive-ins.[46]

In the vein of *The Day of the Locust* (John Schlesinger, 1975), John Carpenter's *Escape from Los Angeles* (1996) is also a satire on Hollywood's preoccupation with the apocalyptic and Christian moralism. When an earthquake strikes a crime-ridden and decadent Los Angeles in 2000, the San Fernando valley is flooded, and the city is turned into an island (from Malibu to Anaheim). A fire and brimstone presidential candidate, Adam (Cliff Robertson) is elected for life when he declares L.A. to be sinful and condemned by God. With echoes of the Prohibition era, he establishes new 'Moral America' laws that prohibit extra-marital sex, atheism as well as the use of recreational drugs and alcoholic beverages. Offenders are stripped of their citizenship and deported to a highly guarded L.A. Island (with echoes of Alcatraz prison). President Adam is modelled on the puritanism of teleevangelists with parallels to Heston's Moses – the patriarchal and righteous lawgiver, and L.A. is depicted as an urban wasteland of inequity recalling *The Last Days of Sodom and Gomorrah* (Robert Aldrich,

1962). To underscore the moral dialectic, L.A. is ruled by Cuervo Jones (Georges Corraface), a Peruvian Communist Revolutionary who closely resembles Che Guevara, the countercultural symbol of anti-American imperialism. While mainstream America is aligned with a punitive, religious fanaticism, L.A. is aligned with Pre-Code, immoral Hollywood. The vision of fallenness is framed by a passing reference to the disaster cycle in the form of Universal Studio (that was responsible for most of the disaster films) as a half-sunken city landmark of the flooded valley.

Despite the dialectic, at first, it is difficult to identify the target of Carpenter's satire. Snake (Kurt Russell) defeats Cuervo and retrieves a device, the Sword of Damocles, that can emasculate America's imperialism. But Snake tricks the president and activates the device that ends all technological activity on the planet and utters the final words: 'Welcome to the human race.' To equalize global power, the world is returned to the pre-technocratic dark ages. As K. R. Phillips argues, visions of a 'horrific frontier' belong to a broader American mythology of the frontier as a 'site of conquest', and, in Carpenter's cinematic logic, 'the frontier mythology lingers, but its trajectory is reversed'.[47] An early example of the return of the repressed in Carpenter's oeuvre is *The Fog* (1980). The so-called primitive outsider, that is meant to be conquered and civilized, is liberated. So, Carpenter inverts the logic of DeMille's apocalypticism by returning moral America to a pre-Christian world, populated with Muslims and transvestites who would have been punished by God's will in the form of natural disaster. Snake, wearing a trench-coat, is modelled on the Western hero, Clint Eastwood, but rather than bringing peace and order to a small frontier town through retributive justice, he sides with a queer subculture. For Mike Davies, the film 'manages to sample (in the hip-hop sense) every mean image and racist undertone of survivalist fiction in the service of an ostensibly liberal plot about Los Angeles as the reverse Ellis Island of a Christian fascist America. The result is a cinematic nervous breakdown.'[48] This is because the Sword of Damocles is a symbolic reminder that America is always vulnerable to the levelling effect of a natural order that does not serve any moral creed.

Whereas Carpenter's film both co-opts and debunks Hollywood apocalypticism, *San Andreas* (Brad Peyton, 2015) is a doomsday extravaganza that exceeds Universal's 1974 super-spectacular movie by following a recent trend in uber-apocalyptic films, such as *Disaster Wars: Earthquake vs Tsunami* (David Palmieri, 2013) and *San Andreas Mega Quake* (H. M. Coakley, 2019), when the 'big one' obliterates cities, or a whole nation, or the entire world. It stars Dwayne Johnson as Ray, a Los Angeles Fire Department helicopter-rescue pilot, and it archetypally focuses on the rescue of a single family. At least this time, a non-white actor is the libertarian-saviour figure, who – as expected – is estranged from his wife, Emma (played by Carla Gugino of Italian and English Irish descent). Their relationship improves when Ray rescues her from a collapsing L.A. skyscraper before negotiating the largest recorded earthquake in history, followed by a tsunami that hits San Francisco Bay. Sadly, Daniel (Ioan Gruffudd), who had abandoned the daughter, Blake (Alexandra Daddario), in a fit of teen-cowardice, is killed on the Golden Gate Bridge when bisected by a container ship. Happily, Blake is eventually rescued by Ray, who performs CPR, and both are rescued from another collapsing building by Emma in a boat. In a relief camp, Ray and Emma talk about their future together. The closing image of an American flag unfolding on the remains of the Golden Gate Bridge recalls *San Francisco* (W. S. Van Dyke, 1936) with a message that a post-9/11 America can recover and be rebuilt.

L.A.: A doomed city, but what about Hollywood?

Many disaster movies are set in New York and Washington, DC, but since the release of *Earthquake* one would be forgiven for thinking that, in the eyes of Hollywood studios, Los Angeles has been singled out as the doomed city. Hollywood takes a special pleasure in destroying Los Angeles, and there are numerous websites that list films in which the city is a prominent site of disaster.[49] Adrian Glick Kudler under the subtitle, 'Filmmakers love to destroy LA', offers the 'complete list' of L.A. destruction, starting with *War of the Worlds* (Bryon Haskin, 1953).[50] Kudler classifies films according to the type of attack, echoing Maurice Yacowar's litany: 'Monster Attacks', 'Climatic Events', 'Geologic Events', 'Infections', 'Mankind', 'Alien Attacks', 'Space Rocks' and 'Superhero Battles'. Mark Fraser's webpage is dedicated to 'Top 10 Films That Share an Apocalyptic View of Los Angeles', which includes: *The Omega Man* (Boris Sagal, 1971), *Volcano* (Mick Jackson, 1997) and *2012* (Roland Emmerich, 2009).[51] Shelby Grad, for *The Los Angeles Times*, ranks movies that destroy Los Angeles.[52] And under the headline, 'Los Angeles: City of Perpetual Cinematic Destruction', Mandalit Del Barco makes the point that Hollywood's focus on L.A. as a cinematic spectacle of destruction is perhaps because the city's filmmakers are 'tapping into a sense of disdain the rest of the world feels for the city's rich and famous'.⁵³ In other words, Hollywood is supposedly satisfying a global principle of envy? Yet, Hollywood is quick to depict global destruction – for example, *Geostorm* (Dean Devlin, 2017) – and monumental mayhem, destroying landmarks such as the Golden Gate, the Statue of Liberty and White House. Nonetheless, very few have shown the actual destruction of a Hollywood studio. Perhaps because, as Pauline Kael saw it when reviewing *Earthquake*, a disaster movie set in Los Angeles is a masochistic gesture.⁵⁴

In the video essay, *Los Angeles Plays Itself* (2004), Thom Andersen states: 'But if you're like me and you identify more with the city of Los Angeles than with the movie industry, it's hard not to resent the idea of Hollywood, the idea the movies as standing apart from and above the city.'⁵⁵ And for Andersen, too, the Hollywood Sign, a metonym for the film business, marks literally the ascendancy of Hollywood over the rest of Los Angeles. The city does not have the landmarks of New York, but certain places feature prominently or frequently in movies. For instance, in *Die Hard* (John McTiernan, 1988) terrorists take over the Nakatomi Plaza, a skyscraper that has featured in other major motion pictures released by Twentieth Century Fox. And in *Two-Minute Warning* (1976) the marksman 'who has a perfect aim for ageing movie stars', positions himself above the spectators in the Los Angeles Memorial Coliseum – a sports arena that has featured in other films.⁵⁶ His elevated position momentarily rivals that of the Hollywood Sign. The city's most iconic landmark has been damaged or destroyed in some movies, such as *Earthquake*, *Superman* and *Demolition Man* (Marco Brambilla, 1993). Perhaps it is a passing symbolic redress to a cinematic industry that has profited so much on apocalypticism?

In *Geo-Disaster* (Thunder Levin, 2017), when Los Angeles is damaged by an earthquake caused by dark matter striking Earth, the Mount Lee letters, 'Hollywood', become 'Hol ood' above what appears to be the devastated remains of Warner Bros. Studios. The film was produced by the mockbuster independent film company, Asylum, known for low-budget, direct-to-video films that capitalize on major studio productions, especially blockbusters. For instance, in *Sharknado* (Anthony C. Ferrante, 2013), which spawned a 'sillier' sequel every year for five years, Los Angeles is flooded by shark-infested seawater.⁵⁷ The franchise has also inspired an irreverent survival guide by Andrew Shaffer, *How to Survive a Sharknado and Other Unnatural Disasters: Fight Back When Monsters and Mother Nature Attack* (2014). Why not be entertained by a convergence of history's greatest disasters, as the world endures the imminent threat of eco-collapse due to irreversible climate change? For the only thing to do is to enjoy the superficial rehearsal. And yet for Mark Bould: 'Real catastrophe lurks beneath the surface. It emerges as out-of-place verité fragments, but is quickly swept away by remorseless torrents of distraction. The repressed, however, always returns.'[58] Once again, nature, as in B-Grade creature features or spoof ecohorror films, such as *Piranha* (Joe Dante, 1978), is the antagonist. It also foreshadows the apocalyptic satire, *Don't Look Up* (Adam McKay, 2021), for as Bould argues: 'the franchise enacts – and speaks to – a habituated desensitisation to the ever-present existential threat of anthropogenic climate destabilisation.'[59] Yet, alongside the points of reference towards Hollywood as unanchored by external reality, mock disaster is a cliché in disaster hyperreality.[60] Imagining the jokey destruction of a self-referential cinema industry that fattens on disaster spectacle was established in *Earthquake,* and has become in itself integral to the hegemonic symbolic order.

Sudden Death (1995): A gladiatorial arena of unreal masculinity

Since the release of *Two-Minute Warning* (Larry Peerce, 1976) and *Black Sunday* (John Frankenheimer, 1977), there have been no Super Bowl disaster movies. However, there has been a glut of gladiator arena movies, exemplified by Ridley Scott's *Gladiator* (2000), as well as *Die Hard* 'clones' that have also perpetuated hyper-masculine tropes of stoicism, revenge and violence.[61] Stephen Keane reads the successful *Die Hard* as derivative of *Inferno*, and *Sudden Death* (Peter Hyams, 1995) is considered, like many studio copies, as following a familiar formula of one 'lone wolf' stopping blackmailing terrorists: *Under Siege* (Andrew Davies, 1992), *Passenger 57* (Kevin Hooks, 1992), *Speed* (Jan de Bont, 1994), *Air Force One* (Wolfgang Petersen, 1997).[62] Instead of the Nakatomi Plaza (Los Angeles), the modern site of potential disaster is the Pittsburgh Civic Arena, a place which has been turned into 'one big bomb'. But *Sudden Death* owes a big debt to *Two-Minute Warning*, with the film's title also being an ironic play on dramatic overtime in a sporting competition, while alluding to the suspense and violence that occur in the film's climax.

The film stars Jean-Claude Van Damme – once a martial artist, and now a 'hard body' encoded in the fighting spectacle of a sporting arena, one that is hosting an ice hockey final and in which the Vice President's box has been invaded by capitalist terrorists. It also dramatizes the familiar disaster subplot of a broken family and a psychologically damaged male who overcomes trauma via masculine heroics. Van Damme plays Darren McCord, who as a firefighter was unable to save a young girl from a house fire and is removed from active service. Two years later, he is separated from his wife, Kathi (Kate McNeil), suggesting that women cannot handle the damaged goods of heroic failure. His two small children, who attend the game, bicker over his new job status as a fire marshal in the arena, suggesting that authentic masculinity is equated to the nature of one's work. His son, Tyler (Ross Malinger) is disappointed to see him change light bulbs in the Arena's kitchen, though his daughter, Emily (Whittni Wright), still believes he is brave and will bring her home. McCord reclaims their admiration and his manhood, by killing the terrorists, preventing the stadium and the spectators from being blown up (in disarming the rigged bombs), saving his daughter, and by also performing 'the save of the year' as a goalie (before punching an opposing player). So, McCord is not only a match for the merciless terrorists but can also compete in a physically demanding sport. Failed masculinity is redeemed in a sporting gladiatorial arena.

The film, in many respects, takes its cue from the extended metaphor of spectated sport exploited in *Two-Minute Warning*. Likewise, *Sudden Death* intercuts between shots of ice hockey action and hand-to-hand fighting. In one scene, borrowed from *Under Siege*, starring Steven Seagal (another martial-artist-turned-anti-terrorist-actor), Van Damme fights Carla (Faith Minton), the only henchwoman and who is disguised in a Penguin mascot outfit, in a kitchen. As Roger Ebert puts it, 'they methodically use every prop in sight: the French fry machine, the hot grill, the meat slicer, the exhaust fan, a jar of hot peppers, the industrial dishwasher, even a bone, which winds up stuck through a guy's neck'.[63] This dark carnivalesque sequence of food butchery mirrors the brutal play of the hockey game. We also get a glimpse of a tech-terrorist, a computer hacker (Michael Gaston), who watches the game and the explosion of bombs on security monitors, playing a violent video game. McCord also says to Joshua Foss (Powers Boothe), the criminal mastermind, to signify the rules of engagement in the theatre of war: 'Okay. Here's the game and here are the rules.' It is a game of male winners and losers. The spectating crowds remain oblivious to the terrorist threat, until the over-hanging score display explodes, and the ensuing scenes of pandemonium echo that of *Two-Minute Warning*. Nonetheless, the spectators are not indiscriminate targets of a motiveless, and anonymous, sniper, and the film eschews the uncomfortable detailing of panic-stricken crowds rushing out of the arena. The only playful dialogue uttered at the expense of the diegetic spectators occurs when a hockey period of 'sudden death' (a game decider) is called that defers sudden death (instantaneous death), Foss says, 'Life is just a shitbox of ironies.' Life and death imitate the action of sport. And this is the exchange between two play-by-play announcers: 'It's so loud in here, I can barely hear myself think. You don't have to think, Mike. It's hockey.' It is a mindless sport. The pyrotechnics of exploding bombs elide into shots of celebratory fireworks. The ice hockey 'face off' is a sporting equivalent to the confrontation of a fight. The comic asides are a part of the film's playful staging of martial-arts-inspired-violence. Yet unlike *Black Sunday*, the film does not critically meditate on the mediation of sport as a big spectacle and its continuities with a Roman circus mentality. Like the hockey game, *Sudden Death* is meant to be watched as a playful, blood-letting, mindless spectacle.

In the spectacular climax, Darren assails the arena and advances upon the VIP box from the opened roof. It is a good opportunity for Darren-Damme to, yet again, show off his superstrength athleticism, and to prove he is superior to the ice hockey players, the Secret Services and the Pittsburgh Bureau of Police. The symbolic ascent of a fireman is indicative of super humans, such as super cops, competing with superheroes. In *Die Hard*, Detective John McClane (Bruce Willis) reconciles with his estranged wife and a high-ranking Nakatomi executive, Holly Gennaro-McClane (Bonnie Bedelia), by demonstrating that his stoical, self-sufficient and violent masculinity is superior to Holly's careerism. As Keane argues, quoting Susan Jeffords: 'US masculinity in Hollywood films of the 1980s was largely transcribed through spectacle and bodies, with the male body itself becoming the most fulfilling form of spectacle.'[64] *Sudden Death* exhibits Van Damme's prowess in a way that *San Andreas* (2015) and *Skyscraper* (Rawson Marshall Thurber, 2018) – hybrid disaster movies indebted to the 70s cycle – are vehicles for Dwayne Johnson, who is also known by his wrestling ring name: 'The Rock'. Hollywood has a long tradition of turning sporting heroes into disaster film actors – for example, O. J. Simpson in *Inferno* and Woody Strode in *The Last Voyage* (Andrew L. Stone, 1960). The cross-over underscores the transformation of the superhero into an ordinary heroic saviour (e.g., a fireman, a Marine veteran, an FBI agent). On the front cover of a DC Comics memorial edition, entitled *9-11: September 11TH 2001*, Superman is depicted as paying respect to the so-called real heroes: ordinary people with extraordinary strength. The speech bubble utters the single word: 'Wow', implying a humbling of the superhero when it comes to genuine disaster heroism. But the image still demonstrates a fixation on unreality. In one story, 'Unreal': 'Superman bemoans that the fact that he's "unreal"', and that he is unable to 'break free from the fictional pages where I live and breathe, become real during times of crisis, and right the wrongs of an unjust world. A world, fortunately, protected by heroes of its own.'[65] The story denudes the fantasy space of superheroes, but the upgrading of 'ordinary' masculine courage into the unreal action drama of disaster is a cinematic legacy of the seventies cycle.

Bee dystopia

The only obvious follow-on from *The Swarm* (1978) is *The Killer Bees* (Penelope Buitenhuis, 2002), a television movie that also bears the hallmarks of Irwin Allen's made-for-television disaster films, as well as 1970s' revenge-of-nature spin-offs, such as *Piranha*. The sheriff, Lyndon Harris (C. Thomas Howell), who echoes police chief Martin Brody (Roy Scheider) in *Jaws*, had witnessed, as a child, the death of his father by stinging bees, and years later attempts to warn local farmers in a small town of the threat posed by a swarm of killer bees. An entomologist, Riley Muir (Fiona Loewi), believes they are African bees, the result of a crossbreeding experiment in Brazil. It soon turns out that they are being delivered to farmers during the pollinating season in a truck, driven by a Mexican (Raimund Stamm) who is suspected of being an illegal immigrant. So, the film alludes to the racist hysteria provoked by the bee scare in the 1970s. Following an escalation of isolated bee-related deaths, the mayor (Doug Abrahams) refuses to heed the warnings because of the up-and-coming 'Sumas Honey Festival'. In this respect, there are parallels to mayor Larry Vaughn (Murray Hamilton) in *Jaws*, who was indirectly responsible for the deaths of swimmers in Amity Waters. However, this mayor, who has sold out to a bank in aiding the foreclosure of farms, is uncaring, and dies a *schadenfreude* death when the swarm attacks the festival. As well as professionals, sceptics and a bee problem, there is a typical Irwin Allen small town family drama. The sheriff, who is estranged from his wife (who is demanding a divorce) and unruly son – Dylan Harris (Noel Fisher), proves his worth when he sets fire to the colony of bees in a community hall – thus saving the occupants. Mr. Harris believes his wife, Audrey Harris (Tracy Nelson), had lost confidence in him when their farm was foreclosed. And so, through the act of eco-sadism and masculine redemption, the family are reunited. Despite its title, this bee movie legacy does not reiterate the beehive gender politics of *Killer Bees* (Curtis Harrington, 1974). Instead of the separatist queen bee, it is the male exterminator of bees who is ultimately respected and valorized. Yet again, disaster is a test of character for the emasculated male.

The Killer Bees exemplifies a modern dystopian representation of bee swarming, as well as bee balling, that has recurred in various film scenes, for instance: *Candyman* (Bernard Rose, 1992), *The X-Files* (Rob Bowman, 1998) and *The Wicker Man* (Neil LaBute, 2006).[66] In the 'lair' scene, the Candyman (Tony Todd) offers immortality to Helen (Virginia Madsen) and opens his coat to reveal a ribcage wreathed in bees, and the bees pour out his mouth and stream down her throat. In the 'swarmed' scene, Special Agents Fox Mulder (David Duchovny) and Dana Scully (Gillian Anderson) flee a glowing dome when grates in the floor open and swarms of bees fly out. In *The Wicker Man* remake, Edward Malus (Nicholas Cage), who does not believe in native pagan gods, becomes a human sacrifice to restore the island's production and to bring back the pollinating bees. This is also revenge for Edward having destroyed the beehives. In the torture scene, a basket of live stinging bees is placed over his head, before he is sacrificed in a giant wicker man. The prevalence of bee dystopia is an indicator that matriarchal bee ecotopias, exemplified by Charlotte Perkins Gilman's short story 'Bee Wise' (1913), do not lend themselves to Hollywood spectacle.[67] Rather than offering an alternative social model or being seen as essential for ecological balance, bees are an instrument of terror.

Conclusion

The focus on the family in the disaster genre, as illustrated by Joe Webb's painting, *Staying In*, and which is evident in, for instance, *2012*, *San Andreas*, *Sudden Death*, *Die Hard*, and *The Killer Bees*, generally veils the justification of male aggression channelled through protectionism. Even though Superman is lacking in a biological family, Superman's heroic anger is provoked by Lois's death, and, in *Superman II*, their romance is consummated, implying an alternate human, and fully embodied, destiny for the superhero. Superman's messianic duty to bring out the good in humanity is momentarily betrayed by sexual and romantic desire. Ultimately, he realizes his selfishness and makes a utilitarian choice, one that echoes Charlotte Perkins Gilman's disaster story, 'The Unnatural Mother' (1895), which tells of a mother saving, rather than her own daughter, the lives in three villages from a flood: 'She neglected her own to look after other folks [...]'.[68] In other words, a disaster only brings out the best in a person if it is self-sacrifice for the collective good.

Notes

Preface

1 Naomi Grimley, Jack Cornish and Nassos Stylianou, 'Covid: World's True Pandemic Death Toll Nearly 15 Million, Says WHO', *BBC News*, 1 May 2022. https://www.bbc.co.uk/news/health-61327778
2 Leicester had to endure special Lockdown measures, isolated from the new freedoms gradually being enjoyed by the rest of the UK.

Introduction

1 Quoted in Judy Klemesrud, 'He's the Master of Disaster: He's the Master of Disaster Bang! Crash! Sizzle!', *The New York Times*, 29 December 1974: 71.
2 'Arnold Schwarzenegger: Climate Change Is Not Science Fiction', *The Guardian*, 21 July 2015. https://www.theguardian.com/environment/2015/jul/21/arnold-schwarzenegger-climate-change-is-not-science-fiction
3 George Monbiot, 'Watching Don't Look Up Made Me See My Whole Life of Campaigning Flash before Me', *The Guardian*, 4 January 2022. https://www.theguardian.com/commentisfree/2022/jan/04/dont-look-up-life-of-campaigning
4 Will Self, 'Rereading Philosophy Books: Guy Debord's *The Society of the Spectacle*', *The Guardian*, 14 November 2013. https://www.theguardian.com/books/2013/nov/14/guy-debord-society-spectacle-will-self
5 Douglas Kellner, *Media Spectacle* (London: Routledge, 2003), 2–3.
6 Kevan Manwaring, 'APOCALYPSE (wow!), 1 March 2019. https://www.stillpointldn.com/articles/kevan-manwaring-apocalypse-wow/
7 Slavoj Žižek, *Event* (London: Penguin Books, 2014), 6.
8 Stephen Keane, *Disaster Movies: The Cinema of Catastrophe* (London: Wallflower, 2001), 19.
9 Zoë Wallin, '"Pictures Seem to Run in Cycles": Industry Discourse and the Economics of Film Cycles in Classical Hollywood', *Film History* 31, no. 1 (2019): 81–101.
10 Michael Ryan and Douglas Kellner, *Camera Politica: The Politics and Ideology of Contemporary Hollywood Film* (Bloomington and Indianapolis: Indiana University Press, 1990), 52.

11 'Disaster films constitute a sufficiently numerous, old, and conventionalized group to be considered a genre rather than a popular cycle that comes and goes'. Maurice Yacowar, 'The Bug in the Rug: Notes on the Disaster Genre', in *Film Genre Reader IV*, ed. B. K. Grant (Austin: University of Texas Press, 2012), 313.
12 Ryan and Kellner, *Camera Politica*, 49; See also David Cook, '1974: Movies and Political Trauma', in *American Cinema of the 1970s: Themes and variations*, ed. L. D. Friedman (New Brunswick: Rutgers University Press, 2007), 124. '*Earthquake* and *The Towering Inferno*, [...] reflect the country's loss of faith in its institutions'.
13 Nick Roddick, 'Only the Stars Survive: Disaster Movies in the Seventies', in *Performance and Politics in Popular Drama*, ed. David Brady, Louis James and Bernard Sharratt (Cambridge: Cambridge University Press, 1981), 245; Roger Ebert, '*The Towering Inferno* (movie review)', *Chicago Sun-Times*, 1 January 1974. https://www.rogerebert.com/reviews/the-towering-inferno-1974
14 Peter Lev, *American Films of the 70s: Conflicting Visions* (Austin: University Texas Press, 2010), 49.
15 Keane, *Disaster Movies*, 50.
16 Ryan and Kellner, *Camera Politica*, 56.
17 John Sutherland, *Bestsellers: Popular Fiction of the 1970s* (London: Routledge & Kegan Paul, 1981), 118.
18 Roddick, 'Only the Stars Survive', 257.
19 Stuart M. Kaminsky, *American Film Genres* (Chicago: Nelson-Hall, 1988), 2.
20 Steve Neale, *Genre and Hollywood* (London: Routledge, 2000), 7.
21 As John Belton puts it: 'Genres help to stabilize an otherwise unstable film industry'. *American Cinema/American Culture* (New York: McGraw-Hill, 2005), 127. List of Universal disaster movies: *Airport* (1970), *The Andromeda Strain* (1971), *Earthquake* (1974), *Airport 1975* (1974), *Jaws* (1975), *The Hindenburg* (1975), *Two-Minute Warning* (1976), *Airport '77* (1977), *Rollercoaster* (1977), *Gray Lady Down* (1978), *Jaws 2* (1978) and *The Concorde ... Airport '79* (1979). *Airport*'s commercial success in 1970 surpassed *Spartacus* (1960) as Universal's 'biggest money maker'. Universal Pictures financial investment in twelve disaster movies proved to be warranted until *Two-Minute Warning* signalled a decline in commercial terms.
22 Rick Altman states: 'The basic, broadly accepted assumption [...] stands: once generically identified by the industry, films are typed for life', in *Film/Genre* (London: BFI, 1999), 19.
23 '[...] the disaster film exploits the spectacular potential of the screen and nourishes the audience's fascination with the vision of massive doom'. Yacowar, 'Notes on the Disaster Genre', 313.
24 *Airport* precipitated a cycle in terms of big-budget disaster films in featuring an all-star cast, a multi-stranded narrative, a time-critical scenario, an impending disaster

as the central feature of its plot and heroic male leadership. See Annette Kuhn and Guy Westwell, *Oxford Dictionary of Film Studies* (Oxford: Oxford University Press, 2012), 143.

25 Roddick, 'Only the Stars Survive', 243.
26 Vincent Canby, 'The Screen: Multi-Plot, Multi-Star "Airport" Opens: Lancaster and Martin in Principal Roles Adaptation of Hailey's Novel at Music Hall', *The New York Times*, 6 March 1970, 34; Vincent Vincent, 'What Makes "Poseidon" Fun?', *The New York Times*, 14 January 1973, 121.
27 Pauline Kael, *Reeling* (London: Marion Boyars, 1977), 385. Kael is commenting on *Earthquake* (2 December 1974).
28 Nat Segaloff, *Stirling Silliphant: The Fingers of God* (Albany: BearManor Media, 2013), 117–18.
29 Andrew Britton, 'Blissing Out: The Politics of Reaganite Entertainment', in *Britton on Film: The Complete Film Criticism of Andrew Britton*, ed. Barry Keith Grant (Detroit: Wayne State University Press, 2008), 97–156, 99.
30 Kael, *Reeling*, 406.
31 'Modern subjects have developed a protective shield, though "the real" has ways of breaking back through', in *Crash Cultures: Modernity, Mediation and the Material*, ed. Jane Arthurs and Iain Grant (Bristol: Intellect Books, 2003), 4.
32 Altman, *Film/Genre*, 61.
33 Joël Magny, Denis Lévy and Stéphane Sorel, 'Films Catastrophiques: Spectateurs Catastrophés', *Positif*, March 1976, 11–14. I am grateful for Hannah May's French-to-English translation.
34 Joel Magny, 'Towards a New Man', in 'Films Catastrophiques: Spectateurs Catastrophés'.
35 Stéphane Sorel, 'Catastrophic Masculinity', in 'Films Catastrophiques: Spectateurs Catastrophés'.
36 Ibid.
37 Ibid.
38 See Tatiana Teslenko, *Feminist Utopian Novels of the 1970s: Joanna Russ and Dorothy Bryant* (London: Routledge, 2003).
39 John Sutherland defined 'eco-sadism', a 'disguised satisfaction of the [disaster] genre', as: 'the justified slaughter of wild things'. *Reading the Decades: Fifty Years of the Nation's Bestselling Books* (London: BBC Worldwide Ltd, 2002), 119.
40 Roddick, 'Only the Stars Survive', 257–62.
41 Yacowar, 'The Bug in the Rug: Notes on the Disaster Genre', 325.
42 Kael, *Reeling*, 385.
43 Vincent Canby, '"The Towering Inferno" First-Rate Visual Spectacle', *The New York Times* (20 December 1974). https://www.nytimes.com/1974/12/20/archives/the-towering-inferno-firstrate-visual-spectacle.html

44 Vincent Canby, 'The Year of the Disaster Movie', *The Times-News* (2 December 1974). https://news.google.com/newspapers?id=g1MaAAAAIBAJ&sjid=vyQEAAAAIBAJ&pg=7166,3828596&hl=en
45 Keane, *Disaster Movies*, 33.
46 Ibid., 48.
47 Roddick, 'Only the Stars Survive', 246.
48 The so-called beginning of the end for the cycle was signalled by United Artists' *Juggernaut* (1974) – the first to lose money – and Universal's *The Hindenburg* (1975), which also lost a significant amount of money. As David A. Cook puts it: '[…] the cycle had run its course'. *Lost Illusions: American Cinema in the Shadow of Watergate and Vietnam, 1970–1979* (Los Angeles: University of California Press, 2000), 254.
49 Roger Ebert, '*The Hindenburg* (movie review)', *Chicago-Sun Times*, 1 January 1975. https://www.rogerebert.com/reviews/the-hindenburg-1975
50 Kael, *Reeling*, 387.
51 Amanda Ann Klein, *American Film Cycles: Reframing Genres, Screening Social Problems, and Defining Subcultures* (Austin: University of Texas Press, 2011), 19.
52 Yacowar defines eight basic types: 'natural attack', 'the ship of fools', 'the city fails', 'the monster', 'survival', 'war', 'the historical', 'the comic'.
53 Ryan and Kellner, *Camera Politica*, 57.
54 Keane, *Disaster Movies*, 49; Britton, 'Blissing Out', 98.
55 Mollie Gregory, *Stuntwomen: The Untold Hollywood Story* (Lexington: University Press of Kentucky, 2015), 109.

Chapter 1

1 T. S. Eliot, *The Dry Salvages* (London: Faber & Faber, 1941), 8.
2 See Jeremy Diaper, *T. S. Eliot & Organicism* (Clemson, South Carolina: Clemson University Press, 2018), 69–72. The tendency to forget the memory of earth's climatic past is also expressed in John Steinbeck's *East of Eden*. B. Lynn Ingram, Frances Malamud-Roam, and Lynn Ingram, *The West without Water: What Past Floods, Droughts, and Other Climatic Clues Tell Us about Tomorrow* (Berkeley: University of California Press, 2013), 31.
3 Ibid., 58.
4 Jess C. Porter, 'What Was the Dust Bowl? Assessing Contemporary Popular Knowledge', *Popul Environ* (2014): 35: 391–416, 361–2.
5 Pauline Kael, *Reeling* (London: Marion Boyars, 1976), 384.
6 Stephen Keane, *Disaster Movies: The Cinema of Catastrophe* (London: Wallflower, 2001).

7   A. A. Iannucci (ed.), 'Dante and Hollywood', in *Dante, Cinema, and Television* (Toronto: University of Toronto Press, 2004), 3–20, 10.
8   See Neil M. Maher, '"A Conflux of Desire and Need": Trees, Boy Scouts, and the Roots of Franklin Roosevelt's Civilian Conservation Corps', in *FDR and the Environment*, ed. Henry L. Henderson and David B. Woolner (New York: Palgrave Macmillan, 2005), 49–84, 56.
9   William H. Brackney, 'Walter Rauschenbusch: Then and Now', *Baptist Quarterly* (2017): 48:1, 23–46.
10 Christopher H. Evans, *The Social Gospel in American Religion: A History* (New York: New York University Press, 2017), 147.
11 See Doug Rossinow, 'The Radicalization of the Social Gospel: Harry F. Ward and the Search for a New Social Order, 1898–1936', *Religion and American Culture: A Journal of Interpretation* 15, no. 1 (Winter 2005): 63–106.
12 David Leeming, *The Oxford Companion to World Mythology* (Oxford: Oxford University Press, 2009), 138.
13 Franks Kermode, *The Sense of an Ending: Studies in the Theory of Fiction* (Oxford: Oxford University Press, 1967), 96.
14 Brian M. Stableford, 'Introduction', in Sydney Fowler Wright, *Deluge*, ed. Brian M. Stableford (Middletown, CT: Wesleyan University Press, 2003), i–iviii, xxiii.
15 Sheldon Hall and Steve Neale, *Epics, Spectacles and Blockbusters* (Detroit: Wayne State University Press, 2010), 98.
16 Ibid., 39–40.
17 T. S. Eliot, 'Ulysses, Order and Myth [1923]', in *Selected Prose of T. S. Eliot*, ed. Frank Kermode (London: A Harvest Book, 1975), 175–8.
18 See Scott Freer, *Modernist Mythopoeia: The Twilight of the Gods* (London: Palgrave, 2015), 45–77.
19 As Brian M. Stableford points out, *Deluge* does not advocate a return to a 'State of Nature' but 'represents the reconstruction of social order as an urgent and difficult problem'. Sydney Fowler Wright, *Deluge* (Skerries, County Dublin: Gilbert Dalton, 1980), xxx.
20 Wright, *Deluge*, 239.
21 Ibid.
22 Arthur J. Pomeroy, *Then It Was Destroyed by the Volcano: The Ancient World in Film and on Television* (London: Gerald Duckworth, 2008), 34.
23 Ibid., 7.
24 Ibid., 34.
25 See Adam Fairclough, 'Historian and the Civil Rights Movement', *Journal of American Studies* 24, no. 3 (1990): 387–98.

26 Robert B. Ray, *A Certain Tendency of the Hollywood Cinema, 1930–1980* (Princeton, NJ: Princeton University Press, 1985), 29.
27 Stephen Fender, 'The Dust Bowl on Film', in *Nature, Class, and New Deal Literature: The Country Poor in the Great Depression* (London: Routledge, 2011), 127–56, 131.
28 Jeffrey Geiger, *American Documentary Film: Projecting the Nation* (Edinburgh: Edinburgh University Press, 2011), 12.
29 Pare Lorentz, *The River* (script), in *Pare Lorentz, FDR's Moviemaker: Memoirs & Scripts* (Reno: Nevada Press, 1992), 60–76, 66.
30 Ibid., 69.
31 Ibid., 71.
32 Pare Lorentz, *The Plow that Broke the Plains* (script), in *Pare Lorentz, FDR's Moviemaker: Memoirs & Scripts*, 44–50, 50.
33 Lorentz, *The River* (script), 74.
34 Ibid., 76.
35 Pare Lorentz, 'The Making of *The River*', in *Pare Lorentz, FDR's Moviemaker: Memoirs & Scripts*, 51–9, 57.
36 See Robin Murray and Joe Heumann, 'Environmental Catastrophe in Pare Lorentz's "The River" and Elia Kazan's "Wild River": The TVA, Politics, and the Environment', *Studies in Popular Culture*, October 2004, Vol. 27, No. 2, *Studies in American Culture* (October 2004), 47–65. 'Lorentz's *The River* claims that the best way to solve the problems humans have caused by their degradation of nature is to implement a technological project driven by culture and mankind: the TVA's construction of enormous dams like the Norris Dam, started in 1933 and finished on 4 March 1936, at the head of the Tennessee River', 48.
37 Geiger, *American Documentary Film*, 111. Here Geiger quotes George Stoney (2007) Interview, special features, *The Plow That Broke the Plains / The River*, dir. Pare Lorentz [DVD], Naxos.
38 John Steinbeck, *The Grapes of Wrath* (London: Penguin Books, 2000), 456–76.
39 Robert DeMott, 'Introduction', in John Steinbeck, *The Grapes of Wrath* (London: Penguin Books, 2000), xl.
40 Ibid.
41 Ibid., xii–xiv.
42 Pare Lorentz, 'The Grapes of Wrath (review)', in *Movies 1927 to 1941: Lorentz on Film* (New York: Hopkinson and Blake, 1975), 185.
43 Vivian C. Sobchack, '*The Grapes of Wrath* (1940): Thematic Emphasis through Visual Style', in *Hollywood as Historian: American Film in a Cultural Context*, ed. Peter C. Rollins (Lexington: University Press of Kentucky, 1983), 68–87, 87.
44 A case may be made for the roots of the 1970s films to have also existed in the 1950s sci-fi and monster movies, in which a community pulls together to confront

and address an external threat. This is the basic Nigel Kneale plotline in, for instance, *The Quatermass Experiment* (1953), which is replicated in *The Blob* (Irvin Yeaworth, 1958). However, the 1930s cycle was reflective of actual flood disasters.

Chapter 2

1. Staff, 'Airport Review', *TV Guide Magazine*. https://www.tvguide.com/movies/airport/review/2030122594/
2. Staff, 'Airport Review', *Variety*, 31 December 1969. https://variety.com/1969/film/reviews/airport-1200422292/
3. Stephen Keane, *Disaster Movies: The Cinema of Catastrophe* (London: Wallflower, 2001), 19.
4. Sheldon Hall and Steve Neale, *Epics, Spectacles and Blockbusters* (Detroit: Wayne State University Press, 2010), 205.
5. Peter Krämer, *The New Hollywood: From Bonnie and Clyde to Star Wars* (London: Wallflower Press, 2005), 108.
6. Vincent Canby, 'What Makes 'Poseidon' Fun?', *The New York Times*, 14 January 1973, 121.
7. David A. Cook, *Lost Illusions: American Cinema in the Shadow of Watergate and Vietnam, 1970–1979* (Los Angeles: University of California Press, 2000), 33–4.
8. George Seaton, *Airport* (1969 script), 42.
9. Krämer, *The New Hollywood*, 107.
10. Ibid., 110.
11. Ibid., 107. I am grateful to Dr Sheldon Hall for sharing and substantiating this information.
12. Vincent Canby sees *Airport* as resembling 'any number of old 'Grand Hotel' movies'. 'The Screen: Multi-Plot, Multi-Star 'Airport' Opens: Lancaster and Martin in Principal Roles Adaptation of Hailey's Novel at Music Hall', *The New York Times*, 6 March 1970: 34.
13. Brenda I. Koerner, *The Skies Belong to Us: Love and Terror in the Golden Age of Hijackings* (New York: Crown Publishers, 2013), 8–10.
14. Stephen Keane, 'The Savage Seventies', in *Disaster Movies: The Cinema of Catastrophe* (London: Wallflower Press, 2001), 19–50; Michael Ryan and Douglas Kellner, 'Disaster Films', in *Camera Politica: The Politics and Ideology of Contemporary Hollywood* (Bloomington: Indiana University Press, 1990), 52–6.
15. Keane, *Disaster Movies*, 31.
16. Ryan and Kellner, *Camera Politica*, 52–3.
17. Grace M. Ferrara (ed.), *The Disaster File: The 1970s* (London: The Macmillan Press Ltd, 1980), 2.

18　Mimi White, 'Movies and the Movement', in *American Cinema of the 1970s: Themes and Variations*, ed. Lester D. Friedman (Oxford: Berg Publishers, 2007), 24.
19　Terry H. Anderson, '1968: The End and the Beginning in the United States and Western Europe', *South Central Review* 16–17, no. 4 (1999): 1.
20　Ibid., 2.
21　Ibid., 3.
22　Ibid., 5.
23　Ibid., 6.
24　Keane, *Disaster Movies*, 24.
25　Koerner, *The Skies Belong to Us*, 8–9.
26　Arthur Hailey, *Airport* (London: Pan Books Ltd, 1970), 473.
27　White, 'Movies and the Movement', 25.
28　Ibid., 34.
29　Keane, *Disaster Movies*, 34.
30　Both *Airport* and *Love Story* are also screen adaptations of top-selling works of fiction: Arthur Hailey's novel stayed for thirty weeks in *The New York Times* best seller list and Erich Segal's novel for forty-one weeks in 1970.
31　White, 'Movies and the Movement', 37.
32　Ibid., 35.
33　I wish to express my gratitude towards Dr Chris Horn for sharing his scholarly expertise in New Hollywood. See *The Lost Decade: Altman, Coppola, Friedkin and The Hollywood Renaissance Auteur in the 1980s* (forthcoming from Bloomsbury).
34　Pauline Kael, *Deeper into Movies* (Boston: Little, Brown and Company, 1973), 132 & 136.
35　Ibid., 136.
36　See Guy Barefoot, *Trash Cinema: The Lure of the Low* (New York: Columbia University Press, 2017), 12.
37　Kael, *Deeper into Movies*, 294.
38　Roger Ebert, '*Airport* (movie review)', *Chicago Sun-Times*, 1 January 1970. https://www.rogerebert.com/reviews/airport-1970
39　Vincent Canby, *Airport* review.
40　Pauline Kael, *Reeling* (London: Marion Boyars, 1976), 72.
41　Pauline Kael, *5001 Nights at the Movies* (London: Marion Boyars, 1993), 591.
42　Ibid., 12 & 299.
43　*Airport* Theatrical Trailer. https://www.youtube.com/watch?v=PACKbKt8MOw
44　Kael, *Deeper into Movies*, 92.
45　Maria del Mar Azcona, *The Multi-Protagonist Film* (Oxford: Wiley-Blackwell, 2010), 47 & 62.
46　Kael, *Reeling*, 447.

47 Ibid., 451.
48 Robin Wood, *Hollywood from Vietnam to Reagan ... Beyond* (New York: Columbia Press, 2003), 25.
49 See Robert Niemi, 'Experiments in Genre Revision', in *The Cinema of Robert Altman Book Subtitle: Hollywood Maverick* (New York: Columbia University Press), 23.
50 Cook, *Lost Illusions*, 251–2.
51 Hailey, *Airport*, 3.
52 Peter Savage, 'Hailey's Commentaries: Best Selling Views on Latter-Day Organizations', *Public Administration Review* 39, no. 2 (1979): 184–7.
53 Peter Guttridge, 'Obituaries: Arthur Hailey', *The Independent*, 27 November 2004. https://www.independent.co.uk/news/obituaries/arthur-hailey-534720.html
54 Ibid.
55 Jenifer Van Vleck, *Empire of the Air: Aviation and the American Ascendancy* (Cambridge: Harvard University Press, 2013), 240–1. '26 October 1958: Pan American World Airways opened the "Jet Age" with the first commercial flight of an American jet airliner.' See Tag Archives: 'Clipper America', *This Day in Aviation: Important Dates in Aviation History*. https://www.thisdayinaviation.com/tag/clipper-america/
56 Vincent Canby, *Airport* review.
57 Seaton, *Airport*, 175.
58 John Woodcock, 'Disaster Thrillers: A Literary Mode of Technology Assessment', *Science, Technology, & Human Values* 4, no. 26 (1979): 38.
59 Hailey, *Airport*, 475.
60 Charles D. Bright, 'Aviation Literature – A Changing Art', *Aerospace Historian* 31, no. 1 (1984): 72.
61 Hailey, *Airport*, 70.
62 Ibid., 160.
63 Ibid., 156.
64 Ibid., 155.
65 Ibid., 156.
66 Ibid., 156–7.
67 Ibid., 157–8.
68 Woodcock, 'Disaster Thrillers', 38.
69 Peter Lev, *American Films of the 70s: Conflicting Visions* (Austin: University of Texas Press, 2000), 43.
70 See Keane, *Disaster Movies*, 21; John Sanders, *Studying Disaster Movies* (Leighton Buzzard: Auteur Publishing Ltd, 2009), 18.
71 Seaton, *Airport*, 89–90.
72 Keane, *Disaster Movies*, 28.

73 Nick Roddick, 'Only the Stars Survive: Disaster Movies in the Seventies', in *Performance and Politics in Popular Drama*, ed. David Brady, Louis James and Bernard Sharratt (Cambridge: Cambridge University Press, 1981), 244.

74 Hailey, *Airport*, 3.

75 Staff, *Airport* (movie review), *Variety*, 31 December 1969. https://variety.com/1969/film/reviews/airport-1200422292/

76 Keane, *Disaster Movies*, 24.

77 Joël Magny, Denis Lévy and Stéphane Sorel, 'Films Catastrophiques: Spectacteurs Catastrophés', *Positif*, March 1976, 11–14.

78 Joan Sangster and Julia Smith, 'From Career Girl to Sexy Stewardess: Popular Culture and Women's Work in the Canadian and American Airline Industries', *Women: A Cultural Review* 30, no. 2 (2019): 150.

79 Peter Lyth, '"Think of Her as Your Mother": Airline Advertising and the Stewardess in America, 1930–1980', *The Journal of Transport History* 30, no. 1 (2009): 11.

80 Seaton, *Airport*, 42.

81 Keane, *Disaster Movies*, 28. See also Ryan and Kellner, *Camera Politica*, 51–5.

82 Seaton, *Airport*, 42.

83 Ibid., 43–4.

84 Ibid., 44–6.

85 Ibid., 15 & 12.

86 Ibid., 18. See Victoria Vantoch, *The Jet Sex: Airline Stewardesses and the Making of an American Icon* (Philadelphia: University of Pennsylvania Press, 2013), 95.

87 Seaton, *Airport*, 63 & 172.

88 Vincent Canby, *Airport* Review.

89 Douglas Keesey, *Brian de Palma's Split-Screen: A Life in Film* (Jackson: University Press of Mississippi, 2019), 4.

90 Ibid.

91 Todd Berliner, 'Hollywood Storytelling and The Aesthetic Pleasure', in *Psychocinematics: Exploring Cognition at the Movies*, ed. Arthur P. Shimamura (Oxford: Oxford University Press, 2013), 195.

92 Peter William Evan, *Written on the Wind* (London: British Film Institute, 2013), 1.

93 Tom Gunning, 'Heard over the Phone: The Lonely Villa and the de Lorde Tradition of the Terrors of Technology', *Screen* 32, no. 2 (1991): 188.

94 Ibid.

95 Ned Schantz, 'Telephonic Film', *Film Quarterly* 56, no. 4 (2003): 23.

96 Ibid., 25.

97 Ibid., 34.

98 Seaton, *Airport*, 1.

99 Ibid., 2.

100 Ibid., 4.
101 Ibid., 21–3.
102 Ibid., 98.
103 Ibid., 101.
104 Ibid., 8.
105 Ibid., 9.
106 Ibid., 104.
107 Ibid., 131.
108 Ibid., 136.

Chapter 3

1 Stephen Keane, *Disaster Movies: The Cinema of Catastrophe* (London: Wallflower, 2001), 29.
2 Vincent Canby, 'What Makes "Poseidon" Fun?', *The New York Times*, 14 January 1973, 121.
3 Nick Roddick, 'The Poseidon Adventure', in *Magill's Survey of Cinema, English Language Films,* ed. Frank Magill (Englewood, NJ: Salem Press, 1980), 1363–4.
4 Peter Lev, *American Films of the 70s: Conflicting Visions* (Austin: University of Texas Press, 2000), 45.
5 Daniel K. Williams, 'Richard Nixon's Religious Right: Catholics, Evangelicals, and the Creation of an Antisecular Alliance', in *The Right Side of the Sixties: Reexamining Conservatism's Decade of Transformation,* ed. Laura Jane Gifford and Daniel K. Williams (Palgrave, 2012), 141–58, 141.
6 Axel R. Schäfer, 'Introduction: Evangelicals and the Sixties: Revisiting the 'Backlash', in *American Evangelicals and the 1960s*, ed. Axel R. Schäfer (Madison: University of Wisconsin Press, 2013), 3–16, 6.
7 Will Kaufmann and Staff Van Oostrum, *American Culture in the 1970s* (Edinburgh: Edinburgh University Press, 2009), 24.
8 Lev, *American Films of the 70s*, 44.
9 Robert Stam, 'The Upside-Down World of the Carnivalesque', in *Keywords in Subversive Film/Media Aesthetics*, ed. Robert Stam, Richard Porton and Leo Goldsmith (Chichester: John Wiley & Sons, 2015), 68–106, 89.
10 Ibid., 70.
11 Ibid., 71–2.
12 Michael DeAngelis, 'Movies and Confession', in *American Cinema of the 1970s: Themes and Variations,* ed. Lester D. Friedman and Margo Natalie Crawford (New Brunswick: Rutgers University Press, 2007), 71–94, 79.

13 Stam, 'The Upside-Down World of the Carnivalesque', 72.
14 Paul Gallico, *The Poseidon Adventure* (London: Pan Books Ltd, 1969), 7–25.
15 Ibid., 7.
16 Ibid., 69.
17 Clarence H. Baily, 'The Wreck of the Valencia', in *The Pacific Monthly*, March 1906, 281.
18 Genesis 28: 11–12.
19 Thomas Hardy, 'The Convergence of the Twain', quoted in *Poetry Foundation*. https://www.poetryfoundation.org/poems/47266/the-convergence-of-the-twain
20 Paul Heyer, *Titanic Legacy: Disaster as Media Event and Myth* (London: Praeger, 1995), 128–9.
21 Ibid., 134.
22 Cited from Staff, 'Obituaries: Irwin Allen, Producer of Disaster Films, Dies', *The Washington Post* (4 November 1991): B6.
23 Jon Abbott, *Irwin Allen Television Productions, 1964–1970: A Critical History of Voyage to the Bottom of the Sea, Lost in Space, the Time Tunnel and Land of the Giants* (Jefferson: McFarland & Co., 2009), 113.
24 Gladwin Hill, 'Hollywood Cycle: Industry Is Gearing for Outer', *The New York Times* (26 March 1961): X9.
25 Keane, *Disaster*, 44.
26 Gallico, *Poseidon*, 234.
27 Bosley Crowther, 'Screen: Disaster at Sea: "Last Voyage" Provides Thrills and Suspense', *The New York Times* (20 February 1960): 14.
28 Staff, 'New Picture: The Last Voyage (M-G-M)', *Time* (29 February 1960), no. 9: 98.
29 Ken Ringle, 'Integrity Goes Down with the Ship; Historical Facts, Including True-Life Gallantry, Lost in *Titanic*', *The Washington Post* (22 March 1998): 140.
30 See Steven F. Lawson, 'Long Origins of the Short Civil Rights Movement, 1954–1968', in *Freedom Right: New Perspectives on the Civil Rights Movement,* ed. Danielle L. McGuire and John Dittmer (Lexington: University Press of Kentucky, 2011), 9–38. I am grateful for David Daverick for sharing his expertise.
31 See Chapter 1 for a more detailed examination of *Dante's Inferno* (1935).
32 Mikhail Bakhtin, *Rabelais and His World,* trans. Helene Iswolsky (Cambridge: MIT Press, 1965), 7–10.
33 Michael Holquist, *Dialogism: Bakhtin and His World* (London: Routledge, 1990), 89.
34 Bakhtin, *Rabelais and His World*, 370.
35 Friedrich Nietzsche, *The Birth of Tragedy Out of the Spirit of Music,* trans. Michael Tanner (London: Penguin Books, 1993), 17.
36 Terence Eagleton, *Holy Terror* (Oxford: Oxford University Press, 2005), 4.

37 Ibid., 3–4.
38 George Seaton, *Airport* (screenplay), 19.
39 Ibid., 25.
40 Ibid.
41 Ibid., 28.
42 Ibid., 29.
43 Ibid., 30–1.
44 Ibid., 34–6a.
45 Ibid., 38.
46 See Stam, 'The Upside-Down World of the Carnivalesque', 71–2.
47 Seaton, *Airport* (screenplay), 39a.
48 Ibid., 41.
49 Stam, 'The Upside-Down World of the Carnivalesque', 78.
50 Stirling Silliphant, *The Poseidon Adventure* Screenplay, Third Revised Shooting Final (24 March 1972), 57.
51 Ibid., 61.
52 Ibid.
53 Gallico, *The Poseidon Adventure*, 50.
54 Seaton, *Airport* (screenplay), 71A.
55 Gallico, *The Poseidon Adventure*, 105–6.
56 Ibid., 21.
57 William Ernest Henley, 'Invictus', in *Book of Verses* (1888), cited from *Poetry Foundation*. https://www.poetryfoundation.org/poems/51642/invictus
58 Gallico, *Poseidon*, 9.
59 Paul Gallico, *Confessions of a Story-Teller* (London: Michael Joseph, 1961), 25.
60 Ibid., 23.
61 Kate Bowler, *Blessed: A History of the American Prosperity Gospel* (Oxford: Oxford University Press, 2003), 78.
62 Ibid., 79.
63 Matthew 17:20.
64 Daniel J. Salinas (ed.), *Prosperity Theology and the Gospel: Good News or Bad News for the Poor?* (Peabody, MA: Hendrickson Publishers, 2017), 9.
65 Ibid., 5.
66 Oral Roberts, *Oral Robert's Life Story: As Told by Himself* (Tulsa 1, OK: Oral Roberts, 1952), 70.
67 Oral Roberts, *The Call: An Autobiography* (London: Hodder and Stoughton, 1972), 215–16.
68 Gallico, *Poseidon*, 14.
69 Ibid., 15.

70 Ibid., 277.
71 'God is no copilot in the current disaster film and probably never was'. Maurice Yacowar, 'The Bug in the Rug: Notes on the Disaster Genre', in *Film Genre Reader IV*, ed. Barry Keith Grant (Austin: University of Texas Press, 2012), 325. However, for Nick Roddick: 'the idea of the disaster as a primitive elemental test sent by God is strongly present in all the movies with the exception of *Juggernaut*'. 'Only the Stars Survive: Disaster Movies in the Seventies', in *Performance and Politics in Popular Drama*, ed. David Brady, Louis James and Bernard Sharratt (Cambridge: Cambridge University Press, 1981), 254.
72 Keane, *Disaster Movies*, 38.
73 Ibid., 32–4.
74 Gallico, *Poseidon*, 237.
75 Ibid., 222.
76 Ibid., 241–2.
77 Ibid., 243.
78 Ibid., 244–5.
79 Ibid., 251.
80 Ibid., 252–3.
81 Ibid., 253–4.
82 Romans 9: 6–8.
83 Gallico, *Poseidon*, 306.
84 Seaton, *Airport* (screenplay), 128.
85 Ibid., 127A–128.
86 Ibid., 129.

Chapter 4

1 John William Law, *Master of Disaster: Irwin Allen – The Disaster Years* (San Francisco: Aplomb Publishing, 2008), 45.
2 Stephen Keane, *Disaster Movies: The Cinema of Catastrophe* (London: Wallflower, 2001), 42–4.
3 Ibid., 42.
4 "'Listen I don't make message movies", he goes on, "but as it turns out I've got the hottest message in the world, in "The Towering Inferno": That there can be a terrible fire disaster in tall buildings. […] It's because of our antiquated fire codes."' Judy Klemesrud, 'He's the Master of Disaster: He's the Master of Disaster Bang! Crash! Sizzle!', *The New York Times*, 29 December (1974): 71.
5 Thomas Stubblefield, *9/11 and the Visual Culture of Disaster* (Bloomington, IN: Indiana University Press, 2015), 3.

6   Ibid., 63.
7   Ibid., 72.
8   See Todd A. Comer and Lloyd Isaac Vayo, 'Introduction: Terror and the (Post) Cinematic Sublime', in *Terror and the Cinematic Sublime: Essays on Violence and the Unpresentable in Post-9/11 Films*, ed. Todd A. Comer and Lloyd Isaac Vayo (London: McFarland & Company, Inc., Publishers, 2013), 5–13.
9   Pauline Kael, *Reeling* (London: Marion Boyars, 1976), 406.
10 See Richard Abel (ed.), *Encyclopedia of Early Cinema* (Taylor & Francis Group, 2005), 577.
11 Ibid., 424.
12 Harvey G. Cohen, 'Chaplin's America, The Essanay and Mutual Years: The Making of an Artist in the Progressive Era, 1915–1917', *Quarterly Review of Film and Video* 33, no. 7 (2016): 585–601, 586.
13 Arthur F. McEvoy, 'The Triangle Shirtwaist Factory Fire of 1911: Social Change, Industrial Accidents, and the Evolution of Common-Sense Causality', *Law & Social Inquiry* 20, no. 2 (1995): 621–51, 629.
14 Louis Waldman, *Labor Lawyer* (New York: E.P. Dutton & Co., 1944), 32–3.
15 David Von Drehle, *Triangle: The Fire that Changed America* (New York: Grove Press, 2004), 3.
16 Ibid., 219.
17 Leon Stein, *The Triangle Fire* (Ithaca, NY: Cornell University Press, 2011), 12.
18 Ibid., 6–7.
19 McEvoy, 'The Triangle Shirtwaist Factory Fire of 1911', 627.
20 Stein, *The Triangle Fire*, 11.
21 Ibid., 20–1.
22 Quoted from Janet Zandy, 'Fire Poetry on the Triangle Shirtwaist Company Fire of March 25, 1911', *College Literature* 24, no. 3, *Diversity and American Poetries* (1997): 33–54, 37.
23 Abel, *Encyclopedia of Early Cinema*, 369.
24 Richard A. Greenwald, '"The Burning Building at 23 Washington Place": The Triangle Fire, Workers and Reformers in Progressive Era New York', *New York History* 83, no. 1 (2002): 55–91, 55.
25 Tom Buckley, 'TV: 'Triangle Fire with Torn Bosley', *The New York Times* (30 January 1979): C12.
26 Quoted from Ken Booth and Tim Dunne, 'Evil', in *Terror in Our Time* (Routledge, 2011), 62–75. 'We are dealing with people, not Monsters', 66.
27 Roland Barthes, 'The Eiffel Tower', in *The Eiffel Tower and Other Mythologies*, trans. Richard Howard (Los Angeles: University of California Press, 1997), 3–18, 3–4.
28 Library of Congress, 'The Skyscrapers of New York'. https://www.loc.gov/item/00694391

29 Merrill Schleier, 'The Empire State Building, Working-Class Masculinity, and "King Kong"', *Mosaic: An Interdisciplinary Critical Journal* 41, no. 2 (2008): 29–54, 30.
30 Ibid., 31.
31 See Åke Bergvall, 'Apocalyptic Imagery in Fritz Lang's Metropolis', *Literature/Film Quarterly* 40, no. 4 (2012): 246–57.
32 T. S. Eliot, *The Waste Land* (New York: Liveright Publishing Corporation, 2013), 64.
33 Geoff King, *Spectacular Narratives: Hollywood in the Age of the Blockbuster* (London: I.B. Tauris, 2000), 146.
34 See Scott G. Bruce (ed.), *The Penguin Book of Hell* (New York: Penguin Books, 2018), xv.
35 Thomas N. Scortia and Frank M. Robinson, *The Glass Inferno* [1974] (New York: Doubleday & Company, Inc.), 5–6 & 374.
36 Ibid., 375.
37 Richard Martin Stern, *The Tower* [1973] (London: Pan Books Ltd, 1974), 12.
38 Ibid., 12.
39 Ibid., 145.
40 Ibid., 145–6.
41 Ibid., 279.
42 See David E. Nye, *American Technological Sublime* (Cambridge: MIT Press, 1994), 103.
43 Ibid., 89.
44 Ibid., 91.
45 Ibid., 100.
46 Vincent Canby, '*The Towering Inferno* First-Rate Visual Spectacle', *The New York Times* (20 December 1974): 20.
47 Terry Eagleton, *Sweet Violence: The Idea of the Tragic* (Oxford: Blackwell Publishing, 2003), 29.
48 Slavoj Žižek, *Event* (London: Penguin Books, 2014), 5.
49 Geoff King, *The Spectacle of the Real: From Hollywood to Reality TV and Beyond* (Bristol: Intellect Books Ltd, 2005), 21.
50 Kael, *Reeling*, 405–7.
51 'I determined to let the fire win – make it the hero – but I always knew that, in the end, the good guys – the Architect and the Fireman – would have to triumph.' Nat Segaloff, *Stirling Silliphant: The Fingers of God* (Albany: BearManor Media, 2013), 117.
52 Richard Neupert, *The End-Narration and Closure in the Cinema* (Detroit: Wayne State University Press, 1995), 178.
53 Stirling Silliphant, '"Towering Inferno": A Bit of Art Too Often Imitated by Life and Death', *Los Angeles Times* (10 May 1988): C7.

54 Ibid.
55 Christopher Lehmann-Haupt, 'Books of the Times: Big City Life and Cold War', *The New York Times* (19 October 1973): 14.
56 CNN, 'Prosecutor: Yousef Aimed to Topple Trade Center Towers' (5 August 1997). http://edition.cnn.com/US/9708/05/wtc.trial/index.html
57 Josh Barbanel, 'Tougher Code May Not Have Helped', *The New York Times* (27 February 1993): 24.
58 James Bennett, 'Explosion at the Twin Towers: Flaws in Emergency Systems Exposed', *The New York Times* (28 February 1993): 37.
59 See Bruce M. Metzger and Michael D. Coogan (eds.), *The Oxford Companion to the Bible* (Oxford: Oxford University Press, 1993), 34–5.

Chapter 5

1 See David Seed, 'Los Angeles' Science Fiction Futures', in *The Cambridge Companion to the Literature of Los Angeles*, ed. Kevin R. McNamara (Cambridge: Cambridge University Press, 2010), 123–34; Michael Cassidy, 'Los Angeles: Promise and Warning', *Official Architecture and Planning* 33, no. 12 (1970): 1057–66.
2 Pauline Kael, *Reeling* (London: Marion Boyars, 1977), 385.
3 Mark Shiel, 'The Southland on Screen', *The Cambridge Companion to the Literature of Los Angeles*, 145–56, 154; R. C. Lutz, 'On the Road to Nowhere? California's Car Culture', *California History* 79, no. 1 (2000): 50–5, 55.
4 Lutz, 'On the Road to Nowhere', 50.
5 T. S. Eliot, *The Dry Salvages* (London: Faber & Faber, 1941), 8.
6 Mike Davis, *Ecology of Fear: Los Angeles and the Imagination of Disaster* (New York: Vintage, 1999), 9.
7 Jack Matthews, 'Universal Shuts Earthquake Attraction for Two Days', *Los Angeles Times* (19 October 1989). https://www.latimes.com/archives/la-xpm-1989-10-19-ca-334-story.html
8 George Fox, *Earthquake: The Story of a Movie* (New York: A Signet Book, 1974), i.
9 David M. Andersen, 'The Los Angeles Earthquake and the Folklore of Disaster', *Western Folklore* 33, no. 4 (1974): 331–6, 331–2.
10 'But there is no doubt anywhere that San Francisco can be rebuilt, larger, better and soon. Just as there would be none at all if all this New York that has so obsessed me with its limitless bigness was itself a blazing ruin. […] The sense of inexhaustible supply, of an ultra-human force behind it all, is, for a time, invincible.' H. G. Wells, 'New York', in *The Future in America: A Search after Realities* (Chapman & Hall, 1906), 35–48, 42.

11 Fox, *The Story of a Movie*, 88.
12 Ibid.
13 Davies, *Ecology of Fear*, 324.
14 Kael, *Reeling*, 387.
15 Ibid., 387 & 363–4.
16 Ibid., 364.
17 Susan Sontag, 'Notes on "Camp"', first published in *Partisan Review*, 31:4, Fall 1964, 515–30. Quoted from Fabio Cleto (ed.), *Queer Aesthetics and the Performing Subject A Reader* (Edinburgh: Edinburgh University Press, 1999), 53–65.
18 See Morris Dickstein, 'Sunset Boulevard', *Grand Street* 7, no. 3 (1988): 176–84, 176.
19 Nora Sayre, 'Screen: "Earthquake" Evokes Feelies', *The New York Times* (16 November 1974). https://www.nytimes.com/1974/11/16/archives/screen-earthquake-evokes-feeliesthe-cast.html
20 Fox, *The Story of a Movie*, 15.
21 Ibid., 109–10.
22 Ibid., 16.
23 Ibid., 31.
24 Claire Jenkins, 'Family Destruction and the Action-Melodrama', in *Home Movies: The American Family in Contemporary Hollywood Cinema* (London: I.B. Tauris, 2014), 101–23, 101.
25 Ibid.
26 Ibid., 103.
27 Fox, *The Story of a Movie*, 96.
28 Kael, *Reeling*, 385.
29 Fox, *The Story of a Movie*, 96.
30 Ibid., 97.
31 Ibid., 33.
32 Ibid., 37.
33 Ibid.
34 Ibid., 106.
35 Kael, *Reeling*, 385.
36 Fox, *The Story of a Movie*, 110.
37 Ibid., 24.
38 Charlton Heston, *In the Arena: The Autobiography* (London: HarperCollins, 1995), 472.
39 Ibid., 427.
40 Nora Sayre, Screen: 'Earthquake' Evokes Feelies'.
41 Kael, *Reeling*, 386.
42 Ibid.

43 Heston, *In the Arena*, 398.
44 Ibid., 133–4.
45 Fox, *The Story of a Movie*, 62.
46 Exodus 14:13.
47 Vincent Canby, 'The Year of the Disaster Movie: Audience Participation Abounds', *The Times-News* (2 December 1974): 10.
48 Heston, *In the Arena*, 426.
49 Nora Sayre, 'Earthquake' Evokes Feelies'; Fox, *The Story of a Movie*, 110.
50 Stephen Holden, 'Theater: Previews and Openings: "*Marjoe*"', *The New York Times* (13 January 2006): E28.
51 Ibid.
52 Kael, *Reeling*, 385.
53 Jans Wager, 'Richard Roundtree: Inventing Shaft', in *Hollywood Reborn: Movie Stars of the 1970s*, ed. James Morrison (New Brunswick: Rutgers University Press, 2010), 101–99, 101.
54 Mark Reid, *Redefining Black Film* (Berkeley: University of California Press, 1993), 83.
55 David Walker, Andrew J. Rausch and Chris Watson (eds.), *Reflections on Blaxploitation: Actors and Directors Speak* (Lanham: Scarecrow Press, 2009), ix.
56 William Lyne, 'No Accident: From Black Power to Black Box Office', *African American Review* 34, no. 1 (2000): 39–59, 39. See also Wager, 'Richard Roundtree: Inventing Shaft', 114.
57 Andy Webster, 'Review: "Being Evel" Examines the Life of a Notorious Stuntman', *The New York Times* (20 August 2015): C6.
58 Ibid.
59 Wager, 'Richard Roundtree: Inventing Shaft', 102–19.
60 See Walker, Rausch and Watson (eds.), *Reflections on Blaxploitation: Actors and Directors Speak*, 121.
61 'If there is an iron law of disaster in Southern California, it is simply that bad news for the region is usually good news for "the industry"'. Davies, *Ecology of Fear*, 323–4.
62 James F. Light, *Nathanael West: An Interpretative Study* (Evanston: Northwestern University Press, 1971), 154–5.
63 Ibid., 190.
64 J. Hoberman, '*Nashville* contra *Jaws*, or "The Imagination of Disaster" Revisited', in *The Last Great American Picture Show: New Hollywood Cinema in the 1970s*, ed. Thomas Elsaesser, Alexander Horwath and Noel King (Amsterdam: Amsterdam University Press), 195–222, 211.
65 Davies, *Ecology of Fear*, 86.

66 Edward T. Jones, 'That's Wormwood: "The Day of the Locust"', *Literature/Film Quarterly* 6, no. 3 (1978): 222–9, 228.
67 Robert Mazzocco, 'Letter from Nashville', *New York Review of Books* (17 July 1975): 180.
68 Shiel, 'The Southland on Screen', 148.
69 Anton Karl Kozlovic, 'What Sort of Scripture Filmmaker was Cecil B. DeMille: Biblical, Religious or Spiritual', *KINEMA: A Journal for Film and Media* 37 (2012): 21–46, 21.
70 Vincent Canby, "Day of Locust' Turns Dross into Gold', *The New York Times* (8 May 1975): 48.
71 Nathanael West, *The Day of the Locust* (London: Penguin Books, 2018), 152.
72 Nancy Pogel and William Chamberlain, 'Self Reflections in Adaptations of Black Comic Novels', *Literature/Film Quarterly* 13, no. 3 (1985): 187–93, 192.
73 John Lennon, 'God', *John Lennon/Plastic Ono Band* (1970).
74 Davis, *Ecology of Fear*, 9.
75 Pogel and Chamberlain, 'Self Reflections in Adaptations of Black Comic Novels', 193.
76 Joseph Leo Koerner, 'The Mortification of the Image: Death as a Hermeneutic in Hans Baldung Grien', *Representations*, no. 10 (Spring, 1985): 52–101, 64.
77 W. H. Auden, 'Interlude: West's Disease', in *The Dyer's Hand and Other Essays* (London: Faber & Faber, 1975), 241.
78 West, *The Day of the Locust*, 155.
79 Light, *Nathanael West*, 171.
80 Ibid., 189–90.
81 Jay Cocks, 'Cinema: The 8th Plague', *Time* (12 May 1975). https://archive.ph/20190821024813/ and http://content.time.com/time/magazine/article/0,9171,917442,00.html?promoid=googlep
82 Roger Ebert, '*Day of the Locust* Review', *Chicago Sun-Times* (23 May 1975). https://www.rogerebert.com/reviews/day-of-the-locust-1975
83 Hoberman, '*Nashville* contra *Jaws*, or "The Imagination of Disaster" Revisited', 203.
84 Ibid., 210–11.
85 Lutz, 'On the Road to Nowhere?', 53.
86 Light, *Nathanael West*, 202.
87 Quoted from Lutz, 'On the Road to Nowhere?', 50.
88 Andy Warhol Interview with Gene Swanson. G. R. Swenson, 'What Is Pop Art? Answers from 8 Painters, Part I', *ARTnews* 62, no. 7 (1963): 24–7, 60–4, and 'What Is Pop Art? Part II', *ARTnews* 62, no. 10 (1964): 40–3, 62–7.
89 National Highway Traffic Safety Administration. http://www-fars.nhtsa.dot.gov/Main/index.aspx
90 Tico Romoa, 'Guns and Gas: Investigating the 1970s Car Chase Film', in *The Action and Adventure Cinema*, ed. Yvonne Tasker (London: Routledge, 2004), 130–52.

91 Jesse Crosse, *The Greatest Movie Car Chases of All Time* (St. Paul: Motorbooks International, 2006), 47.
92 Ibid., 151.

Chapter 6

1   See David A. Cook, *Lost Illusions: American Cinema in the Shadow of Watergate and Vietnam, 1970–1979* (Los Angeles: University of California Press, 2000), 255.
2   Pauline Kael, *Reeling* (London: Marion Boyars, 1976), 387.
3   Maurice Yacowar, 'The Bug in the Rug: Notes on the Disaster Genre', in *Film Genre Reader IV*, ed. B. K. Grant (Austin: University of Texas Press, 2012), 313.
4   Kael, *Reeling*, 385.
5   Ibid., 387.
6   Ibid., 406.
7   Jim Kendrick, *Film Violence: History, Ideology, Genre* (New York: Columbia University Press, 2010), 61.
8   Amy Rust, *Passionate Detachments: Technologies of Vision and Violence in American Cinema, 1967–1974* (Albany: State University of New York, 2017), 4.
9   Cook, *Lost Illusions*, 254.
10 Roger Ebert, *The Hindenburg* (movie review)', *Chicago-Sun Times* (1 January 1975). https://www.rogerebert.com/reviews/the-hindenburg-1975
11 Herbert Morrison, WLS radio broadcast (6 May 1937). https://weinterruptthisbroadcast.org/2021/04/21/episode-one-the-hindenburg-disaster/
12 Guy Flatley, 'At the Movies: Producer Sets Hoffman's Sail for Popeye', *The New York Times* (October 14, 1977), 58.
13 Roy Scranton, '*Star Wars* and the Fantasy of American Violence', *The New York Times* (2 July 2016). https://www.nytimes.com/2016/07/03/opinion/sunday/star-wars-and-the-fantasy-of-american-violence.html
14 Ibid.
15 Murray Pomerance, *The Eyes Have It: Cinema and the Reality Effect* (New Brunswick: Rutgers University Press, 2013), 23.
16 Paula J. Massood, 'Movies and a Nation in Transformation', in *American cinema of the 1970s: Themes and Variations,* ed. L. D. Friedman (New Brunswick: Rutgers University Press (2007), 184–204, 182–3.
17 See J. David Slocum, 'Film Violence and the Institutionalization of the Cinema', *Social Research* 67, no. 3 (2000): 649–81, 659 & 661.
18 Mathias Clasen, 'Never Go Swimming Again: *Jaws* (1975)', in *Why Horror Seduces* (Oxford: Oxford University Press, 2017), 103–11, 106.

19. Ethan Alter, *Film Firsts: The 25 Movies that Created Contemporary American Cinema* (Santa Barbara: Praeger, 2014), 3.
20. Andrew Britton, 'Jaws (1979)', in *Britton on Film: The Complete Film Criticism of Andrew Britton*, ed. Barry Keith Grant (Detroit: Wayne State University Press, 2008), 248–51, 248.
21. *Jaws* Official Trailer. https://www.youtube.com/watch?v=U1fu_sA7XhE&t=31
22. Clasen, 'Never Go Swimming Again: *Jaws* (1975)', 107.
23. Mark Bould, 'Film and Television', in *The Cambridge Companion to Science Fiction*, ed. James Edward (Cambridge: Cambridge University Press, 2003), 8–9, 79–95.
24. Stephen Keane, *Disaster Movies: The Cinema of Catastrophe* (London: Wallflower, 2001), 48.
25. Jane Arthurs and Iain Grant, *Crash Cultures: Modernity, Mediation and the Material* (Bristol: Intellect Books, 2003), 1; Jean Baudrillard, (trans.) Chris Turner, *America* (New York: Verso, 1989), 55.
26. Pauline Kael, 'Killing Time', in *Screen Violence*, ed. Karl French (London: Bloomsbury, 1997), 171–8, 171.
27. Ibid., 172.
28. William Rosenau, '"Our Backs Are against the Wall": The Black Liberation Army and Domestic Terrorism in 1970s America', *Studies in Conflict & Terrorism* 36, no. 2 (2013): 176–92, 176.
29. L. Stampnitzky, *Disciplining Terror: How Experts Invented 'Terrorism'* (Cambridge: Cambridge University Press, 2013), 21.
30. Christopher Falzon, 'Dirty Harry Ethics', *SubStance* 45, no. 3 (2016): 49–65, 54–5.
31. Ibid., 52.
32. Joe Street, 'Dirty Harry's San Francisco', *The Sixties: A Journal of History, Politics and Culture* 5, no. 1 (2012): 1–21, 1.
33. Roger Ebert, '*Dirty Harry* (movie review)', *Chicago-Sun Times* (1 January 1971). https://www.rogerebert.com/reviews/dirty-harry-1971
34. Christian Keathley, 'Trapped in the Affection Image: Hollywood's Post-Traumatic Cycle (1970–1976)', in *Last Great American Picture Show: New Hollywood Cinema in the 1970s*, ed. Thomas Elsaesser, Noel King and Alexander Horwath (Amsterdam: Amsterdam University Press, 2004), 238–51, 241.
35. Stephen Prince, *Screening Violence* (London: The Athlone Press, 2000), 176.
36. Ibid.
37. Quoted from Staff, 'Irwin Allen, Big-Budget Producer of Disaster Movies, is Dead at 75', *The New York Times* (4 November 1991): D9.
38. John R. Blakinger, '"Death in America" and "Life" Magazine: Sources for Andy Warhol's "Disaster" Paintings', *Artibus et Historiae* 33, no. 66 (2012): 269–85, 270.
39. Andy Warhol, *Electric Chair* (1964), The Tate. https://www.tate.org.uk/art/artworks/warhol-electric-chair-t07145

40 Bennett Capers, 'On Andy Warhol's "Electric Chair"', *California Law Review* 94, no. 1 (2006): 243–60.
41 James Fiumara, 'Electrocuting an Elephant at Coney Island: Attraction, Story, and the Curious Spectator', *Film History* 28, no. 1 (2016): 43–70, 43.
42 Jim Kendrick, *Film Violence: History, Ideology, Genre* (New York: Columbia University Press, 2010), 33.
43 Ibid., 34.
44 Thomas Elsaesser, 'The Pathos of Failure: American Films in the 1970s: Notes on the Unmotivated Hero [1975]', in *The Last Great American Picture* Show, 279–92, 281–2.
45 Keathley, 'Trapped in the Affection Image', 302.
46 J. Hoberman, 'Nashville Contra Jaws', in *The Last Great American Picture Show*, 195–222, 196.
47 Jan Campbell, *Film Cinema Spectatorship: Melodrama and Mimesis* (Cambridge: Polity Press, 2005), 138.
48 Gemma Blackwood, 'Dream Factory Tours: The Universal Pictures Movie Tour Attraction in the 1960s', *Historical Journal of Film, Radio and Television* 38, no. 3 (2018): 516–35, 518.
49 Mary Murphy, 'Jumping on the Disaster Bandwagon', *Los Angeles Times* (3 May 1974): E1.
50 Nora Sayre, 'Screen: "Earthquake" Evokes Feelies', *The New York Times* (16 November 1974). https://www.nytimes.com/1974/11/16/archives/screen-earthquake-evokes-feeliesthe-cast.html
51 Lauren Rabinovitz, *Electric Dreamland: Amusement Parks, Movies and American Modernity* (New York: Columbia University Press, 2012), 35–6 & 173.
52 Vincent Canby, 'Screen: "Rollercoaster" on Track: Suspense Melodrama Stars Widmark and Fonda', *The New York Times* (11 June 1977): 12.
53 Arwen P. Mohun, 'Designed for Thrills and Safety: Amusement Parks and the Commodification of Risk, 1880–1929', *Journal of Design History* 14, no. 4 (2001): 291–306, 292.
54 See Thomas Riegler, 'Through the Lenses of Hollywood: Depictions of Terrorism in American Movies', *Perspectives on Terrorism* 4, no. 2 (2010): 35–45, 36.
55 Mohun, 'Designed for Thrills and Safety', 304.
56 Canby, 'Screen: "Rollercoaster" on Track'.
57 Lee Edelman and Joseph Litvak, 'Two Much: Excess, Enjoyment, and Estrangement in Hitchcock's Strangers on a Train', *GLQ: A Journal of Lesbian and Gay Studies* 25, no. 2 (2019): 297–314, 302.
58 Ibid., 304.
59 Mircea Eliade, *Cosmos and History: The Myth of the Eternal Return*, trans. Willard R. Task (New York: Harper Torchbooks, 1959), 62.

60 Amilcare A. Iannucci, 'Dante and Hollywood', in *Dante, Cinema, and Television,* ed. A. A. Iannucci (Toronto: University of Toronto Press, 2004), 3–20, 10.
61 Ibid.
62 Ibid.
63 Kael, *Reeling*, 406.
64 A. M. Butler, *Solar Flares: Science Fiction in the 1970s* (Liverpool: Liverpool University Press, 2012), 216.
65 Ibid., 215.
66 J. B. South and K. S. Engels (eds.), *Westworld and Philosophy: If You Go Looking for the Truth, Get the Whole Thing* (New Jersey: John Wiley & Sons, 2018), 191.
67 Butler, *Solar Flares*, 214.
68 Baudrillard, *America*, 108.
69 Falzon, 'Dirty Harry Ethics', 52.
70 Roger Ebert, 'Two-Minute Warning (movie review)', *Chicago Sun-Times* (15 November 1976). https://www.rogerebert.com/reviews/two-minute-warning-1976
71 Ibid.
72 Richard Eder, 'Be Warned about "Two Minute Warning"', *The New York Times* (13 November 1976): 11.
73 Charlton Heston, *In the Arena* (London: HarperCollins, 1996), 473.
74 Charlton Heston, *The Actor's Life: Journals 1956–1976*, ed. Hollis Alpert (New York: A Henry Robbins Book, 1978), 480.
75 Newgate Callendar, '*Black Sunday* (movie review)', *The New York Times* (2 February 1975): 4.
76 Yair Galily, Moran Yarchi and Ilan Tamir, 'From Munich to Boston, and from Theater to Social Media: The Evolutionary Landscape of World Sporting Terror', *Studies in Conflict & Terrorism* 38, no. 12 (2015): 998–1007.
77 Corey K. Creekmur, 'John Frankenheimer's "War on Terror"', in *A Little Solitaire: John Frankenheimer and American Film,* ed. Murray Pomerance and R. Barton Palmer (New Brunswick: Rutgers University Press, 2011), 103–66, 104. See also Jason Grant McKahan, *Hollywood Counterterrorism: Violence, Protest and the Middle East in U.S. Action Feature Films,* Florida State University (Thesis, 2009).
78 Guy Flatley, 'At the Movies: Bruce Dern Plays Veteran Tormented by Love and War', *The New York Times* (7 January 1977): 43.
79 Stephen Prince, *Firestorm: American Film in the Age of Terrorism* (New York: Columbia University Press, 2009), 27.
80 Stephen B. Armstrong, *Pictures about Extremes: The Films of John Frankenheimer* (Jefferson: McFarland & Company, 2008), 2.
81 Daniel Varndell, 'The Little Deaths of John Frankenheimer', in *The Other Hollywood Renaissance,* ed. Dominic Lennard, R. Barton Palmer and Murray Pomerance (Edinburgh: Edinburgh University Press, 2022), 134–47.

82 See also Raya Morag, 'Defeated Masculinity: Post-Traumatic Cinema in the Aftermath of the Vietnam War', *The Communication Review* 9, no. 3 (2006): 189–219.
83 Keathley, 'Trapped in the Affection Image', 296–7.
84 Frank Sweeney, '"What Mean Expendable?": Myth, Ideology, and Meaning in First Blood and Rambo', *Journal of American Culture* 22, no. 3 (1999): 63–9, 63.
85 Ibid., 64.
86 Fred Pfeil, *White Guys: Studies in Postmodern Domination & Difference* (London: Verso, 1995), 4. See also Morag, 'Defeated Masculinity', 206.
87 Thomas Riegler, 'Through the Lenses of Hollywood: Depictions of Terrorism in American Movies', *Perspectives on Terrorism* 4, no. 2 (2010): 35–45, 37.
88 A 'brutal utilitarian logic, in which the ends justify any means'. Falzon: 'Dirty Harry Ethics', 49.
89 Quoted from David Scott Diffrient, 'Spectator Sports and Terrorist Reports: Filming the Munich Olympics, (Re)imagining the Munich Massacre', *Sport in Society* 11, no. 2–3 (2008): 311–29, 322.
90 Ibid.
91 Quoted from Stephen Prince, *Savage Cinema: Sam Peckinpah and the Rise of Ultraviolent Movies* (London: The Athlone Press, 1998), 108.
92 Creekmur, 'John Frankenheimer's "War on Terror"', 108.

Chapter 7

1 Scott Hughes, 'The Worst Movie Ever?', *The Guardian* (26 April 2001): A15.
2 Constantine Verevis, 'Vicious Cycle: Jaws and Revenge-of-Nature Films of the 1970s', in *Cycles, Sequels, Spin-offs, Remakes, and Reboots: Multiplicities in Film and Television,* ed. A. A. Klein and R. B. Palmer (Austin: University of Texas Press, 2016), 96–111, 101.
3 Vincent Canby, 'The Swarm – A Bumbling "B"', *The New York Times* (23 July 1978): D13. https://www.nytimes.com/1978/07/23/archives/film-view-the-swarm-a-bumbling-b-film-view-a-bumbling-b.html
4 Ibid.
5 Staff, 'Irwin Allen, Warners Sign Production Deal', *Los Angeles Times* (21 July 1975): E13.
6 Arthur Herzog, *The Swarm* (London: Pan Books Ltd, 1974), 26.
7 Ibid., 10.
8 Ibid., 13.
9 'The Killer Bee', *Saturday Night Live* (11 October 1975).
10 Canby, 'The Swarm – A Bumbling "B"'.

11 John Sutherland, *Reading the Decades: Fifty Years of the Nation's Bestselling Books* (London: BBC Worldwide Ltd, 2002), 100.
12 John Sutherland, *Bestsellers: Popular Fiction of the 1970s* (London: Routledge & Kegan Paul, 1981), 119.
13 Alison Benjamin, 'Carol Ann Duffy – the Newest of the Bee Poets', *The Guardian* (28 October 2011). https://www.theguardian.com/environment/blog/2011/oct/28/carol-ann-duffy-bee-poetry?newsfeed=true
14 Herzog, *The Swarm*, 10.
15 Ibid., 17.
16 Ibid.
17 Ibid., 20.
18 Ibid.
19 Ibid.
20 'Many had come to believe in the supremacy of the devil, whose hell seemed to have arrived.' Arthur Herzog, *Heat* (London: Pan Books Ltd, 1978), 187.
21 The term 'ecofeminism' was coined in *Le Féminisme ou la Mort* (1974) by Françoise d'Eaubonne.
22 'Disbelieving, uncomprehending, he watched the whale back off and vanish. Moments passed and then, in the distance, the orca leaped, filling the sky with majesty.' Arthur Herzog, *Orca* (London: Pan Books Ltd, 1977), 191.
23 I am grateful for Christopher George Harrington's feedback on my chapter and for sharing his PhD thesis, *Creatures Like the Bee: The Social Insect in the Social Problem Novel*, submitted to the Department of Creative Arts and English La Trobe University, Australia (December 2019).
24 See Hilda M. Ransome, *The Sacred Bee in Ancient Times and Folklore* (New York: Dover Publications, 2004). See also Claire Preston, *Bee* (London: Reaktion Books, 2015), 92.
25 Maurice Maeterlinck, *The Life of the Bee*, trans. Alfred Sutro (New York: Dover Publications, 2015), 32.
26 Bosley Crowther, 'The Screen: "Queen Bee"; New Film at Loew's State Drones Along', *The New York Times* (November 23, 1955): 18.
27 Sir Arthur Conan Doyle, 'His Last Bow', in *His Last Bow: Some Reminiscences of Sherlock Holmes* (London: Penguin Books, 1997), 194.
28 Bee Wilson, *The Hive: The Story of the Honeybee and Us* (London: John Murray, 2005), 231.
29 Maeterlinck, *The Life of the Bee*, 34.
30 H. F. Heard, *A Taste of Honey* (Nevada City: Blue Dolphin Publishing, 2009), 132.
31 Otto Plath, *Bumblebees and Their Ways* (New York: The Macmillan Company Publishers, 1934).

32 Sylvia Plath, 'Stings', in *Ariel: The Restored Edition* (London: Faber & Faber, 2004), 86.
33 'Tomorrow I will be sweet God, I will set them free.' Plath, 'The Arrival of the Bee Box', 83.
34 Herzog, *The Swarm*, 36.
35 Ibid., 36.
36 Ibid., 160.
37 See Barbara Creed, *The Monstrous-Feminine: Film, Feminism, Psychoanalysis* (London: Routledge, 1993), 105–21.
38 Plath, 'Wintering', 88.
39 Plath, 'The Bee Meeting', 80.
40 The term 'deep ecology' was coined by Arne Næss in 1973.
41 Herzog, *The Swarm*, 204.
42 Charlotte Sleigh, 'Empire of the Ants: H. G. Wells and Tropical Entomology', *Science as Culture* 10, no. 1 (2001): 33–71.
43 Charlotte Sleigh, *Ant* (London: Reaktion Book, 2003), 144.
44 Stephen D. Arata, 'The Occidental Tourist: Dracula and the Anxiety of Reverse Colonization', in *The Nineteenth-Century Novel: A Critical Reader*, ed. Stephen Regan (London: Routledge, 2001), 457–64.
45 See John Kenneth Muir, *Horror Films of the 1970s* (Jefferson: McFarland, 2007), 292–4.
46 Plath, 'The Arrival of the Bee Box', 82.
47 Ibid.
48 See Alf Pratte, 'When my bees swarm …', from *Negro History Bulletin*, published in *Association for the Study of African American Life and History* 49, no. 4 (October–December, 1986): 13–16.
49 Randolph B. 'Mike' Campbell, 'Slavery', *Texas State Historical Association*. https://www.tshaonline.org/handbook/entries/slavery
50 Sue Monk Kidd, *The Secret Lives of Bees* (New York: Penguin Books, 2001).
51 'They had this all-star cast and a geriatric love story between Olivia de Havilland and Fred MacMurray, which didn't make much sense.' Tom Weaver, *Double Feature Creature Attack* (Jefferson: McFarland and Co., 2003), 221.
52 See Robin Wood, 'The American Nightmare: Horror in the 70s', in *Horror: The Film Reader*, ed. Mark Jancovich (London: Routledge, 2002), 25–32.
53 'Return of the Repressed', in *Robin Wood on the Horror Film: Collected Essays and Reviews*, ed. Barry Keith Grant (Detroit: Wayne State University Press, 2018), 62.
54 Sutherland, *Bestsellers*, 119.
55 See Timothy Clark, *Literature and the Environment* (Cambridge: Cambridge University Press, 2014), 55–62.
56 Maland, '1978: Movies and Changing Times', 226.

57　Herzog, *The Swarm*, 214.
58　Ibid., 217.
59　Ibid., 218.
60　Ibid.
61　'[…] Hollywood films can be seen as exemplifying, and often actually promoting, [a] loosely educational and ethical agenda, particularly through the use of ecological/mythic expression, evidenced in a range of narrative closures'. Patrick Brereton, *Hollywood Utopia: Ecology in Contemporary American Cinema* (Bristol: Intellect Books Ltd, 2004), 11.
62　John Gray, *The Silence of Animals: On Progress and Other Modern Myths* (London: Penguin Books, 2014), 31–2.
63　Eleanor Heartney, 'How the Ecological Art Practices of Today Were Born in 1970s Feminism', *Art in America*, 22 May 2020. https://www.artnews.com/art-in-america/features/ecofeminism-women-in-environmental-art-1202688298/

Chapter 8

1　See Kim Newman, *Nightmare Movies: Critical History of the Horror Film, 1968–88* (London: Bloomsbury, 1988).
2　Vincent Canby, 'Screen: Medusa without Perseus: Life on the Couch', *The New York Times* (14 April 1978): C9.
3　The book of Amos: 5:24.
4　Ovid, *Metamorphoses*, trans. Rolfe Humphries and (annotated) Joseph D. Reed (Bloomington: Indiana University Press, 2018), 262–3.
5　Peter Van Greenaway, *The Medusa Touch* (St. Albans: Panther Granada, 1975), 116.
6　Eman El Nouhy, 'Redeeming the Medusa: An Archetypal Examination of Ted Hughes', *The Iron Woman*', *Children's Literature in Education* 50 (2019): 347–63.
7　Sigmund Freud, 'The "Uncanny"', in *The Complete Psychological Works of Sigmund Freud Volume XVII (1917–1919)*, trans. James Strachey (London: The Hogarth Press, 1925), 219–53, 231.
8　Jacques Lacan, *The Four Fundamental Concepts of Psycho-Analysis*, trans. Alan Sheridan (London: Penguin Books, 1994), 92.
9　Ibid., 118.
10　Susan Sontag, 'The Imagination of Disaster', in *Against Interpretation* (New York: Delta, 1966), 209–25. Nick Roddick, 'Only the Stars Survive: Disaster Movies in the Seventies', in *Performance and Politics in Popular Drama*, ed. David Bradby, Louis James and Bernard Sharratt (Cambridge: Cambridge University Press, 1981), 243–70, 259.

11 '[...] the films are both reactionary and radical, both a closing off of significant desires and a blueprint for the inevitable reopening of them'. Michael Ryan and Douglas Kellner, *Camera Politica: The Politics and Ideology of Contemporary Hollywood Film* (Bloomington and Indianapolis: Indiana University Press, 1990), 57.
12 Nick Roddick, 'Only the Stars Survive: Disaster Movies in the Seventies', 258.
13 'Modern subjects have developed a protective shield, though "the real" has ways of breaking back through.' Jane Arthurs and Iain Grant (eds.), *Crash Cultures: Modernity, Mediation and the Material* (Bristol: Intellect Books, 2003), 4.
14 Ibid., 1.
15 Maurice Yacowar, 'The Bug in the Rug: Notes on the Disaster Genre', in *Film Genre Reader IV*, ed. B. K. Grant (Austin: University of Texas Press, 2012), 317.
16 Roddick, 'Only the Stars Survive', 246.
17 Pauline Kael, 'Killing Time', in *Screen Violence*, ed. Karl French (London: Bloomsbury, 1997), 171–8.
18 Percy Bysshe Shelley 'Ozymandias' (1817), quoted from *Poetry Foundation*. https://www.poetryfoundation.org/poems/46565/ozymandias
19 'But when you see a gruesome picture over and over again, it doesn't really have any effect.' Gene Swenson, 'What Is Pop Art? Answers from 8 Painters, Part I', *ARTnews* 62, no. 7 (November 1963): 24–7, 60–4.
20 I am grateful to Professor Phil Shaw for this phrase.
21 'It is easier to imagine an end to the world than an end to capitalism.' Quoted from Jodi Dean, 'Realism', *Mediations* 33, no. 1–2 (2019–20): i. 'It's easier to imagine an end to the world than an end to capitalism because capitalism is the end of the world.' https://mediationsjournal.org/articles/end-of-world
22 H. G. Wells, 'Human Evolution, an Artificial Process', in *The Gothic Body: Sexuality, Materialism, and Degeneration at the Fin de Siècle,* ed. Kelly Hurley (Cambridge: Cambridge University Press, 2009), 66.

Chapter 9

1 Quoted from Stephen Keane, *Disaster Movies: The Cinema of Catastrophe* (London: Wallflower, 2001), 51.
2 Ibid., 52.
3 Will Kaufman, *American Culture of the 1970s* (Edinburgh: Edinburgh University Press, 2009), 88.
4 Julian C. Chambliss, William Svitavsky, Thomas Donaldson and Julian C. Chambliss (eds.), *Ages of Heroes, Eras of Men: Superheroes and the American Experience* (Cambridge: Cambridge Scholars Publisher, 2013), 18.

5   Ibid., 19.
6   Judges 16: 15–17.
7   *Ages of Heroes*, 20.
8   Garrett Martin, 'The Original Superhero Movie Isn't Really a Superhero Movie', *Paste* (18 November 2018). https://www.pastemagazine.com/movies/4k/superman-the-original-superhero-movie-isnt-really/
9   In using a 'motion line' to indicate Superman flying around the world, Dru Jeffries sees the scene as representative of the film respecting the comic book aesthetic. Dru Jeffries, *Comic Book Film Style: Cinema at 24 Panels per Second* (Austin: University of Texas Press, 2017), 145.
10 See Kaufman, *American Culture the 1970s*, 93.
11 Geoff King, *Spectacular Narratives: Hollywood in the Age of the Blockbuster* (London: I.B. Tauris, 2000), 79.
12 See Michael J. Lecker, 'Superhero Fantasy in a Post 9-11 World: Marvel Comics and Army Recruitment', in *Ages of Heroes, Eras of Men: Superheroes and the American Experience*, 299–40, 237–8.
13 I am grateful to David Watts, film and media studies tutor at Wyggeston and Queen Elizabeth I College (Leicester), for sharing his expertise in comic book blockbusters.
14 See Menaka Philips, 'Violence in the American Imaginary: Gender, Race, and the Politics of Superheroes', *American Political Science Review* (2022): 470–483.
15 Delip Menon, 'Fifty Shades of Blackness: Recovering an Aesthetics of the Afrifuge', *Cambridge Journal of Postcolonial Literary Inquiry* 7, no. 2 (April 2020): 107–20, 107. I am grateful for Dr Zoe Groves.
16 Ibid., 120.
17 Tom Pollard, *Hollywood 9/11: Superheroes, Supervillains, and Super Disasters* (London: Routledge, 2011), 5.
18 Kevin J. Wanner, 'In a World of Super-Violence, Can Pacifism Pack a Punch?', *The Journal of American Culture* 39, no. 2 (June 2016): 177–92.
19 Rick Moody, 'Frank Miller and the Rise of Cryptofascist Hollywood', 24 November 2011, *The Guardian*. https://www.theguardian.com/culture/2011/nov/24/frank-miller-hollywood-fascism
20 Menaka Philips, 'Violence in the American Imaginary: Gender, Race, and the Politics of Superheroes', 470–83.
21 'Disaster movies are especially prone to unintentional camp for the way they juxtapose low, trivial pop culture sensationalism with the high and important fight for group survival [...]'. Ken Fiel, *Dying for a Laugh: Disaster Movies and the Camp Imagination* (Middleton, CT: Wesleyan University Press, 2005), xiv.
22 Pauline Kael, *Reeling* (London: Marion Boyars, 1977), 364–5.

23 Susan Sontag, 'Notes on "Camp"', first published in *Partisan Review*, 31:4, Fall 1964, 515–30. Quoted from Fabio Cleto (ed.), *Queer Aesthetics and the Performing Subject A Reader* (Edinburgh: Edinburgh University Press, 1999), 53–65.
24 See Andrea Austin, 'Roland Emmerich's 2012: A Simple Truth', in *2012: Decoding the Countercultural Apocalypse*, ed. Joseph Gelfer (London: Routledge, 2014), 108–9, 108–22.
25 See Robert Pierro, 'Aesthetic Legacies and Dashed Political Hopes: Caspar David Friedrich Motifs in Roland Emmerich's Post-9/11 Popcorn Message Movies', *The Germanic Review: Literature, Culture, Theory* 88, no. 4 (2013): 400–17, 401.
26 Muhammad Abukarar Pirzada, Letter to *The Guardian* (31 October 2022).
27 Merrill Schleier, *Skyscraper Cinema: Architecture and Gender in American Film* (Minneapolis: University of Minnesota Press), 265.
28 Thomas Stubblefield, *9/11 and the Visual Culture of Disaster* (Bloomington, IN: Indiana University Press, 2015), 3.
29 Letters page: '11 September', *London Review of Books* 23, no. 19 (4 October 2001). https://www.lrb.co.uk/the-paper/v23/n19/nine-eleven-writers/11-september
30 Ibid., Neal Ascherson.
31 Ibid., Mary Beard.
32 Jean Baudrillard, *The Spirit of Terrorism and Other Essays*, trans. Chris Turner (London and New York: Verso, 2002), 3–34, 5.
33 Bruno Latour, 'Why Has Critique Run Out of Steam? From Matters of Fact to Matters of Concern', *Critical Inquiry* 30 (2004): 225–48, 231.
34 Hal Foster, Letters page: '11 September'.
35 Slavoj Žižek, *Welcome to the Desert of the Real: Five Essays on September 11 and Related Dates* (London: Verso Books, 2002), 71.
36 Eric Foner, Letters page: '11 September'.
37 Slavoj Žižek, 'Welcome to the Desert of the Real!', in *Cultures of Fear: A Critical Reader* ed. Uli Linke and Danielle Taana Smith (London: Pluto Press, 2009), 70–7, 77.
38 Karen Randall, '"It Was Like a Movie": The Impossibility of Representation in Oliver Stone's World Trade Center', in *Reframing 9/11: Film, Popular Culture and the War on Terror*, ed. Jeff Birkenstein, Anna Froula and Karen Randell (London: Bloomsbury, 2010), 141–52, 142.
39 Douglas Kellner, *Cinema Wars: Hollywood Film and Politics in the Bush-Cheney Era* (Hoboken, NJ: John Wiley & Sons, Incorporated, 2009), 104–5.
40 See Ken Booth and Tim Dunne, *Terror in Our Time* (London: Routledge, 2011), 64.
41 Ric Gentry, 'Another Meditation on Death: An Interview with Oliver Stone', *Film Quarterly* 60, no. 4 (2007): 54–60, 56.
42 Ibid.

43 Ibid.
44 Žižek, 'Welcome to the Desert of the Real!', 77.
45 The cycle prompted numerous parodies in book as well as film form, including *The Making of the Goodies' Disaster Movie: The Greatest Story Ever Blown to Bits!* (London: Weidenfeld & Nicolson Ltd, 1977).
46 The film was released on condition that it was shown for two weeks. It was a big draw at Little Rock drive-ins. In 1959, it was again released to drive-ins for one week. The film, two years after its release, drew in a big audience. I am grateful to Dr Guy Barefoot for sharing his expertise. See: *The Drive-in: Outdoor Cinema in 1950s American and the Popular Imagination* (Bloomsbury, 2024).
47 K. R. Phillips, 'Desolate Frontiers in the Films of John Carpenter', *Dark Directions: Romero, Craven, Carpenter, and the Modern Horror Film* (Carbondale: Southern Illinois University Press, 2012), 123–6, 124–5.
48 Mike Davies, *Ecology of Fear: Los Angeles and the Imagination of Disaster* (New York: Vintage, 1999), 338.
49 Ibid.
50 Adrian Glick Kudler, 'The Complete List of Los Angeles Destruction Movies: Filmmakers Love to Destroy LA', *Curbed LA* (19 April 2018). https://la.curbed.com/2014/3/21/10129198/los-angeles-destruction-disaster-movies
51 Mark Fraser, 'Top 10 Films That Share an Apocalyptic View of Los Angeles', *Top Ten Films* (25 May 2014). https://www.top10films.co.uk/21163-top-10-films-share-apocalyptic-view-los-angeles/
52 Shelby Grad, 'Ranking Movies that Destroy Los Angeles: Did "San Andreas" Do It Best?', *Los Angeles Times* (1 June 2015). https://www.latimes.com/local/california/la-me-hollywood-disasters-20150529-story.html
53 Mandalit Del Barco, 'Los Angeles: City of Perpetual Cinematic Destruction', *npr*, 9 August 2011. https://www.npr.org/2011/08/09/138985693/los-angeles-city-of-perpetual-cinematic-destruction
54 See Chapter 6.
55 Thom Andersen, *Los Angeles Plays Itself* (2014).
56 Ibid.
57 Mark Bould, *The Anthropocene Unconscious: Climate Catastrophe Culture* (London: Verso, 2021), 43.
58 Ibid., 53.
59 Ibid., 54.
60 See Katarzyna Nowak-mcniece and Agata Zarzycka (eds.), *A Dark California: Essays on Dystopian Depictions in Popular Culture* (Jefferson, NC: McFarland, 2017).

61 'The formula is familiar: Blackmailing terrorists gain control of a high-rise, or let's say, a sports arena, and threaten to destroy it unless megabucks are transferred to their account. One brave man finds out about the plan, and works as a lone wolf to stop them. (Threads almost always end with the dramatic line, " … but they didn't count on – one man!") There are a lot of special effects, many fights and chases, and a sensational climax.' Roger Ebert, 'Sudden Death', *Chicago Sun-Times* (22 December 1995). https://www.rogerebert.com/reviews/sudden-death-1995
62 Keane, *Disaster Movies*, 48–53.
63 Roger Ebert.
64 Keane, 58.
65 Steven T. Seagle, 'Unreal', *9/11* (New York: D C Comics, 2002), 15–16.
66 I am grateful for the film suggestions from Christopher Harrington and David Watts.
67 Charlotte Perkins Gilman, 'Bee Wise', in *Herland and Related Writings*, ed. Beth Sutton-Ramspeck (Peterborough, Canada: Broadview Editions, 2013), 187–196.
68 I wish to express my gratitude towards Dr Rebecca Styler for sharing her expertise in feminist utopian literature. Charlotte Perkins Gilman, 'The Unnatural Mother', in *Herland and Related Writings*, 177, 170–7.

Bibliography

Abbott, Jon. *Irwin Allen Television Productions, 1964–1970: A Critical History of Voyage to the Bottom of the Sea, Lost in Space, the Time Tunnel and Land of the Giants*. Jefferson: McFarland & Co., 2009.

Abel, Richard (ed.). *Encyclopedia of Early Cinema*. Taylor & Francis Group, 2005.

Airport Theatrical Trailer: https://www.youtube.com/watch?v=PACKbKt8MOw

Alter, Ethan. *Film Firsts: The 25 Movies that Created Contemporary American Cinema*. Santa Barbara: Praeger, 2014.

Altman, Rick. *Film/Genre*. London: BFI, 1999.

Andersen, David M. 'The Los Angeles Earthquake and the Folklore of Disaster'. *Western Folklore* 33, no. 4 (1974): 331–6.

Anderson, Terry H. '1968: The End and the Beginning in the United States and Western Europe'. *South Central Review* 16.4–17.1 (Winter 1999–Spring 2000): 1–15.

Andrews, Hazel. 'Feeling at Home: Embodying Britishness in a Spanish Charter Tourist Resort'. *Tourist Studies* 5, no. 3 (2005): 247–66.

Ann Klein, Amanda. *American Film Cycles: Reframing Genres, Screening Social Problems, and Defining Subcultures*. Austin: University of Texas Press, 2011.

Arata, Stephen D. 'The Occidental Tourist: Dracula and the Anxiety of Reverse Colonization'. In *The Nineteenth-Century Novel: A Critical Reader*, edited by Stephen Regan, 457–64. London: Routledge, 2001.

Armstrong, Stephen B. *Pictures about Extremes: The Films of John Frankenheimer*. Jefferson: McFarland & Company, 2008.

Arthurs, Jane and Iain Grant (eds.). *Crash Cultures: Modernity, Mediation and the Material*. Bristol: Intellect Books, 2003.

Auden, W. H. 'Interlude: West's Disease'. In *The Dyer's Hand & Other Essays*, edited by W. H. Auden, 238–45. London: Faber & Faber, 1975.

Austin, Andrea. 'Roland Emmerich's 2012: A Simple Truth'. In *2012: Decoding the Countercultural Apocalypse*, edited by Joseph Gelfer, 108–22. London: Routledge, 2014.

Azcona, Maria del Mar. *The Multi-Protagonist Film*. Oxford: Wiley-Blackwell, 2010.

Baily, Clarence H. 'The Wreck of the Valencia', *The Pacific Monthly*, March 1906: 28.

Bakhtin, Mikhail. *Rabelais and His World*. Translated by Helene Iswolsky. Cambridge: MIT Press, 1965.

Barbanel, Josh. 'Tougher Code May Not Have Helped: Fire Safety', *The New York Times*, 27 February 1993: 24.

Barefoot, Guy. *Trash Cinema: The Lure of the Low*. New York: Columbia University Press, 2017.

Barthes, Roland. *The Eiffel Tower and Other Mythologies*. Translated by Richard Howard. Los Angeles: University of California Press, 1997.

Baudrillard, Jean. *America*. Translated by Chris Turner. New York: Verso, 1989.

Baudrillard, Jean. *The Spirit of Terrorism and Other Essays,* trans. Chris Turner. London and New York: Verso, 2002.

BBC News. 'Covid: World's True Pandemic Death Toll Nearly 15 Million, Says WHO'. https://www.bbc.co.uk/news/health-61327778

Belton, John. *American Cinema/American Culture*. New York: McGraw-Hill, 2005.

Benjamin, Alison. 'Carol Ann Duffy – the Newest of the Bee Poets', *The Guardian* (28 October 2011). https://www.theguardian.com/environment/blog/2011/oct/28/carol-ann-duffy-bee-poetry?newsfeed=true

Benjamin, Alison and Brian McCallum. *A World without Bees*. Guardian Books, 2009.

Bennet, James. 'Explosion at the Twin Towers: Flaws in Emergency Systems Exposed', *The New York Times*, 28 February 1993: 37.

Bergvall, Åke. 'Apocalyptic Imagery in Fritz Lang's Metropolis'. *Literature/Film Quarterly* 40, no. 4 (2012): 246–57.

Berliner, Todd. 'Hollywood Storytelling and The Aesthetic Pleasure'. In *Psychocinematics: Exploring Cognition at the Movies*, edited by Arthur P. Shimamura, 195–213. Oxford: Oxford University Press, 2013.

Blackwood, Gemma. 'Dream Factory Tours: The Universal Pictures Movie Tour Attraction in the 1960s'. *Historical Journal of Film, Radio and Television* 38, no. 3 (2018): 516–35.

Blakinger, John R. '"Death in America" and "Life" Magazine: Sources for Andy Warhol's "Disaster" Paintings'. *Artibus et Historiae* 33, no. 66 (2012): 269–85.

Booth, Ken and Tim Dunne. *Terror in Our Time*. London: Routledge, 2011.

Bould, Mark. 'Film and Television'. In *The Cambridge Companion to Science Fiction*, edited by Edward James, 79–95. Cambridge: Cambridge University Press, 2003).

Bould, Mark. *The Anthropocene Unconscious: Climate Catastrophe Culture*. London: Verso, 2021.

Bowler, Kate. *Blessed: A History of the American Prosperity Gospel*. Oxford: Oxford University Press, 2003.

Brackney, William H. 'Walter Rauschenbusch: Then and Now'. *Baptist Quarterly* 48, no. 1 (2017): 23–46.

Brereton, Patrick. *Hollywood Utopia: Ecology in Contemporary American Cinema*. Bristol: Intellect Books Ltd, 2004.

Bright, Charles D. 'Aviation Literature – A Changing Art'. *Aerospace Historian* 31, no. 1 (Spring/March 1984): 68–73.

Britton, Andrew. 'Blissing Out: The Politics of Reaganite Entertainment (1986)'. In *Britton on Film: The Complete Film Criticism of Andrew Britton*, edited by Barry Keith Grant and Robin Wood, 97–156. Detroit: Wayne State University Press, 2008.

Britton, Andrew. 'Jaws (1979)'. In *Britton on Film: The Complete Film Criticism of Andrew Britton*, edited by Barry Keith Grant and Robin Wood, 248–51. Detroit: Wayne State University Press, 2008.

Brooke-Taylor, Tim, Graeme Garden and Bill Oddie. *The Making of the Goodies' Disaster Movie: The Greatest Story Ever Blown to Bits!* London: Weidenfeld & Nicolson Ltd, 1977.

Bruce, Scott G. (ed.). *The Penguin Book of Hell*. New York: Penguin Books, 2018.

Buckley, Tom. 'TV: "Triangle Fire" with Tom Bosley', *The New York Times*, 30 January 1979: C12.

Butler, A. M. *Solar Flares: Science Fiction in the 1970s*. Liverpool: Liverpool University Press, 2012.

Callendar, Newgate. '*Black Sunday (movie review)*', *The New York Times*, 2 February 1975: 4.

Campbell, Jan. *Film Cinema Spectatorship: Melodrama and Mimesis*. Cambridge: Polity Press, 2005.

Canby, Vincent. 'The Screen: Multi-Plot, Multi-Star "Airport" Opens: Lancaster and Martin in Principal Roles Adaptation of Hailey's Novel at Music Hall', *The New York Times*, 6 March 1970: 34.

Canby, Vincent. 'What Makes "Poseidon" Fun?', *The New York Times*, 14 January 1973: 121.

Canby, Vincent. 'The Year of the Disaster Movie: Audience Participation Abounds', *The Times-News* (2 December 1974). https://news.google.com/newspapers?id=g1MaAA AAIBAJ&sjid=vyQEAAAAIBAJ&pg=7166,3828596&hl=en

Canby, Vincent. '*The Towering Inferno First-Rate Visual Spectacle*', *The New York Times*, 20 December 1974: 20.

Canby, Vincent. ''Day of Locust' Turns Dross into Gold', *The New York Times*, 8 May 1975: 48.

Canby, Vincent. 'Screen: "Rollercoaster" on Track: Suspense Melodrama Stars Widmark and Fonda', *The New York Times*, 11 June 1977: 12.

Canby, Vincent. 'Screen: Medusa without Perseus: Life on the Couch', *The New York Times*, 14 April 1978: C9.

Canby, Vincent. 'The Swarm – A Bumbling 'B'. *The New York Times*, 23 July 1978: D13.

Capers, Bennett. 'On Andy Warhol's "Electric Chair"'. *California Law Review* 94, no. 1 (January 2006): 243–60.

Cassidy, Michael. 'Los Angeles: Promise and Warning'. *Official Architecture and Planning* 33, no. 12 (December 1970): 1057–66.

Chambliss, C. Julian, William Svitavsky, Thomas Donaldson and Julian C. Chambliss (eds.). *Ages of Heroes, Eras of Men: Superheroes and the American Experience*. Cambridge: Cambridge Scholars Publisher, 2013.

Clark, Timothy. *Literature and the Environment*. Cambridge: Cambridge University Press, 2014.

Clasen, Mathias. 'Never Go Swimming Again: Jaws (1975)'. In *Why Horror Seduces*, edited by Mathias Clasen, 103–11. Oxford: Oxford University Press, 2017.

Cleto, Fabio (ed.). *Queer Aesthetics and the Performing Subject A Reader*. Edinburgh: Edinburgh University Press, 1999.

CNN. 'Prosecutor: Yousef Aimed to Topple Trade Center Towers', 5 August 1997. http://edition.cnn.com/US/9708/05/wtc.trial/index.html

Cocks, Jay. 'Cinema: The 8th Plague', *Time*, 12 May 1975. https://archive.ph/20190821024813/ and http://content.time.com/time/magazine/article/0,9171,917442,00.html?promoid=googlep

Cohen, Harvey G. 'Chaplin's America, The Essanay and Mutual Years: The Making of an Artist in the Progressive Era, 1915–1917'. *Quarterly Review of Film and Video* 33, no. 7 (2016): 585–601.

Comer, Todd A. and Lloyd Vayo (eds.). *Terror and the Cinematic Sublime: Essays on Violence and the Unpresentable in Post-9/11 Films*. London: McFarland & Company, Inc., Publishers, 2013.

Cook, David A. *Lost Illusions: American Cinema in the Shadow of Watergate and Vietnam, 1970–1979*. Los Angeles: University of California Press, 2000.

Cook, David. '1974: Movies and Political Trauma'. In *American Cinema of the 1970s: Themes and Variations*, edited by L. D. Friedman, 116–34. New Brunswick: Rutgers University Press, 2007.

Creed, Barbara. *The Monstrous-Feminine: Film, Feminism, Psychoanalysis*. London: Routledge, 1993.

Creekmur, Corey K. 'John Frankenheimer's "War on Terror"'. In *A Little Solitaire: John Frankenheimer and American Film*, edited by Murray Pomerance and R. Barton Palmer, 103–66. New Brunswick: Rutgers University Press, 2011.

Crosse, Jesse. *The Greatest Movie Car Chases of All Time*. St. Paul: Motorbooks International, 2006.

Crowther, Bosley. 'The Screen: "Queen Bee"; New Film at Loew's State Drones Along', *The New York Times*, 23 November 1955: 18.

Crowther, Bosley. 'Screen: Disaster at Sea: "Last Voyage" Provides Thrills and Suspense', *The New York Times*, 20 February 1960: 14.

Davis, Mike. *Ecology of Fear: Los Angeles and the Imagination of Disaster*. New York: Vintage, 1999.

Dean, Jodi. 'Realism'. *Mediations* 33, nos. 1–2 (2019–2020). https://mediationsjournal.org/articles/end-of-world.

DeAngelis, Michael. 'Movies and Confession'. In *American Cinema of the 1970s: Themes and Variations*, edited by Lester D. Friedman and Margo Natalie Crawford, 71–94. New Brunswick: Rutgers University Press, 2007.

DeMott, Robert. 'Introduction'. In *The Grapes of Wrath*, edited by John Steinbeck. London: Penguin Books, 2000.

Diaper, Jeremy. *T. S. Eliot & Organicism*. Clemson, South Carolina: Clemson University Press, 2018.

Dickstein, Morris. 'Sunset Boulevard'. *Grand Street* 7, no. 3 (Spring 1988): 176–84.

Diffrient, David Scott. 'Spectator Sports and Terrorist Reports: Filming the Munich Olympics, (Re)imagining the Munich Massacre'. *Sport in Society* 11, nos. 2–3 (2008): 311–29.

Doyle, Sir Arthur Conan Doyle. 'His Last Bow'. In *His Last Bow: Some Reminiscences of Sherlock Holmes*, 181–98. London: Penguin Books, 1997.

Drehle, David Von. *Triangle: The Fire that Changed America*. Grove Press, 2004.

Eagleton, Terence. *Holy Terror*. Oxford: Oxford University Press, 2005.

Eagleton, Terry. *Sweet Violence: The Idea of the Tragic*. Oxford: Blackwell Publishing, 2003.

Ebert, Roger. 'Airport (movie review)', *Chicago Sun-Times*, 1 January 1970. https://www.rogerebert.com/reviews/airport-1970

Ebert, Roger. 'Dirty Harry (movie review)', *Chicago-Sun Times*, 1 January 1971. https://www.rogerebert.com/reviews/dirty-harry-1971

Ebert, Roger. 'The Towering Inferno (movie review)', *Chicago Sun-Times*, 1 January 1974. https://www.rogerebert.com/reviews/the-towering-inferno-1974

Ebert, Roger. 'The Hindenburg (movie review)', *Chicago-Sun Times*, 1 January 1975. https://www.rogerebert.com/reviews/the-hindenburg-1975

Ebert, Roger. 'Day of the Locust (movie review)', *Chicago Sun-Times*, 23 May 1975. https://www.rogerebert.com/reviews/day-of-the-locust-1975

Ebert, Roger. 'Two-Minute Warning (movie review)', *Chicago Sun-Times*, 15 November 1976. https://www.rogerebert.com/reviews/two-minute-warning-1976

Ebert, Roger. 'Sudden Death (movie review)'. *Chicago Sun-Times*, 22 December 1995. https://www.rogerebert.com/reviews/sudden-death-1995

Edelman, Lee and Joseph Litvak. 'Two Much: Excess, Enjoyment, and Estrangement in Hitchcock's Strangers on a Train'. *GLQ: A Journal of Lesbian and Gay Studies* 25, no. 2 (April 2019): 297–314.

Eder, Richard. 'Be Warned about 'Two Minute Warning'. *The New York Times*, 13 November 1976: 11.

Eliade, Mircea. *Cosmos and History: The Myth of the Eternal Return*. Translated by Willard R. Task. New York: Harper Torchbooks, 1959.

Eliot, T. S. *The Dry Salvages*. London: Faber & Faber, 1941.

Eliot, T. S. 'Ulysses, Order and Myth [1923]'. In *Selected Prose of T. S. Eliot*, edited by Frank Kermode, 175–8. London: A Harvest Book, 1975.

Eliot, T. S. *The Waste Land* [1922]. New York: Liveright Publishing Corporation, 2013.

Elsaesser, Thomas. 'The Pathos of Failure: American Films in the 1970s: Notes on the Unmotivated Hero [1975]'. In *The Last Great American Picture Show: New Hollywood Cinema in the 1970s*, edited by Thomas Elsaesser, Alexander Horwath and Noel King, 279–92. Amsterdam: Amsterdam University Press, 2004.

Erickson, Glen. 'Panic in Year Zero! and Last Man on Earth', DVD Savant Review, 8 April 2005. https://www.dvdtalk.com/dvdsavant/s1571pani.html

Evans, Peter William. *Written on the Wind*. London: British Film Institute, 2013.

Evans, Christopher H. *The Social Gospel in American Religion: A History*. New York University Press, 2017.

Fairclough, Adam. 'Historian and the Civil Rights Movement'. *Journal of American Studies* 24, no. 3 (1990): 387–98.

Falzon, Christopher. 'Dirty Harry Ethics'. *SubStance* 45, no. 3 (2016): 49–65.

Fender, Stephen. *Nature, Class, and New Deal Literature: The Country Poor in the Great Depression*. London: Routledge, 2011.

Fiel, Ken. *Dying for a Laugh: Disaster Movies and the Camp Imagination*. Middleton, CT: Wesleyan University Press, 2005.

Fisher, Mark. *Capitalist Realism: Is There an Alternative?* Winchester: Zero Books, 2009.

Fiumara, James. 'Electrocuting an Elephant at Coney Island: Attraction, Story, and the Curious Spectator'. *Film History* 28, no. 1 (2016): 43–70.

Flatley, Guy. 'At the Movies: Bruce Dern Plays Veteran Tormented by Love and War', *The New York Times*, 7 January 1977: 43.

Flatley, Guy. 'At the Movies: Producer Sets Hoffman's Sail for Popeye', *The New York Times*, 14 October 1977: 58.

Fox, George. *Earthquake: The Story of a Movie*. New York: A Signet Book, 1974.

Fraser, Mark. 'Top 10 Films That Share an Apocalyptic View of Los Angeles'. *Top Ten Films*. 25 May 2014. https://www.top10films.co.uk/21163-top-10-films-share-apocalyptic-view-los-angeles/

Freer, Scott Freer. *Modernist Mythopoeia: The Twilight of the Gods*. London: Palgrave, 2015.

Freud, Sigmund. 'The 'Uncanny''. In *The Complete Psychological Works of Sigmund Freud Volume XVII (1917–1919)*, translated by James Strachey, 219–53. London: The Hogarth Press, 1925.

Galily, Yair, Moran Yarchi and Ilan Tamir. 'From Munich to Boston, and from Theater to Social Media: The Evolutionary Landscape of World Sporting Terror'. *Studies in Conflict & Terrorism* 38, no. 12 (2015): 998–1007.

Gallico, Paul. *Confessions of a Story-Teller*. London: Michael Joseph, 1961.

Gallico, Paul. *The Poseidon Adventure*. London: Pan Books Ltd, 1969.

Garrard, Greg. *Ecocriticism*. London: Routledge, 2012.

Geiger, Jeffrey. *American Documentary Film: Projecting the Nation*. Edinburgh University Press, 2011.

Gentry, Ric. 'Another Meditation on Death: An Interview with Oliver Stone'. *Film Quarterly* 60, no. 4 (2007): 54–60.

Gilman, Charlotte Perkins. *Herland and Related Writings*. Edited by Beth Sutton-Ramspeck. New York: Broadview Editions, 2013.

Grad, Shelby. 'Ranking Movies that Destroy Los Angeles: Did "San Andreas" Do It Best?'. *Los Angeles Times*. 1 June 2015. https://www.latimes.com/local/california/la-me-hollywood-disasters-20150529-story.html

Gray, John. *The Silence of Animals: On Progress and Other Modern Myths*. London: Penguin Books, 2014.

Greenaway, Peter Van. *The Medusa Touch*. St. Albans: Panther Granada, 1975.

Greenwald, Richard A. '"The Burning Building at 23 Washington Place": The Triangle Fire, Workers and Reformers in Progressive Era New York'. *New York History* 83, no. 1 (Winter 2002): 55–91.

Gregory, Mollie. *Stuntwomen: The Untold Hollywood Story*. Lexington: University Press of Kentucky, 2015.

Gunning, Tom. 'Heard over the Phone: The Lonely Villa and the de Lorde Tradition of the Terrors of Technology'. *Screen* 32, no. 2 (Summer 1991): 184–96.

Guttridge, Peter. 'Obituaries: Arthur Hailey', *The Independent*, 27 November 2004. https://www.independent.co.uk/news/obituaries/arthur-hailey-534720.html

Hailey, Arthur. *Airport*. London: Pan Books Ltd, 1970.

Hall, Sheldon and Steve Neale. *Epics, Spectacles and Blockbusters*. Detroit: Wayne State University Press, 2010.

Hardy, Thomas. 'The Convergence of the Twain', *Poetry Foundation*. https://www.poetryfoundation.org/poems/47266/the-convergence-of-the-twain

Heard, H. F. *A Taste of Honey* [1941]. Nevada City: Blue Dolphin Publishing, 2009.

Henley, William Ernest. 'Invictus'. *Book of Verses* (1888), in *Poetry Foundation*. https://www.poetryfoundation.org/poems/51642/invictus

Herzog, Arthur. *The Swarm*. London: Pan Books Ltd, 1974.

Herzog, Arthur. *Orca*. London: Pan Books Ltd, 1977.

Herzog, Arthur. *Heat*. London: Pan Books Ltd, 1978.

Heston, Charlton. *The Actor's Life: Journals 1956–1976*. Edited by Hollis Alpert. New York: A Henry Robbins Book, 1978.

Heston, Charlton. *In the Arena: The Autobiography*. London: HarperCollins, 1995.

Heyer, Paul. *Titanic Legacy: Disaster as Media Event and Myth*. London: Praeger, 1995.

Hill, Gladwin. 'Hollywood Cycle: Industry Is Gearing for Outer', *The New York Times*, 26 March 1961: X9.

Hoberman, J. '*Nashville contra Jaws*, or "The Imagination of Disaster" Revisited'. In *The Last Great American Picture Show: New Hollywood Cinema in the 1970s*, edited by Thomas Elsaesser, Alexander Horwath and Noel King, 195–222. Amsterdam: Amsterdam University Press, 2004.

Holden, Stephen. 'Theater: Previews and Openings: "*Marjoe*"', *The New York Times*, 13 January 2006: E 28.

Holquist, Michael. *Dialogism: Bakhtin and His World*. London: Routledge, 1990.

Hughes, Scott. 'The Worst Movie Ever?', *The Guardian*, 26 April 2001: A15. https://www.theguardian.com/culture/2001/apr/26/artsfeatures2

Hurley, Kelly. *The Gothic Body: Sexuality, Materialism, and Degeneration at the Fin de Siècle*. Cambridge: Cambridge University Press, 2009.

Iannucci, Amilcare A. 'Dante and Hollywood'. In *Dante, Cinema, and Television*, edited by A. A. Iannucci, 3–20. Toronto: University of Toronto Press, 2004.

Ingram, Lynn and Frances Malamud-Roam. *The West without Water: What Past Floods, Droughts, and Other Climatic Clues Tell Us about Tomorrow*. Berkeley: University of California Press, 2013.

Jaws Official Trailer. https://www.youtube.com/watch?v=U1fu_sA7XhE&t=31

Jeffries, Dru. *Comic Book Film Style: Cinema at 24 Panels per Second*. Austin: University of Texas Press, 2017.

Jenkins, Claire. 'Family Destruction and the Action-Melodrama'. In *Home Movies: The American Family in Contemporary Hollywood Cinema*, 101–23. London: I.B. Tauris, 2014.

Jones, Edward T. 'That's Wormwood: "The Day of the Locust"'. *Literature/Film Quarterly* 6, no. 3 (1978): 222–9.

Kael, Pauline. *Deeper into Movies*. Boston: Little, Brown and Company, 1973.

Kael, Pauline. *Reeling*. London: Marion Boyars, 1977.

Kael, Pauline. *Going Steady: Film Writings 1968–1969*. New York: Marion Boyars, 1994.

Kael, Pauline. 'Killing Time'. In *Screen Violence*, edited by Karl French, 171–8. London: Bloomsbury, 1997.

Kaminsky, Stuart M. *American Film Genres*. Chicago: Nelson-Hall, 1988.

Kaufmann, Will and Staff Van Oostrum. *American Culture in the 1970s*. Edinburgh: Edinburgh University Press, 2009.

Keane, Stephen. *Disaster Movies: The Cinema of Catastrophe*. London: Wallflower, 2001.

Keathley, Christian. 'Trapped in the Affection Image: Hollywood's Post-Traumatic Cycle (1970–1976)'. In *Last Great American Picture Show: New Hollywood Cinema in the 1970s*, edited by Thomas Elsaesser, Noel King and Alexander Horwath, 238–51. Amsterdam: Amsterdam University Press, 2004.

Keesey, Douglas. *Brian de Palma's Split-Screen: A Life in Film*. Jackson: University Press of Mississippi, 2019.

Kellner, Douglas. *Media Spectacle*. London: Routledge, 2003.

Kellner, Douglas. *Cinema Wars: Hollywood Film and Politics in the Bush-Cheney Era*. Hoboken, NJ: John Wiley & Sons, Incorporated, 2009.

Kendrick, Jim. *Film Violence: History, Ideology, Genre*. New York: Columbia University Press, 2010.

Kermode, Frank. *The Sense of an Ending: Studies in the Theory of Fiction*. Oxford: Oxford University Press, 1967.

Kidd, Sue Monk. *The Secret Lives of Bees*. New York: Penguin Books, 2001.

King, Geoff. *Spectacular Narratives: Hollywood in the Age of the Blockbuster*. London: I.B. Tauris, 2000.

King, Geoff. *The Spectacle of the Real: From Hollywood to Reality TV and Beyond.* Bristol: Intellect Books Ltd, 2005.

Klemesrud, Judy. 'He's the Master of Disaster: He's the Master of Disaster Bang! Crash! Sizzle!'. *The New York Times*, 29 December 1974: 71.

Koerner, Brenda I. *The Skies Belong to Us: Love and Terror in the Golden Age of Hijackings.* New York: Crown Publishers, 2013.

Koerner, Joseph Leo. 'The Mortification of the Image: Death as a Hermeneutic in Hans Baldung Grien'. *Representations*, no. 10 (1985): 52–101.

Kozlovic, Anton Karl. 'What Sort of Scripture Filmmaker was Cecil B. DeMille: Biblical, Religious or Spiritual'. *KINEMA: A Journal for Film and Media* 37 (2012): 21–46.

Kramer, Peter. *The New Hollywood: From Bonnie and Clyde to Star Wars.* London: Wallflower Press, 2005.

Kudler, Adrian Glick Kudler. 'The Complete List of Los Angeles Destruction Movies: Filmmakers Love to Destroy LA'. *Curbed LA*, 19 April 2018. https://la.curbed.com/2014/3/21/10129198/los-angeles-destruction-disaster-movies

Kuhn, Annette and Guy Westwell (eds.). *Oxford Dictionary of Film Studies.* Oxford: Oxford University Press, 2012.

Lacan, Jacques. *The Four Fundamental Concepts of Psycho-Analysis.* Translated by Alan Sheridan. London: Penguin Books, 1994.

Latour, Bruno. 'Why Has Critique Run Out of Steam? From Matters of Fact to Matters of Concern'. *Critical Inquiry* 30 (Winter 2004): 225–48.

Law, John William. *Master of Disaster: Irwin Allen – The Disaster Years.* San Francisco: Aplomb Publishing, 2008.

Lawson, Stephen F. 'Long Origins of the Short Civil Rights Movement, 1954–1968'. In *Freedom Right: New Perspectives on the Civil Rights Movement*, edited by Danielle L. McGuire and John Dittmer, 9–38. Lexington: University Press of Kentucky, 2011.

Lecker, Michael J. Lecker. 'Superhero Fantasy in a Post 9-11 World: Marvel Comics and Army Recruitment'. In *Ages of Heroes, Eras of Men: Superheroes and the American Experience*, edited by Julian C. Chambliss, William Svitavsky, Thomas Donaldson and Julian C. Chambliss, 299–40. Cambridge: Cambridge Scholars Publisher, 2013.

Leeming, David. *The Oxford Companion to World Mythology.* Oxford: Oxford University Press, 2009.

Lehmann-Haupt, Christopher. 'Books of the Times: Big City Life and Cold War', *The New York Times*, 19 October 1973: 41.

Lennon, John. 'God', *John Lennon/Plastic Ono Band* (Apple Record, 1970).

'Letters page: '11 September', *London Review of Books*, 4 October 2001. https://www.lrb.co.uk/the-paper/v23/n19/nine-eleven-writers/11-september

Lev, Peter. *American Films of the 70s: Conflicting Visions.* Austin: University of Texas Press, 2000.

Library of Congress. 'The Skyscrapers of New York'. https://www.loc.gov/item/00694391

Light, James F. *Nathanael West: An Interpretative Study*. Evanston: Northwestern University Press, 1971.

Lorentz, Pare. 'The Grapes of Wrath (review)'. In *Movies 1927 to 1941: Lorentz on Film*, edited by Pare Lorentz, 183–6. New York: Hopkinson and Blake, 1975.

Lorentz, Pare. *Pare Lorentz, FDR's Moviemaker: Memoirs & Scripts*. Reno: Nevada Press, 1992.

Lutz, R. C. 'On the Road to Nowhere? California's Car Culture'. *California History* 79, no. 1 (Spring, 2000): 50–5.

Lyne, William. 'No Accident: From Black Power to Black Box Office'. *African American Review* 34, no. 1 (2000): 39–59.

Lyth, Peter. '"Think of Her as Your Mother": Airline Advertising and the Stewardess in America, 1930–1980'. *The Journal of Transport History* 30, no. 1 (2009): 1–21.

Maeterlinck, Maurice. *The Life of the Bee*. Translated by Alfred Sutro. New York: Dover Publications, 2015.

Magny, Joël, Denis Lévy and Stéphane Sorel. 'Films Catastrophiques: Spectacteurs Catastrophés', *Positif*, March 1976, 11–14.

Maher, Neil M. '"A Conflux of Desire and Need": Trees, Boy Scouts, and the Roots of Franklin Roosevelt's Civilian Conservation Corps'. In *FDR and the Environment*, edited by Henry L. Henderson and David B. Woolner, 49–84. New York: Palgrave Macmillan, 2005.

Maland, Charles J. '1978: Movies and Changing Times'. In *American Cinema of the 1970s: Themes and Variation*, edited by Lester D. Friedman and Margo Natalie Crawford, 205–27. Oxford: Berg, 2007.

Mandalit, Del Barco. 'Los Angeles: City of Perpetual Cinematic Destruction'. *npr*. 9 August 2011. https://www.npr.org/2011/08/09/138985693/los-angeles-city-of-perpetual-cinematic-destruction

Manwaring, Kevan. 'APOCALYPSE (wow!)'. *Still Point*, 1 March 2019. https://www.stillpointldn.com/articles/kevan-manwaring-apocalypse-wow/

Martin, Garrett. 'The Original Superhero Movie Isn't Really a Superhero Movie'. *Paste*, 18 November 2018. https://www.pastemagazine.com/movies/4k/superman-the-original-superhero-movie-isnt-really/

Massood, Paula J. 'Movies and a Nation in Transformation'. In *American Cinema of the 1970s: Themes and Variations*, edited by L. D. Friedman, 184–204. New Brunswick: Rutgers University Press, 2007.

Matthews, Jack. 'Universal Shuts Earthquake Attraction for Two Days', *Los Angeles Times* (19 October 1989). https://www.latimes.com/archives/la-xpm-1989-10-19-ca-334-story.html

Mazzocco, Robert. 'Letter from Nashville'. *New York Review of Books*, 17 July 1975: 180.

McEvoy, Arthur F. 'The Triangle Shirtwaist Factory Fire of 1911: Social Change, Industrial Accidents, and the Evolution of Common-Sense Causality'. *Law & Social Inquiry* 20, no. 2 (Spring, 1995): 621–51.

McKahan, Jason Grant. *Hollywood Counterterrorism: Violence, Protest and the Middle East in U.S. Action Feature Films*. Florida State University (Thesis), 2009.

Menon, Delip. 'Fifty Shades of Blackness: Recovering an Aesthetics of the Afrifuge'. *Cambridge Journal of Postcolonial Literary Inquiry* 7, no. 2 (April 2020): 107–20.

Metzger, Bruce M. and Michael D. Coogan (eds.). *The Oxford Companion to the Bible*. Oxford: Oxford University Press, 1993.

Mohun, Arwen P. 'Designed for Thrills and Safety: Amusement Parks and the Commodification of Risk, 1880–1929'. *Journal of Design History* 14, no. 4 (2001): 291–306.

Monbiot, George. 'Watching Don't Look Up Made Me See My Whole Life of Campaigning Flash before Me'. *The Guardian*, 4 January 2022. https://www.theguardian.com/commentisfree/2022/jan/04/dont-look-up-life-of-campaigning

Moody, Rick. 'Frank Miller and the Rise of Cryptofascist Hollywood'. *The Guardian*. 24 November 2011. https://www.theguardian.com/culture/2011/nov/24/frank-miller-hollywood-fascism

Morag, Raya. 'Defeated Masculinity: Post-Traumatic Cinema in the Aftermath of the Vietnam War'. *The Communication Review* 9, no. 3 (2006): 189–219.

Morrison, Herbert. WLS radio broadcast, 6 May 1937. https://weinterruptthisbroadcast.org/2021/04/21/episode-one-the-hindenburg-disaster/

Muir, John Kenneth. *Horror Films of the 1970s*. Jefferson: McFarland, 2007.

Murphy, Mary. 'Jumping on the Disaster Bandwagon', *Los Angeles Times*, 3 May (1974): E1.

Murray, Robin and Joe Heumann. 'Environmental Catastrophe in Pare Lorentz's "The River" and Elia Kazan's "Wild River": The TVA, Politics, and the Environment'. *Studies in Popular Culture* 27, no. 2 (October 2004): 47–65.

National Highway Traffic Safety Administration. http://www-fars.nhtsa.dot.gov/Main/index.aspx.

Neale, Steve. *Genre and Hollywood*. London: Routledge, 2000.

Neupert, Richard. *The End-Narration and Closure in the Cinema*. Detroit: Wayne State University Press, 1995.

Newman, Kim. *Nightmare Movies: Critical History of the Horror Film, 1968–88*. London: Bloomsbury, 1988.

Niemi, Robert. 'Experiments in Genre Revision'. In *The Cinema of Robert Altman Book Subtitle: Hollywood Maverick*, edited by Robert Niemi, 23–72. New York: Columbia University Press, 2016.

Nietzsche, Friedrich. *The Birth of Tragedy Out of the Spirit of Music*. Translated by Michael Tanner. London: Penguin Books, 1993.

Nouhy, Eman El. 'Redeeming the Medusa: An Archetypal Examination of Ted Hughes' *The Iron Woman*'. *Children's Literature in Education* 50 (2019): 347–363.

Nowak-mcniece, Katarzyna and Agata Zarzycka (eds.). *A Dark California: Essays on Dystopian Depictions in Popular Culture*. Jefferson, NC: McFarland, 2017.

Nye, David E. *American Technological Sublime*. Cambridge: MIT Press, 1994.

Ovid. *Metamorphoses*. Translated by Rolfe Humphries and annotated by Joseph D. Reed. Bloomington: Indiana University Press, 2018.

Pfeil, Fred. *White Guys: Studies in Postmodern Domination & Difference*. London: Verso, 1995.

Phillips, K. R. *Dark Directions: Romero, Craven, Carpenter, and the Modern Horror Film*. Carbondale: Southern Illinois University Press, 2012.

Philips, Menaka. 'Violence in the American Imaginary: Gender, Race, and the Politics of Superheroes'. *American Political Science Review* 116, no. 2 (2022): 470–83.

Pierro, Robert. 'Aesthetic Legacies and Dashed Political Hopes: Caspar David Friedrich Motifs in Roland Emmerich's Post-9/11 Popcorn Message Movies'. *The Germanic Review: Literature, Culture, Theory* 88, no. 4 (2013): 400–17.

Pirzada, Muhammad Abukarar. Letter to *The Guardian*. 31 October 2022.

Plath, Otto. *Bumblebees and Their Ways*. New York: The Macmillan Company Publishers, 1934.

Plath, Sylvia. *Ariel: The Restored* Edition. London: Faber & Faber, 2004.

Pogel, Nancy and William Chamberlain. 'Self Reflections in Adaptations of Black Comic Novels'. *Literature/Film Quarterly* 13, no. 3 (1985): 187–93.

Pollard, Tom. *Hollywood 9/11: Superheroes, Supervillains, and Super Disasters*. London: Routledge, 2011.

Pomerance, Murray. *The Eyes Have It: Cinema and the Reality Effect*. New Brunswick: Rutgers University Press, 2013.

Pomeroy, Arthur J. *Then It Was Destroyed by the Volcano: The Ancient World in Film and on Television*. London: Gerald Duckworth, 2008.

Porter, Jess C. 'What Was the Dust Bowl? Assessing Contemporary Popular Knowledge'. *Popul Environ*, no. 35 (2014): 391–416.

Preston, Claire. *Bee*. London: Reaktion Books, 2015.

Prince, Stephen. *Savage Cinema: Sam Peckinpah and the Rise of Ultraviolent Movies*. London: The Athlone Press, 1998.

Prince, Stephen. *Screening Violence*. London: The Athlone Press, 2000.

Prince, Stephen. *Firestorm: American Film in the Age of Terrorism*. New York: Columbia University Press, 2009.

Rabinovitz, Lauren. *Electric Dreamland: Amusement Parks, Movies and American Modernity*. New York: Columbia University Press, 2012.

Randall, Karen. '"It Was Like a Movie": The Impossibility of Representation in Oliver Stone's World Trade Center'. In *Reframing 9/11: Film, Popular Culture and the War on Terror*, edited by Jeff Birkenstein, Anna Froula and Karen Randell, 141–52. London: Bloomsbury, 2010.

Ransome, Hilda M. *The Sacred Bee in Ancient Times and Folklore*. New York, Dover Publications, 2004.

Ray, Robert B. *A Certain Tendency of the Hollywood Cinema, 1930–1980*. Princeton, NJ: Princeton University Press, 1985.

Reid, Mark. *Redefining Black Film*. Berkeley: University of California Press, 1993.

Riegler, Thomas. 'Through the Lenses of Hollywood: Depictions of Terrorism in American Movies'. *Perspectives on Terrorism* 4, no. 2 (May 2010): 35–45.

Ringle, Ken. 'Integrity Goes Down with the Ship: Historical Facts, Including True-Life Gallantry, Lost in Titanic'. *The Washington Post*, 22 March 1998: 140.

Roberts, Oral. *Oral Roberts's Life Story: As Told by Himself* (Tulsa 1, OK: Oral Roberts, 1952).

Roberts, Oral. *The Call: An Autobiography*. London: Hodder and Stoughton, 1972.

Roddick, Nick. 'The Poseidon Adventure'. In *Magill's Survey of Cinema, English Language Films*, edited by Frank Magill, 1363–4. Englewood, NJ: Salem Press, 1980.

Roddick, Nick. 'Only the Stars Survive: Disaster Movies in the Seventies'. In *Performance and Politics in Popular Drama*, edited by David Brady, Louis James and Bernard Sharratt, 243–70. Cambridge: Cambridge University Press, 1981.

Romoa, Tico. 'Guns and Gas: Investigating the 1970s Car Chase Film'. In *The Action and Adventure Cinema*, edited by Yvonne Tasker, 130–52. London: Routledge, 2004.

Rosenau, William. '"Our Backs Are against the Wall": The Black Liberation Army and Domestic Terrorism in 1970s America'. *Studies in Conflict & Terrorism* 36, no. 2 (2013): 176–92.

Rossinow, Doug. 'The Radicalization of the Social Gospel: Harry F. Ward and the Search for a New Social Order, 1898–1936'. *Religion and American Culture: A Journal of Interpretation* 15, no. 1 (Winter 2005): 63–106.

Rust, Amy. *Passionate Detachments: Technologies of Vision and Violence in American Cinema, 1967–1974*. Albany: State University of New York, 2017.

Ryan, Michael and Douglas Kellner. *Camera Politica: The Politics and Ideology of Contemporary Hollywood Film*. Bloomington and Indianapolis: Indiana University Press, 1990.

Salinas, David J. (ed.). *Prosperity Theology and the Gospel: Good News or Bad News for the Poor?* Peabody, MA: Hendrickson Publishers, 2017.

Sanders, John. *Studying Disaster Movies*. Leighton Buzzard: Auteur Publishing Ltd, 2009.

Sangster, Joan and Julia Smith. 'From Career Girl to Sexy Stewardess: Popular Culture and Women's Work in the Canadian and American Airline Industries'. *Women: A Cultural Review* 30, no. 2 (2019): 141–61.

Savage, Peter. 'Hailey's Commentaries: Best Selling Views on Latter-Day Organizations'. *Public Administration Review* 39, no. 2 (March–April 1979): 184–7.

Sayre, Nora. 'Screen: "Earthquake" Evokes Feelies', *The New York Times*, 16 November 1974. https://www.nytimes.com/1974/11/16/archives/screen-earthquake-evokes-feeliesthe-cast.html

Schäfer, Axel R. 'Introduction: *Evangelicals and the Sixties: Revisiting the 'Backlash'*. In *American Evangelicals and The 1960s*, edited by Axel R. Schäfer, 3–16. Madison: University of Wisconsin Press, 2013.

Schantz, Ned. 'Telephonic Film'. *Film Quarterly* 56, no. 4 (2003): 23–35.

Schleier, Merrill. *Skyscraper Cinema: Architecture and Gender in American Film.* Minneapolis: University of Minnesota Press.

Schleier, Merrill. 'The Empire State Building, Working-Class Masculinity, and "King Kong"'. *Mosaic: An Interdisciplinary Critical Journal* 41, no. 2 (June 2008): 29–54.

Schwarzenegger, Arnold. 'Climate Change Is Not Science Fiction', *The Guardian*, 21 July 2015. https://www.theguardian.com/environment/2015/jul/21/arnold-schwarzenegger-climate-change-is-not-science-fiction

Scortia, Thomas N. and Frank M. Robinson. *The Glass Inferno* [1974]. New York: Doubleday & Company.

Scranton, Roy. 'Star Wars and the Fantasy of American Violence', *The New York Times*, 2 July 2016. https://www.nytimes.com/2016/07/03/opinion/sunday/star-wars-and-the-fantasy-of-american-violence.html

Seagle, Steven T. 'Unreal'. In *9/11*, 15–16. New York: D C Comics, 2002.

Seaton, George. *Airport*. 1969 script.

Seed, David. 'Los Angeles' Science Fiction Futures'. In *The Cambridge Companion to the Literature of Los Angeles*, edited by Kevin R. McNamara, 123–34. Cambridge: Cambridge University Press, 2010.

Segaloff, Nat. *Stirling Silliphant: The Fingers of God*. Albany: BearManor Media, 2013.

Self, Will. 'Rereading Philosophy Books: Guy Debord's The Society of the Spectacle'. *The Guardian*, 14 November 2013. https://www.theguardian.com/books/2013/nov/14/guy-debord-society-spectacle-will-self

Shelley, Percy Bysshe. 'Ozymandias' (1817). In *Poetry Foundation*. https://www.poetryfoundation.org/poems/46565/ozymandias

Shiel, Mark. 'The Southland on Screen'. In *The Cambridge Companion to the Literature of Los Angeles*, edited by Kevin R. McNamara, 145–56. Cambridge: Cambridge University Press, 2010.

Silliphant, Stirling. *Airport* Screenplay: Third Revised Shooting Final. 24 March 1972.

Silliphant, Stirling. '"Towering Inferno": A Bit of Art Too Often Imitated by Life and Death', *Los Angeles Times* (10 May 1988): C7.

Slocum, David. 'Film Violence and the Institutionalization of the Cinema'. *Social Research* 67, no. 3 (2000): 649–81.

Sobchack, Vivian C. 'The Grapes of Wrath (1940): Thematic Emphasis through Visual Style'. In *Hollywood as Historian: American Film in a Cultural Context*, edited by Peter C. Rollins, 68–87. Lexington: University Press of Kentucky, 1983.

Sontag, Susan. 'The Imagination of Disaster'. In *Against Interpretation*, edited by Susan Sontag, 209–25. New York: Delta, 1966.

South, J. S. and K. S. Engels (eds.). *Westworld and Philosophy: If You Go Looking for the Truth, Get the Whole Thing*. New Jersey: John Wiley & Sons, 2018.

Stableford, Brian M. 'Introduction'. In *Deluge*, by Sydney Fowler Wright, i–iviii, xxiii. Middletown, CT: Wesleyan University Press, 2003.

Staff. 'New Picture: The Last Voyage (M-G-M)'. *Time*, 29 February 1960 (no. 9): 98. https://time.com/vault/issue/1960-02-29/page/92/

Staff. *Airport* (movie review), *Variety*, 31 December 1969. https://web.archive.org/web/20190722211352/ and https://variety.com/1969/film/reviews/airport-1200422292/

Staff. '*Airport Review*', *TV Guide Magazine*, 1970. https://www.tvguide.com/movies/airport/review/2030122594/

Staff. 'Irwin Allen, Warners Sign Production Deal'. *Los Angeles Times*, 21 July 1975: E13.

Staff. 'Irwin Allen, Big-Budget Producer of Disaster Movies, Is Dead at 75'. *The New York Times*, 4 November 1991: D9.

Staff. 'Obituaries: Irwin Allen, Producer of Disaster Films, Dies'. *The Washington Post*, 4 November 1991: B6. https://www.washingtonpost.com/archive/local/1991/11/04/irwin-allen-producer-of-disaster-films-dies/4008a607-accd-4638-b1a6-6ac2929a68ea/

Stam, Robert, Richard Porton and Leo Goldsmith (eds.). *Keywords in Subversive Film/Media Aesthetics*. Chichester: John Wiley & Sons, 2015.

Stampnitzky, L. *Disciplining Terror: How Experts Invented 'Terrorism'*. Cambridge: Cambridge University Press, 2013.

Stein, Leon. *The Triangle Fire*. Ithaca, NY: Cornell University Press, 2011.

Steinbeck, John. *The Grapes of Wrath*. London: Penguin Books, 2000.

Stern, Richard Martin. *The Tower* [1973]. London: Pan Books Ltd, 1974.

Street, Joe. 'Dirty Harry's San Francisco'. *The Sixties: A Journal of History, Politics and Culture* 5, no. 1 (June 2012): 1–21.

Stubblefield, Thomas. *9/11 and the Visual Culture of Disaster*. Bloomington, IN: Indiana University Press, 2015.

Sutherland, John. *Bestsellers: Popular Fiction of the 1970s*. London: Routledge & Kegan Paul, 1981.

Sutherland, John. *Reading the Decades: Fifty Years of the Nation's Bestselling Books*. London: BBC Worldwide Ltd, 2002.

Sweeney, Frank. '"What Mean Expendable?": Myth, Ideology, and Meaning in First Blood and Rambo'. *Journal of American Culture* 22, no. 3 (1999): 63–9.

Swenson, G. R. 'What Is Pop Art? Answers from 8 Painters, Part I'. *ARTnews* 62, no. 7 (November 1963): 24–7, 60–4.

Swenson, G. R. 'What Is Pop Art? Part II'. *ARTnews* 62, no. 10 (February 1964): 40–3, 62–7.

Tag Archives: 'Clipper America', *This Day in Aviation: Important Dates in Aviation History*. https://www.thisdayinaviation.com/tag/clipper-america/

Teslenko, Tatiana. *Feminist Utopian Novels of the 1970s: Joanna Russ and Dorothy Bryant*. London: Routledge, 2003.

Vantoch, Victoria. *The Jet Sex: Airline Stewardesses and the Making of an American Icon*. Philadelphia: University of Pennsylvania Press, 2013.

Varndell, Daniel. 'The Little Deaths of John Frankenheimer'. In *The Other Hollywood Renaissance*, edited by Dominic Lennard, R. Barton Palmer and Murray Pomerance, 134–47. Edinburgh: Edinburgh University Press, 2022.

Verevis, Constantine. 'Vicious Cycle: Jaws and Revenge-of-Nature Films of the 1970s'. In *Cycles, Sequels, Spin-offs, Remakes, and Reboots: Multiplicities in Film and Television*, edited by A. A. Klein and R. B. Palmer, 96–111. Austin: University of Texas Press, 2016.

Vleck, Jenifer Van. 'The Jet Age and the Limits of American Power'. In *Empire of the Air: Aviation and the American Ascendancy*, edited by Jennifer Van Vleck, 239–80. Cambridge: Harvard University Press, 2013.

Wager, Jans. 'Richard Roundtree: Inventing Shaft'. In *Hollywood Reborn: Movie Stars of The 1970s*, edited by James Morrison, 101–19. New Brunswick: Rutgers University Press, 2010.

Waldman, Louis. *Labor Lawyer*. New York: E.P. Dutton & Co., 1944.

Walker, David, Andrew J. Rausch and Chris Watson (eds.). *Reflections on Blaxploitation: Actors and Directors Speak*. Lanham: Scarecrow Press, 2009.

Wallin, Zoë. '"Pictures Seem to Run in Cycles": Industry Discourse and the Economics of Film Cycles in Classical Hollywood'. *Film History* 31, no.1 (2019): 81–101.

Wanner, Kevin J. 'In a World of Super-Violence, Can Pacifism Pack a Punch?'. *The Journal of American Culture* 39, no. 2 (June 2016): 177–92.

Warhol, Andy. 'Electric Chair' (1964). Tate: https://www.tate.org.uk/art/artworks/warhol-electric-chair-t07145

Weaver, Tom. *Double Feature Creature Attack*. Jefferson: McFarland and Co., 2003.

Webster, Andy. 'Review: "Being Evel" Examines the Life of a Notorious Stuntman', *The New York Times*, 20 August 2015: C6.

Wells, H. G. 'New York'. In *The Future in America: A Search after Realities*, edited by H. G. Wells, 35–48. London: Chapman & Hall, 1906.

West, Nathanael. *The Day of the Locust*. London: Penguin Books, 2018.

White, Mimi 'Movies and the Movement'. In *American Cinema of the 1970s: Themes and Variations*, edited by Lester D. Friedman, 24–47. Oxford: Berg Publishers, 2007.

Williams, Daniel K. 'Richard Nixon's Religious Right: Catholics, Evangelicals, and the Creation of an Antisecular Alliance'. In *The Right Side of the Sixties: Reexamining Conservatism's Decade of Transformation*, 141–58. London: Palgrave, 2012.

Wilson, Bee. *The Hive: The Story of the Honeybee and Us*. London: John Murray, 2005.

Wood, Robin. *Hollywood from Vietnam to Reagan ... Beyond*. New York: Columbia Press, 2003.

Woodcock, John. 'Disaster Thrillers: A Literary Mode of Technology Assessment'. *Science, Technology, & Human Values* 4, no. 26 (Winter 1979): 37–45.

Wright, Sydney Fowler Wright. *Deluge*. Skerries. County Dublin: Gilbert Dalton, 1980.

Yacowar, Maurice. 'The Bug in the Rug: Notes on the Disaster Genre'. In *Film Genre Reader IV*, edited by Barry Keith Grant, 313–31. Austin: University of Texas Press, 2012.

Zandy, Janet. 'Fire Poetry on the Triangle Shirtwaist Company Fire of March 25, 1911'. *College Literature* 24, no. 3 (October 1997): 33–54.

Žižek, Slavoj. *Welcome to the Desert of the Real: Five Essays on September 11 and Related Dates*. London: Verso Books, 2002.

Žižek, Slavoj. 'Welcome to the Desert of the Real!'. In *Cultures of Fear: A Critical Reader*, edited by Uli Linke and Danielle Taana Smith, 70–7. London: Pluto Press, 2009.

Žižek, Slavoj. *Event*. London: Penguin Books, 2014.

Index

9/11 (2017) 189–90
2001: A Space Odyssey (1968) 57
2012 (2009) 175, 186–7, 193, 199

Aftermath (2017) 185–6
Air Force One (1997) 185, 195
Airplane! (1980) 1, 184
Airport (1970) 4, 5, 6, 8, 30, 31–54, 55, 101, 103, 124, 174, 183, 185, 186, 189
Airport 1975 (1974) 6, 7, 37, 101, 105, 124, 184
Airport '77 (1977) 33, 124, 189
Alice's Restaurant (1969) 56, 57
All That Heaven Allows (1955) 49
All the President's Men (1975) 131
Andromeda Strain, The (1971) 5, 48, 55, 130, 176
A Night to Remember (1958) 60, 63–4
Anne of the Thousand Days (1969) 102
Armageddon (1998) 103

Ben-Hur (1959) 68, 106
Beyond the Poseidon Adventure (1979) 186
Big Bus, The (1976) 1, 190
Birds, The (1963) 158
Black Panther (2018) 182
Black Panther: Wakanda Forever (2022) 182
Black Sunday (1977) 5, 10, 45, 124, 125, 126, 132, 139–44, 172, 174, 175–6, 195, 197
Blacula (1972) 111, 161–2, 163
Blazing Stewardesses (1975) 46
Bonnie and Clyde (1967) 35, 130, 131
Boston Strangler, The (1968) 48
Breathless (1960) 44
Brighton Rock (1948) 134
Buccaneer (1938) 112
Buck and the Preacher (1972) 163, 182
Bullitt (1968) 47, 119

Candyman (1992) 199
Carnival of Souls (1962) 136
Carrie (1976) 172

Cars That Ate Paris, The (1974) 121
Catch-22 (1970) 57
Cave-In! (1979) 30, 54, 60
Ceiling Zero (1936) 37
Children of Men (2006) 187
China Syndrome, The (1979) 176
Chinatown (1974) 94
Close Encounters of the Third Kind (1977) 177, 145
Colossus: The Forbin Project (1970) 176
Coming Home (1978) 125
Conversation, The (1974) 131
Crime of Carelessness, The (1912) 11, 83–4
Crisis in Mid-Air (1979) 183, 185

Day After Tomorrow, The (2004) 103, 123
Day of the Animals, The (1977) 145
Day of the Locust, The (1975) 5, 58, 100, 111–16, 150, 171, 191
Dante's Inferno (1935) 11, 14, 25, 64, 135–6
Deadly Bees (1966) 154
Dead Zone (1983) 177
Death of Ocean View Park, The (1979) 134
Death Race 2000 (1975) 121, 136
Death Wish (1974) 176
Deep Impact (1998) 103
Deer Hunter, The (1978) 125
Deluge (1933) 8, 14, 15–20, 25, 27, 67, 88, 175
Demolition Man (1993) 194
Devil at 4 O'Clock, The (1961) 8
Devil Rides Out, The (1968) 57
Devils, The (1971) 57
Die Hard (1988) 75–6, 77
Dionysus in '69 (1970) 48
Dirty Harry (1971) 128–30, 137
Disaster Wars: Earthquake vs Tsunami (2013) 192
Dog Day Afternoon (1975) 131
Dolemite (1975) 164
Don't Look Up (2021) 1–3, 195

Drive-In (1976) 190–1
Dr. Strangelove or: How I Stopped Worrying and Learned to Love the Bomb (1964) 57

Earthquake (1974) 6, 7, 8, 9, 34, 37, 45, 99–111, 112, 116, 120, 123, 124, 132–3, 136, 139, 164, 174, 179, 193, 194, 195
Easy Rider (1969) 57, 94, 102, 132
El-Cid (1961) 106
Electrocuting an Elephant (1903) 131
Elysium (2013) 175, 187
Empire of the Ants (1977) 7, 151
Enforcer, The (1976) 128, 142
Escape from Los Angeles (1996) 191–2
Evel Knievel (1971) 110–11
Exorcist, The (1973) 57, 127

Fiddler on the Roof (1971) 35
Final Destination (2000) 177
Fire! (1977) 30, 54, 60
Fireman, The (1916) 11, 80, 81
First Blood (1982) 142
Flight (2012) 184
Flight 93 (2006) 185
Flight into Danger (1956) 39, 40
Flood! (1976) 29–30, 53
Fly Me (1973) 46
Fog, The (1980) 192
Food of the Gods (1976) 145
French Connection, The (1971) 119, 178
French Connection II (1975) 141
Fountainhead, The (1949) 91
Fury, The (1978) 172–3
Futureworld (1976) 136

Geo-Disaster (2017) 194
Geostorm (2017) 194
Get to Know Your Rabbit (1970) 49
Gladiator (2000) 195
Godfather, The (1972) 31, 56, 57
Gone in 60 Seconds (1974) 121
Graduate, The (1967) 35, 45, 57, 94, 116, 131
Grand Hotel (1932) 5, 9, 31, 36, 40
Grand Prix (1966) 48, 53, 119
Grapes of Wrath, The (1940) 14, 23, 27–29
Grease (1978) 145, 166, 178

Greatest Story Ever Told, The (1965) 106
Greenland (2020) 123, 175, 187

Hanging by a Thread (1979) 30, 54, 60
High and the Mighty, The (1954) 37, 38–9, 184
High Plains Drifter (1973) 103
Hindenburg, The (1975) 10, 90, 125
How the West Was Won (1962) 49, 99–100, 116
Human Tornado, The (1976) 164

Imitation of Life (1959) 49
Initiation of Sarah, The (1978) 172
In Old Chicago (1938) 22, 24–26, 27, 28, 80–1
It Came from Outer Space (1953) 151
Intolerance (1916) 16
Invasion of the Bee Girls (1973) 146, 155–6, 157
Invasion of the Body Snatchers (1956) 48, 155
Invasion of the Body Snatchers (1978) 176
Island in the Sky (1953) 38

Jaws (1975) 5, 9, 10, 94, 112, 116, 125, 127, 133, 134, 137, 142, 145, 148, 149, 166, 177, 179, 184, 198
Jet Storm (1959) 39
Joe (1970) 35, 176

Killer Bees (1974) 146, 157–8, 164
Killer Bees, The (2002) 198–9
King of Kings, The (1927) 22, 100, 174
King Kong (1933) 88, 90
King Kong (1976) 123, 180
Krakatoa, East of Java (1969) 88

Lady from Shanghai, The (1947) 134
Last Days of Pompeii, The (1935) 21–2
Last Days of Sodom and Gomorrah, The (1962) 192
Last House on the Left, The (1972)
Last Movie, The (1971) 57
Last Picture Show, The (1971) 35, 94, 132
Last Voyage, The (1960) 62–4
Legend of Nigger Charley, The (1972) 163
Le Mans (1971) 119

Life of an American Fireman, The (1903) 11, 79–80, 83
Logan's Run (1976) 45, 136, 165
Lost World, The (1960) 11, 60, 61
Love Story (1970) 31, 34–5

Magnum Force (1973) 128
Malatesta's Carnival of Blood (1973) 134
Manhattan (1979) 178
Man of Steel (2013) 181
Marjoe (1972) 107
M*A*S*H (1970) 11, 32, 34, 36, 57, 130
McCabe and Mrs. Miller (1971) 57
Medium Cool (1969) 130
Medusa Touch, The (1978) 8, 169–76
Metropolis (1927) 89
Midnight Cowboy (1969) 94, 130
Mildred Pierce (1945) 151
Munich (2005) 142

Nashville (1975) 36, 112, 113, 116, 119, 131, 190
Naughty Stewardesses, The (1974) 46
Night Flight (1933) 37
Night the Bridge Fell Down, The (1979) 30, 54, 60
Noah's Ark (1928) 16–18

Omega Man, The (1971) 106
Omen, The (1976) 57, 169
One Flew Over the Cuckoo's Nest (1975) 131
Orca (1977) 145, 148, 149, 161, 166

Panic in Year Zero! (1962) 160
Passenger 57 (1992) 185, 195
Peeping Tom (1960) 138
Phase IV (1974) 168
Pillow Talk (1959) 40, 49–50
Piranha (1978) 145, 195
Planet of the Apes (1968) 2, 34, 106, 161
Plow that Broke the Plains, The (1936) 27, 28
Point Blank (1967) 130
Poseidon (2006) 186
Poseidon Adventure, The (1972) 5, 6, 7, 8, 11, 29, 31, 36, 37, 54, 55–76, 91, 98, 100, 103, 174, 179, 186
Psycho (1960) 158

Queen Bee (1955) 151–3

Raid on Entebbe (1977) 142
Rebel Without a Cause (1955) 102, 117
River, The (1938) 26–7, 29
Rollerball (1975) 136
Rollercoaster (1977) 9–10, 45, 123, 124, 125, 132–4
Rosemary's Baby (1968) 57

Samson and Delilah (1949) 68, 113, 178
San Andreas (2015) 192–3
San Andreas Mega Quake (2019) 192
San Francisco (1936) 22–4, 25, 27, 28
Savage Bees, The (1976) 159
Scream, Blacula, Scream! (1973) 162
Seven-Ups, The (1973) 119
Shaft (1971) 108, 110
Shaft in Africa (1973) 109
Shampoo (1975) 131
Sharknado (2013) 194
Sign of the Cross, The (1932) 21, 123, 131, 138
Silent Running (1972) 168
Singin' in The Rain (1952) 90, 112–13
Skyjacked (1972) 32, 33, 108, 141–2, 174, 183
Skyscraper (2018) 197
Smash-Up on Interstate-5 (1976) 5, 100, 116–21
Snakes on a Plane (2006) 185
Soylent Green (1973) 2, 106, 109, 150
Spartacus (1960) 64
Speed (1994) 195
SST Death Flight (1977) 184
Star Wars (1977) 9, 35, 94, 123, 125, 126, 127, 145, 177, 179, 181
Stewardesses, The (1969) 46
Stewardesses Report (1971) 46
Strangers on a Train (1951) 134
Straw Dogs (1972) 126
Stepford Wives, The (1975) 136
Sting of Death (1955) 153–4
Street Angel (1928) 21
Sudden Death (1995) 195–8
Sully: Miracle on Hudson (2016) 184–5
Sunset Boulevard (1950) 102, 113
Superman (1978) 9, 177–182, 194

Superman II (1980) 181
Superman III (1983) 181
Superman Returns (2006) 181
Super Fly (1972) 110
Suspense (1913) 49–50
Swarm, The (1978) 4, 7, 10, 45, 60, 145–68, 174, 198
Sweet Ride, The (1968) 47

Taking of Pelham One Two Three, The (1974) 33, 134
Taxi Driver (1976) 131, 141, 178
Ten Commandments, The (1923) 16
Ten Commandments, The (1956) 9, 16, 67, 105, 106, 174, 178, 179, 191
Terror in the Sky (1971) 38
Terror on the 40th Floor (1974)
Terror Out of the Sky (1978) 159
Them! (1954) 146
They Died with their Boots on (1941) 164
Thing from Another World, The (1951) 151
Third Man, The (1949) 134
Thomas Crown Affair, The (1968) 48, 53
Three Days of the Condor (1975) 131
Titanic (1943) 59
Titanic (1953) 11, 23, 58–60
Towering Inferno, The (1974) 5–6, 7, 11, 29, 31, 37, 60, 76, 77–98, 99, 109, 174, 177, 187
Triangle Factory Fire Scandal, The (1979) 1, 85–7

Twelve O'Clock High (1949) 38
Two-Minute Warning (1976) 10, 124, 125, 132, 134, 137–9, 142, 172, 194, 195, 196

Under Siege (1992) 195, 196
United 93 (2006) 185

Vanishing Point (1971) 120
Victory at Entebbe (1976) 142
Volcano (1997) 193

War of the Worlds, The (1953) 8, 167, 193
War of the Worlds (2005) 103
Westworld (1973) 114, 136, 143
When Time Ran Out (1980) 11, 60
Who's That Knocking at My Door (1967) 57
Wicker Man, The (1973) 199
Wild Bunch, The (1969) 119, 126, 130
Willard (1971) 148
With These Hands (85)
Wizard of Oz, The (1939) 26
Woodstock (1970) 48
Workman's Lesson, The (1912) 11, 83
World Trade Center (2006) 79, 188–9
Written on the Wind (1956) 49

X-Files, The (1998) 199

Zero Hour! (1957) 38, 39

www.ingramcontent.com/pod-product-compliance
Lightning Source LLC
Chambersburg PA
CBHW070026010526
44117CB00011B/1729